*ANALYSTS IN THE TRENCHES*

D1445899

# ANALYSTS IN THE TRENCHES

## STREETS, SCHOOLS, WAR ZONES

*Edited by*

Bruce Sklarew

Stuart W. Twemlow

Sallye M. Wilkinson

**THE ANALYTIC PRESS**

2004   Hillsdale, NJ                    London

Published by
   The Analytic Press, Inc., Publishers
   Editorial Offices:
   101 West Street
   Hillsdale, NJ 07642

   www.analyticpress.com

   Designed and typeset by CompuDesign, Charlottesville, VA.

   Index by Writers Anonymous, Inc., Phoenix, AZ.


   **Library of Congress Cataloging-in-Publication Data**

Analysts in the trenches : streets, schools, war zones / edited by Bruce Sklarew, Stuart W. Twemlow, Sallye Wilkinson.
      p. cm.
      Includes bibliographical references and index.
      ISBN 0-88163-345-3

   1.   Psychiatric emergencies.   2. Psychoanalysts.
   I. Sklarew, Bruce.   II. Twemlow, Stuart W.
   III. Wilkinson, Sallye M.

   RC480.6.P79 2003
   362.2'04251-dc22                                      2003062841


Printed in the United States of America

10 9 8 7 6 5 4 3 2 1

In memory of Viola W. Bernard, M.D. (1907–1998)

*"Assuming that it is our social responsibility to increase the understanding of psychological aspects of social issues, it is also our social responsibility to seek effective utilization of such knowledge in the shaping of relevant policies and decision-making at the many organizational, institutional, and governmental levels of our society."*

Viola Bernard, 1983 APA Distinguished Psychiatrists Series

# Contents

# Contributors

**Maurice Apprey, Ph.D.** is Professor of Psychiatry, University of Virginia School of Medicine, Charlottesville, and coauthor, *Intersubjectivity, Projective Identification, and Otherness*.

**Martha Bragin, M.S.W., Ph.D.** is Clinical and Research Faculty in Social Work, International Program on Refugee Trauma at Columbia University College of Physicians and Surgeons, New York City, and consultant to programs for women and children affected by war and violence around the world.

**Melissa J. Brymer, Psy.D.** is Terrorism and Disaster Branch Manager, UCLA/Duke University National Center for Child Traumatic Stress.

**Sue-Huei Chen, Ph.D.** is Assistant Professor, Clinical Psychology Program, Department of Psychology, National Taiwan University, Taipei, Taiwan.

**Grete Dyb, M.D.** is Faculty of Medicine, Department of Psychiatry and Behavioral Medicine, Norwegian University of Science and Technology, Trondheim, Norway.

**Alan D. Felix, M.D.** is Director, Critical Time Intervention Mental Health Program, and Associate Clinical Professor of Psychiatry, Columbia University College of Physicians and Surgeons, New York City.

**Peter Fonagy, Ph.D.** is Freud Memorial Professor and Director, Psychoanalysis Unit, University College London.

**Armen K. Goenjian, M.D.** is Research Professor of Psychiatry, Department of Psychiatry and Biobehavioral Sciences, University of California, Los Angeles, and Medical Director of Psychiatry, Pacific and Community Hospitals of Long Beach.

**William L. Granatir, M.D.**, retired, is former Training and Supervising Analyst, Washington Psychoanalytic Institute, and former Director, School-Based Mental Health Project, Washington, DC.

**Anna Higgitt, M.D.** is Consultant Psychiatrist and Senior Policy Advisor for the Department of Health, UK, and an Honorary Senior Lecturer, Imperial College of Science Technology and Medicine, University of London.

**Janice Krupnick, Ph.D.** is Research Professor of Psychiatry, Georgetown University School of Medicine, Washington, DC.

**Steven Marans, Ph.D.** is the Harris Associate Professor of Child Psychoanalysis at the Child Study Center, Yale University School of Medicine, New Haven, CT and Director, Trauma Programs for the National Center for Children Exposed to Violence and the Child Development-Community Policing Program.

**Carol B. Napoli, R.N., M.A.** is Staff Counselor, Wendt Center for Loss and Healing, Children's Program, Washington, DC.

**Howard J. Osofsky, M.D., Ph.D.** is Kathleen and John Bricker Chair and Professor and Head of the Department of Psychiatry, Louisiana State University Health Sciences Center, and teaches at the New Orleans Psychoanalytic Institute.

**Joy D. Osofsky, Ph.D.** is Professor of Public Health and Psychiatry, Louisiana State University Health Sciences Center, and Adjunct Professor of Psychology, University of New Orleans.

**Robert S. Pynoos, M.D.** is Codirector, UCLA/Duke University National Center for Child Traumatic Stress, and Director, UCLA Trauma Psychiatry Program.

**Bruce Sklarew, M.D.** (editor), a psychoanalyst in private practice, is Principal Investigator, School-Based Mourning Project, Wendt Center for Loss and Healing, Washington, DC, and Cochair, Forum for the Psychoanalytic Study of Film.

**Alan M. Steinberg, Ph.D.** is Associate Director, UCLA/Duke University National Center for Child Traumatic Stress, and Director of Research, UCLA Trauma Psychiatry Program.

**Jeffrey Taxman, M.D.** is a psychoanalyst in private practice in Milwaukee, WI and teaches at the Medical College of Wisconsin.

**Stuart W. Twemlow, M.D.** (editor), is Director, Peaceful Schools and Communities research program, Menninger Clinic, and Professor of Psychiatry, Baylor School of Medicine, Houston, TX.

**Vamik D. Volkan, M.D.** is Founding Director, Center for the Study of Mind and Human Interaction, and Professor Emeritus of Psychiatric Medicine, University of Virginia, Charlottesville, VA.

**Dottie Ward-Wimmer, R.N., M.A.** is Senior Therapist, Wendt Center for Loss and Healing, Washington, DC and Adjunct Associate Professor, George Washington University School of Medicine and Health Sciences.

**Sallye M. Wilkinson, Ph.D.** (editor), a psychoanalyst in private practice, teaches at the Greater Kansas City Psychoanalytic Institute.

# Introduction

## THE COMMUNITY PSYCHOANALYST

As we began inviting psychoanalysts who had distinguished themselves for help given outside the consultation room to contribute to this collection, we realized that there were strongly, if not passionately, held views about what makes their work truly psychoanalytic: a field of endeavor we have chosen to call community psychoanalysis. The conventional application of psychoanalysis is limited to a clinical scenario involving one patient and one psychoanalyst. The unconventional application of psychoanalysis to social problems immediately sparks two divergent views about psychoanalytic technique. Comparing and contrasting these views sometimes generates more heat than light. The stakes seem high because relatively few psychoanalysts have come out from behind the couch and explicitly frame psychoanalytic interventions targeting community problems. Even fewer articles and books have been written about such efforts. In this volume, we intend to shed more light (and less heat) on the creative strategies that psychoanalysts employ when assisting communities to overcome violence and the transmission of trauma.

The point of divergence in approach occurs when a psychoanalyst contemplating such actions begins to make choices between a clinical stance and an active-interventionist/group-focused stance. The more conventional, clinical approach, described by Bracher (1992) from a Lacanian perspective, holds the analyst to the role of passive interpreter of group functioning. Interpretive insights uncover problems and can prepare the way for the group to collaborate on solutions. According to this viewpoint, active participation by an analyst verges on seduction, manipulation, or unhealthy gratification. The analyst remains separate from the group, and the method is expressive, as the use of the Group Relations-Tavistock model in organizational consultation exemplifies. The active-interventionist, group-focused approach equally values understanding the transference-based expectations of group participants to ascertain etiology. However, as is evident in the many examples presented in this volume, the primary intervention is actively to change how the group functions more than to interpret underlying dynamics. This method is actively engaging but no less informed by the analyst's understanding of the existing conflicts and compromises. For example, Angolan war-bred youth who had evolved into highway bandits began to repair their damaged sense of themselves when enlisted to secure the roads for the delivery of supplies and medicine (see Bragin, chapter 8). The opportunity to fantasize about violence while simultaneously protecting themselves and others from its effects transformed a lifetime accrual of unconscious guilt, thus allowing for reparations.

Vamik Volkan (1988, 1997, 1999, 2001; Volkan and Harris, 1992) has opened up new horizons for analysts interested in the active-interventionist/group-focused stance by articulating how large-scale problems at the level of international conflict or interethnic strife can be understood, in part, as manifestations of unconscious process. Volkan has clearly articulated that nations and communities must deal with unconscious processes in order to forge lasting solutions to intergenerational conflicts. The point that Volkan makes, which is repeatedly illustrated in this book, is that individual members of a community are best able to identify a community's pressing concerns, and that these individuals must be engaged if they are to provide the point of entry for the most effective assistance.

The mode of action employed by an analyst to initiate problem-solving dialogues between community stakeholders, and to draw out of the participants helpful approaches toward the reframing of questions and solutions, offers a unique take on the traditional approach to violence and trauma. The following principles elaborate the active-interventionist/group-focused approach (Volkan, 1999; Twemlow, 2000):

1. To establish a point of similarity between participants that allows for toleration of differences in others and acceptance of negative emotions without reacting impulsively or angrily.

2. To develop the habit of collaboration by initially addressing nonconflictual issues to help establish common ground and agreement.
3. To develop personal relationships and perceptions of each other, so that the people and the process become humanized.
4. To establish mutual respect for differences that have the potential to trigger racial, religious, gender or ethnic stereotypes.
5. To develop an agreed-upon common language to communicate ideas.
6. To understand that the process is not a magic bullet and requires continued maintenance.
7. To understand that only a collaborative, nonblaming, rather than competitive, partnership will result in change.
8. To achieve an understanding by all participants that the facilitator(s) must remain neutral in the psychoanalytic sense; that is, they must not adopt sides or advocate a particular position but instead should encourage mutual problem solving.

As these points illustrate, the community psychoanalyst relies more on active engagement than on interpretation, but the psychoanalytic basis remains.

## History of Psychoanalytic Interventions in the Community

Many early psychoanalysts championed psychoanalytic applications addressing the transmission of trauma and the prevention of violence. For example, Anna Freud, D.W. Winnicott, August Aichhorn, Hermine Hug-Hellmuth, and Dorothy Burlingham, to name only a few, actively worked to help parents, educators, physicians, lawyers, and social workers better understand children. John Bowlby (1944) carefully evaluated 44 juvenile thieves (by assessing character style, capacity for attachment, history of separations, quality of relationship with parents, and other factors) and vigorously recommended early intervention and preventative measures. He also consulted with the World Health Organization and wrote his classic, three-volume study, *Attachment and Loss*, under their sponsorship (Bowlby, 1969, 1973, 1980).

In the United States, the lay analyst Erik Erikson, in concert with culturalists like Erich Fromm and Karen Horney, were the vanguard for community psychoanalysis. They built on the example of the European analysts, particularly as articulated by Wilhelm Reich

(1937): the individual had to be treated within the larger social context while simultaneously addressing the societal pressures that created the individual's problems (see also Danto, 1998, 2000). Erikson capitalized on the person-in-environment model by elaborating how children, families, groups, and communities could be understood as varying across normal social phenomena (Wallerstein and Goldberger, 1998).

Fritz Redl was among the analysts devoted to addressing the effects of violence on people within their environment. Redl (1945) articulated a means for understanding children's behaviors in groups and in gangs. His descriptions of how a group's "magical seduction" not only reinforced delinquent traits but made them more daring and intensive, established psychoanalytic reference points for understanding gang violence and the transmission of trauma. Redl's observations about the gang's ability to provide "guilt insurance" by virtue of its code, demands for segregation and the accompanying hatred for those outside the group, and ability symbolically to depersonalize nonmembers takes on chilling relevance with the increase of terrorism worldwide.

Karl Menninger (1968) also had an abiding interest in criminal behavior, law, and justice. He argued for prison reform and strongly advocated the abolition of capital punishment. Corresponding regularly with prisoners, he offered them hope for solving their problems and turning their lives around. He insisted that the prevention of mental illness was the best means of reducing crime and founded The Villages, Inc., a nationwide, nonprofit organization providing safe, nurturing homes to troubled youth. Angered by the high cost of psychiatric care, Menninger devoted himself to making services available to the indigent. His insights into law enforcement supported the community's need for police while emphasizing the need for psychological mindedness as part of officer selection criteria.

Developments outside mainstream American psychoanalysis in the mid-1960s—in the form of the burgeoning community psychiatry movement—slowed the acceptance within the American Psychoanalytic Association of psychoanalytic interventions outside the consulting room. In forming and initially chairing a committee on "Psychoanalysis, Community and Society," Viola Bernard recalled: "In setting up this Committee, the Association sought to counteract this adversary situation and to give affirmative organizational support to community-oriented analysts for working toward synergistic relationships between community psychiatry and psychoanalysis" (*The American Psychoanalyst,* 1978). On behalf of the committee, Ruth Fuller drafted a paper on consultation in an effort to articulate how psychoanalysts could collaborate with the emerging community psychiatry movement. In the mid-1970s, under the leadership of Moisy Shopper, an impressive 12-week course called "Psychoanalysis and the Community" was developed and employed in the curriculum of the Cincinnati, Topeka, and Baltimore-Washington Institutes. But these initial attempts to formalize psychoanalytic practice and training for community interventions receded into the background. In the last 10 years, committee chairs Bruce Sklarew and Stuart Twemlow have taken a more activist stance, both within and outside the American Psychoanalytic Association, reflected in a revised mission statement stating that psychoanalysts have a role *and a responsibility* to address the complex issues and problems created by external reality. The compilation of this book, a suggestion by Gladys Topkis, formerly of Yale Univeristy Press, is one effort to exercise that responsibility.

## Psychoanalytic Identity Derived from a Mode of Action

It has been our observation that when psychoanalysts gather to discuss community psychoanalysis, the subject of the analyst's professional identity inevitably takes center stage. For example, at a conference where analysts reviewed efforts to inform the public about psychoanalytic ideas in 20 different countries, the discourse returned repeatedly to the topic of the psychoanalyst's "identity" as a professional highly trained in procedures designed to alleviate mental suffering and how that "identity" as expert could be successfully represented to, and embraced by, the public. Embedded in these concerns about analytic identity are beliefs that the psychoanalyst's expertise is reason enough for the world to beat a path to the consultation room door.

The contributors to this book have, by and large, taken a different approach to the issue of the analyst's identity. Rather than trying to package for public consumption the analyst's identity by dint of training, theoretical persuasion, or clinical method, as if credentials were sufficient recommendations in and of themselves, the progenitors of the projects described here simply advocate being helpful. Readers will see how identity derived from a mode of action frees an analyst from having to distinguish between applications that are "truly" analytic and those that are not. Being helpful may be the best way psychoanalysts can make their mission known to the lay public. When people feel they are being helped, they often become curious about the background and training of the person who has been helpful.

A community analyst is required to exercise flexibility in technique and personal humility when embracing an analytic identity derived from a mode of action. This is especially true of applications addressing community violence. Interpretation may not be the most desirable intervention; transference may be more important to leverage than to understand. Analytic abstinence may be undesirable, and neutrality may need to be defined along entirely different dimensions than it is now. The analyst may not be involved with delivering the intervention but, rather, may be a member of a team, not the leader. Other team members may approach community problems in a manner that is counteranalytic, if not antianalytic. Such stakeholders are just as important to the team functioning as the analyst is, and it is incumbent on the analyst to accept a limited role in attempts to solve complex social problems. Clearly, psychoanalysts have much to contribute by virtue of their understanding of unconscious determinants of irrational actions within groups and by virtue of their appreciation of process over outcome.

To a greater or lesser degree, all the chapters in this book illustrate how psychoanalytic ideas are employed painlessly and without fanfare in schools, homeless shelters, war-torn communities, and politics. These "community psychoanalysts" are applying their knowledge of the influences of unconscious processes, including transference, externalization, projection, and other defenses, to population groups. They articulate and integrate theory with observable phenomena in considering how internal and external factors interact to influence development and adaptation. They are addressing the problems and the emotional sequelae of violence, sexual and physical abuse, traumatic loss, learning inhibitions, scapegoating of classes and groups, teenage pregnancy, homelessness, and variations in family structures. As community consultants and change agents, these analysts spell out the basic principles of community psychoanalytic work underlying their successes.

This book brings together the experiences of community psychoanalysts, their methods and recommendations for community work, difficulties they have encountered, and their program successes.

## References

*American Psychoanalyst* (1978), Newsletter, the American Psycho-analytic Association, July.

Bowlby, J. (1944), Forty-four juvenile thieves: Their characters and home-life. *Internat. J. Psycho-Anal.*, 25:19–53.

——— (1969), *Attachment and Loss: Vol. 1.* New York: Basic Books.

——— (1973), *Attachment and Loss: Vol. 2.* New York: Basic Books.

——— (1980), *Attachment and Loss: Vol. 3.* New York: Basic Books.

Bracher, M. (1992), Psychoanalysis and social change. *Humanity & Soc.*, 6:461–479.

Danto, E. A. (1998), The ambulatorium: Freud's free clinic in Vienna. *Internat. J. Psycho-Anal.*, 79:287–300.

——— (2000), The Berlin Poliklinik: Psychoanalytic innovation in Weimar Germany, *J. Amer. Psychoanal. Assn.*, 47:1269–1292.

Menninger, K. (1968), *The Crime of Punishment.* New York: Viking Press.

Pyles, R. (1999), President's column. *Amer. Psychoanalyst*, 33:3.

Redl, F. (1945), The psychology of gang formation and the treatment of juvenile delinquents. *The Psychoanalytic Study of the Child*, 1:367–377. New York: International Universities Press.

Reich, W. (1937), This is Politics! *The Emotional Plague of Mankind, Vol. 2*, trans. M. Higgins & P. Schmitz. New York: Farrar, Straus & Giroux, 1976, pp. 77–117.

Twemlow, S. W. (2000), The roots of violence: Converging psychoanalytic explanatory models for power struggles and violence in schools. *Psychoanal. Quart.*, 69:741–785.

Volkan, V. D. (1988), *The Need to Have Enemies and Allies.* Northvale, NJ: Aronson.

——— (1997), *Bloodlines: From Ethnic Pride to Ethnic Terror.* New York: Farrar, Straus & Giroux.

——— (1999), Presenter. From dialogue to action: Models of ethnic reconciliation and civil society-building in Estonia. Center for the Study of Mind and Human Interaction, University of Virginia, Charlottesville, April 30–May 1, 2001.

——— & Harris, M. (1992), Negotiating a peaceful separation: A psychopolitical analysis of current relationships between Russia and the Baltic Republics. *Mind & Human Interaction*, 4:20–39.

Wallerstein, R. & Goldberger, L. (1998), *Ideas and Identities: The Life and Work of Erik Erikson.* Madison, CT: International Universities Press.

## ❖ 1 ❖

# Reverberations of Danger, Trauma, and PTSD on Group Dynamics

Robert S. Pynoos • Alan M. Steinberg • Grete Dyb

Armen K. Goenjian • Sue-Huei Chen • Melissa J. Brymer

Individuals, families, groups, organizations, communities, and societies face an ever-present and ever-changing ecology of natural and man-made dangers. Tragically, catastrophic situations occur that may affect only one person or an entire population. Trauma resulting from human violence encompasses childhood physical and sexual abuse, domestic and community violence, political violence and torture, and war. Trauma can also unfold from natural or man-made disasters, serious accidental injury, occupational or transportation catastrophes, and life-threatening medical illness (Pynoos, Steinberg, and Wraith, 1995). Over the life cycle, an individual may experience different types or a series of traumas, and, within a group, members may endure a wide range of traumatic situations. As a result of traumatic experiences, including witnessing injury and traumatic death, individuals develop posttraumatic stress and complicated grief reactions, are often faced with ubiquitous post-

Additional support for the writing of this chapter was provided by the Bing Fund.

trauma reminders and adversities, and live with trauma-generated expectations that reverberate in complex ways through their various group affiliations. An understanding of the interactions of danger, trauma, and PTSD among group members can elucidate the impact of trauma on groups at various levels and suggest strategies of response that promote individual and group recovery.

There is an intricate reciprocal relationship between an individual's traumatic experience and his or her wider group affiliations. Consideration of a number of aspects of trauma will help to explicate this interrelationship: (1) the human appraisal and response to danger; (2) the nature of trauma and the complexity of traumatic experiences; (3) the role of trauma reminders in posttrauma behavior; (4) posttraumatic stress disorder; (5) posttrauma adversities; and (6) traumatic expectations.

Over the past decade, we have refined a developmental psychopathology model of traumatic stress that incorporates these features (Steinberg and Ritzmann, 1990; Pynoos et al., 1995; Pynoos, Steinberg, and Piacentini, 1999). Building on this perspective on the individual, we hope to illuminate selected issues that illuminate the impact of trauma on parent–child relationships; family, peer, school, and occupational groups; and the broader community and society.

## Human Appraisal and Response to Danger

Our developmental framework assigns a prominent role to the ontogenesis of the human appraisal and response to danger. This framework includes three principal components: (1) estimation of the nature and magnitude of external and internal danger; (2) emotional and physical reactions and efforts at their regulation; and (3) estimation of the needed type, degree, and efficacy of protective intervention. These three operations are strongly influenced by the individual's developmental stage, including neurobiological maturation, and by experiential history, learning, current affiliative attachments, and the social ecology. In addition, families, school communities, social groups, nations and international alliances also evaluate dangers, shape the parameters of emotional response and regulation, and form strategies of preventive and protective intervention. Culture permeates each of these levels of individual affiliation and group behavior. Intercultural differences in estimation of danger and response can lead to intense conflicts among groups within a society and to extreme forms of violence. Miscalculations in the perception of threat and mobilization of resources for protective intervention between nations can lead to massive catastrophic consequences.

With respect to child development, for example, young children rely on a parent for social referencing of danger, for assistance in emotional regulation of fear responses, and for provision of a protective shield (Lieberman and Pawl, 1990). While school-age children begin to test their own appraisal of danger, to develop private means to regulate fear responses, and to play at protective self-efficacy, in situations of serious danger they remain primarily reliant on parent, teacher, or older caretaker to successfully appraise and protectively intervene. By midadolescence, there is significant reliance on self- and peer appraisal of threat, consequence, and protection, and sufficient emotional regulation to permit decision making about direct interventions on behalf of self and others. Successive developmental transitions, including marriage, having children, occupational and community life, and political and cultural affiliations, are additional dimensions that broaden the scope of appraisal of danger, complicate emotional responses and regulation, and elicit a wide range of considerations for preventive and protective action.

## Trauma and the Complexity of Traumatic Experiences

### Trauma

Trauma refers to the actualization of an expected or unexpected danger. It involves both objective and subjective features. The objective features include circumstances of extreme life-threat to self and other, actual injury or death, and exposure to grotesque features of mutilating injury, even indirectly. Trauma usually entails an experience of physical helplessness, where imagined or attempted protective interventions have failed. The subjective features include the experience of terror, horror, helplessness, and a range of extremely negative emotions (e.g., feelings of shame, guilt, rage, betrayal, and profound loss). Of particular note for traumatic situations, the reappraisal process, if it is to remain reality based, serves only to confirm the extreme magnitude of danger, the appropriateness of the emotional responses, and the absence of effective protective intervention.

The impact of trauma on family and groups can be categorized according to the agent of the trauma, affiliative assumptions, and expectations regarding sources of protective intervention. Issues of accountability are embedded in traumatic situations. Through various cultural means, among them historical narratives, witness accounts, modes of artistic representation, religious doctrine, and political ideology, groups maintain versions of traumatic situations that assign accountability. Intrafamilial agency can generate intense conflicts of loyalty, severe challenges to basic affiliative assumptions, and profound estrangement among family members (Green, 1993). Extrafamilial agency can provoke extreme fantasies of retaliation and counterretaliation. Preoccupation with revenge can be transmitted across generations, maintaining feuds and vendettas. If affecting a sufficient number within the population, revenge can be mobilized by societal or governmental agencies to engage group members in organized aggression. In addition, since judicial proceedings adjudicate blame, there is a link between judicial outcome, reparation and reconciliation, and the resolution of individual and group dynamics motivated by revenge. Even natural disasters are often imbued with issues of human agency and accountability within and outside the group (Pynoos, Goenjian, and Steinberg, 1998; Goenjian et al., 2001). These phenomena appear to operate across the levels of family, school, workplace, community, and nation.

As one example of extrafamilial agency, one of the authors (GD) and her colleagues developed and implemented a psychiatric response for parents and children after alleged sexual abuse at a community day-care center in a rural Norwegian community. The traumatic impact on parents encompassed extreme concern about their children's physical and mental health and a sense of failure and guilt for having placed their children in danger. Because the school had closed after the reports of the abuse, the children lost their playmates and their daily routine was disturbed. They displayed posttraumatic reactions, confusion, anger, and withdrawal.

There was a two-fold impact on the family matrix. Parents became united in their efforts to insure appropriate physical examinations and mental health care for their children; participated with authorities in conducting the police investigation; and supported one another when testifying in court proceedings. At the same time, there were differences in spousal response to the ongoing police investigation, legal proceedings, and media coverage. Fathers were generally more inclined than mothers to engage with police, to follow the media reports, and to meet with local authorities to generate community resources for their family. Spousal disputes arose over whether to relocate the family out of the community or to send their child to another day-care center. Some mothers left their employment or reduced their working hours so as to be able to stay home with their children.

Siblings of the day-care children felt that they were getting much less attention from their parents than before, and they were at a loss as to how to respond to their affected sibling. The family dynamics were disturbed; parents became overprotective of their older children, not allowing them to go on field trips or to sleep over at a friend's house. About half the affected families relocated from the community. Other families reduced their social activities and changed their constellation of friends.

The parents of the day-care children took on a group identity with the school community. They met on a number of occasions and elected several spokespersons to represent them to the media and community agencies. The formation of this group allowed members to exchange information, share their experiences, and support one another emotionally. Sometimes, however, hearing traumatic details from other parents proved quite distressing for parents whose children had not reported highly intrusive abuse.

The school administration and staff faced many difficult issues, such as conflict over whether the abuse had actually occurred and guilt over failure in their responsibility for the care and supervision of the children. Not only was the school closed after the reported abuse, but also the headmaster took an immediate leave of absence with subsequent early retirement. The teachers were subjected to intense questioning from parents and police, and were the focus of media attention.

Like the school community, the wider community suffered from an extreme split about whether or not the alleged abuse actually occurred. This conflict filtered through workplace interactions and a variety of social situations. Moreover, an extreme disruption to the community arose from the intense media coverage, both during the investigation and for months during the trial. The story was broadcast across the nation, and community members suffered from the stigma of identification of their town with this event.

To help remediate disturbances in family functioning, the psychiatric program provided group counseling to children and parents. Given the finding of "not guilty" for the accused in this case, mental health services after the trial and verdict were needed for parents and children to address anger over the verdict, the ultimate absence of human accountability, and disillusionment and loss of trust in social institutions.

### Complexity of Traumatic Experiences

The complexity of traumatic experiences complicates the intersubjective experience of family or group members. Commonly, a family or group is challenged by the repercussions of variable experiences among members to the same traumatic situation. Some family or group members will have been present, while others not. Even members who were present during a traumatic situation will have had disparate moment-to-moment experiences. There will inevitably be differences in the initial and ongoing appraisal of danger and estimation of effective intervention by self and others. These differences often correspond to different vantagepoints and changing concerns for self and other. As members try to regulate their own emotional reactions, their efforts are strongly influenced by the emotional reaction of others and the success or failure of mutual emotional assistance. Members often evaluate the actions of self and other as successfully protective, passive, disorganized, or more endangering. They often simultaneously or serially confront direct life-threat, and they witness threat, injury, or death to others. They may have to contend with ongoing life-threat even in the midst of loss of significant others. Circumstances may result in temporary or prolonged separations from significant others and intense worry about their safety. Traumatic experiences contain additional features that extend after the cessation of violence or threat, including efforts at rescue, evacuation, and medical care.

The concatenation of these highly individual, yet group-shared experiences inevitably leads to a Rashomon-like phenomenon that complicates the interpersonal life of the family or group. The intense contrast in experience between those present and those who were not can create an emotional divide that interferes with mutual reintegration, despite genuine efforts at communication and comfort. There is often a discordance in the ongoing reappraisal of threat and intervention because the mind of the nonexposed person is not as confined to the traumatic situation as it unfolded as is the mind of the person who was there. Even when shared, the experience is highly privatized, with important consequences to family or group dynamics. In families or groups, violent assault can lead to a radical break in concern for others when the threat to self is imminent. As this profound sense of estrangement persists into the posttrauma milieu, the sense of closeness in pretrauma relationships may be disturbed. Within the adolescent group, we have described the added element of an "existential dilemma" as friends have to choose, under life-threat, between self-protective actions and intervention on behalf of a peer (Layne, Pynoos, and Cardenas, 2001). We have observed how, after such experiences, best friendships can be lost and not replaced.

As another example, we provided consultation to a school where a fifth-grade classroom had been taken hostage by a psychotic woman who made the class write out a suicide note for her, then shot and killed herself in front of the students and teacher. Although the students were together, often sitting next to close friends, they each felt extremely alone during the episode. The children described inhibiting their wish to comfort one another for fear that such an action might draw attention to them and provoke a violent response. This was a group experience. But afterward, one of the most intense trauma reminders involved moments when children felt alone, even at home. To address the fragmented posttrauma classroom milieu, it was critical to elicit a shared understanding of this common feature of their experience. At the same time, to address the regressive reverberations in the children's family life, it was essential to enhance parental appreciation and support for the children's difficulty in being alone.

Radical shifts in self-object representation can occur as a result of traumatic situations. This shift can occur when a family member suddenly becomes the agent of violence in the family, for example, when a parent attempts a murder-suicide. However, similar radical shifts can occur when a parent is seen as ineffectual, or a teacher is viewed as having endangered students by misappraisal of a life-threatening situation. For instance, we have seen how a child can become severely estranged from a father who, with the child, was made to watch the mother being raped. Moreover, in one of the earliest school shootings we studied, a classroom of students was sent out to the playground by a teacher who misinterpreted the sound of a semiautomatic weapon for the backfire of a car. Over the next year, the students reported a deep distrust of this teacher. These radical shifts can occur in the relationship of traumatized members to the action or inaction of outside social agencies responsible for prevention, protection, and reparative interventions. As happened at Columbine High School, failures in rescue efforts continue to be a source of profound disillusionment to students in a classroom who had tried to keep a teacher alive until help arrived.

In the acute aftermath of trauma, the interpersonal matrix of the family or group may not only be severely altered by injury and loss, but, as is often overlooked, by differing psychological agendas arising from each member's unique experience and posttrauma reactions. Family dynamics are challenged by members who have different psychological agendas with different sets of traumatic reminders, different courses of recovery, and differences in posttrauma stress and adaptation to posttrauma adversities.

Group, institutional, and intergroup accounts of trauma often introduce versions of the traumatic situation that do not capture the complexity of the individual's experience. Indeed, over time, they may introduce conflicting accounts, misunderstandings, distortions, misattributions, or new information that affect the individual's or traumatized group's relationship with other group members, their wider community, official agencies, and other groups. To traumatized members of a group, there is nothing more important than "getting it right" when it comes to validating their own private experience and its traumatic consequences (Meichenbaum, 1995).

### Trauma Reminders

Trauma reminders derive from the trauma-specific features of a traumatic situation and subjective reactions. They are ubiquitous in the aftermath of trauma and constitute an additional source of ongoing distress. Psychological and physiological reactivity to reminders contributes to the periodic or phasic nature of renewed traumatic anxiety and traumatic expectations that often elicit maladaptive reenactment and avoidant behavior. The interplay of trauma reminders, their effects on interpersonal behavior, and group forms of remembering and commemoration are pervasive influences on group dynamics.

It has been our consistent observation that the powerful influence of trauma reminders on group behavior is too often overlooked. As groups move from mobilization during the trauma and crisis responses in the immediate aftermath to more sustained efforts at recovery, they often fail to incorporate interventions to mitigate the pernicious impact of trauma reminders. Simply introducing the concept of "trauma reminder" can stimulate a valuable shift in perspective in appreciating the impact of trauma reminders on daily life.

The consequence sometimes can be dramatic. For example, in an intervention program after the Taiwan Chi-Chi Earthquake in 1999, one of our colleagues (S-HC) introduced the concept of trauma reminder to a group of residents from a rural community in Pu-Li, a town near the epicenter. One traumatized housewife began to experience more frequent posttraumatic symptoms a year after the earthquake. She and her family attributed her problems to a mild traffic accident she had witnessed. With the help of the group discussion, she made a quick perspective shift and realized that the "chanting" coming from a shrine located on a hillside near her house was a powerful trauma reminder of the earthquake. Over the past months, she had suffered from frequent intrusion of earthquake images and felt annoyed at the shrine for no apparent reason. Importantly, the hillside shrine, which had collapsed during the earthquake, was reopened one year later. She came to realize that the chanting from the rebuilt shrine, a persistent, low-keyed, monotonous hum, was similar to the noise of the earthquake. The trauma reminder, rather than the woman's witnessing an accident, accounted for the exacerbation of her PTSD symptoms.

We often find ourselves telling a group that they are now living in a world of reminders. We had this experience in Bosnia-Herzegovina. Rune Stuvland, Director of the UNICEF Psychosocial Program, asked the UCLA Trauma Psychiatry Program to consult on how to revise the wartime program to address postwar needs. Focus on the role of trauma reminders in family dynamics, school behavior and academic performance, and occupational functioning proved to be a critical first step in planning a long-term mental health recovery program (Layne et al., 2001). Government officials, school personnel, and health and mental health providers readily described their own continued reactivity to reminders and consequent altered role performance.

By their own policies governments often exacerbate the problem of reminders. In Sarajevo, the government turned the streets into avenues of recurrent renewed distress by filling mortar holes in sidewalks with red plastic material to commemorate where people had been killed. After the Iraqi occupation of Kuwait, the Kuwaiti government widely posted and broadcast images of Iraqi atrocities to keep the population vigilant to the ongoing risks of Iraqi aggression. Our study indicated that this strategy had a cohort effect. While these images had no measurable adverse impact on children who had temporarily taken residence outside the country during the occupation, they served as significant, powerful, unwelcome reminders to the cohort who remained in country (Nader et al., 1993). These reminders contributed significantly to the severity of the cohort's posttrauma distress.

The reverberations of trauma reminders on interpersonal life and group dynamics can best be observed up close as they echo through family life. What is remarkable is how little family members are aware of, or even consider, the role of trauma reminders. Equally remarkable is how helpful it is to introduce this consideration into their mutual understanding, which can then be followed by efforts at mutual identification and support. Reactivity to trauma reminders often underlies withdrawn, avoidant, irritable, or agitated behaviors that are mystifying, frustrating, frightening, and anger provoking to other family members. Over time, nontraumatized family members can become impatient with their traumatized relatives, with a "get over it" attitude, and impose a self-protective reluctance to revisit traumatic features that make sense of these reactive behaviors. The most profound impact on family dynamics occurs when family members serve as trauma reminders to each other. Family members often struggle with their reactivity to one another, leading to conflicts over avoidant and affiliative emotions.

Similar phenomena can be observed in school and work settings when there has been trauma. Without the same strength of affiliative bonds, group responses can easily lead to intolerance, divisive behavior, and transfers from school or leaving the workplace. Nontraumatized members' inquiries or comforting remarks can be ill-timed reminders to traumatized group members; they leave traumatized members feeling rude or discourteous to other group members if they are curt or dismissive, or they may feel open to renewed distress if they recount the traumatic details. Over time, serious tension can arise over group memory; many members may try to rid themselves of group identification with the trauma. Without reference to the trauma, reminder-reactive behavior of traumatized members will come to be labeled as deviant or characterological. The variance in exposure among group members can lead to conflicts over rebuilding efforts designed to eliminate the most upsetting physical reminders (for example, to rebuild a school library where students and faculty were killed) and efforts to preserve a physical reminder as part of a commemoration. In one case, parents of children who had been killed at school and parents of other students became involved in a lawsuit over where to place a commemorative plaque. The traumatized and bereaved parents insisted it be placed at the entrance to the school. Other parents, arguing that this would be an ill-advised, unavoidable reminder, insisted it be placed where students had more choice to visit it or not.

With regard to group recovery, we have learned that traumatized families and group members are often required to take the lead in making others aware of their reminders and of how to provide useful and timely support. The support can be as simple as taking a hand, being understanding of a momentary reaction, or permitting a temporary period of reconstitution. An important component of our recovery programs for families, schools and workplaces is the enhancement of the social skills to deal with social questioning and interactions about the trauma that permit appropriate disclosure and genuine communication. We have worked with school systems to have children's trauma history included as part of their school health records so that future trauma-reactive behavior could be recognized and appropriately managed. Workplaces present more difficult issues because there is often less flexibility to accommodate temporary reminder-induced changes in work performance and because of employee concern over the inclusion of trauma-related mental health information in their employment records.

## PTSD

Posttraumatic stress disorder refers to a constellation of psychiatric symptoms with serious biopsychosocial manifestations and consequences. Its impact on group dynamics depends on the number of members impaired by PTSD, the severity and chronicity of symptoms, the role functions that are disturbed, and the degree to which specific cohorts may be affected.

Within any group, there is a tendency to view the symptomatic behavior of traumatized members as "deviant." This characterization may occur for several reasons. The interpersonal behavior of traumatized individuals—for example, irritable, aggressive or vigilant behavior—may be taxing to nontraumatized members. As with other anxiety disorders, vigilance to danger and avoidant behavior can dictate or restrict the behavior of family or friends. Nontraumatized members typically underestimate the length of time required for recovery, even of severely traumatized family members or peers. Nontraumatized members often become impatient with the course of recovery, especially if PTSD symptoms continue to interfere with the individual's role performance in the group. A tension can easily arise between returning to "business as usual," in educational goals or work productivity, and modifying these expectations while devoting resources to group recovery. Perceived unfairness or a lack of appropriate consideration from governmental agencies, employers, and supervisors can provoke a profound sense of disenfranchisement that can damage group identification and affiliation.

A single PTSD symptom can have a profound effect on parent–child interactions. We previously reported how a mother who was raped, with her son as a witness, would respond with an exaggerated startle to the son's entering her room for comfort after having his own traumatic nightmare (Pynoos and Nader, 1988). Her hyperarousal interfered with her ability to comfort her son, while he interpreted her behavior as if he represented a threat to her. Within a family, the regressive behavior of children, who, say, want to sleep with their parents and who consequently cause a change in family sleeping routines, becomes resented by the nontraumatized members, whether siblings or parents.

When only one member or a few group members are affected, any exposure to traumatic details through intrusive reexperiencing, whether manifested in traumatic play or obsessive recounting, is typically disturbing to other members. On the playground, for example, sexually abused children may exhibit their symptoms by engaging other children in overly sexualized traumatic play, or they may use trauma-specific precocious sexual references (Friedrich, 1993; Cosentino et al., 1995). Parents may then object to their children playing with those children, the school may label the children's behavior as deviant, rather than symptomatic, and peer rejection may follow. Peer rejection carries its own independent risk of subsequent psychopathology and maladaptive peer selection that may lead to outright deviant group behavior.

PTSD-related impairments in role performance can lead to intragroup conflicts. Following school violence or disaster, tensions may grow between the most traumatized teachers and those less directly affected, as the latter become impatient with the compromised professional functioning of their colleagues and the accommodations needed to assist their recovery. An increased turnover of students and school personnel may further challenge the resilience of the school community. Similar group disturbances can occur in other occupational settings.

Traumatic death precipitates both PTSD and complicated bereavement. The course of trauma and grief responses may place group members on quite different psychological trajectories. Family members or friends who were not at the scene, and thus were spared direct traumatic exposure, may more immediately engage in grieving the loss. Those directly exposed are likely to be preoccupied with their own traumatic experience with the death of another, as well as with their sense of life-threat. PTSD symptoms such as numbing, may also directly interfere with the course of bereavement, though as the symptoms of PSTD are alleviated, the grief process may be facilitated. However, this course may not coincide well with family, religious and societal practices assisting and supporting mourning. This dissynchrony in timing and the offering of support places strains on the cohesion of the group, be it family, school, or workplace.

A significant effect of PTSD on role performance may be seen in the decision-making of those in leadership roles. Whether parents, teachers, school administrators, business executives, or governmental officials, leaders are reluctant to acknowledge their own trauma symptoms because of a perceived need to preserve their authority, especially under posttrauma conditions in which their leadership is critical. This effect is often apparent in tasks and decisions that face them in rapid succession outside their usual purview. Traumatized leaders may make inopportune public remarks, underappreciate the impact of trauma on their subordinates, misallocate financial resources in safety and recovery efforts, and misunderstand the changed group dynamics generated by the variations in exposure, consequence, and symptomatic response of group members.

After the catastrophic earthquake in Armenia in 1988, one of the authors (AKG) devoted much time during implementation of the mental health intervention program to treating the school principals in Spitak. All the principals had had their own lives endangered by collapsing school buildings, experienced a profound sense of professional failure to save the lives of the majority of their students, and suffered the personal loss of family members. The PTSD-related passivity, anger, avoidance, and pessimism pervasive among the principals threatened their decision-making ability to support and sustain a successful school-based postdisaster mental health recovery program. In addition, many high-ranking officials in the earthquake zone who were in charge of organizing and coordinating relief efforts had other difficulties, including inertia in making major decisions and prioritizing the needs of the victims (Goenjian, 1993).

Epidemics of violence can generate specific cohorts with high rates of PTSD-related functional impairments. In the United States, the 1980 emergence of a crack cocaine market led to a proliferation of guns in the inner cities, which, in turn, spawned an inordinate increase in youth homicide, leaving in the high schools a reservoir of untreated youths who were exposed to exceedingly high rates of community violence. The current heated political debate about the apparent failure of our public schools, especially in our inner cities, to promote academic achievement overlooks the significant ways in which violence-related PTSD has impaired students' ability to learn. The classroom milieu and the educational environment have been compromised. The impact on this cohort of youngsters has repercussions beyond the school setting; it affects their investment in the wider social contract, especially trust in social agencies and institutions that govern social behavior.

Where a significant segment of the population within a large region is suffering from PTSD and other comorbid conditions, the repercussions may alter the individual and social character of the people (Goenjian et al., 1999). We found widespread, chronic, severe PTSD among children and adolescents in the earthquake zone many years after the 1988 Spitak earthquake in Armenia (Goenjian et al., 1995). These findings raise questions about how the functioning of society is affected by so many traumatized children in different stages of recovery with regard to schooling, intrafamilial and peer interactions, and adaptation to future stress. Similar considerations underlie the UNICEF decision to invest in a major postwar, school-based mental health adolescent program in Bosnia-Herzegovina. The adolescent population is the first generation to enter adulthood in the postwar period. Their academic achievement and economic productivity as well as the stability they bring to marriage and family life, their views of their social institutions, and their role in society, are all vital to the future of this region.

## Secondary Stress and Adversities

Traumatic situations are commonly associated with secondary adversities that vary considerably with the type of trauma, group resources, and group priorities. They complicate individual and group efforts at recovery, alter or unbalance role assignments and performance, often evoke frustration and dissatisfaction with group members or agencies seen as responsible for addressing adversities, and exacerbate competition for limited resources.

Among secondary adversities are changes in family constellation and function, changes in family living circumstances and resources, and posttrauma medical or surgical care and rehabilitation. There is often a need to assume new responsibilities; a strain on community resources, such as the basic infrastructure (transportation, electricity, gas, drinking water, youth centers); a change in the availability and utilization of social support; altered role performance and issues of accountability (Hobfoll, Briggs, and Wells, 1995). In large-scale disasters, secondary stress may be associated with dealing with governmental and nongovernmental relief agencies.

These stresses and adversities can interfere with the resolution of PTSD symptoms (Goenjian et al., 1995), initiate or exacerbate depressive reactions, and cause feelings of ineffectualness and demoralization. Frequently, conflicts arise over allocation of recovery resources, accompanied by mistrust of government and others. When hardships persist, there is often a downward spiral of worsening inter-related adversities with loss of motivation to overcome adversity.

The 1988 Spitak earthquake in Armenia was associated with extremely harsh and persistent postearthquake stresses and adversities. A powerfully adverse influence on family functioning was the pervasiveness situation of families living in crowded inadequate housing. Nuclear and extended families lived together, with a consequent lack of privacy, without a place for children to study, and with young children regularly sleeping with their parents. Family dynamics were affected in many ways—disturbances in separation and individuation of children from parents, disturbance in the parents' sexual relationship, and altered family responsibilities among all family members.

The postearthquake adversities for the schools were evidenced in a profound shortage of school buildings and playgrounds, lack of heat for the tents that were set up as schools, overcrowded classrooms, inadequate school supplies, compromised role performance of principals and teachers, and disturbances in the children's ability to concentrate and learn. The impact of these adversities on the school community could be seen in the disruptive classroom behaviors of the children, who were angry, irritable, and frustrated; increasingly harsh and punitive responses by teachers; loss of motivation of teachers; and lowered school-wide academic achievement. Postearthquake adversity also affected the workplace—many employees had died in the earthquake and others had subsequently moved out of the earthquake zone. These losses placed increased productivity demands on a smaller workforce. The increased demand on workers was compounded in one factory by the losses of other factories producing the same basic necessity. In the primary hospital in Spitak, there was a shortage of medical specialists, medical supplies, hospital beds, and facilities—all factors producing a frustrated and deeply demoralized hospital staff.

Adversity-related demoralization and resignation severely affected community life. Postearthquake saw increases in marital discord, alcohol abuse, and juvenile delinquency and decreases in the numbers of cultural functions. It was as if the entire community was in a state of prolonged mourning. The multitude and severity of postearthquake adversities quickly overwhelmed local government. Government officials were criticized by the community, and became ineffective; their decision making was impaired. This disruption of governmental functioning further compromised the recovery of the community.

## Traumatic Expectations

Beyond PTSD, traumatic experiences often generate traumatic expectations: catastrophic expectations for the future, safety, and security of interpersonal life and measures needed to insure preventive and protective intervention. Traumatic expectations operate and are transmitted on many levels: between and among children, adults, families, generations, groups, communities, societal institutions, and nations. Traumatic expectations, reflected in responses to trauma reminders, often serve as occasions for intergenerational transmission of trauma. For example, when parents respond to reminders, children often receive direct instruction about protective behavior.

For individuals, these expectations are manifested in thought, emotions, behavior, and biology. They often involve preoccupation with imagined strategies of protective or retributive action that addresses details of the individual's traumatic experience. Through social leadership or a sufficient number of individuals with shared traumatic expectations, they may become embodied in group beliefs, group appraisals of danger, group preventive behavior, and group strategies or propensity to intervene in response to perceived threat. These traumatic expectations can propel individuals and groups toward constructive prosocial action and improvements in public safety. Conversely, they may propel groups into violent aggression and self-endangering behavior.

Traumatic expectations in thought are reflected in beliefs that incorporate schemas of a dangerous physical and social world, the lack of trustworthiness of others, and the unfairness of the social contract and the behavior of agents of social institutions. Cultural representations extend traumatic expectations among a cohort to the wider society and future generations. Geographical representations may include control over a buffer zone, which, for example, in the case of Russia and Germany, influenced the autocratic control of Eastern Europe for more than 50 years following World War II. Verbal expressions that embody such expectations usually also imply protective interventions. The motto of the survivors of Pearl Harbor is "Remember Pearl Harbor and Keep America Alert." "Never Again" is perhaps the 20th century's most poignant and powerful verbal expression of a traumatic expectation that carries a transgenerational imperative.

A recent clinical case illustrates the conflicts that arise from differences in cross-generational expectations. A family experienced an armed robbery in which the father, legally armed, repelled the assailants with gunfire. Afterwards, over the mother's and son's objections, the father insisted on teaching his son to shoot a gun, while becoming openly dismissing of his son's wish to have the police arrest and punish the perpetrators. The father had been badly abused as a child and had left home as an adolescent to live with an uncle. He had witnessed his uncle use extreme physical force to collect protection money for an organized crime ring. The father grew up not believing in a social contract that has laws to deter violence and agents of the law to prevent harm and insure justice. His insistence that his son see the world through the father's expectations generated severe posttrauma conflict within the family. In treatment, the father came to understand that, by having raised his son in a loving, nonabusive home and in a law-abiding community, he had enabled his son to have expectations different from his own. Indeed, these divergent expectations were a sign of his success as a father. He gained more empathic understanding of his son's responses to the robbery and respect for his son's investment in the social contract.

History is replete with examples of what happens when traumatic expectations of leaders are played out on the geopolitical stage. Mapping the complex motivations of Peter the Great's moving the capital of Russia from Moscow to St. Petersburg, his Pulitzer Prize–winning biographer (Massie, 1980) attributed the relocation primarily to a terrifying violent traumatic event in Peter's childhood. As a young boy, the prince was present during a revolt during which the palace was brutally and savagely attacked by Kremlin guards. Peter witnessed the horrific murder of Matveev, the Tsar's prime minister, a close and trusted friend and protector of the family. His sister dropped Peter's hand and, placing herself in extreme danger, threw her arms around Matveev to protect him. The rioters threw her off, and, before Peter's very eyes, cut Matveev to pieces with their swords. They went on to drag off and bloodily massacre statesmen and nobles from throughout the Kremlin. As Massie notes, the Strelsky revolt marked Peter for life, left him with extreme traumatic aversion and a revulsion for the Kremlin that extended to all of Moscow, inspired the building of a new capital far away on the Baltic, and thus had a profound impact on Russian history.

One of the authors has previously discussed the traumatic role of the assassination attempt on President Reagan and his subsequent unrelenting commitment to the development of a Strategic Defense Initiative (SDI) (Pynoos, 1992). SDI was a defense plan to create an impenetrable umbrella against incoming objects, in this case not bullets but, rather, intercontinental ballistic missiles. The pursuit of a missile defense system remains a part of United States military policy; it placed competing budgetary demands on the U.S.S.R. that are said to have contributed to its dissolution.

From a sociobiological perspective, there is the question of the usefulness to the individual, and to the group, of such intense, complex, and enduring traumatic expectations. Traumatized persons have ongoing traumatic expectations, and continued vigilance and reactivity to reminders, out of proportion to current danger and at a great personal cost. Often enough, however, their prosocial actions to prevent future occurrences may benefit the group or social system. Victims of an airplane disaster may suffer for a prolonged period of time from having lived in the immediacy of that disaster, but their persistent efforts to ensure changes in Federal Aviation Administration policy may improve the standards of aviation safety from which we all benefit.

## Concluding Remarks

Over the past two decades, exposure to violence, disaster, and traumatic death has taken a heavy toll on school communities around the world. As a consequence, students and school personnel alike have suffered significant ongoing psychological distress, often in the form of intrusive daytime disturbing images, reactivity to reminders, sleep disturbances, always being on the alert, and interference with concentration, attention and learning. In addition, youth and school personnel often emerge from horrifying encounters with violence, injury, and traumatic death with altered expectations regarding the safety and security of interpersonal life, and diminished confidence in the social contract by which human life is protected and valued.

There is increasing evidence that state-of-the-art school-based interventions that address these psychological and interpersonal consequences can enhance the recovery of traumatized students and school personnel; improve academic, interpersonal, and occupational functioning; and contribute to a healthy school community (Saltzman et al., 2001). Such mental health efforts must be part of a national educational strategy to break the cycle of violence and to promote a school environment in which school personnel and students can offer their best to one another, their own futures, and society.

## References

Cosentino, C. E., Meyer-Bahlburg, H. F. L., Alpert, J. L., Weinberg, S. L. & Gaines, R. (1995), Sexual behavior problems and psychopathology symptoms in sexually abused girls. *J. Amer. Acad. Child & Adolesc. Psychiat.*, 34:1033–1042.

Friedrich, W. N. (1993), Sexual victimization and sexual behavior in children: A review of recent literature. *Child Abuse & Neglect*, 17:59–66.

Goenjian, A. K. (1993), A mental health relief program in Armenia after the 1988 earthquake: Implementation and clinical observations. *Brit. J. Psychiat.*, 163:230–239.

——— Molina, L., Steinberg, A. M., Fairbanks, L. A., Alvarez, M. L., Goenjian, H. A. & Pynoos, R. S. (2001), Posttraumatic stress and depressive reactions among Nicaraguan adolescents after Hurricane Mitch. *Amer. J. Psychiat.*, 158:788–794.

——— Pynoos, R. S., Steinberg, A. M., Najarian, L. M., Asarnow. J. R., Karayan, I., Ghurabi, M. & Fairbanks, L. A. (1995), Psychiatric co-morbidity in children after the 1988 earthquake in Armenia. *J. Amer. Acad. Child & Adolesc. Psychiat.*, 34:1174–1184.

——— Stilwell, B. M., Steinberg, A. M., Fairbanks, L. A., Galvin, M., Karayan, I. & Pynoos, R. S. (1999), Moral development and psychopathological interference with conscience function among adolescents after trauma. *J. Amer. Child & Adolesc. Psychiat.*, 38:376–384.

Green, A. (1993), Childhood sexual and physical abuse. In: *International Handbook of Traumatic Stress Syndromes*, ed. J. P. Wilson. New York: Plenum Press, pp. 577–592.

Hobfoll, S. E., Briggs, S. & Wells, J. (1995), Community stress and resources. In: *Stress and Communities*, ed. S. E. Hobfoll & M. V. de Vries. Dordrecht, The Netherlands: Kluwer, pp. 137–158.

Layne, C. M., Pynoos, R. S. & Cardenas, J. (2001), Wounded adolescence: School-based group psychotherapy for adolescents who sustained or witnessed violent injury. In: *School Violence: Assessment, Management and Prevention*, ed. M. Shafil & S. Shafil. Washington, DC: American Psychiatric Press, pp. 163–186.

———— Saltzman, W. R., Arslanagic, B., Stuvland, R., Savjak, N., Popovic, T., Durakovic, E., Compara, N., Muftic, M., Steinberg, A. M. & Pynoos, R. S. (2001), Trauma/grief focused group psychotherapy: School-based postwar intervention with traumatized Bosnian adolescents. *Group Dynam.*, 5:277–290.

Lieberman, A. F. & Pawl, J. H. (1990), Disorders of attachment and secure base behavior in the second year of life: Conceptual issues and clinical intervention. In: *Attachment in the Preschool Years: Theory, Research, and Intervention*, ed. M. T. Greenberg, C. Dante & E. Mark. Chicago: University of Chicago Press, pp. 375–397.

Massie, R. K. (1980), *Peter the Great: His Life and World*. New York: Wings Books.

Meichenbaum, D. (1995), Disasters, stress and cognition. In *Stress and Communities*, ed. S. E. Hobfoll & M. W. de Vries. Dordrecht, The Netherlands: Kluwer, pp. 33–61.

Nader, K. O., Pynoos, R. S., Fairbanks, L. A., al Ajeel, M. & al Asfour, A. (1993), A preliminary study of PTSD and grief among the children of Kuwait following the Gulf crisis. *Brit. J. Clin. Psychol.*, 32:407–416.

Pynoos, R. S. (1992), Violence, personality and post-traumatic stress disorder: Developmental and political perspectives. In: *The Mosaic of Contemporary Psychiatry in Perspective*, ed. A. Kales, C. M. Pierce & M. Greenblatt. New York: Springer, pp. 53–65.

———— Goenjian, A. K. & Steinberg, A. M. (1998), A public mental health approach to the post-disaster treatment of children and adolescents. *Psychiat. Clin. N. Amer.*, 7:195–210.

—— & Nader, K. (1988), Children who witness the sexual assaults of their mothers. *J. Amer. Acad. Child & Adolesc. Psychiat.*, 27:567–572.

—— Steinberg, A. M. & Piacentini, J. C. (1999), Developmental psychopathology of childhood traumatic stress and implications for associated anxiety disorders. *Biolog. Psychiat.*, 46:1542–1554.

—— Steinberg, A. M. & Wraith, R. (1995), A developmental model of childhood traumatic stress. In: *Manual of Developmental Psychopathology*, ed. D. Cicchetti & D. J. Cohen. New York: Wiley, pp. 72–93.

Saltzman, W. R., Pynoos, R. S., Layne, C. M., Steinberg, A. M. & Aisenberg, E. (2001), Trauma- and grief-focused intervention for adolescents exposed to community violence: Results of a school-based screening and group treatment protocol. *Group Dynam.*, 5:291–303.

Steinberg, A. M. & Ritzmann, R. F. (1990), A living systems approach to understanding the concept of stress. *Behav. Sci.*, 35:138–146.

# ❖ 2 ❖

---

# Life Without Walls
## *Violence and Trauma Among the Homeless*

Alan D. Felix

While poverty alone exposes individuals to high rates of violence and trauma, rates of victimization are even greater for those who are homeless. Perhaps more than any group in America and much of the world, the homeless illustrate how the effects of violence and trauma are transmitted from one generation to the next.

Prior to the 1970s, the homeless population of the United States consisted largely of Caucasian, middle-aged, alcoholic men. Then, in the 1970s, various economic and policy changes fueled a rapid growth and change in the homeless population. The loss of industry-based jobs, decline in affordable housing, deinstitutionalization, and reform of the social security and welfare systems have been cited as forces contributing to this change (Caton, 1990). The face of the homeless that emerged in the last decades of the 20th century tended to be that of a young, minority, single male or single mother with her children. Often, mental illness, substance abuse, or both were evident in homeless adolescent runaways and adults.

Some evidence exists that the numbers of homeless persons in the United States may have been underestimated in early reports

(Caton, 1990). By contrast, one survey (Link et al., 1995) looking at the prevalence of homelessness found that a startling 14% of Americans had been homeless or doubled-up with other families in their lifetimes; 7.4%, or 13.5 million, Americans had been literally homeless (sleeping in shelters, on the street, or in stations or abandoned buildings).

A number of epidemiological studies examining childhood risk factors for homelessness point to such factors as foster care placement, shifting caretakers, parental mental illness or substance abuse, and exposure to violence (Caton et al., 1994; Bassuk et al., 1997; Herman et al., 1997). Now a "second generation" of homeless adults has emerged who may have grown up homeless or who may have been exposed to a number of these risk factors. This intergenerational effect is perhaps best illustrated by foster care and the neglect, abuse, or abandonment that frequently precedes placement. Not only is foster care a risk factor for adult homelessness, but also many foster children have parents who are homeless (Roman and Wolfe, 1995; Zlotnick, Kronstadt, and Klee, 1998).

We are concerned here with the importance of analytically informed interventions to help homeless people make the transition to stable, domiciled lives. The critical periods of transition faced by anyone who experiences homelessness are, first, engaging with service providers in the early stages of homelessness; then, making the transition from homelessness into housing. Also drawn from analytic theory is the centrality of the engagement process with a primary caregiver/therapist (or "case manager"), which entails commonly encountered transference and countertransference reactions.

### Prevalence of Violence and Trauma in Homeless Populations

Studies of homeless populations generally focus on a specific subgroup of homeless individuals, such as single mothers, mentally ill adults, or runaway children. To speak of "the homeless" as an entity is about as meaningful as speaking of "the domiciled." Nevertheless, there is a remarkable and tragic consistency across studies of homeless populations. Homeless persons have a high incidence of violence and trauma during childhood, and being homeless is a definite risk factor for further trauma and violence. Thus, it is often the case that trauma begets homelessness and homelessness begets further trauma.

A number of studies have examined the role of childhood risk factors for adult homelessness. Herman et al. (1997) compared nationally representative samples of homeless and never-homeless adults. The researchers concluded that lack of care from a parent or physical abuse during childhood significantly increases the risk of subsequent homelessness; sexual abuse was associated with a tendency toward homelessness. Several studies (Susser, Lin, and Conover, 1991; Caton et al., 1994; North, Smith, and Spitznagel, 1994; Koegel, Melamid, and Burnam, 1995) found high degrees of poverty, residential instability, out-of-home placement, violence, and other family problems in the childhood of homeless adults. While Koegel et al. (1995) did not find that the homeless adults in their sample of 1563 had suffered increased rates of physical abuse in childhood, many of the women in the sample had been sexually abused. Consistent with most studies, however, almost half the homeless sample had spent a portion of their childhood living apart from their parents.

Some studies have looked specifically at homeless persons who suffer severe mental illnesses. Susser et al. (1991) found a 28% life-time prevalence of homelessness among state-hospital patients. Drug abuse and urban residence were also found to be associated with homelessness. Caton et al. compared homeless with never-homeless men (1994) and women (1995) with schizophrenia to determine risk factors for homelessness. The men had higher degrees of family disorganization in childhood and less current family support. The women demonstrated only the latter. Both groups were more likely to have coexisting substance abuse and antisocial personality disorders. In a similarly designed case-control study of nonpsychotic adults, Caton et al. (2000) found that good family support in adulthood is a protective factor against homelessness.

Looking at dually diagnosed (mental illness plus substance abuse) homeless adults, Blankertz, Cnaan, and Freedman (1993) found that nearly 90% of the sample had at least one of the generally recognized childhood risk factors for homelessness: sexual abuse, physical abuse, parental mental illness, parental substance abuse, or out-of-home placement. The most common risk factor was physical abuse, present in over 50% of the sample.

Netzley, Hurlburt, and Hough (1996) looked specifically at child abuse in the history of homeless women with severe mental illness.

They found significantly higher rates of abuse when compared to homeless women in general. The women who were victims of child abuse were more likely to become homeless in childhood and had higher rates of suicidality and posttraumatic stress disorder as well. In a comparison of homeless and poor domiciled families in Los Angeles, Wood et al. (1990) found that homeless mothers reported more spousal abuse, child abuse, drug use, mental illness, and weaker support systems than their domiciled counterparts. The homeless mothers generally came from families in which their parents abused substances, or they had backgrounds of foster care and other out-of-home placements.

Building on these findings of childhood trauma in homeless adults, Zorus and Zax (1991) studied the perceptions of childhood of 90 homeless men in Rochester, New York. Not surprisingly, compared with a control group, the homeless men perceived a greater lack of maternal warmth or involvement during childhood. Another large study of homeless men and women in St. Louis, by North et al. (1994), reported high rates of family problems and violence predating the onset of homelessness. Over 60% of the men and women in that study had not been reared by both parents. Twenty-one percent of the women reported having been raped. In further studies of the St. Louis population, North and Smith (1992) found a high lifetime prevalence of posttraumatic stress disorder (PTSD) in homeless men (18%) and women (34%). Childhood histories of abuse and fighting were predictive of PTSD and led the authors to conclude that trauma and violence long preceded the onset of homelessness.

The victimization of women, both preceding and following the onset of homelessness, has been well documented. Browne (1993; Browne and Bassuk, 1997) and Wenzel, Koegel, and Gelberg (2000) document the childhood victimization of homeless women, and the repetition of this trauma that results from the combination of being homeless and having poor survival skills. Likewise, the family problems of homeless and runaway adolescents are well known. Not surprisingly, this population has higher levels of parental rejection, family violence, and abuse and lower levels of parental monitoring, support, and warmth when compared with controls (Powers, Eckenrode, and Jaklitsch, 1990; Whitbeck, Hoyt, and Ackley, 1997; Ryan et al., 2000).

Exposure to trauma on the street and in shelters comes in many forms for homeless persons. Studies have shown high rates of battery, rape, and HIV infection in homeless women (Fisher et al., 1995), exposure to violence among pregnant homeless women (Robrecht and Anderson, 1998), high rates of trauma in homeless adults (Buhrich, Hodder, and Teesson, 2000), a high incidence of physical and sexual abuse among homeless women with severe mental illness (Goodman, Dutton, and Harris, 1997), other forms of victimization among mentally ill men (Padgett and Struening, 1992), and exposure to violence both in adults (Fitzpatrick, LaGory, and Ritchey, 1999) and in youths (Kipke et al., 1997) as a consequence of being homeless.

Clearly, the experience of severe trauma and neglect in childhood is common across most subpopulations of homeless. Further victimization occurs in adulthood as a result of being homeless. This legacy of violence and neglect is often passed along to the children of homeless adults, perpetuating a tragic intergenerational transmission of violence and trauma.

## Using Psychoanalytically Informed Techniques to Help Homeless People[1]

The first phase of providing services to people who are homeless usually involves outreach.

The recipient of outreach services may refuse help for any number of reasons. People who are homeless frequently do not trust providers. A mother may fear that her children will be taken away. Someone with mental illness may have experienced coercive measures in a hospital setting or may suffer from paranoia as a symptom of the illness. A survivor of street life may have been raped or mugged on more than one occasion. Even when a client voluntarily seeks services, it is essential that a case manager or other provider remain aware of the complexities of forming a treatment alliance.

Levy (1998) has described a model of homeless outreach based on the ecological approach of "The Life Model" (Germain, 1991) and Erickson's (1950) developmental stages. How to develop a trusting relationship while maintaining appropriate boundaries is at the heart of Levy's work and is a fundamental aspect of psychoanalysis.

---

1. For the sake of convenience, we refer to recipients of services as "he" and case manager/providers as "she."

To maximize the opportunity that a successful alliance will form with a homeless person, it is usually necessary that there be a milieu similar to Winnicott's (1965) holding environment, in which the engagement is fostered at a pace tolerable to the client. This is especially true for persons suffering from chronic mental illness, substance abuse disorders, or severe personality disorders. The holding environment may be a shelter-based day treatment program (Felix, 1997), a drop-in center, or a clinic. A mobile team meeting a client in the same park location week after week may serve the same function. The essential condition is that the client be made to feel safe to express his needs to the outreach worker, who is there to empathize with the client, remain nonjudgmental, and strive to meet those needs from the client's perspective. While Winnicott's holding environment emphasizes the fostering of a trusting and loving transference, Bion's (1977) concept of the "container" adds the dimension of tolerance of the client's aggression in the treatment setting. The provision of safety and the setting of boundaries to allow appropriate verbal expression of aggression are critical in working with a population so victimized by violence and trauma.

As initial outreach efforts progress into a working alliance between a homeless client and the case manager, the next phase of treatment required careful attention to how the client–case manager relationship unfolds. Here again, psychoanalysis provides a rich and comprehensive framework for understanding the complexities of this relationship under the broad conceptualizations of transference and countertransference (Gill, 1982). Specific theories (e.g., object relations, self psychology, interpersonal) emphasize different aspects of the dyad, but each can be useful. The merit of one particular theoretical framework over another is not my concern here. Rather, I am arguing in favor of the usefulness of the general psychoanalytic concepts of transference and countertransference, including inward and outward, real and distorted reactions of the client and case manager.

In settings where case managers lack the clinical training to manage the transference, it is important that senior staff be present as supervisors. A number of common transference–countertransferece pairings may be encountered in work with persons with histories of violence, neglect, abandonment, and other forms of severe trauma. For example, a client who feels helpless may elicit either helplessness or feelings of omnipotence in the case manager. Under the former circumstances, the case manager may withdraw in frustration, whereas in the latter case, fantasies of heroic rescue will ultimately turn to feelings of disappointment for both the client and the case manager.

Given the prevalence of trauma and violence across homeless populations, it is not surprising that aggressive transference reactions are commonly encountered in outreach or treatment settings. The client may react to any perceived rejection with verbal, or even physical, aggression. It is of utmost importance to any program that these reactions be dealt with effectively, preferably before they are acted out.

Treatment typically begins with the taking of a history. Obtaining a life history from a person who is homeless serves many therapeutic purposes (Sherman, 1998). It may help the case manager to connect to a homeless client when there is an unconscious tendency to pull away, as if to say, "I cannot possibly be like this person before me." Fear of entering the psychic world of an angry victim–victimizer dyad is likely to be perceived as a rejection and trigger anger in the client. Winnicott (1947) entered new territory by applying his experiences in community mental health to the analytic setting to better understand hate in the countertransference. Chafetz (1990) specifically addressed how hatred toward homeless persons may be manifested.

One of the more poignant personal accounts of the horrors of being homeless and mentally ill was written by a woman under the pseudonym Rose (Bachrach, 1997). Rose, who was raped three times while homeless and assaulted many times more, describes the hate she frequently encountered: "Another remembrance also involves the illogical hate others felt towards me because I was not part of society's norm" (p. 442).

Sharing the history humanizes the homeless person. It brings to light his needs, his frailties and strengths, his defensive operations, and the sources of his anger, frustrations, or perhaps rage. By providing services to homeless persons, even those with the most severe mental illnesses, we can empathically observe that their anger is understandable given all that they have been through. At the same time, it may be helpful to point out how the expression of that anger might lead to self-defeating outcomes. Maintaining an empathic stance will often lessen the intensity of the client's anger, allowing productive case management or treatment to proceed.

A key function of supervision is to recognize countertransference reactions in the case manager. Just as the client must feel safe to express his feelings freely, the case manager must be safe to express her reactions to the client and the frustrations that often accompany work with the homeless.

A review of the client's history usually opens a path to understanding the transference and countertransference. For example, a case manager might become impatient with a client who sabotages a move from shelter to housing. The case manager views a placement into housing as an indicator of her effectiveness and feels defeated by the client. Understanding that the client has been repeatedly passed along from one reluctant caretaker to the next during his childhood will help make sense of the patient's apparently self-defeating behavior. The new understanding of the client's behavior as a means of dealing with separation anxiety will help the case manager regain a feeling of competence and enable her to empathize with the client.

In most treatment settings, case management does not include psychotherapy in a formal sense. However, effective case management always involves supportive counseling, which comprises primarily empathic interventions. Confrontation has a place but should be used cautiously and guided by empathy. More expressive interventions can be used as well, particularly in the service of managing acting-out behaviors. As in psychoanalysis, the verbal expression of affect should be encouraged over acting out. Occasionally, under the guidance of a trained supervisor, a case manager might make use of interpretation. For the client who was sabotaging a move to housing, for instance, an interpretation might be, "Given all the moving around and rejection you experienced in your childhood, it is understandable why you might not want to leave the shelter." A treatment intervention that incorporates continuity of care, such as the Critical Time Intervention (discussed later in this chapter), reinforces the case manager's empathy for and interpretation of the client's separation anxiety by making the separation process a gradual one.

An effective holding environment will provide the necessary physical and psychological safety for providers and clients. The physical requirements for safety go beyond the scope of this chapter. Here we concern ourselves with some of the key elements in creating emotional safety for the appropriate expression of aggression in a homeless program. Psychoanalytic theory can provide a framework for managing and limiting aggressive transferences and countertransference reactions.

For example, managing aggression in the case management or treatment setting with homeless persons requires an understanding of the use of primitive defensive operations. Earlier, I referred to how feelings of helplessness can be projected onto the case manager. Often, this projection is accompanied by feelings of rage toward a caregiver who may have abandoned the client, abused him, or failed to protect him from abuse. Through the process of projective identification, the case manager may be made to feel and contain the rage the client cannot tolerate. If the case manager cannot tolerate these feelings, she will feel frustrated with the client, overwhelmed, and eventually resentful. The resentment may lead to subtle forms of avoidance of the client or to more overt and potentially dangerous confrontations.

When situations such as these occur, it is important that a supervisor or clinical team provide the case manager with the opportunity to express her feelings about the client and to work to clarify the transference and countertransference. Thus, programs serving the homeless should have at least weekly staff meetings where the dynamics of the case management relationship can be examined. The typical task-oriented case management treatment plan becomes more effective when these psychodynamic issues are considered. Other aspects of transference and countertransference encountered in work with people who are homeless, as well as discussions of specific cases, have been provided elsewhere (Felix and Wine, 2001).

Once a working alliance is formed and the homeless client is ready to move into housing, case management enters the third phase, transition to the community. Whether a working alliance is a necessary precursor for the accomplishment of a number of tasks that must precede the move into housing, or is simply a descriptor of such activities, remains an unanswered question. In my experience, an emotional alliance between case manager and client precedes the working alliance, in which client motivation increases and the tasks leading to housing are completed. Depending on the subpopulation of homeless persons, these tasks might include the acceptance of substance abuse and mental health treatment, obtaining benefits and budgeting money, reconciling with family members, or obtaining employment.

As noted earlier, during this third phase of case management it is extremely helpful, if not critical, for care to be continuous. The challenge presented during this phase of treatment is to help the client move into a more independent life in the community and to begin to separate from the relationship that he and the case manager have worked so hard to foster. The Critical Time Intervention, or CTI (Valencia et al., 1997) is one such model of continuous case management during the transition into housing. CTI has been tested in a shelter setting for men with severe mental illness and is currently under investigation for homeless families in a shelter and for mentally ill patients in a state-hospital setting.

Under the CTI model, case management and other services specific to the target population are provided before, during, and after the transition into housing. CTI services, however, last for only nine months after housing is obtained. The idea is to move from assertive, direct provision of services, to linking to appropriate community-based providers, aided by bolstering of the client's life skills.

In working with people who experienced traumatic losses and separations during childhood, it is of paramount importance not to repeat this pattern in treatment. Unfortunately, many systems that serve homeless people, such as hospitals, shelters, and the criminal justice system, operate as institutions isolated from each other and the community and offer little if any continuity of care. The childhood experience of being passed along from one reluctant caretaker to another is repeated.

CTI incorporates principles of separation and individuation described by Mahler's (1972) developmental psychology. Guided by these principles, a case manager can anticipate a reaction to leaving homelessness akin to what Mahler described as the "rapprochement crisis." The client begins to explore new communities, a life outside homelessness, but senses danger as he separates from familiar providers. Often, clients seek to return to a familiar street or shelter setting when confronted by perceived dangers of a new world. For example, someone prone to paranoia might flee living in decent housing with a single roommate only to return to what in reality is a more dangerous congregate setting in a shelter.

Prior to CTI, as many as 50% of clients placed into housing from a shelter returned to homelessness within 18 months (Caton et al., 1993). Some clients returned to the "mother" shelter by relapsing into substance abuse, acting aggressively toward new roommates, or refusing services in the community. By making the separation gradual and by guiding the client through a "practicing phase" once he is housed (Felix and Wine, 2001), the CTI case manager fosters a healthy process of individuation. Like the "good-enough mother" described by Winnicott (1975), the "good-enough case manager" hovers by the client as he adapts to housing. The intensity of the intervention is titrated to fit the needs of the client. Ideally, this is accomplished over the nine months of CTI by gradually transforming from an active role of "doing for" the client, to one of "doing with," and finally to one of observation. The goal at the end of the nine months is that the client will have access to necessary services in the community while maximizing his independent living skills.

For example, the good-enough case manager actively intervenes to prevent crises and loss of housing during the transition to housing (approximately the first three months of CTI). In the case of a homeless client with schizophrenia, the case manager might accompany the client to the first few clinic appointments after housing is obtained. Guided by empathy and a clear understanding of the client's strengths and needs, the case manager then steps back and observes the fit between the client and the new community-based providers. Does the client make it to the appointment on his own? Does the clinic provide medications when the Medicaid card is temporarily suspended? Do they offer transportation reimbursement to the client, who could not otherwise afford the cost of travel? In other words, the good-enough case manager helps facilitate an adaptation between client and the community. In the final stage of CTI, the service plan is fine-tuned, and the client's reactions to termination of the relationship with the CTI case manager are thoroughly explored.

### Developing Preventive Services for Children at Risk

Knowing some of the risk factors for adult homelessness, it is possible to recognize children at risk for homelessness and some of its comorbidities, such as trauma and violence. Prevention, in this case, ideally means prevention of homelessness but also refers to the prevention of the consequences of homelessness in those already without homes. Interventions must be comprehensive to be effective and should consider the psychological, social, family, educational, medical, cultural, and religious or spiritual needs of the child.

While little has been documented about effective preventative interventions for children at risk for homelessness and its consequences, we do know something about what can be protective against harmful outcomes in these children. In a study of 39 offspring of indigent parents (almost exclusively mothers) with schizophrenia, Caton et al. (1998) were surprised by the remarkable adjustment of the offspring, ranging in age from 13 to 48. Despite their residential instability in childhood (being raised in an average of three different settings, with 29% of the sample entering foster care), these offspring did not exhibit a level of dysfunction anticipated by the authors. None was currently homeless, 87% had at least one close relationship, nearly half had attended college, 61% were employed full- or part-time, and the median score on the Global Assessment of Functioning (DSM IV) was 74. Only three of the 39 offspring ever had been incarcerated, and only two were ever psychiatrically hospitalized.

However, some problems were apparent. About one fifth of the sample had a previous history of homelessness, often while living with the ill parent. The prevalence of lifetime depression, as well as that of substance abuse, was double that of the general population. Posttraumatic stress disorder also occurred in 13%. Yet only one subject met the criteria for schizophrenia or schizoaffective disorder. While 59% of the offspring had children of their own, most were single parents. Owing to the selection process of subjects, the authors believe that this study may have been overrepresented by well-adjusted offspring. For example, the parents, who were subjects of an earlier study, tended to be residentially stable. Homeless parents and their offspring were much more difficult to find for this follow-up study. Nevertheless, the offspring studied did have childhood backgrounds of poverty, residential instability, parental mental illness, and, in at least 21% of the cases, physical or sexual abuse. Perhaps, something can be learned from the apparent resiliency of the offspring of these indigent parents with schizophrenia.

The authors approached this finding by looking at the presence of nurturing caretakers. Significantly, only 5% of the sample identified their nonschizophrenic parent (primarily the father) as their most significant nurturing adult, whereas 28% said that the ill parent satisfied this role. A full 60% identified another relative, typi-cally a grandparent. Despite the high incidence of foster care among the subjects, only one reported that a foster parent served this impor-tant function.

A fundamental tenet of psychoanalysis is that early childhood experiences, especially the relationship with a primary nurturing figure, shapes many aspects of a person's emotional development. In the study of these at-risk offspring, it appears that the presence of a nurturing relative to compensate for the limitations of an ill parent is a critical protective factor. Sadly, in this sample, foster care did not seem to meet this need.

**Case Illustration**

Ms. Reeves is a 23-year-old African-American woman living in a family shelter with her daughters, aged one and six. Because of her mother's dependency on intravenous drugs and her father's absence, other relatives had cared for Ms. Reeves during her childhood. First a grandmother, then an aunt took care of her and her three younger siblings. When the aunt remarried, she could no longer care for her nieces and nephews and placed them in foster care. As the oldest of the four children, Ms. Reeves felt she was never treated as well as her siblings were while in foster care. From age 9 to 16, she stayed with one family. During that time, a family friend sexually abused her. Her foster family never knew, and Ms. Reeves remained silent, fearing punishment.

When she reached the age of 16, Ms. Reeves signed herself out of foster care, entered a summer job-training program, and got her own apartment. A year later she was pregnant with the child of an older man who abandoned her. She managed to support her child for a few years on public assistance and with temporary employment. In her early 20s, Ms. Reeves met a man from another state. She again became pregnant, but this time moved into the man's home. He reluc-tantly agreed to support her for a limited time. There were many problems. He was drinking heavily and physically abusive. He also had trouble holding jobs, so there were financial pressures.

After a year, Ms. Reeves moved back to her hometown to live with and help nurse the now ailing aunt who had raised her for some time. When the aunt died, the landlord pressured Ms. Reeves into leaving, and, with no place else to go, she entered the family shelter with her two daughters. In the shelter, Ms. Reeves was given psychiatric and substance-abuse assessments. Her parenting skills were evaluated, her vocational needs determined, and her children's needs assessed. She met her CTI case manager, who began to implement a service plan and apply for an emergency apartment subsidized by the county.

When I interviewed Ms. Reeves at the shelter, she seemed very connected to her CTI case manager and very determined to move into housing. She appeared to be taking good care of her children, and she was well into a training program to become a security guard. She denied using drugs, and urine tests confirmed this. There was no evidence of depression, active PTSD symptoms, or other Axis I psychiatric disorders. However, she did recognize that she made poor choices for relationships with men and was dealing with this problem by avoiding relationships. She was reluctant to discuss the past abuse she had suffered and was not receptive to being in psychotherapy. However, once situated in housing and supporting her family, she said, she might consider it.

I was impressed with Ms. Reeves's strengths but concerned about her tendency to become involved with abusive men, thus repeating her past trauma. When I told her of my concern, she seemed aware of her vulnerability but was too overwhelmed by trying to survive the present to delve into it further. She cited her relationships with her aunt and grandmother as being the source of her strength, her resolve, her dedication to her children, and her hope for a better life. Above all, she did not want her children to grow up without a loving mother, the way she had.

Several weeks after our interview, Ms. Reeves obtained an apartment and graduated from her job training. She was very happy, proud of her accomplishments, and looking forward to working. Her six-year-old completed first grade and would be going to a summer camp for underprivileged children. The one-year-old was thriving. Ms. Reeves had a very positive attachment to her CTI case manager. Not only did the case manager help her deal with various appointments, applications, and assorted bureaucratic hurdles, she was someone Ms. Reeves trusted and "could talk to about anything."

This case illustrates how important a nurturing relationship can be in early childhood even when there are multiple losses and trauma. Consistent with the studies previously discussed, it is likely that the relationships with the grandmother and the aunt saved her life, as Ms. Reeves herself recognizes. Furthermore, her capacity to seek help, form a good alliance with her case manager, and provide her children with good mothering will likely help prevent them from falling victim to abuse and homelessness.

Several questions emerge from this case and the studies of children at risk for homelessness. Do the findings of Caton et al. (1998) apply to other populations of at-risk children, including, for example, those with homeless, mentally ill parents? How do subjects with a nurturing figure compare with those who lack one? Studies with adequate numbers of subjects and control groups can be designed to examine these questions.

Finally, when relatives are lacking, or unable to cope with the demands of caring for a child at risk, can case management and other social programs fill the void? Tragically, the foster care system has yet to reach this goal (Roman and Wolfe, 1995). Can we develop school-based programs, outreach methods, and home care that will provide nurturance where it is lacking, and support and services to family members who desperately need them? Again, to answer these questions definitively, we must await further studies of the Critical Time Intervention and other services for homeless families and at-risk children.

One direct study of high-risk children (Wymann et al., 1992) and one that looked specifically at children in homeless shelters (Zima et al., 1999) give us some indications of the importance of good early childhood care as a reducer of risk. Both found that perception of one or more adult relatives as a source of help leads to fewer behavioral problems and depressive symptoms in the children. In a small study of the effect of parenting education on parents who are homeless, Gorzka (1999) found that her intervention led to significant decreases in parenting stress and in the level of unrealistic expectations for the children. Furthermore, these changes predict a decrease in the potential for parental abuse after the intervention. Peer support in homeless and runaway adolescents may potentially serve a therapeutic function. In a study of over 600 homeless youths across several sites, Bao Whitbeck, and Hoyt (2000) found that peer support from friends on the street reduced depressive symptoms typically associated with family abuse and early separation. However, association with deviant peers increased depressive symptoms.

These findings suggest that interventions for children and adolescents may be bolstered by group processes and constructive peer support. The latter has demonstrated efficacy in adult populations of homeless persons (Dixon, Hackman, and Lehman, 1997). Instead of leaving it to chance that a runaway or homeless youth will find the right kind of peer support, outreach teams can insure it by including peers who themselves have overcome similar trauma in their lives.

### Applying Psychoanalytically Informed Interventions to Those Living Without Walls

Enough is known now for us to recognize at-risk children and to predict the consequences of homelessness. Psychoanalytic theories of attachment, separation and individuation, object relations, and self psychology give us frameworks to understand the psychological impact of homelessness, violence, and trauma. Furthermore, these theories usefully guide the planning and implementation of treatment strategies. Applications of these theories (Moses, 2000; Grizenko et al., 2000) to interventions with domiciled children and adolescents must be extended to those who are homeless. We will then be on our way to addressing the goals set forth by one of the pioneers in the study of homeless families, Ellen Bassuk (1986), who wrote:

> Our major goal should be to rescue these families, particularly the children, from a lifetime of deprivation and violence and to interfere with a newly emergent cycle of intergenerational homelessness. Without long-term solutions that focus on both the seriousness of the housing crisis and the emotional problems of the mothers and children the plight of these families will continue to be desperate [p. 52].

Psychoanalysts who bring their unique knowledge and perspectives to challenging populations in the community can serve a vital role in fulfilling Bassuk's vision. The client–case manager relationship has become central to any service system providing for homeless individuals and families. A psychoanalytic perspective converts case management from a static, task-oriented process into a dynamic, interpersonal one that aims to promote emotional development, break the repetitive, intergenerational cycle of violence and trauma, and facilitate the transition from a life without walls to the security of home.

## References

Bachrach, L. L. (1997), "Rose" guest editorial: My life on the street. *Bull. Menninger Clin..* 61:425–445.

Bao, W., Whitbeck, L. B., & Hoyt, D. R. (2000), Abuse, support and depression among homeless and runaway adolescents. *J. Health & Soc. Behav.*, 41:408–420.

Bassuk, E. L., ed. (1986), The mental health needs of homeless persons. *New Directions for Mental Health Services*. San Francisco: Jossey-Bass, 45–53.

——— Buckner, J. C., Weinreb, L. F., Browne, A., Bassuk, S. S., Dawson, R. & Perloff, J. N. (1997), Homelessness in female-headed families: Childhood and adult risk and protective factors. *Amer. J. Pub. Health*, 87:241–248.

Bion, W. R. (1977), *Seven Servants*. New York: Aronson.

Blankertz, L. E., Cnaan, R. A. & Freedman, E. (1993), Childhood risk factors in dually diagnosed homeless adults. *Soc. Work*, 38:587–596.

Browne, A. (1993), Family violence and homelessness: The relevance of trauma histories in the lives of homeless women. *Amer. J. Orthopsychiat.*, 63:370–384.

——— & Bassuk, S. S. (1997), Intimate violence in the lives of homeless and poor housed women: Prevalence and patterns in an ethnically diverse sample. *Amer. J. Orthopsychiat.*, 67:261–278.

Buhrich, N., Hodder, T. & Teesson, M. (2000), Lifetime prevalence of trauma among homeless people in Sydney. *Australi. & New Zeal. J. Psychiat.*, 34:963–966.

Caton, C. L. M. (1990), *Homelessness in America*. New York: Oxford University Press.

——— Cournos, F., Felix, A. & Wyatt, R. J. (1998), Childhood experiences and current adjustment of offspring of indigent patients with schizophrenia. *Families & Mental Health Treatment*, 49:86–90.

———— Hasin, D., Shrout, P. E., Opler, L. A., Hirshield, S., Dominguez, B. & Felix, A. (2000), Risk factors for homelessness among indigent urban adults with no history of psychotic illness: A case-control study. *Amer. J. Pub. Health*, 90:258–263.

———— Shrout, P. E., Boanerges, D., Eagle, P. F., Opler, L. A. & Cournos, F. (1995), Risk factors for homelessness among women with schizophrenia. *Amer. J. Pub. Health*, 85:1153–1156.

———— ———— Eagle, P. F., Opler, L. A., Felix, A. & Dominguez, B. (1994), Risk factors for homelessness among schizophrenic men: A case-control study. *Amer. J. Pub. Health*, 84:265–270.

———— Wyatt, R. J., Felix, A., Grunberg, I. & Dominhuez, B. (1993), Follow-up of chronically homeless mentally ill men. *Amer. J. Psychiat.*, 150:1639–1642.

Chafetz, L. (1990). Withdrawal from the homeless mentally ill. *Commun. Mental Health J.*, 36:227–254.

Davies-Netzley, S., Hurlburt, M. S. & Hough, R. L. (1996), Childhood abuse as a precursor to homelessness for homeless women with severe mental illness. *Violence & Victims*, 11:129–142.

Dixon, L., Hackman, A. & Lehman, A. (1997), Consumers as staff in assertive community treatment programs. *Adm. Policy Mental Health*, 25:199–208.

Erikson, E. H. (1950), *Childhood and Society*. New York: Norton.

Felix, A. D. (1997), Treating the homeless mentally ill. *Amer. Psychoanal.*, 31:21–23.

———— & Wine, P. (2001), From the couch to the street: Applications of psychoanalysis to work with individuals who are homeless and mentally ill. *J. Appl. Psychoanal. Stud.*, 1:17–32.

Fisher, B., Hovell, M., Hofstetter, R. & Hough, R. (1995), Risks associated with long-term homelessness among women: Battery, rape, and HIV infection. *Internat. J. Health. Serv.*, 25:351–369.

Fitzpatrick, K. M., LaGory, M. E. & Ritchey, F. J. (1999), Dangerous places: Exposure to violence and its mental health consequences for the homeless. *Amer. J. Orthopsychiat.*, 69:438–447.

Germain, C. B. (1991), *Human Behavior in the Social Environment: An Ecological View*. New York: Columbia University Press.

Gill, M. (1982), *Analysis of Transference*. New York: International Universities Press.

Goodman, L. A., Dutton, M. A. & Harris, M. (1997), The relationship between violence dimensions and symptom severity among homeless, mentally ill women. *J. Trauma. Stress*, 10:51–71.

Gorzka, P. A. (1999), Homeless parents: Parenting education to prevent abusive behaviors. *J. Child Adolesc. Psychiat. Nursing*, 12:101–109.

Grizenko, N., Zappitelli, M., Langevin, J. P., Hrychko, S., Messidi, A. E., Kaminester, D., Pawliuk, N. & Stephanian, M. T. (2000), Effectiveness of a social skills training program using self/other perspective-taking: A nine-month follow-up. *Amer. J. Orthopsychiat.*, 70:501–509.

Herman, D. B., Susser, E. S., Struening, E. L. & Link, B. L. (1997), Adverse childhood experiences: Are they risk factors for adult homelessness? *Amer. J. Pub. Health*, 87:249–255.

Kipke, M. D., Simon, T. R., Montgomery, S. B., Unger, J. B. & Iversen, E. F. (1997), Homeless youth and their exposure to and involvement in violence while living on the streets. *J. Adolesc. Health*, 20:360–367.

Kogel, P., Melamid, E. & Burnam, A. (1995), Childhood risk factors for homelessness among homeless adults. *Amer. J. Pub. Health*, 85:1642–1649.

Levy, J. S. (1998), Homeless outreach: A developmental model. *Psychiat. Rehab. J.*, 22:123–131.

Link, B., Phelan, J., Bresnahan, M., Stueve, A., Moore, R. & Susser, E. (1995), Lifetime and five-year prevalence of homelessness in the United States: New evidence on an old debate. *Amer. J. Orthopsychiat.*, 65:347–354.

Mahler, M. S. (1972), On the first three subphases of the separation-individuation process. *Internat. J. Psychoanal.*, 53:333–338.

Moses, T. (2000), Attachment theory and residential treatment: A study of staff-client relationship. *Amer. J. Orthopsychiat.*, 70:474–490.

North, C. S. & Smith, E. M. (1992), Posttraumatic stress disorder among homeless men and women. *Hosp. Commun. Psychiat.*, 43:1010–1016.

———— ———— & Spitznagel, E. L. (1994), Violence and the homeless: Epidemiologic study of victimization and aggression. *J. Trauma. Stress*, 7:95–111.

Padgett, D. K. & Struening, E. L. (1992), Victimization and traumatic injuries among the homeless: Associations with alcohol, drug, and mental problems. *Amer. J. Orthopsychiat.*, 62:525–534.

Powers, J. L., Eckenrode, J. & Jaklitsch, B. (1990), Maltreatment among runaway and homeless youth. *Child Abuse & Neglect*, 14:87–98.

Robrecht, L. C. & Anderson, D. G. (1998), Interpersonal violence and the pregnant homeless woman. *J. Obstet. Gynecol. Neonatal Nurs.*, 27:684–691.

Roman, N. P. & Wolfe, P. B. (1995), Web of failure: The relationship between foster care and homelessness. *National Alliance to End Homelessness* (report), pp. 2–15.

Ryan, K. D., Kilmer, R. P., Cauce, A. M., Watanabe, H. & Hoyt, D. R. (2000), Psychological consequences of child maltreatment in homeless adolescents: Untangling the unique effects of maltreatment and family environment. *Child Abuse & Neglect*, 24:333–352.

Sherman, C. (1998), History is important in dealing with homeless. *Clin. Psychiat. News*, p. 31.

Susser, E. S., Lin, S. P. & Conover, S. A. (1991), Risk factors for homelessness among patients admitted to a state mental hospital. *Amer. J. Psychiat.*, 148:1659–1664.

Valencia, E., Susser, E., Torres, J., Felix, A. & Conover, S. (1997), Critical time intervention for individuals in transition from shelter to community living. In: *Mentally Ill and Homeless: Special Programs for Special Needs*, ed. W. R. Breakey & J. W. Thompson. Amsterdam, NY: Harwood Academic, pp. 75–94.

Wenzel, S. L., Koegel, P. & Gelberg, L. (2000), Antecedents of physical and sexual victimization among homeless women: A comparison to homeless men. *Amer. J. Commun. Psychol.*, 28:367–391.

Whitbeck, L. B., Hoyt, D. R. & Ackley, K. A. (1997), Families of homeless and runaway adolescents: A comparison of parent/caretaker and adolescent perspectives on parenting, family violence, and adolescent conduct. *Child Abuse & Neglect*, 21:517–528.

Winnicott, D. W. (1949), Hate in the countertransference. *Internat. J. Psycho-Anal.*, 30:69–74.

———— (1965), *The Motivational Processes and the Facilitating Environment*. New York: International Universities Press.

———— (1975), Primary maternal preoccupation. In: *Through Pediatrics to Psychoanalysis*. London: Hogarth Press, pp. 300–305.

Wood, D., Valdez, B., Hayashi, T. & Shen, A. (1990), Homeless and housed families in Los Angeles: A study comparing demographic, economic, and family function characteristics. *Amer. J. Pub. Health*, 80:1049–1052.

Wymann, P. A., Cowen, E. L., Work, W. C., Raoff, A., Gribble, P. A., Parker, G. R. & Wannon, M. (1992), Interviews with children who experience major street life: Family and child attributes that predict resilient outcomes. *J. Amer. Acad. Child Adolesc. Psychiat.*, 31:904–910.

Zima, B. T., Bussing, R., Bystritsky, M., Widawski, M. H., Belin, T. R. & Benjamin, B. (1999), Psychosocial stressors among sheltered homeless children: Relationship to behavior problems and depressive symptoms. *Amer. J. Orthopsychiat.*, 69:127–133.

Zlotnock, C., Kronstrandt, D. & Klee, L. (1998), Public health briefs: Foster care children and family homelessness. *Amer. J. Pub. Health*, 88:1368–1370.

Zozus, R. T. & Zax, M. (1991), Perceptions of childhood: Exploring possible etiological factors in homelessness. *Hosp. & Commun. Psychiat.*, 42:535–537.

# ❖ 3 ❖

# From the Events of History
# to a Sense of History
## Aspects of Transgenerational Trauma and
## Brutality in the African-American Experience

Maurice Apprey

There are many clinical methods for understanding and transforming the impact of historical trauma and reinventing the self in the clinical process. The approach advocated here, however, requires that, regardless of which clinical method of intervention is chosen, a particular strand must run through the process of treatment to produce durable and meaningful change. This strand must run through psychoanalysis and creative and expressive art therapies, as well as many forms of intervention in aggrieved communities. The strand involves understanding human suffering and the way that particular suffering is mentalized by the victimized group and is subsequently reenacted by generations to come.

There must first be many profiles of understanding of the historical injury. Then there must be an understanding of how the aggrieved community has stored in its communal memory those psychological hurts—those feelings of humiliation—along with changing historical accounts of the actual injuries. Subsequently these sedimentations of historical grievances are enacted within the transference in the clinical situation where the grievances are not only staged, but restaged, distorted, or extended. Then comes the most decisive obligation that the clinician has toward the analysand, patient, client, or community that is attempting to transform itself. That decisive obligation is to extract the errand toward extinction—the ambush of the self—and to undergo the unpleasant drudgery of constantly engaging the mandate to die or destroy oneself in order to find new and more flexible forms of adaptation.

Clinicians must shift from conceptualizing history as nuances of social and political evolution to a sense of history inscribed traumatically in individuals, and they must do so in ways that link that history to the potential for psychological change in our communities. Here concepts like introjection with the aggressor (Ferenczi, 1909) and identification with the aggressor (Freud, 1946) are, in my view, incomplete although they are correct and meaningful in their rightful places in psychoanalytic practice. In working with aggrieved communities and encountering pooled communal memories that continue to have a destructive impact in the present, a description of shared communal injury must include (a) the fact of historical injury, (b) the potential for transformation of that history, and (c) a constant reminder that each person, family, and ethnic group must come to know the motivations that lie behind the perpetuation of the historical injury caused by the original transgressor.

The issue of "transgenerational haunting" (Abraham, 1988) is a complex one. The study of it is not new in the clinical literature, but the topic is seldom developed to the point that it actually achieves the heuristic status it deserves. This chapter is not intended as an exhaustive explication of the concept of transgenerational haunting, for fuller expatiation may be found elsewhere (see Abraham, 1988; Apprey, 1991, 1992). Instead, I take a cue from a powerful passage in which Abraham (1988) defines the concept, in a prelude to an examination of a powerful and most instructive account of transgenerational haunting by Carolivia Herron. With his words, Abraham casts us all under the spell of transgenerational drama:

> The belief that the spirits of the dead can return to haunt the living exists either as a tenet or as a marginal conviction in all civilizations, whether ancient or modern. More often than not, the dead do not return to reunite the living with their loved ones but rather to lead them into some dreadful snare, entrapping them with disastrous consequences. To be sure,

all the departed may return, but some are predestined to haunt: the dead who have been shamed during their lifetime or those who took unspeakable secrets to the grave [p. 75].

For Abraham, the phantom associated with transgenerational haunting is an invention of the living. This invention objectifies "the gap that the concealment of some part of a loved one's life produced in us" (p. 75). What haunts, therefore, are not the dead; what haunts are those gaps left within us by the secrets of others.

Abraham tried to distinguish unsuccessful mourning of loved ones from the construction of phantoms through the secrets of the traumatized. In his view, "it is the children's or descendants' lot to objectify these buried tombs through diverse species of ghosts. What comes back to haunt are the tombs of others. The phantoms of folklore merely objectify a metaphor active within the unconscious: The burial of an unspeakable fact within the loved one" (p. 76).

When we think of the African-American experience of exilic alienation and transgenerational haunting and its aftermath, do we not see representations of phantoms? How these gaps—wherein the phantoms dwell—show themselves is the subject of this chapter. To elucidate the vicissitudes of transgenerational haunting in the context of the African-American experience, I refer to the story of one family, as portrayed in the novel *Thereafter Johnnie* by Carolivia Herron (1991). Herron is an associate professor of English at Mount Holyoke College; her novel is a biographical account of herself, as a product of incest and as a product of the five generations preceding her, which began in rape.

## The Story

Briefly told, Herron's story tells us that first there was the original black slave, called the nameless one, who was shipped to Virginia, dead. Her surviving daughter was placed in a special cart along with a few other black exiles and transported to Richmond, Virginia; there she was delivered to a select group of slavemasters. This special *order* of slaves included "black chiefs, black cherubs, and black ladies of the chamber" (Herron, 1991, p. 235).

So first was the nameless one, then her daughter, the special one, who was regarded as her master's sexual slave. With her master, the special one begat Laetitia, a child with brown eyes and alabaster skin. At the same time, the master married a white southern woman (who had blond hair and blue eyes), with whom he had a son. Laetitia grew into a beautiful and desirable young woman, and by the time she was 20 years old "had received within herself the sperm of both her white father and of the white male child, her father's son, her half brother" (pp. 235–236).

Laetitia, now the concubine of both father and son, was placed in her own home as a white widow. She was taught "proper language, diction, speech, and the long tale of the wandering God who begat Jesus Christ upon Mary his daughter—the masters giving Laetitia of their own library, books to read that she might well portray what she was not" (p. 237). When Laetitia became impregnated, the two masters, father and son, grew anxious. Each feared his child by Laetitia would be born dark skinned. Much to their relief, the child was a girl with white skin, sandy silk hair, and blue eyes. She was named Rowena, and the decision was made to raise her as a white child; she was told that her mother was a widow and that her father had been a soldier.

Despite frequent visits by the two masters, Rowena remained innocent of their relationship with her mother. For her part, Laetitia continued to submit to her fate with recalcitrant resignation, receiving upon her body the slavemaster and his son. She would not tell herself that she derived no pleasure from them, but she acknowledged that she had sinned greatly by submitting sexually to father and to son, to give birth to Rowena. That sin, however, served as ransom, for it formed the basis for the bargain she forced the slavemaster and his son to make—the promise that Rowena would never be touched by them.

Rowena was reared in a virginal manner: she read her Bible, spent time in her garden, and attended a private finishing school for southern girls. Her father's true identity remained unbeknownst to her and to others, as was the fact that she was of mixed African- and Euro-American parentage. The deception continued until one day, when Rowena found the two masters seducing her mother, "standing with their private parts exposed, holding the naked Laetitia horizontal between them" (p. 238). Without shame, the masters boasted, while "pumping themselves into her mother" and crying out in passion, "Yeah, now you know, you and your Ma are both nigger. . . . We can sell you or rape you any day of the week" (p. 238). In sorrow, Rowena left to begin a new life "up north" in Pennsylvania.

Sometime after her arrival in Pennsylvania, Rowena married a man of Indian ancestry; she gave birth to a female child. In time, this girl gave birth to Camille, who married John Christopher. Camille and John Christopher begat three children: Cynthia Jane, Eva, and Patricia. Cynthia Jane became a nun; Eva became hooked on drugs and survived as a prostitute in urban America; and Patricia became a suicide, but not before committing incest with her father, John Christopher. Johnnie, the issue of their union, is a very dark-skinned child, who in Herron's novel lives to tell the story of all six generations, including her own:

> And from these origins has there come this great curse upon our house: The females shall be raped and the males shall be murdered! And the males that are not murdered shall be sold, and to certain ones of the males that are neither murdered nor sold, to certain of those few males come late into the house marrying, and to certain of the males born to the house but who nevertheless survive murder and slavery—to these shall be given the power of revenge upon the females of their own house who consented with the white males for their destruction, these males shall be given the female children of their own house, and these shall be raped. And raped again [pp. 239–240].

To appreciate the relevance of this chilling passage, one must first unpack certain preconceptions. Paradoxically, this is best achieved by referring to two altogether tame concepts from psychoanalysis describing the ego's defensive operations: change of function and secondary autonomy. Thus, murder as an original form of destructive behavior may be committed in one generation, but it may change function in the next generation and appear as incestuous behavior; the latter then may assume a secondary autonomy.

## The Shift from Rape and Murder to Incest

Hartmann (1958) explicated his view of "the historical-developmental factor" entailed in transgenerational dramas in the following two passages:

> Man does not come to terms with his environment anew in every generation; his relation to the environment is guaran-

teed by . . . an evolution peculiar to man, namely, the influence of tradition and the survival of works of man. We take
over from others . . . a great many of our methods for solving problems. . . . The works of man objectify the methods
he has discovered for solving problems and thereby become
factors of continuity, so that man lives, so to speak, in past
generations as well as in his own [p. 30].

A network of appropriations operates between families, ethnic
groups, and institutions. This network is perpetuated and transformed in peculiar ways. It is adopted and maintained for psychological reasons "inasmuch as certain social phenomena which
originated as expressions of definite psychological tendencies can
become the expressions of different tendencies during historical
development" (Hartmann, 1964, p. 33).

Thus, psychological trends of antecedent generations show themselves and impose themselves on individuals in consequent generations as new realities. In Hartmann's view, in following generations
frequently, but not always, the psychological trends of antecedent
generations "continue to satisfy along broad lines the same psychological needs to which they originally owed their creation" (p.
33). Dread of infanticide and an impulse toward it may linger simultaneously in a lineage. They may appear as diffuse or circumscribed
anxiety or as a misread danger; or the impulse may persist through
the erection of defenses against the accompanying anxiety—over-
solicitude in one family, a belief that children must be toughened
and hardened in another—in ways that permit the defensive organization to develop a life of its own. Through a change of function,
then, the resulting defensive organization can become stable or irre-
versible. This newly developed organization can serve autonomous
functions in a secondary way, as opposed to a primary autonomy
that is "originary" (of its own origins).

What, then, are some twists and turns of history that may evolve
into an entirely different representation? Herron's (1991) interpretation of the African-American experience draws attention to the
following set of traumatic axioms that become realized finally as
transgenerational phantoms:

• The females shall be raped by slavemasters; the males shall be
murdered by slavemasters.

- The males who are not murdered shall be sold away.
- The males who are neither murdered nor sold away shall marry the females who are not murdered or sold away.
- In marriage, enslaved males and former slaves shall have revenge over females perceived to have consented to the destruction of males.
- Women and their daughters shall, therefore, be raped over and over again by enslaved men or former slaves.

Herron calls this psychic legacy "the curse." In it, incest is presented as a derivative of, and as being continuous with, rape and murder. This abiding legacy involves a three-fold process: (1) in the first instance, the historical facts of rape and murder; (2) appropriation by an ethnic group of a transgressor's cruelty, to serve a secondary purpose of revenge; and (3) ossification of a structure of experience that holds that victims may heap cruelty, which originated with external transgressors, onto their own kind. This process is a literary version of the transfer of the events of history to an appropriated and mentalized sense of history that clinicians observe in the psychoanalytic process. It is also consistent with Hartmann's (1958) idea of a developmental history of instinctual goals. In psychoanalytically informed field work, the staging of the destructive-aggressive aspects of slavery may present itself as "black-on-black" crime, in which the transgressed has lost sight of the original enemy.

Herron's (1991) story accounts for the murder of African-American males and for the rape of African-American women and demonstrates how incest became a derivative of this behavior. The character Rowena dreamed of escaping from slavery and its trajectories and of starting life anew; her dream coincides with those of her ancestral fathers. Juxtaposed with Rowena's dream is Laetitia's wish for her daughter to return to the south. The dying Laetitia wants her daughter by her side—but not Rowena's black child, who was born of African-American and Indian parentage, for the child's presence would publicize her blackness. To this request, Rowena insists repeatedly: "I shall not come. This is the dream of my father" (p. 240). In short, the phantom as a metapsychological construct must not be actualized by acceding to a peremptory or insidious demand by the transgressor, who is now internalized. A break with history as remembered must occur so that the self may be freed to make new and ethical choices.

## The Juxtaposition of Lost Narcissism and Collective Megalomania

The declaration of Rowena's father's dream "to be free" represents injured narcissism on a collective basis. It speaks to the loss of the idealized self, which will never again be found, due to incest, rape, and other transgressions (Apprey, 1991). In other words, the structure of experience originally constituted by the destructive aggression of historical events that subserve feelings of humiliation must, in the clinical situation, be expanded to include multiple constructions of the self beyond the damaged internalized self and other representations.

Positioned on the other side of this equation are a number of questions. What was it that drove Euro-Americans to seek to obliterate the identity of African Americans? What drove the Euro-American to "kill" the men in the lives of African-American women? What drives the members of one group to regard member of another group as nameless ones? What drives one group to designate certain members of another group the special ones, and then rape and humiliate them? In short, what drives one side to dehumanize another, to foster secrets in the lives of the other, and psychically to scotomize and obliterate the existence of the other as human amongst humans?

In the story of the collective injury to African Americans as conveyed by Herron, injured narcissism is stretched across generations. The author traces the devastation of the narcissism of African-American women, who, as a group, were either raped or victimized by incest. This destruction resulted in their loss of an image of their ideal selves as a people with proud origins. Superimposed on this portrait of the injured narcissism of a once-proud people is a picture of destructive narcissism, of the kind that permits men— whether colonial governors or slavemasters—to think that they have dominion over an endless array of sexual consorts toward whom they may act out their sexual and destructive impulses at will.

### A System Based on Delusion

*Thereafter Johnnie* demonstrates how a structure of patriarchal power became entrenched, building on a most destructive narcissism that resisted disillusion. In this respect, narcissism, in the special form of megalomania, converged with the once-positive narcissism of the enslaved (now lost) to fill the gap in the ruptured lives owed to transgenerational trauma, enslavement, and deracination from West Africa to the United States.

What is this megalomania that preys on the injury of others? It shows itself as a "double delusion—a delusional inferiority, on one hand, and a delusional superiority on the other" (Money-Kyrle, 1978, p. 380). Compassion toward one who is supposed to be inferior becomes suspect, for empathy toward a tired and weary slave does not end the enslavement. Rather it conceals arrogance and contempt. At the same time, "pleasant feelings of admiration and gratitude may override painful feelings of inferiority, hate, and envy" (p. 380). The sense of inferiority that dwells in the slavemaster is thus projected onto the person who is enslaved, resulting in insults such as those portraying the slave as being dirty. The slave then becomes the custodian of the slavemaster's own stench.

Megalomania may thus mask a delusional arrogance that is responsible for the creation of barriers between the self and the other and that causes the other to be treated as though he or she does not possess human qualities, special merits, or any merit at all. This megalomania splits off as inferiority that must be translocated into another race; this inferiority, in turn, drives a delusional superiority. Delusional inferiority and delusional superiority appear and disappear together. Like outer garments, they act as a second skin. As a second skin, delusional arrogance cannot bear rebellion against itself, however. Recognition of the other might cause the illusory garment to fall away and shatter one's aggrandized and false reality. Like an embodiment of Narcissus, one would die if one were to know oneself. Again, as for Narcissus, any recognition of the presence of Echo would spell one's demise, because one would have to acknowledge one's self as being dependent on the other.

### Finding Representations of the Phantom

Understanding the interstices between recognizing one's dependence on another human and recognizing one's own capacity for destructiveness is, therefore, an obligatory first step to comprehending transgenerational haunting in African-American families and communities. The intersubjectivity within the interstices, of Narcissus and Echo (who once was part of him), allows us to come to grips with the dire consequences of transgenerational haunting as they appear in contemporary African-American families but in disguised forms. Thus, we see that there really is a phantom behind black-on-black crime. And there is a phantom behind adolescent pregnancies among blacks and behind other displays of appropriations of hatred. If we are to find a way to give these phantoms a decent burial, we must not blame African Americans for inflicting harm on their own selves; nor should we hold Euro-Americans entirely responsible for planting every seed of hatred. Rather, as we trace this particular branch of human behavior, we must locate the point where it forks off into injured narcissism, on one side, and megalomania on the other. There we may find that the phantom is a collaged and constructed image, composed of acts of destructive aggression, hostile dependence on the other, megalomania, and other destructive agents of transmission.

*Thereafter Johnnie* awakens us from our slumber to face vicissitudes of aggression committed by one race against another; destructive aggression which may otherwise surface as intraracial incest, black-on-black crime, or adolescent pregnancies. The road to resolution, however, is not to branch left or right at the fork (of the road), but to stop, interrogate, and, with a discerning eye, cross the bridge that already is there, beckoning us.

## Notes

Anna Freud (1936) analyzed the ego's defensive operations and determined that they involve the following: defense against instinct that shows itself as resistance, defense against painful affects; and the manifestation of both in permanent defense phenomena. Hartmann (1958) refined Reich's (1933) observations about the change of function of instincts that defensively and permanently come to have a life of their own. That is, change of function refers to a form of defensive behavior that begins in one realm of life, but appears in a distinctly different realm in a future state, where it performs a different role and acts as though it were an independent structure. As an independent structure, it serves other adaptational functions by turning a means into a goal. When a function changes, it takes on a secondary autonomy, whereby it achieves a level of stability and irreversibility.

Here I apply the language of Edmund Husserl, the father of phenomenology.

## References

Abraham, M. (1988), Notes on the phantom. In: *The Trials of Psychoanalysis*, ed. F. Meltzer. Chicago, IL: Chicago University Press, pp. 75–80.

Apprey, M. (1991), Psychical transformations by a child of incest. In: *The Trauma of Transgression*, ed. S. Kramer & S. Akhtar. Northvale, NJ: Aronson, pp. 115–147.

——— (1992), Dreams of urgent/voluntary errands and transgenerational haunting in transsexualism. *Melanie Klein & Object Relations*, 10:1–29.

Ferenczi, S. (1909), Introjection and transference. In: *Sex in Psychoanalysis*. New York: Basic Books, 1950, pp. 422–457.

Freud, A. (1936), *The Ego and the Mechanisms of Defense*. New York: International Universities Press, 1966.

Hartmann, H. (1958), *The Ego and the Problem of Adaptation*. New York: International Universities Press.

——— (1964), *Essays on Ego Psychology*. New York: International Universities Press.

Herron, C. (1991), *Thereafter Johnnie*. New York: Random House.

Money-Kyrle, R. (1978), Megalomania. In: *The Collected Papers of Roger Money-Kyrle*. Perth, Scotland: Clunie Press, pp. 376–388.

## ❖ 4 ❖

# Concurrent Intervention During Massive Community Trauma
## An Analyst's Experience at Ground Zero

Jeffrey Taxman

On September 11, 2001, every man, woman, and child in the United States was assaulted by unbridled aggression. We were witnesses to the type of death and destruction previously relegated to fantasy or the Unconscious. The twin towers of the World Trade Center, the tallest, sleekest testaments to our technological prowess, at the center of the West's financial strength in the heart of our greatest city, were cut down and reduced to fiery rubble as two airliners, one after the other, crashed into them. An unseen, unknown force killed thousands. Among those killed were hundreds to whom we usually turn for protection: the uniformed police, fire fighters, and Port Authority officers. We soon learned that one of the great bastions of our strength, the Pentagon, had also been attacked and was in flames.

Immediately following the collapse of the towers, smoking ash covered the area. Primitive collective fears spread like wildfire: Who did this? Will there be another attack? Are there more hijacker-pilots? Is there radiation? Are there toxins? Has the retaining wall holding back the Hudson River been breached? Will lower Manhattan be flooded? Tens of thousands of suddenly displaced persons fled on foot for miles—they did not know where they were going or from what they were fleeing. Hundreds of thousands worried about the safety of their loved ones and friends but were unable to contact them. Everyone ultimately came to realize that a naive but deeply ingrained element of our identity was gone forever: we, and our way of life, were not untouchable; the oceans, after all, did not insulate us from harm. We had been attacked on our own soil.

The violence and horror of September 11 caused pain and trauma both in tragically familiar and in shocking new ways. In the past, we have witnessed images of war only in film clips, prepared and delayed for news broadcasts. In the postmodern technological era, however, information and image transfer can be instantaneous and widespread. On September 11, 2001, our entire nation witnessed the graphic horrors of war unfold. This unparalleled death and destruction was viewed by tens of millions, repeatedly, in slow motion and in real time. Millions watched live as the second plane slammed into the second tower. We all watched as the towers collapsed, trapping and crushing what was then presumed to be at least ten thousand people. The immediacy of this event led to unique psychological trauma for those at Ground Zero, in New York City, and throughout the rest of the United States. For caregivers to the rescuers, an understanding of the dynamic mind and the world of the unconscious facilitated understanding and assisting those affected by these traumatic events.

### Setting up at Ground Zero

Like many Americans, I awoke on September 11, 2001, to the unfolding of a tragedy. As the shock, disbelief, and horror settled, a sense of impotence transformed into a need to do something—anything—to help those caught in the disaster. Having trained at New York Hospital, I contacted a number of my colleagues there, and after a series of phone calls, I was put in touch with a well-organized group called Disaster Psychiatry Outreach (DPO). I explained that I had worked with police officers, fire fighters and FBI agents and had an understanding of the different nuances of psychotherapy that working with this close-knit band of men and women demanded. Two days later I was on a nearly empty airplane headed for New York City and Ground Zero.

Descending toward LaGuardia airport, I could see smoke billowing from lower Manhattan. An angry, dark wound was now where the center of the West's financial capital once stood. Walking to get my luggage was an eerie, disquieting experience. The airport resembled a ghost town, with more guards and soldiers than passengers or tourists. After a short bus ride, I made my way to New York's West Side.

Pier 94 had become the emergency resource center for those individuals, families, and rescuers who had been affected by the destruction of the World Trade Center and surrounding areas. Outside the respite center were hundreds of yards of fencing plastered with photographs of loved ones inscribed with identifying information, phone numbers, and desperate hope regarding the whereabouts of people last seen in the World Trade Center buildings. Inside the building, the City of New York had assembled an enormous array of resources for survivors of the bombing. The resources ranged from police and medical personnel, to international telephone and e-mail access, to information about lost or stranded pets. Food was available as were emergency medical and psychiatric referrals.

It soon became apparent there were very few, if any, police, military, or fire personnel using the respite center. Most of these rescue workers were remaining at the site. Therefore, the following day, DPO sent me and Dr. Laura Sherman, a psychiatrist who had experience with smaller disasters, to Ground Zero to work with the people still on site. We were given space in one of the respite centers on Wall Street. Not knowing what to expect, we brought with us forms and rudimentary medications, including anxiolytics and hypnotics. We would quickly discover that in this population we would not use the forms or the medications nor the standard techniques that one usually employs in an analyst's office.

## The Use of Different Techniques

At the respite center there was, of course, no office. We were working in what had been a downtown fitness center that was now a dusty, makeshift food and rest center for steel workers, fire fighters, police officers, and the military. On the ground level were chairs and television sets, as well as twenty-four-hour hot-and-cold-food tables supplied by the Red Cross. Upstairs were fifty or more cots for around-the-clock shifts of rescue workers. We realized that this population was not going to come seeking out a "therapy session," nor would we get very far if we started with an information sheet taking down name, address, rank, and "chief complaint." We also realized that normal business attire or even "Friday casual" not only would set us apart, but also would be viewed with derisive distaste, much as a politician coming to tour the battle field in his pristine suit might be viewed by combat-weary soldiers. Thus, dressed in jeans, T-shirts, and workboots, but wearing identification and security passes as well as hard hats and ventilator masks, we mingled among the rescue workers. Mostly we made small talk. We asked how people were doing or if they wanted coffee. Inevitably, the workers' eyes would drop down to our ID badges. Often we would hear a comment like, "Ah ha, so you're a shrink! Man, you should talk to THAT guy! He's REALLY crazy!" Of course "that guy" would inevitably be his or her partner. A humorous comment acted as an icebreaker and more often than not eventually led to a more private conversation about the stresses, traumas, and difficulties that the person was experiencing.

After we had mingled for a day or so, the rescue workers began to recognize and become more comfortable with us. Still, defensive bravado and a reluctance to look "weak," kept many of them from engaging us in candid conversation. If the lower-ranking members of a squad saw an officer talking with us, however, the rest of the squad began to feel free to approach us.

This acceptance was poignantly brought home to me on the second day, when I walked out to meet three senior members of the National Guard in a military transport. As I approached with an early morning smile and a greeting, their disdainful stares spoke volumes. It was clear that they wanted nothing to do with me or with anything I had to offer. About an hour later, while I was standing in the doorway watching the sky clearing from a light rain, I noticed from the corner of my eye one of the three, a squat, powerfully built, dark-complexioned man in his 50s, approaching me. Recalling the morning's encounter I gave him wide berth and was surprised a few minutes later when he began to make small talk.

The small talk led to talk about the events of the past week and their nonstop, 20-hour days. He told me with pride of his decades of service in the National Guard and his years of active duty in the military. He then began to talk about the pain he and his family were suffering now from the backlash against people that appeared to be foreigners. He recounted how his son had been mistaken for someone of Middle Eastern descent and had been beaten by a group of youths. He also angrily reported how his wife had been asked for special identification and her passport when she was shopping at a local appliance store. I could hear the anger and frustration in his voice but was surprised, as I turned, to see tears rolling down his cheeks.

We spent the next hour talking about the prejudice and isolation that he and his Dominican Republican family had endured despite his lifetime of service to this country. He went on to relate painful memories of feeling helpless and impotent when his son's friend died of a drug overdose after being turned away from rehab centers because of insurance problems. For this soldier, past issues of violence, death, prejudice, and xenophobia were brought to the surface by the terror attacks. He smiled and reflected on the relief of being able to unburden some of these festering issues to an "outsider."

A number of the soldiers in his unit saw him talking with me and witnessed his emotional reaction. Within an hour from the time the officer and I had finished talking, three of the men from his unit approached either my colleague or me. In fact, on subsequent days these soldiers, once skeptical, brought in many buddies and civilians who appeared to be in distress. This experience reinforced the technique of establishing a therapeutic alliance with superiors in a hierarchical system. We found that, in this highly charged, traumatic situation, establishing such an alliance created a permissive environment much more conducive for therapeutic engagement than random or compulsory interaction (for example, mandatory "debriefing") would be. It was also crucial that we were "out-of-town civilians" with no ties to government or their department administration.

The unique circumstances and population we were working with demanded that we develop and employ techniques different from those we ordinarily use in the consultation office. Standard parameters, or frames, of therapy were nonexistent. The situation was fluid. It was ongoing, and we were intervening with people as they concurrently carried out their jobs. It was a unique situation in which we were interacting with people enduring extreme stress and prolonged trauma, while we ourselves were in the midst of the ongoing traumatic event. Everything about the interactions was different from the day-to-day analytic or insight-oriented psychotherapy interaction. There were no offices or desks and frequently no chairs. No notes were taken. Verbal interactions were casual and to the outside observer took on the appearance of conversation or "schmoozing."

Many of the techniques we used working with the rescue workers "on the fly" seemed diametrically opposed to what we as analysts have been taught and what classical analytic theory endorses. For example, the complete interaction—introduction, engagement, depth, understanding, intervention, and termination—might take place in 15 minutes to an hour. This required incisive flexibility, rigorous focus, maximum empathic attunement, and a willingness to be, at times, quite self-revealing and interactive. For example, late one evening I stopped to ask an officer at his post if he knew where I could get some soup. He gave me directions, noticed my identification, and after some small talk began to tell me about many of the horrors he had witnessed during the collapse of the buildings and its aftermath. They were without doubt horrific recollections, but his demeanor and affect remained quite professional.

It was only when we found ourselves talking responsively and almost conversationally about our families, marriages, and children that his more central concerns and distressed affect emerged: The sudden loss of life and the realization that time and opportunities are not endless brought to the surface a long-smoldering worry about his marriage and his relationship with his children. He spoke with despair about the helplessness and futility he had felt, standing there, seemingly unable to do anything or save anyone. This relatively young officer, who was continuing a family tradition of police work, had for the past few days begun to think about quitting. He said it was impossible to see any good that he could do or any use for the uniform. After all, "What can I do for anyone?" he said. I was struck by this question, for I had heard him speak earlier, quite passionately, about the values and honor in law enforcement, which he had shared all his life with his familial predecessors, and, especially, with the close friends who had died in the buildings. I spoke to him about those friends who had just died in the uniforms that they loved, doing what they believed in. Although intervening this quickly was a calculated risk, I decided to go even further. I told him that to me his standing there, at his post—in his uniform, at midnight and doing the job that he believed in, even though he felt devastated—was a testament to the beliefs and the values that his friends lived and died for in *their* uniforms. He looked at me and smiled. Then he chuckled and said, "You should have been a cop." I laughed and said something self-deprecating about my long hair. He laughed again and said, "Well, you could always work undercover."

As we shook hands and I started to leave, he said he would like to stop by the respite center later and chat a bit, which he did. In addition, he brought along two friends to "chat." Faced with the horrors and devastation of the first days following the bombing, many of this man's integrating beliefs and values began to falter. He felt alone with his fears and self doubts. An empathic exchange of personal experiences helped him feel less isolated, while reframing his values gave him validation and support. Validation for *me* was in his response. Telling me that I "should have been a cop" was at once letting me know he felt I understood him, as well as allowing me into his revered peer group. The "undercover" allusion was a fascinating approximation of how he saw the actual work I was doing: I was one of the good guys, dressed in plain clothes, finding important, hidden information that was not otherwise available.

At Ground Zero every interaction had the potential to be significant, although it might not have appeared so until halfway into it. This kind of interaction occurred around 3:00 one morning as I was taking a break and sitting down to watch a few minutes of television. A young, African-American enlisted man was sitting next to me and appeared to be asleep. There was a heavyweight boxing match on the television. One of the boxers delivered a thunderous right to the other man's head, and I muttered some involuntary exclamation. The soldier responded, "Oh man, I know. I don't know how they stay standing. I think I'd get killed if I were in that ring. People think we're so tough 'cause we're soldiers. I'm pretty tough, but I don't think I could take something like that." I told him that I felt the same way, and we began to talk about a hero we had in common, Muhammad Ali. We spoke about the kind of skill and preparation Ali had committed to his sport. He not only transformed boxing but also transcended it, and he had a dramatic effect on American society. The soldier talked about how Ali had given him someone to look up to and had given him hope.

This seemingly casual conversation about a boxing match took place over approximately 10 minutes, with both of us watching television. We never once looked at each other. When one of his buddies called him over to go back to his shift, he stood up, held out his hand, and said, "Thank you. It was nice meeting you." His words at first struck me as odd because we had not "met." We had not looked at each other, introduced ourselves, or known each other's name. I was well aware of the many parallels our conversation had to the situation surrounding us both. I was not aware of how profound and close to the surface these parallels were for him until I noticed the tears in his eyes.

As he grasped my hand, smiled, and said "Thank you," I was reminded that in that kind of setting every interaction had the potential for significant meaning and must be approached with that possibility in mind. Like any utterance in analysis, these interactions need to be scrutinized respectfully for deeper meaning. At Ground Zero, the manifest content of the here-and-now was so highly charged and experience-near that it shared a greater part of the stage with the more hidden issues. I took great care to avoid the appearance of dismissing immediate issues while looking for "deeper psychological meaning."

In contradistinction to usual psychoanalytic practice, my colleague and I became adept at spotting and exploiting any "hook," or prop, to help engage those who looked distressed. For example, we might approach someone who looked particularly bedraggled or distressed to ask for a match or a cigarette. I almost always had a cup of coffee in my hand and would either offer it or let the person know about the food and showers back at the respite center. Dr. Sherman, who had worked with children in the past, brought many of her supplies in a child's Dr. Seuss backpack. Within a day or two, most of the workers at Ground Zero had seen the incongruous sight of a woman in a white coat and hard hat with a Dr. Seuss backpack. She would often be greeted with calls of "Hey, Dr. Seuss" or "There goes Dr. Seuss." At once both disarming and engaging, the backpack was a potent transitional object, linking pleasant childhood memories to the bearer of the backpack.

### Early Psychological Impact of the Terror Attack

Thousands of rescue workers and others in New York City were exposed to the traumas of a massive terror attack. Witnesses reported seeing sudden death and destruction, finding dead bodies and severed limbs, watching helplessly as people jumped from one hundred stories high and seeing and hearing what happened when they hit the ground. Rampant among these rescue workers and witnesses were less obvious sequelae of this attack. As so often is the case in our analytic work, many of the psychological conflicts and traumas were not what one might expect based on initial appearances. Some areas of conflict included survivor guilt, frustration, family and marital conflicts, doubts about self-worth, and a sense of impotence and futility.

One of the most poignant expressions of the crushing sense of frustration and impotence came from a police officer summoned from his uptown precinct after the first jetliner struck. He and hundreds of others were put into buses and vans and were brought to a staging area. After the second plane hit, they were not allowed off the buses because the situation was still fluid, and it was unknown if there were still planes not accounted for. Not being allowed off the buses, of course, frustrated these men and women of action, who were there to assist their fellow officers in evacuating and aiding citizens. As they saw the first building collapse, their frustration turned to frantic anger, as their commanders would still not allow them to run into the unstable situation.

Making matters worse, they were all wearing their emergency radios, as were the men and women trapped in the first building. They could hear the cries, pleas, and confusion. They sometimes recognized voices, but could do nothing except watch the second building collapse. After a short while they were allowed out to try to help rescue those who were still alive. The officer described a disorienting, hellish scene of twisted metal, fire, incredible heat, and dense smoke. At one point, after the dust had settled some, he was standing in wreckage when he suddenly heard hundreds of crickets. He thought this was quite bizarre and could not understand what crickets were doing in lower Manhattan in the middle of a war zone. It was then that he noticed a flurry of activity from the firefighters near him, and he asked what was happening. He was told that all firefighters have an electronic locator that sets off an electronic chirp when there is no movement or communication for a set period of time. As he looked around, he realized that all those "crickets" were dead or dying fire fighters buried somewhere under the rubble.

Reflecting on this nightmarish imagery added a powerful dimension to concerns about the future for many of the firefighters, especially with regard to posttraumatic stress disorder. As spring and summer bring real crickets out, their chirping in the night may act as a powerful trigger for many firefighters' memories and unbidden recollections of death.

Many of the soldiers and police officers experienced a mounting level of frustration. Some of this frustration was apparent as feelings of helplessness and futility. In addition, many aspects of the trauma replayed childhood struggles and frustrations. A knowledge of early childhood struggles around learning and incorporating parental and societal rules, versus enacting drive impulses—especially aggressive impulses—shed light on the officers' mounting anxiety, frustration, and anger. This internal struggle was particularly highly charged for the officers on the buses in the staging area when their superiors held to protocol and would not let them off. Such a situation might bring to mind the lessons of a playground, a classroom, or a sports field when a child is taught that he needs to follow the rules even if the opponent is cheating. Developmental models also offer a framework for understanding the mounting anger expressed by those wishing to strike back. Many of the soldiers I spoke to were seething and were well aware of the United States' capability of delivering a devastating blow in retaliation. Aware of the rules governing the use of deadly force, they were very frustrated by having to face an enemy that followed no such rules.

The numbing awareness of the magnitude of loss of life continually found ways to seep into the minds of those at and near Ground Zero. Initially, awareness came with brutally concrete exposure to death. There were the horrifying sights and sounds of people either blown out of buildings or jumping out of windows a quarter of a mile in the air to certain death below. Many people jumped in groups of two or more, some holding hands or embracing. At least one rescue worker reported seeing one of his buddies hit by a falling body. Many reported that the sound and sight of bodies hitting the concrete remained like a stain in their memories.

Delayed or less direct reminders of the enormous loss of life continued for weeks. One ironic indirect reminder, or reinforcer, of the enormity of the loss of life was the empty emergency rooms in the surrounding hospitals. Within hours of the disaster, emergency mobilization plans had scores of hospitals in New York and New Jersey ready with their disaster preparedness protocol. Trauma surgeons, internists, anesthesiologists, nurses, and others were all assembled and ready for the expected waves of thousands of wounded citizens. As the hours ticked away, the onslaught of injured patients never materialized. The realization spread from hospital to hospital: this assault had been terribly effective. There would be relatively few treatable injuries and almost everyone who did not make it out of the buildings was dead.

Many of the rescuers spoke of self-recriminating thoughts that they could have done more. This was a disorientingly strange disaster for many rescuers: the magnitude of destruction was enormous, covering many acres of total destruction, yet there were relatively few people to be rescued. Most either escaped more or less unharmed, or died. One of the firefighters ruminated with despair about a voice that he heard calling for help but could not locate. He searched diligently but was unable to find the source of the voice, though it sounded close to him. Eventually the voice faded and was not heard again. This was a firefighter who found and escorted five or six people out of that same area, yet all he could say to me was, "I couldn't find the voice. I couldn't find it." While he likely saved all those lives, what stuck with him and tormented him was the voice that he could not find.

I heard from police officers and firefighters who harbored tremendous guilt for having switched shifts with someone who never made it out of the rubble. Often this guilt took the form of needing to apologize for the switch, or to explain it, as though they would be blamed for their colleague's death. Some expressed guilt for having survived without a scratch while many in their company or squad perished. Some would ask what they could say to a fallen buddy's spouse or children. Many had rapid associations to quitting their jobs, perhaps revealing a form of self-punishment to help assuage guilt.

Psychoanalysts are trained to work with paradoxes, such as conscious, rational thought coexisting with unconscious, irrational inner life. The rescue workers, however, were not prepared for the ambivalent paradoxes they faced at Ground Zero. Many reflected on the tremendous euphoria and ego gratification they experienced when passing by crowds of cheering, grateful citizens lining the streets. At the same time, they were at a loss to understand why that gratification prompted pangs of guilt and thoughts of having done nothing and thus being undeserving of the hero's mantel.

The "two minds"—the rational and the irrational—at odds with each other was most apparent among the firefighters during the second week after the collapse of the buildings. It was around this time that the rescue phase switched to recovery. Dysphoria did not set in until the hope of rescue had formally shifted by administrative fiat to the despair of recovery. Quite early on, however, the calculating, rational side of the mind recognized that virtually nobody was going to survive who had not gotten out early. The incredible heat kept girders glowing for weeks, the force crushed all concrete to powder, and the pressure condensed 110 floors of soaring modern technology into ten. There would be no miracle stories of survival after a few days.

Hope and the struggle against despair kept the firefighters, National Guard, police, and steelworkers working well beyond what the rational mind and physical limitations would normally have allowed. Once administrators officially announced what everyone knew but could not say, the psychological gates were opened for ten days' worth of suppressed affect. Despair was palpable. Irritability and distraction were increasingly apparent. Fights occasionally broke out. Exhaustion, so long denied, was now allowed to overwhelm. Somber respect for those few bodies recovered, however, never wavered. When a body was found, all work would stop in the vicinity. If the body was that of a fellow officer, a long, silent, respectful line of officers would form along the path of recovery.

### Parallel Processes

There were many challenges in the work done at Ground Zero. There were also many rewards. As is often the case in our analytic work, the difficulties were frequently not those expected, and mine often paralleled the experiences and processes of those rescuers with whom I was working. Much of the work was grim and unsettling. It was also, surprisingly, exhilarating and rewarding. I discovered in this setting and in this situation that my greatest risk for "burning out" was not from being overwhelmed by horror, fear, or pathos. Rather, it was from being unable to disengage and pull away. It seemed as if there was always one more shift that might need help or that I should take one more walk around the perimeter or through the crowded, smoky areas adjacent to the rubble. Sleep became expendable, yet I never felt fatigued. Even as I needed to catch transportation to the airport to go home, I felt the urgent need to talk to one more person and make one more pass through the respite center. I felt a nearly irresistible urge to call and reschedule my patients, to tell my wife I would be gone longer, and to stay for another week. There was still so much to do and so much unfinished work.

Then, in the quiet of the bus heading to the airport, I found myself thinking, "What have I accomplished? Nothing really. Maybe I helped some people, but there were thousands that I didn't get a chance to help." I realized then, of course, the striking parallel between my thoughts of futility and uselessness and those I had heard for days from the rescuers. I could then look back and recognize the parallel experience and process: feelings of futility, being unable to leave, hoping and searching for one more person to help rather than leaving the scene to rest or be with friends. This was strikingly similar to the reactions so easily recognized in others but not immediately seen in myself.

### Terror's Toll in the Living

Terrorists become visible when they hurt people, damage things, and disrupt lives. This, however, is only the terrorists' currency: Lives are exchanged to purchase fear among the living. Terrorism is aimed directly at the intended victims' psyches. Its express purpose and very nature is not only to kill but also to inflict maximum fear and cause changes in the minds, emotions, and actions of others. It is not assassination. Rather, like an effective parasite, it is intended to infect and spread fear among the living witnesses to the action. The actual, effective weapon used by a terrorist is not the bullet or explosive, but the psychological and symbolic assault. While witnesses tend to focus on the loss of life or injury to individuals, for the purposes of terrorism the individual is merely an instrument. This was never borne out so clearly as on September 11. The hundreds of people who were murdered on those airplanes used as guided missiles were truly inconsequential to the terrorists—they just happened to be there. As with sociopathy, the human life involved has no value to the terrorist other than as an object to effect the terrorist's purpose. The purpose of the September 11 terrorists' hijacking of the airplanes was to destroy iconical buildings and make an impact on the entire United States, indeed, on the world. It would most likely have mattered little to the terrorists if there were one hundred people on the planes, or no one other than the pilots.

This faceless aspect of terrorism is an effective communication in and of itself. It is a clear, cold statement that our lives have no meaning to the terrorists. It also conveys the message that the terrorists have complete control, can strike at anyone at any time, and can come out of shadows without being seen or known. This message is aimed too, at the psyche of the intended victim, who is placed in a subservient position and a state of utter helplessness. The message resonates with very early fears of the unknown and children's almost universal fear of imagined monsters or "bad guys" lurking in the dark. The pervasiveness, and lasting impression, of the September 11 traumatic events was borne out by how long afterward it took for people to overcome a new fear of flying. When flights were resumed, airplanes were viewed differently when seen or heard overhead. Many people, no longer taking flight for granted, looked to the sky, and wondered, "Will it stay up there?"

The intentional striking at the World Trade Center and the Pentagon were devastatingly effective in actual human, cultural, and financial damage. It was also horribly efficient at inflicting widespread psychological injury. The choice of the Twin Towers was not a random one. Functionally, the Towers housed an enormous concentration of the West's financial dealmakers and were also the nerve center for electronic communication for the United States and the Western world's financial business. The Towers housed the offices that made the majority of bond deals for the West. Symbolically the Twin Towers were an extremely effective psychological choice for a terror attack. They were a testament to American industry and technology. Their sleek, straight, soaring lines captured the imagination and awe of most who saw them. In addition, their inescapable phallic shape (which was not unintentional, according to architects who worked in the design stages of the buildings) resonated with early developmental conflicts and exacerbated unconscious distress for many witnesses of the destruction.

There are many developmental models we use to help us understand and operationalize the impact of parents and guardians on the nascent ego. Whether viewed from the framework of Freud's Oedipus, Mahler's rapprochement, or Kohut's self-object, the internalized image and experience of a strong, ever-present caretaker is a vital, central theme for human growth. Thus, the attack on the Pentagon sends a powerful symbolic message. The Pentagon is America's symbol of its military might, and to attack it face-on sends a message that the enemy is not cowed by our strength. Hence, the potential unconscious reverberations of the cutting down of the Twin Towers and the defiant assault on the Pentagon—on which we had relied as an untouchable military might—had a very powerful yet hidden effect on those citizens of the United States who witnessed this ordeal.

Further worsening the potential psychological trauma was the sudden loss of fire, police, and Port Authority personnel. These are people to whom we turn for help and protection, not unlike a strong parent. On one level, seeing or hearing about them being killed may reawaken fears of abandonment, or loss of a parent, from childhood. Unlike many irrational fantasies, however, these protectors *were* lost and people may have been left feeling unprotected in the city of New York, a feeling that could further shake early foundations of self-reliance and autonomy.

On a more subtle psychological level, most of the uniformed officers who were killed died while doing their jobs. This sacrifice while doing the job of protecting others and guiding others out of danger may additionally strengthen the unconscious tie to parents who may have been seen to sacrifice "for their children." Long-buried guilt or childhood rage at parents may have been frighteningly reawakened by this unconscious connection.

For many, especially those at Ground Zero or elsewhere in New York City, this exacerbated a sense of vulnerability and helplessness. For most, including me, there was a gnawing yet unspoken anxiety when in subways or on bridges in Manhattan. I believe this sense of vulnerability also explains one aspect of the exuberant, heartfelt cheers and hero status for the uniformed defenders of public safety. I was very aware of my own feelings of comfort and relief when I saw a soldier or police officer every few yards in lower Manhattan. This feeling of relief was profound, yet it was clear that there was no immediate danger near me. Rational assessment of the situation would have also made clear that the presence of the police or the army would not truly protect me from the type of onslaught wrought on September 11.

This feeling of vulnerability was echoed in the National Guard's frequently mentioned frustration and anxiety about not having live ammunition loaded in their automatic rifles. They, like all of us, had a sense of the potential for an unseen, violent attacker who could strike at any time. While they did have sidearms, they continued to feel more vulnerable and exposed because they did not have bigger, more powerful weapons ready to use.

I was also witness to many high-functioning responses and caring interactions between people. People went out of their way to help one another. Victims and survivors shared information and support. Tens of thousands gave time and money, food and shelter, without looking for an external reward. Humor was frequently used by rescuers, survivors, and victims' families. Interpersonal conflict was seldom seen, and there was an abundance of generosity and altruism.

## Impact on Psychotherapy

Witnessing the violence of September 11 also had a far-reaching impact on psychotherapy. The trauma affected patients and therapists alike; it had immediate, early, and long-term effects. These effects should also be seen and understood in terms of depth, ranging from superficial impact to unconscious responses played out in both the transference and countertransference arenas. The most immediate effect of witnessing the violence was, as with many traumatic experiences, distraction and preoccupation. For the first few days, I found it extremely difficult to focus on my job, my patients, or other matters at hand. Certainly on September 11 almost all my thoughts were focused on the events that were unfolding, and I was extremely distracted by a desire to listen endlessly to or watch the news. I found that I, and other therapists I spoke to, seemed to be more uniformly distracted from our work than our patients seemed to be distracted from their therapy sessions. Some of this discrepancy may have been due to a level of comfort or relief attained by patients going to their therapists' offices, where they could process some of the feelings about the event. Moreover, some of the patients' central therapeutic issues may have been further mobilized by the witnessed violence.

The material presented by patients may have been influenced by the events of September 11, as evidenced in their manifest content, fantasies, dreams, and associations. For the early period following September 11, the environment may have served as a ready source of aggressive or affectively charged material. In addition, elements of the transference were likely to have been affected by the events of September 11. In general, the witnessed violence may have had a permissive effect on, or mobilization of, aggressive material. On the other hand, there may have been a suppression or repression of aggressive material from a patient in a more frightened or vulnerable condition. To the extent that there was a positive parental transference, coming to the therapy session may have had an organizing or anxiolytic aspect not necessarily experienced by the therapist.

Further, oedipal issues in the transference may have changed, particularly if a patient felt the parental role of the therapist in the transference resonate with the terrorists. One patient presented dream material equating the terrorists with her father; she thus revealed deeply hidden fears about her father's hurting her mother and the patient's being unable to protect the mother. Another patient, a married man, chillingly exposed the depth of his narcissism when his only comment about the disaster was his dismay that his "favorite restaurant to take chicks to was gone now."

Among the rescue workers, as well as with patients in my office, I saw an increase in what might be called "enlisting the superego in the service of the id"—that is, allowing unbridled aggressive and violent impulses, wishes, and fantasies to be expressed as long as they flowed through the permissive guise of punishing wrongdoers or avenging innocents. Normally, superego prohibition would inhibit such raw expressions of violence. Following the assault on September 11, such desires for retribution were not only allowed, but were seen as acceptable, even righteous and patriotic. The assault had been felt by virtually the entire United States, and a group mentality normalized expression of such aggressive wishes.

Some patients felt that their issues or problems paled in comparison to the events of September 11, and thus they felt uncomfortable or resisted bringing their issues to their therapists. After I returned from Ground Zero, a number of patients reported fears that I would no longer be interested in them and would find working with them too trivial or mundane. I was also surprised that a few patients were angry at my going to Ground Zero. Some reported worry that I might be hurt and not come back, and others were angry that I might be doing this for my own professional or personal gain or prestige.

Another impact on the practice of psychotherapy was that therapists were affected in their ability to listen. Initially, as I have mentioned, the ability to listen at all was compromised by marked distraction by the day's events. Beyond the initial distraction, however, witnessing or being part of the events at Ground Zero may have had a longer-lasting effect on our ability to listen neutrally to our patients. In the weeks or even months following September 11, many therapists found it difficult to attend evenly to their patients' transference, particularly those elements of the transference leading to seeing themselves as an aggressor. Similarly, immediately following the assault on the World Trade Center, some therapists found it difficult to tolerate patients' aggressive fantasies toward them.

Surprisingly, I found an interesting example of the effect on my ability to hear neutrally. One of my analysands made an associative parallel between the events of September 11 and her parents and her. As this woman's analysis had been filled with examples of mistreatment and ad hominem behavior from her mother toward her, I assumed that in the association, the patient was the United States being attacked by the terrorists. I was wrong. Her understanding of and identification with the terrorists was a strong indicator of the depth of her anger toward her mother and her infantile feelings of impotent rage. It was striking to me that, in the aftermath of the attack on the World Trade Center, I had thoroughly overlooked this possibility and how difficult it was at first for me to grasp. Normally this paradigm would have been an obvious consideration. Exposure to the assault of September 11—*as a personal assault*—led to a countertransference blind spot.

## Summary

On September 11, 2001, we were all witness to massive violence and assault. The destruction of the World Trade Center complex, the bombing of the Pentagon, and the crashing of United States commercial jets full of passengers shocked the world and caused unprecedented damage to the United States in terms of the human toll, the economy, and our individual psyches. As psychoanalysts we are particularly qualified to render aid to a traumatized community struggling as the recipient of such unbridled aggression. We have studied and worked with the unconscious processes that contribute a hidden and often seemingly paradoxical layer of psychological meaning to the more obvious physical and emotional injuries. As observers we are accustomed to looking for meaning beyond the manifest content, searching for how the manifest content and the obvious injury might apply specifically to an individual's life story. We are aware of certain developmental conflicts and processes that may be reawakened by their resonance with current events. We are practiced at the art of patient, emotional attunement even in the face of affective lability or displaced anger. We have also learned from our own analytic searches to look within ourselves, to employ our own affective experience to gain further information, and to communicate effectively with our patients.

On the surface, an observer of my work with the rescuers and survivors at Ground Zero, amid the smoke and litter-strewn streets, might not see similarities to the work of the stereotypical psychoanalyst. On the contrary, at every moment and with every person with whom I interacted, I used everything I learned from my years of analytic training and my experience with my analysands and my own analyst. These experiences allowed me to be a better therapeutic observer and caregiver by giving me a better understanding of some of the powerful dynamic forces affecting those around me and, of course, myself. Many psychoanalysts are taking their analytic experiences into the community. It is incumbent on us to use our particular knowledge and experience to render relief to communities stricken by the violence of terrorism.

# ❖ 5 ❖

## After the Violence
### *The Internal World and Linking Objects of a Refugee Family*

Vamik D. Volkan

There are numerous variables to consider when speaking of the immigrant experience. One factor to take into account is the amount of choice a person has in the immigration process. Levels of dislocation appear on a spectrum ranging from forced emigration—associated with violence—to voluntary emigration—associated with the hope of finding a better life. Newcomers also differ in respect to their ages, their internal psychological organizations, and the support systems that are available to them. In addition, the unconscious fantasies that are linked to traumatic events vary from one individual to another (Parens, 2001).

This chapter describes the drastic effects that forced migration has on refugees' identities and explores their difficulty in mourning. The internal world of a refugee family who was driven out of their homes after massive ethnic violence illustrates the aftermath of forced migration. It took nine years from the time of their dislocation experience for them to be able to "relibidinalize" their self-representations. The relibidinalization process allowed them to resolve their sense of helplessness and humiliation. Only after working through these feelings could they tame the derivatives of their aggression and bring the mourning process to a practical end, and thus improve their abilities to test reality and adapt to their new environment.

## A Brief Review of the Psychoanalytic Literature on Immigrants

Psychoanalysts have not extensively studied the psychology of immigrants and refugees. This lapse is surprising given that many psychoanalysts, especially in North and South America, were immigrants themselves after World War II. There are exceptions of course (see, for example, Ticho, 1971; Garza-Guerrero, 1974; Volkan, 1979; Grinberg and Grinberg, 1989; Wangh, 1992; Akhtar, 1999; Parens, 2001). Most of these studies depict emigration as a traumatic experience. The trauma is, of course, more likely and more severe in cases of forced emigration than in voluntary emigration. The aforementioned immigrant studies explored various types of anxiety, "culture shock" (Ticho, 1971; Garza-Guerrero, 1974) and guilt, as well as the mourning entailed during and after dislocation.

Initially, an immigrant experiences anxiety and "culture shock" owing to sudden change from an "average expectable environment"—as described by Hartmann (1939)—to a strange and unpredictable one. Most often, the immigrant activates a fantasy that the past—the time before the immigration and the violence—contained all "good" self-images coupled with gratifying internal links to "good" object images. When the reality of dislocation begins to set in, such positive images are felt to be missing. At this point, the immigrant feels disconnected from his or her "good" self- and object images and experiences an internal discontinuity.

Anxiety and culture shock are accompanied by feelings of guilt over the loss of what was left behind. Following Kleinian terminology, Grinberg and Grinberg (1989) describe how the guilt an immigrant or refugee suffers may be "depressive" or "persecutory." Refugees who have "depressive" guilt can recognize the loss of their past life intrapsychically, can acknowledge pain, and can exhibit sorrow and nostalgia. They can also discriminate between past and present and develop perspective on the future. Refugees with "depressive" guilt are better equipped to go through the mourning process and adjust to a new life.

On the other hand, when the guilt is "persecutory," persons driven by it expect internal punishment, and their principal emotions are "resentment, pain, fear, and self-reproach" (Grinberg, 1992, p. 79). They face the complicated "work of mourning" (Freud, 1917). In cases of forced emigration following violence, a person's own psychological organization—even if it is cohesive—generates more "persecutory" guilt than may be found in one who emigrates by choice. The refugee's guilt is reinforced by the knowledge that relatives and friends remain in danger even after he or she is in relative safety. If the immigrant faces discrimination within the "host" society, a correlation then arises between internal expectations of punishment and ill treatment in the external environment. Thus, persecutory anxieties are kept alive or may be rekindled (Wangh, 1992).

If dislocated persons still feel accepted in the country or region left behind, on completion of mourning, they may possess a genuine sense of biculturalism, a sense of belonging to neither culture to the exclusion of the other. In fact, they will belong "totally to both" (Julius, 1992, p. 56). This coexistent cultural identity reflects a constructive adaptation. Writing about his own experiences, Julius, a Greek American, states: I slowly came to an appreciation of the importance of intrapsychic cultural complementarity and, more significantly, to an acceptance of the vast cultural differences of the two countries [Greece and the United States]. I began to accept certain psychological paradoxes and to feel myself truly bicultural" (p. 56).

Akhtar (1999) has presented a new theoretical conceptualization regarding the adaptation of an immigrant. He calls it "the third individuation," after the first one, in childhood, and the second one, in adolescence. Mahler (1968) originally described the separation-individuation process and the first individuation that young children complete, for practical purposes, around the age of 36 months. Blos (1979) characterized the second individuation as the time when adolescents undergo an obligatory regression and reexamine and modify their emotional investment in childhood self- and object images. According to Akhtar, immigrants must go through a third individuation if they are to adapt successfully.

Many determinants complicate the first and second individuations, and the same is true for the third individuation. Such factors as forced dislocation, accompanied by violence and survival guilt, add to the complexity of the third individuation. I (Volkan, 1993) suggest that many refugees, who are subjected to life-threatening violence at the time of exile, cannot fully adapt, or in Akhtar's

(1999) words, achieve a third individuation. Instead they become what I call "perennial mourners" who chronically and exaggeratedly use linking objects, externalized images of the deceased connected with the corresponding image of the mourner. The family that I describe here were perennial mourners during their first nine years in their new environment.

## Perennial Mourners and Linking Objects

Mourning is an inevitable reaction to the actual loss of or the threat of losing meaningful objects. This subject has been studied considerably in our literature. When a loved one dies, an adult goes through various phases of mourning, which can be divided into two categories (Volkan, 1981; Pollock, 1989): (1) the initial mourning and (2) the work of mourning. The initial mourning includes such responses as denial, shock, bargaining, pain, and anger, which eventually lead to the beginning of an emotional "knowledge" that the deceased is gone forever. Under normal circumstances, the initial mourning process lasts for three or four months. Before it is completed, however, the "work of mourning" (Freud, 1917) begins. This second category of mourning involves a slow process of revisiting, reviewing, and transforming the mourner's emotional investment in the mental representation of the lost object. In other words, the work of mourning refers to an internal encounter, and its effects, between the images of the lost object and the corresponding self-images of the mourner. The work of mourning can follow any of three major avenues (or a combination of them): "normal" mourning, depression (melancholia), and perennial mourning.

### "Normal" Mourning

After the initial acute grief, the mourner examines a host of different images of the deceased. Slowly, within a year or so, the mourner tames the influence of these images on his or her self-representation. The mourner no longer uses these images as if they still responded to his or her wishes or performed certain tasks for the mourner; the images of the lost object eventually become "future-less" (Tähkä, 1993). "Normal" mourning comes to a practical end after the mourner experiences the anniversaries of meaningful events without the deceased (or lost person or thing). Only during certain occasions, such as anniversaries of the death, religious holidays, weddings, or other funerals, do the mental images of the deceased become temporarily "hot" again. A significant aspect of the normal mourning process is the mourner's selective and unconscious identification with certain enriching functions of the lost object. This identification, of course, influences the mourner's existing self-representation and modifies his or her sense of identity and ego functions to a certain degree. A young man who had been a rather irresponsible person before the loss of his father, for example, can afterwards become a serious businessman like the deceased. After normal mourning—a painful process—we enrich ourselves. In a sense, "loss" is balanced with "gain," and changes occur in our identities and ego functions.

### Depression (Melancholia)

Adults who have had a complicated and ambivalent (love or hate) relationship with the now-deceased end up identifying *totally* (Ritvo and Solnit, 1958) with the mental representation of the lost object. In simple terms, we can say that the mourner makes "unhealthy, not enriching" identifications with the images of the deceased, who was both loved and hated. The struggle that the mourner had with the one who is lost now becomes an internal struggle between himself or herself and the mental representation of the deceased. Such a mourner's internal world becomes a battleground. The mourner wants, unconsciously, to destroy (hate) the lost object's representation and feels guilty. At the same time, the mourner feels obliged to hold on to it (love) because he or she still feels dependent on the representation of the lost object, as if it still had a "future." The mourner experiences depression (melancholia) and may even become suicidal as a result of the guilt and self-punishment that arise from the wish to destroy the mental representation of the lost object. The mourner also feels exhausted and withdrawn from the external world because of the constant inner struggle between these competing processes.

We have known about the psychodynamics of normal mourning and depression since Freud's (1917) work. A third avenue, much less studied (except see Volkan, 1981; Volkan and Zintl, 1993), is perennial mourning.

### Perennial Mourning

Some people are involved in psychological processes that lead them to postpone completion of their normal mourning process or prevent them from evolving melancholia. In a sense, they put the deceased person's mental representation in an envelope (in the old days, we technically called such an envelope an *introject*) and carry this envelope in their minds. They have an illusion that the deceased's image in this envelope can be brought back to life. If, however, the envelope is never opened, the deceased stays "dead." An introject is an "object-image" that strives to be assimilated into the mourner's self-representation. This assimilation (identification) does not actually occur, but the introject remains as a specific object-image that constantly relates to and stimulates the mourner's corresponding self-image. I have seen some people who actually conduct conversations with their introjects as they drive to work, for example. Even when, on the surface, such people appear to be suffering from hallucinations or delusions, they are, in fact, not suffering from a full-blown psychosis; they are simply perennial mourners.

Adult perennial mourners chronically employ linking objects, tangible, externalized versions of the introject, a mental meeting point between the mental representation of the deceased and the corresponding self-image of the mourner. When I began my research on complex mourning processes, I noted that many people who suffered from complications of losing someone "symbolize certain objects which belonged to the dead one" and how "through this process, they are able to control a tie with him" (Volkan, 1970, p. 242). Other clinicians had also briefly mentioned such objects, but none of us had studied their meanings carefully. I became intrigued by these objects. One of my patients would isolate himself in a room with a photograph of his dead father and look at it closely until he began to feel that his father was coming back to life toward him through the frame. Another patient was attached for eight years to the clothing of his brother, who had been shot and killed in a holdup. He was obsessed with the idea that he would grow to a point where these garments would fit him. Still another patient kept his deceased father's soiled handkerchief and treated it as if it were the most important thing on earth.

I coined the term linking objects to describe these symbolic items (Volkan, 1972) and began to examine them descriptively and theoretically. A wide variety of items could be described as linking objects. I have seen the following used as such.

1. *Personal possession of the deceased:* A personal possession of the deceased, often something he or she used routinely or wore on his or her person, like a watch. Usually the mourner chooses an item that requires repairs. For example, if a watch is chosen, it is most likely broken. The mourner becomes preoccupied with fixing it but never finds the time to have the watch repaired. It stays in a state of limbo, if you will, between being repaired and being broken.
2. *Gift or symbolic farewell note:* A gift or a symbolic farewell note to the mourner from the deceased before his or her death, such as something a husband gave his wife before perishing in an accident, or a letter from a war zone written by a soldier before he is killed.
3. *Something the deceased used to extend his or her senses or bodily functions:* For example, a camera (an extension of seeing). Again, the mourner will likely choose a broken camera rather than an operating one as a linking object.
4. *Realistic or symbolic representation of the deceased:* The simplest is a photograph. A symbolic representation might be used instead, such as an identification bracelet.
5. *"Last-minute object":* An object that was at hand when the mourner first learned of the death or saw the deceased's body. For example, a patient was about to play a stack of his favorite records when the phone rang with the news that his half-brother had drowned. The records became his "last minute objects." Telegrams received from the military informing relatives of the death of a son or husband also serve as "last minute objects."
6. *Created linking objects:* Objects that did not exist before the loss. For example, the mourner paints his or her memories of the deceased, and the painting becomes a linking object.

I also observed in my patients what I call *linking phenomena:* sensations, songs, and behavior patterns that perpetuate the possibility of contact between the mourner and the one he or she mourns, without reference to anything tangible. One example of a linking phenomenon has to do with a young woman whose father committed suicide by shooting himself in the head. While attending her father's funeral, the young woman stood in the rain. The song "Rain-drops Keep Falling on My Head" came into her mind during the funeral, and this song functioned as her linking phenomenon for years.

Slowly, I came to understand that the linking object is more than a simple symbol. A symbol is something that represents something else. Linking objects, on the other hand, are protosymbols (Werner and Kaplan, 1963) or at least an amalgamation of symbols and pro-tosymbols. In other words, for mourners, linking objects essentially become what they represent. Unconsciously these linking objects, or protosymbols, are an "actual" meeting place between the mourner and the dead.

A brief clinical vignette illustrates the function of linking objects. A woman in her early 30s, Judith, devoted herself to caring for her ill mother. Judith had not achieved a full separation-individuation in her childhood. During her mother's illness, which lasted for years, Judith became almost like a slave to her mother. She slept in her mother's room and responded to the sick woman's every demand. Once, a few months before her mother died, Judith took a short vacation, during which she bought a pink nightgown. When she returned home, her mother ordered Judith to give the nightgown to her. The daughter was obliged, and soon after, the older woman died while wearing the pink nightgown. After the funeral Judith took the nightgown, put it in a paper shopping bag, and tightly twisted the bag so that the garment was secure inside. The night-gown became her linking object.

Judith was preoccupied with her linking object for the next two years. She had to know where the nightgown was at all times (usu-ally in a closet), and it had to be under her control. When Judith became my patient, I learned that she had an illusion. She believed that if she opened the bag, her dead mother would come back to life. She could not get rid of the nightgown, because such an action would mean that she would be "killing" her mother. Thus, she kept control over her linking object, which externalized and froze her mourning process.

When I was writing about linking objects in the 1980s, I natu-rally focused on their pathological aspects. After all, I was observ-ing them among patients experiencing complicated mourning. Over time I became aware of the "progressive," or beneficial, aspects of these items. While linking objects are employed to postpone and freeze the mourning process, they can also be used to initiate future mourning. When circumstances are right, the mourner may go back, if you will, to his or her linking object, internalize its function, and begin the mourning process as if the loss had just happened. For example, a woman had a daughter who died in a car accident when a college student. This woman kept her daughter's bedroom unchanged as a linking object for 12 years. The daughter's bedroom was locked except on Saturdays. The daughter had attended college in a nearby city and would return home on Saturdays. She was killed while driving home on a Saturday. After her death, her mother would open the deceased girl's bedroom door on Saturdays and clean the room. During the rest of the week, the room would remain a locked-up "secret."

Twelve years after her daughter's death, the woman was driving on a highway and saw a number of people gathered around a smashed car. She stopped to see what had happened and saw two dead persons in the crashed car. She later recalled thinking at the time, "Yes, there is such a thing as death. Death is a reality." After this incident, the woman allowed herself to grieve over her dead child, particularly by using the linking object, her daughter's "magical room." She opened the door of the room, went in, and for many weeks recalled images of her daughter and cried. Slowly she removed the furniture and gave away her daughter's clothes. After experiencing an acute grief, she was able to initiate a successful work of mourning, and the room lost its "magic."

## The World of a Refugee Family

Now, having described how people use linking objects or phenomena after the death of their loved ones, I can turn my attention to the internal world of a refugee family, from the Republic of Georgia, the Kachavaras, and describe their various types of losses, including aspects of their identities.

The Republic of Georgia, with a population of 5.3 million, is located in the Caucasus region. When the Soviet empire began to collapse, Georgia broke away and declared its sovereignty on March 9, 1990. They adopted a declaration of independence a year later on April 9, 1991. Georgia's independence was followed by conflict not only amongst the Georgians themselves, but also among other groups within the state's boundaries. Discord arose between the Georgians and the South Ossetians as well as between the Georgians and the Abkhazians. Abkhazia and South Ossetia are within the legal boundaries of the Republic of Georgia; both declared themselves "independent."

The Kachavara family lived in Gagra in Abkhazia. When war broke out between the Abkhazians and the Georgians, the family moved to a former resort location called Tbilisi Sea, on the outskirts of Tbilisi, the capital of the Republic of Georgia. Officially, they are not called "refugees" but "internally displaced people" (IDPs), since they migrated from one location within the legal boundaries of a state to another within the same state. They also remain among Georgians, their own ethnic group.

There are today 300,000 internally displaced persons in Georgia who have been living as IDPs for the last nine years. The local Georgian sentiments toward IDPs, even if they are Georgians themselves, is "Refugees, go home." The IDPs feel that they are being discriminated against by the locals, despite the fact that the locals are fellow Georgians. IDP children go to school in the late afternoon, after the local Georgian children have left the school for home. Thus, segregation is practiced in the schools.

Of the 300,000 IDPs, 3000 have been living at Tbilisi Sea for the last nine years. Tbilisi Sea consists of three once-luxurious hotels surrounding a man-made lake. One of these hotels is called "Okros Satsmisi" ("Golden Fleece"). This former luxury hotel looks as though it has been hit by a devastating tornado; some walls have been obliterated; windows are covered by plywood or plastic sheets; stairways have become treacherous; paint is long gone; and hallways are cluttered with junk and dirt. Some of the IDPs have become beggars owing to poverty.

### The Kachavara Family

The Kachavara family lives in two former hotel suites, one above the other, on the fourth and fifth floors, at the far end of the Golden Fleece, closest to the lake. In 1998, there was only one telephone for the 3000 IDPs at Tbilisi Sea, and it was in the Kachavara family's "apartment."

Since May 1998, I visited the Kachavara family an average of once every five months through 2001. Each time, I spent many hours in their cramped "apartment" conducting in-depth interviews with each member of the family, alone, one member at a time, or with others present. I collected data about their activities, thoughts, wishes, fantasies, and dreams, as well as their anxieties and their defenses against their anxieties. When I thought it would be useful, I also shared with them my understanding of their psychological states. A female Georgian psychologist accompanied me each time I visited the Kachavara family and functioned as my interpreter since I do not speak Georgian.

Dali, the mother of the family, was a teacher when the family lived in Abkhazia. She has been the primary source of my information. Dali, her husband Mamuka, their two sons (now in their 20s and recently married), their teenage daughter, Tamuna, and Dali's parents live together in the two former hotel suites.

Before their forced exile to Tbilisi Sea, Dali and Mamuka, then a soccer star and policeman, had a house in Gagra. Building and owning their own home during Communist rule had been an almost impossible dream come true for them.

Dali's father, Nodar, is a well-known novelist; Dali is his only daughter. When a heated ethnic conflict broke out between the Georgians and the Abkhazians in 1992, Mamuka left the house to join other local Georgians to fight against the Abkhazians. Mamuka knew that his family and other Georgian families in Gagra were in danger. He arranged for a helicopter to fly into the soccer stadium where he used to play and carry some Georgians, including his wife, children, parents, and in-laws, to safety in Georgia proper.

Dali and her three children (at the time, 1992, the boys were in their early teens and Tamuna was a preteenager) had only 15 minutes to escape; they ran to the stadium under great peril and were able to evacuate. When the helicopter that had taken them to safety went back to rescue more Georgians, it was shot down, killing its young Ukranian pilot. Dali and her three children were the last people brought to safety by this dead pilot. On the way to settling at Tbilisi Sea, Dali and her children saw dead bodies and immense destruction in the border region (Gali region) between Georgia and Abkhazia. "So many people got killed. Thank God we are alive," she told me. Eventually all the family members, including Mamuka, joined one another at Tbilisi Sea. One day, while watching Russian television, Dali saw their home in Gagra burned down by Abkhazians. She also thought that she had a glimpse of "Charlie," the family dog left behind when they escaped.

The Kachavara family had been IDPs for six years when I first visited Tbilisi Sea and met them. At that time I headed the Center for the Study of Mind and Human Interaction (CSMHI), which had a grant to study the ethnic conflict and refugee problems in Georgia. On arriving at the Golden Fleece, I first saw Mamuka, dressed in a paramilitary uniform, getting ready to drive with younger IDP men from Tbilisi Sea to Gali, where renewed fighting had broken out. They were setting out to take part in a miniwar with the Abkhazians—such miniwars between Georgia and Abkhazia have continued for many years, and ceased only within the last four years. As soon as my colleagues and I interviewed Mamuka, the men entered paramilitary vehicles parked near the hotel and left. We later learned that one of them was killed in the fighting, and the rest returned about a week later.

I also interviewed Dali for the first time as her husband was getting ready to go to war. I met with her again two days later while her husband was still away, and a third interview took place after Mamuka returned. During my initial contact with Dali, I noted that she was a very intelligent woman. She was also psychologically minded. For instance, while Mamuka was away taking part in the miniwar, she dreamed that someone else's husband had died and his widow was in grief. When she reported this dream to me, she quickly realized that she was displacing her own expected predicament onto others. Her ability to understand some of her own psychological reactions was one reason why I chose to study Dali and her family. Furthermore, it seemed that the Kachavara family were perceived as leaders by other IDPs at Tbilisi Sea. Their "apartment" was an important meeting place in the settlement, since they had the yellow telephone.

### Observations from the Kachavara Family

Recall that when I met the Kachavara family, they had been refugees for six years, and their mourning process was frozen. Mamuka's sporadic returns to the Gali region for miniwars sustained their belief that the Georgians would recapture the Gali region and that they would return home. Each miniwar, however, retraumatized the family members. Their grief would then become acute. "We have a wound that will remain open forever," Dali told me. These shared feelings were reflected in their political attitudes. Nodar, who began writing poetry only after becoming a refugee, wrote one poem a day describing the conditions and emotions of the IDPs. The following is one of Nodar's poems:

I feel there is betrayal in my motherland
Dishonesty wins
I am leaving all that I have here
And I am coming to you, the sun.

Everything around me is in darkness
I do not see a thing
A snake is biting me bitterly
And, is achieving its betraying aim.

We could not realize what was happening
Everything appeared to be confused
But, I know the enemy is in Tbilisi
Oh! Oh! Let my enemy's life be short.

I see my motherland's suffering from betrayal
Oh, the devil wins
Depression conquers my soul
I pray you, the sun, help us.

This poem, written after a miniwar, reflects the retraumatization as well as its political aftermath. It expresses Nodar's reaction to the agreement made between the Georgian government (Tbilisi) and the Abkhzians to stop this particular miniwar. The agreement shattered the refugees' illusions that if the war went on they would win and the families would return home. Out of anger at the perceived loss of such a possibility, they turned against President Shevardnadze for a while.

Aside from these retraumatizing events and the resulting acute grief, the family members remained perennial mourners, preoccupied with controlling "links" to their past lives. If a present symbol did not have a connection to a symbol of the past, the use of the contemporary symbol was rejected. Tamuna, for example, refused to swim in the man-made lake, Tbilisi Sea, because the lake water did not look like the water in the Black Sea, where she swam as a child when they lived in Gagra.

The first aspect of the Kachavaras' perennial mourning I would like to discuss is their need for someone whom they considered significant to recognize and acknowledge the trauma they had undergone. As I became involved with this family as a "participant observer," I noted that the very fact of their being "recognized" regularly by someone coming from so far away had a significant impact on their lives. Soon they began calling me "our Vamık," the one who "tolerated" their regressions to orality and anality. Being realistically deprived and needy stimulates the oral wishes as well as defenses against them. Such wishes, and especially the defenses against them, were directly expressed in many of Nodar's poems. In one remarkable poem, for example, Nodar rails against the IDP beggars in Tbilisi:

### Children Beggars

When I see your hand begging
My dignity suffers.
I cannot give you my soul (suli)
Since it is impossible to give one's soul to someone.
But, I have nothing left except my soul.

I am pressing against prison bars
If you need my life,
I can give it to you.

In this poem, refugees from Abkhazia (like Nodar himself) are expressly communicating their oral needs by begging in the streets of the capital city. Nodar wants them to stop begging, to disappear, because it is so humiliating to see them. Unconsciously, he connects his own helplessness and need to be fed emotionally, if not physically, with theirs and cannot bear to see it.

I have observed increased orality as well as anality among members of traumatized societies in a variety of locations. As the rage is turned against the rejecting "mother earth," the traumatized people, including various types of refugees, literally dirty their communities, creating ruin and decay (also see Šebek, 1992). They also become "collectors" of junk. Even though what they collect may one day be useful, the aim is to clutter their environment as though they lived in an "anal" field of garbage. In other words, they not only regress into oral preoccupations, but also turn their anal sadism against the area in which they live. Of course, I do not mean to minimize the reality of their financial deprivation and their lack of means to clean up and protect their environment; I am simply focusing on the psychological aspects of such behavior patterns. In the case of the Kachavara family, I noted during my initial visits that they piled their collected junk on their balcony.

People like Dali and the other members of the Kachavara family need to move up internally from oral and anal regression to the genital/oedipal phase in order to start to accept fully their dislocation and find an adaptive solution to their refugee status. I came to realize that their third individuation required a "regenitalization" or "reoedipalization" of their internal worlds. Their attempts to resolve reactivated genitalized/oedipal themes were necessary and accompanied the refugees' efforts at more adaptive living.

My interviews with Dali and other members of her family entailed efforts to understand their dreams and daydreams. Soon after my work with the family started, Dali began dreaming about me; I appeared most often in her dreams in an undisguised fashion when she had been informed of my upcoming visits by my Georgian contacts. When we met she would recite these dreams. I now have a collection of Dali's dreams, which evolved from references to gratification of oral and anal wishes to expressions of gratification of oedipal wishes. Obviously, Dali was not my analysand, and I could not understand her dreams without the benefit of a transference neurosis within the frame of an analytic setting. Nevertheless, the manifest content of her dreams was sufficient to suggest the nature of her transference (nonanalytic, of course) to me. While in the initial dreams I brought her goods that would satisfy her oral needs or I accompanied her in creating explosions (anal sadism), she later began to dream of me (undisguised) as someone who would sleep in her bed next to her and her husband. She was embarrassed to tell me this. Interestingly enough, her daughter, who was 16 when I first met her, exhibited the same pattern in her dreams. Tamuna's dreams slowly changed from my bringing her food to my bringing her a baby.

As Dali said, since, in reality, it would not be proper for me to sleep in the same bed with her and Mamuka, the family should do something else instead. So, in late 1999, they began to build a room for me. They walled off a section of the hallway adjacent to their suite of rooms and turned it into living space. It took almost a year to complete this addition to their "apartment." Dali worked with Mamuka and the children building and finishing the room; they called it "our Vamik's room." The members of the family were involved in "therapeutic play" (Volkan and Ast, 2001), repairing their external world and their corresponding inner world. Solnit (1987) has suggested that "play is best described by its functions" (p. 205) and Neubauer (1993) considers play to be an attempt at a solution of conflicts, at the establishment of ego mastery. The Kachavara family "played" together as they constructed the new room. By naming it "our Vamik's room," they kept my image with them as they "played." In contrast to most of its surroundings, this room would be clean and inviting. They even decided to add a fireplace and finish the floors with beautiful wood. Dali dreamed that I would sleep there. "Our Vamik's room" was like a jewel in the middle of a garbage pile; it would be the external expression of what I call their relibidinalization of their internal world.

Before discussing further Dali's process of relibidinalization through the building of "our Vamik's room," let us turn to another significant aspect of the Kachavaras' perennial mourning—their use and creation of linking objects and linking phenomena. When I first met the Kachavara family, I observed something that, on the surface, did not make sense. As an IDP, Dali was eligible to apply for assistance from authorities in Tbilisi, and by doing so she would receive about five dollars per month to support the family. I must add here that five dollars was a far more substantial sum for the IDPs than it might appear to outsiders. What seemed odd to me was that Dali, then an IDP for six years, refused to do what was necessary to receive this money. Yet every night she would have a hard time falling asleep as she worried about how to feed her children and her husband. Put simply, Dali seemed to be "paralyzed" and unable to take action to secure the much-needed funds. I considered her inhibition a sign of an internal conflict and slowly understood that her inhibition was connected to her identity issues.

To explain Dali's dilemma, we must go back to the escape from Gagra made by her and the children. During their flight, Dali "lost" her "internal passport" (identity card), which symbolized the loss of prerefugee identity. During Soviet times, Soviet citizens had "internal passports"—a person was not free to move from one location to another without permission. Individuals' ethnic identities were written on their passports; one was, for example, Estonian, Kazak, Armenian, Abkhazian, or Georgian. Since the Communist ideology specified "equality" among people, the Soviets were free to keep the citizens' ethnicities alive to demonstrate that Communism was capable of uniting people from different ethnic backgrounds. As the Soviet empire began to collapse, people in different locations began to ask, "Who are we now?" Ethnic sentiments increased, and in Abkhazia they took a malevolent turn in Gagra, where the Kachavara family lived. Dali and her three children were flown out by the helicopter secured by her husband on September 20, 1992, before the fury of war between the Abkhazians and the Georgians swept Gagra. Dali did not even have time to collect her jewelry, but she took her identity card.

As she and her children began to run toward the stadium to board the waiting helicopter, Dali had second thoughts about carrying her identity card. Along with her ethnicity, her husband's name was inscribed on her internal passport. She thought that, if she were captured by Abkhazians, her captors would know who she was, since everyone knew that Mamuka, a famous soccer player, had married Nodar's daughter. Nodar had, in his writing, protested Abkhazian treatment of Georgians for some time before this event and at this time was in hiding. Dali knew that the Abkhazians were looking for her father and indeed, thinking that an older man was Nodar, had once wrongly captured and tortured him. Dali was afraid that, if she were caught, the captors would torture her until she revealed Nodar's whereabouts. Dali was sufficiently scared into concealing her identity. She ran back to the house and left her internal passport there before boarding the helicopter. Presumably the passport was destroyed when their house was burned down. Fortunately, Nodar and his wife were eventually able to escape and join Dali at Tbilisi Sea, but it is clear that Dali's fears were legitimate.

Eventually Dali arrived at Tbilisi Sea without an identity card, a document that also indicated, she emphasized to me, her birthplace. She was a "daughter of Gagra." IDPs had to show their identity cards in order to receive monthly assistance money from Georgian authorities. Dali no longer had hers, but she could go to an office in Tbilisi and register for a new one. However, the new one would not have a statement indicating that Abkhazia was her home. For Dali, it was more important to retain her former identity as a Georgian from Abkhazia than to obtain the needed money. Dali used her internal passport, though destroyed, as a symbol of her personal identity as a Georgian born and raised in Abkhazia. Since the passport no longer existed, it became a kind of linking phenomenon. Getting a new identity card would mean symbolically eradicating her identity as a Georgian from Abkhazia. It would solidify the loss of her "old" identity, a loss she could not accept.

Like other linking objects and phenomena, the image of the lost identity card acted as both a hindrance and an aid in the healing process. After this story came to light and Dali and I discussed it extensively, she waited at least one more year before allowing herself to get a new identity card. She did finally apply for one, and in so doing she became a model for other IDPs at Tbilisi Sea who, like her, had refused to replace their lost cards. For all of them, this bureaucratic step was a true and drastic "new adjustment," and it enabled them to receive the funds to which they were entitled.

The entire Kachavara family also employed poems written by Nodar as linking objects. As I mentioned earlier, after he became an IDP, Nodar began writing one poem every day. He ritualistically shared it with the other family members every morning, and Dali habitually filed the poems in a special place. These poems became concrete symbols both of the loss of their former lives in Gagra and of their hope to return home. Their prerefugee identities and refugee identities were linked. They could not commit themselves fully to any of these identities, so they remained in an indeterminate state.

Another linking object employed by the family pertained to their dog, Charlie, who had been left behind when they fled. Dali, through considerable effort, had learned his fate. She found that, after their house was burned down, Charlie had been hit by a car and killed. During their second year as IDPs at Tbilisi Sea, Dali found a black dog that looked very like the original Charlie. She brought the dog to live with them in their miserable quarters and named him Charlie. I remember this dog very well from my first visit to the Kachavara family's "apartment." The new Charlie was always present during my later visits as well. He would lie at Dali's feet. Everyone was to some extent conscious of his psychological significance; the dog was a "living linking object," a "created" type of linking object that I described earlier. Through the new Charlie, the old Charlie was kept "alive," and through this mechanism the illusion of bringing the images of lost objects (home, dead friends, Gagra, and the Gali region in general) back was, psychologically speaking, possible. Thus, the Kachavara family first made plans to return to Gagra and rebuild their house in three years. When I met them for the first time, they were still holding on to their three-year plan even though six years had passed since they left Gagra. When Dali obtained a new identity card, it was a sign that she and her family members were doing some work of mourning. Then they began to speak of a five-year plan.

The completion of "our Vamik's room" took place, by coincidence, just before the second Charlie died of natural causes. The two events became connected and ushered in, in early 2000, a period of "illness" for Dali. She lost weight and withdrew from her environment. A Georgian doctor was called and diagnosed her condition as a cerebral stroke. I was in the United States when this happened and had received no information about Dali's condition. When I arrived in Georgia a short time later, my Georgian contacts told me of the diagnosis and declared that, unfortunately, there was not much that I could do. They told me that Dali was having a hard time speaking.

After hearing the news, I rushed to the Golden Fleece and indeed found Dali looking like a ghost, wasting away. Her mind seemed sharp, however. I began to realize that she had not had a cerebral stroke but, rather, was suffering from severe depression and suicidal behavior. She was able to talk with me. I spent some hours with her during which I interpreted the meaning of Charlie's death for her. I explained that, without her living linking object, she could no longer postpone her mourning—in her case a melancholic type of mourning. She was fully facing both her sadness and guilt over her beloved Abkhazia, her home, the first and second Charlie, the pilot who had saved her life, and her own survival. Dali's severe melancholia was complicated not only by the loss of the new Charlie, the living linking object, but also by her replacing the dog and becoming herself a living linking object for the other family members. Here is how she became this living linking object.

Around the time of Charlie's death and the completion of "our Vamik's room," Mamuka, Nodar, and the three Kachavara children experienced other events that assisted them in adapting to their refugee status. The process that I call the "verification" of the refugee's new identity as a continuation of his or her previous identity by psychologically significant others is a substantial element in the refugee's adaptation to the new environment. Soon after the second Charlie's death, Mamuka received symbolic verification from others that put his prerefugee identity on a continuum with his identity as a dislocated person. The Georgian Ministry of Internal Affairs organized a soccer match between local soccer players from Tbilisi and IDP soccer players from Abkhazia to honor the memory of a Georgian soccer player from Abkhazia who had been tortured and killed by the Abkhazians. Mamuka took part in this soccer match and scored two goals, establishing himself as a hero among the spectators. More important, the authorities gave him a trophy inscribed with his name and the date of the match. As "our Vamik's room" was almost complete, Mamuka put his trophy on the mantel.

At this time Mamuka was working as a policeman in Tbilisi, in command of lower ranked policemen, all of whom were IDPs from Tbilisi Sea. His local boss treated Mamuka with respect, restoring his self-esteem and verifying and extending his prerefugee identity as a policeman in Gagra. He changed his five-year plan to return to Abkhazia to a ten-year plan, indicating his further acceptance of the loss of his prerefugee identity, his home, and Abkhazia in general.

Nodar also received verification of his continued identity as a vital literary figure. The poems that he began writing when he became an IDP were published in book form and were recognized as an important piece of literature. Nodar was given an award for his book and was transformed by the experience. I can say that his internal world was relibidinalized; he who previously was an ever-angry man was now a man who smiled frequently.

Meanwhile, Dali's children were expanding their environment by leaving the settlement during the day to attend college. The boys began dating local women who were also IDP's; they fell in love; and the oldest got married. These events helped to verify their identity and increase their self-esteem.

Even after Nodar received his award, he continued to write a poem a day. He would still ritualistically bring his poems to the breakfast table every day, but now no one but Dali would sit down and listen to him recite. Dali continued to file the new poems, which still included references to the refugees' lamentable situations, but now Nodar would give them to Dali, smile, and leave the room.

Dali became the only person who functioned as the "reservoir" for Nodar's daily dose of sadness, depression, and guilt. I told her that she had become the linking object for the family, a replacement for the new Charlie. Dali understood my "interpretation."

Still another factor was intruding into Dali's inner world and contributing to her severe depression. "Our Vamik's room" was structurally complete but not yet decorated. Dali told me that, as the room was approaching completion, she had to give up her illusion that I would sleep in there. She came face to face with the reality that I was not a family member and would never actually sleep in the room. Psychologically, it meant that she could not really possess me as an idealized "libidinalizing" object, perhaps as an "oedipal father." She had to give me up and mourn this "loss," much in the same way that an oedipal girl "mourns" the loss of her oedipal father as she resolves the Oedipus complex. We discussed this too in detail. Knowing of Dali's positive transference feelings for me, I told her I could still care for her even though I would not sleep in "our Vamik's room" and that this room really belonged to her and her family. Repeating my understanding of the psychological factors that had led to her severe depression, I told her that, by becoming a living linking object for the family, she was responsible for breaking or maintaining the family's ties to the past; this obligation was stressful for her. Her "power" to cut off this bond, in other words to "kill" the family's prerefugee identity, was causing her guilt.

There was a funeral almost every time I went to Tbilisi Sea. People Dali's age, or even younger, would drop dead, often for no apparent reason. I told Dali that there were others among the IDP's who were killing themselves, and I added that, if she did not die, she could be a model for other depressed refugees as someone who could survive and adjust.

When I returned about five months later, I could not recognize Dali. She had gained weight and was smiling. There was a new dog in the apartment, a female named Linda. Dali told me that she had given up being a living linking object herself and was determined to avoid acquiring another "Charlie" as a living linking object. Linda was female and was not black.

During this visit Mamuka, who was dressed in his best civilian clothes, wanted Dali to set up a table for us in "our Vamik's room," which was now completely finished and furnished. However, Dali told me that she did not wish to break our tradition of meeting in the original room of the "apartment," which had also been renovated. In addition, Dali told me that the new room was no longer "our Vamik's room"—it was theirs. They took me to see their finished new room. The soccer trophy was still on the mantel. Mamuka wanted me to hold it to feel how solid and heavy it was. Above the fireplace there was a painting of the Hotel Gagribsh.

When Mamuka received his soccer trophy, another IDP player was given a painting of the Hotel Gagribsh. At that moment, Mamuka thought he should have such a painting himself. He found out who had painted the picture and made arrangements for the artist to paint another Hotel Gagribsh for the Kachavara family. Mamuka and other family members were fully aware that the painting in the new room was a memorial to their prerefugee identities. Hotel Gagribsh was the best-known location in Gagra when the Kachavara family lived there. Now it was in the former "our Vamik's room," like a tombstone that helps mourners complete their mourning. The painting was *not* a linking object, for, they told me, it symbolized there would be no return to Gagra. The family informed me that they had given up their ten-year plan to go back to Gagra. Now they had no plans to return. The painting was a "futureless memory" (Tähkä, 1993).

Spurred by my interest in the painting, Mamuka discussed his last mission to Abkhazia as a paramilitary man in 1998. The Georgians were called back only a few days after their miniwar. Mamuka was furious with President Shevarnadze, as he felt that the leader should give them permission to continue fighting. Now he explained how his own thoughts of reconquering Abkhazia had been fanciful. "To harbor such wishes and dreams was senseless," he added. He described to me how he was much calmer now but still smoked heavily. His nightmares were gone, and he had given up his plans to return to Abkhazia. Perhaps as an expression of lingering but "silent" depression, he had some difficulty falling asleep, though he was "normal" during the day.

My visit this time followed by one week the marriage of the Kachavaras' youngest son. I was introduced to the new bride, as I had been introduced to the first bride months earlier. There was an atmosphere of festivity in the Kachavara family's home, but Dali wanted to speak with me alone (through the present interpreter, of course).

During our long private conversation, Dali explained how happy she was with her youngest son's marriage. She had, however, had an anxiety attack the day after her son got married, and she wanted to understand why. The Kachavara family's "apartment," the old hotel suite, was small. Dali and Mamuka separated the main room into two sections with a curtain; the space behind the curtain was their "bedroom." The youngest son, before his marriage, slept on a cot in the other section, where I usually conducted my interviews with them. The son and his wife moved elsewhere after their marriage.

Dali woke up on the day after her son's marriage and came out from her "bedroom" to find her son's cot empty. She immediately had an anxiety attack. She knew that separation from her son would be difficult, but she felt that her anxiety attack was connected to a sense that someone was going to die. She recalled how her children huddled around her in the helicopter that had flown them to safety. Her recent attack was connected to her anxiety during that helicopter flight. She now recalled this event in great detail and visualized herself crying, fearing for her children's lives. She remembered feeling that she would die if she lost one of them. She realized that seeing her son's empty cot had rekindled the old fear that had overwhelmed her on that trip. Separation and a sense of actual death were connected in her mind.

At this point Dali told me something that I had not known before. The helicopter pilot who was killed had the same name as her son. She described the physical characteristics of this pilot. He was young and handsome, like Dali's two sons. Not finding her son lying in his cot symbolized her guilt over "killing" the young pilot. Dali fully recognized how guilty she felt over the pilot's death. She told me that, when the IDPs at Tbilisi Sea got together, the pilot's name would on occasion come up, since he had saved some of the IDPs living at the Tbilisi Sea, but there was no memorial or public mourning for him.

I suggested that perhaps she could attend church and perform a funeral rite for the dead pilot and that doing so could decrease her feelings of guilt and help her to separate her son(s) from the dead pilot. She readily agreed. A week later, when I had returned to the United States, Dali sent me a message through our interpreter. She wanted me to know that she had indeed gone to church, lit candles for the pilot, prayed for his soul, and was feeling much better.

In the past two years I have not visited Georgia. During this period, I have received a few e-mail messages from Tamuna, who now speaks fluent English. Dali's new love is her granddaughter, and the Kachavara family is doing well.

## Conclusion

This chapter describes a psychoanalyst's work outside of his office. Obviously, under such conditions a psychoanalyst cannot carry out psychoanalytic treatment of the individuals with whom he or she is involved. However, clinical experience training in psychoanalytic theory can provide psychoanalysts with tools that allow them to help refugees in unique ways. Psychoanalysts are also able to train local mental health professionals to notice issues that may otherwise escape routine refugee aides, such as the meaning of Dali's identity card and of Charlie, the dog, which proved to be both obstacles and catalysts for the Kachavaras' adaptation to their dislocation.

When I started working with the Kachavara family, I had no idea that this type of work could evolve into a "methodology" for helping other individuals within a refugee settlement. Since the Kachavara family members were perceived as leaders of the Tbilisi Sea community, their improvement in adapting to dislocation provided a model for others at Tbilisi Sea. When some men from this area went off to fight the miniwars, their wives and other relatives would gather in or around the Kachavara apartment, waiting for the telephone to ring. As Dali began to observe certain psychological processes in herself, she subsequently became a kind of "consultant" to other refugees. When the Kachavaras finished "our Vamik's room," others began to copy the Kachavara family and built expansions onto their lodgings. Most important, I believe that, when Dali survived after her "stroke" (many at Tbilisi Sea followed the progress of her health), she became a model for "defeating" depression. It was impossible for me to obtain scientific statistical data on Tbilisi Sea, but the general consensus is that the number of people dropping dead for "no apparent reason" at this settlement has decreased considerably.

Anyone who comes from another country to help a massively traumatized refugee community is overwhelmed. He or she will not be able to deal therapeutically, in depth, with many individuals. Thus, the "methodology" that we started at Tbilisi Sea focuses on working in depth with one (or a few) selected families an helping them to evolove into a model for others in their community.

I have described my findings regarding a condition that I call perennial mourning. After working in Cyprus, Georgia, Albania, and elsewhere with dislocated persons who suffered massive trauma and violence, I came to the conclusion that the adjustment we see in refugees following such disasters points to their adjustment to life as perennial mourners. Their linking objects have both regressive and progressive possibilities. Psychoanalysts can help local mental health workers to utilize the progressive aspects of refugees' linking objects (or phenomena) in order to help them adjust to their situations in a better way.

## References

Akhtar, S. (1999), *Immigration and Identity.* Northvale, NJ: Aronson.

Blos, P. (1979), *The Adolescent Passage.* New York: International Universities Press.

Freud, S. (1917), Mourning and melancholia. *Standard Edition,* 14:237–260. London: Hogarth Press, 1957.

Garza-Guerrero, A. C. (1974), Culture shock: Its mourning and vicissitudes of identity. *J. Amer. Psychoanal. Assn.,* 22:400–429.

Grinberg, L. (1992), *Guilt and Depression,* trans. C. Trollope. London: Karnac Books.

———— & Grinberg, R. (1989), *Psychoanalytic Perspectives on Migration and Exile,* trans. N. Festinger. New Haven, CT: Yale University Press.

Hartmann, H. (1939), *Ego Psychology and Problems of Adaptation.* New York: International Universities Press, 1950.

Julius, D. A. (1992), Biculturalism and international interdependence. *Mind & Human Interact.,* 3:53–56.

Mahler, M. (1968), *On Human Symbiosis and the Vicissitudes of Individuation.* New York: International Universities Press.

Neubauer, P. B. (1993), Playing: Technical implications. In: *The Many Meanings of Play,* ed. A. J. Solnit, D. J. Cohen & P. B. Neubauer. New Haven, CT: Yale University Press.

Parens, H. (2001), On society's crimes against itself. *J. Appl. Psychoanal. Studies,* 3:221–229.

Pollock, G. H. (1989), *The Mourning–Liberation Process*, 2 vols. Madison, CT: International Universities Press.

Ritvo, S. & Solnit, A. (1958), Influences of early mother–child interaction on the identification process. *The Psychoanalytic Study of the Child*, 13:64–85. New York: International Universities Press.

Šebek, M. (1992), Anality in the totalitarian system and the psychology of post-totalitarian society. *Mind & Human Interact.*, 4:52–59.

Solnit, A. J. (1987), A psychoanalytic view of play. *The Psychoanalytic Study of the Child*, 42:205–219. New Haven, CT: Yale University Press.

Tähkä, V. (1993), *Mind and Its Treatment*. Madison, CT: International Universities Press.

Ticho, G. (1971), Cultural aspects of transference and countertransference. *Bull. Menninger Clin.*, 35:313–334.

Volkan, V. D. (1970), Typical findings in pathological grief. *Psychiat. Quart.*, 44:231–250.

—— (1972), The linking objects of pathological mourners. *Arch. Gen. Psychiat.*, 27:215–222.

—— (1979), *Cyprus—War and Adaptation*. Charlottesville: University Press of Virginia.

—— (1981), *Linking Objects and Linking Phenomena*. New York: International Universities Press.

—— (1993), Immigrants and refugees: A psychoanalytic perspective. *Mind & Human Interact.*, 4:63–69.

—— & Ast, G. (2001), Curing Gitta's "leaking body": Actualized unconscious fantasies and therapeutic play. *J. Clin. Psychoanal.*, 10:557–596.

—— & Zintl, E. (1993), *Life After Loss: The Lessons of Grief*. New York: Charles Scribner's Sons.

Wangh, M. (1992), Being a refugee and being an immigrant. *Internat. Psychoanal.*, winter: 15–17.

Werner, H. & Kaplan, B. (1963), *Symbol Formation*. New York: Wiley.

# Topeka's Healthy Community Initiative

## *A Psychoanalytic Model for Change*

Stuart W. Twemlow  ◆  Sallye M. Wilkinson

*A good community is a community where the people understand what is going on and take responsibility for what happens.*

—David Mathews

*The greatest achievement of the human spirit is to live up to one's opportunities, and to make the most of one's resources.*

—Vauvenargues

## Isn't Psychoanalysis of the Community a Self-Cancelling Phrase?

Obviously psychoanalysts cannot put an entire community on the couch! Key psychoanalytic techniques—regression in the service of the ego and transference analysis, for example—are hard to implement at the community level. The thought of a city regressed raises the specter of wild bacchanals or frightful riots; regression unchecked by ego. Deepening the transference toward a central figure in the worst-case scenario shades into control by political fiat or fanatical conversion; that is, as Freud (1921) pointed out, surrender of one's superego to the group leader in exchange for a measure of protection and relief from personal accountability. Interpretation, a psychoanalyst's most basic intervention, would neither stem a riot nor dispel a large group's dependence on a leader. Action would sweep away the opportunity for reflection. Psychoanalysts are much more adept at helping neurotic persons to break the confines of unconscious fantasies than at helping communities divest themselves of the dynamic underpinnings of violence, trauma, and strife.

Muddying the waters, the question arises whether psychoanalysts can legitimately diagnose a community. On this matter there are many more questions than answers. This book is an effort to launch such inquiry within the field of psychoanalysis. In particular, this chapter about the psychoanalytic model employed by Topeka's Healthy Community Initiative describes one such probe. Most psychoanalysts would be quite comfortable with the diagnostic process described by Karl Menninger, a native Topekan:

> It is diagnosis in the sense of understanding just *how* the patient is ill and *how* ill the patient is, *how* he became ill and *how* his illness serves him. From this knowledge one may draw logical conclusions regarding how changes might be brought about in or around the patient which would affect his illness [Menninger, Mayman, and Pruyser, 1963, pp. 6–7; emphasis added].

Menninger's description highlights the analyst's detailed observation of the workings of a person's inner world. When using a *clinical approach*, the analyst is at the hub of an extremely intimate relationship with the analysand. When addressing social problems, the analyst is no longer at the hub, but is one among many collaborators. No longer rooted in the clinical situation, perhaps the contributions of the psychoanalyst are now best described as a *group involvement approach* (Bracher, 1992). Borrowing from Dr. Karl and his colleagues, in this approach psychoanalysts apply the same keen capacities for observation and understanding: the community psychoanalyst assesses just how the community functions and how functional or dysfunctional the community is, how the community became dysfunctional and how the community's dysfunction serves it. From this information one may draw logical conclusions about how community members may be engaged to solve their own problems. To conclude that psychoanalysts should remain in the consulting room undervalues the power of a discipline trained to understand dynamic root causes and the associated compromises that can prevent resolution of social ills.

To understand how a community psychoanalytic process unfolds, consider that a great deal of the work in clinical psychoanalysis is subversive. As analysts we strive to make the unconscious, conscious, or to cause what is ego syntonic to become ego dystonic. We do this by interpreting to our patients how their unconscious compromises are enacted in the transference. A premium is placed on the *shared experience* between analyst and analysand. For in telling the story of that mutual experience we gain insight, expose compromises, and encourage growth. Resolution of neurotic conflicts requires retelling the story in a new and creative way. This retelling is not easily accomplished, and motivation for change emerges as problems take on the value of symptoms.

Community psychoanalysts, as in the clinical situation, must capitalize on shared experiences to achieve subversive aims. Sometimes community problems must infiltrate the lives of the majority of the populace before the problems of a few become sufficiently dystonic for the community to address. The new story begins to acknowledge the community's blind spots, maladaptive compromises, loyalty binds, and the like, as well as its underappreciated strengths. A different kind of outcome can be imagined. The Topeka Healthy Community Initiative is one such effort.

## Psychoanalytic Underpinnings for Topeka's Healthy Community Initiative

Topeka's Healthy Community Initiative (HCI) is an experiment in bringing psychoanalytic strategies to bear on solving community problems. Analysts will be familiar with the HCI use of psychoanalytic understanding of transference–countertransference, compromise formation, ego strength, resistance to change, developmental capacities, and interpersonal process. What is different, both for psychoanalysis and for community improvement projects across the nation, is the HCI's effort to use these psychoanalytic concepts as leverage to mobilize a pragmatic form of altruism, in which neighbors help each other solve shared problems. What is pragmatic altruism?

Research into the practical value of altruistic behavior appears in diverse places. For example, an economist (Clotfelter, 1980) surveyed 1299 households to determine the motivation of citizens who had provided help to victims of crime. Using hypothetical situations, this analysis supported the hypothesis that purely altruistic behavior and behavior based on self-interest, as well as behavior guided by social norms, are important in these helpful-bystander actions, with individuals with higher incomes and those with higher education tending to be most helpful. Several observational studies on children helping each other when school playground bullying and fighting occurs have yielded a variety of interesting results, summarized by Ginsberg (1977). Such studies indicate that children who see continued aggressive behavior on the playground are more likely to respond for the benefit of the victim especially if the victim/child communicates submission or distress.

In stark contrast, the Genovese case in New York in 1964 was a chilling example of the absence of any apparent concern for others (Milgram and Hollander, 1964). In this instance, neighbors in a Kew Gardens apartment building in New York City watched as a woman, Kitty Genovese, was stabbed to death in the early hours of the morning in a horrendous knifing lasting over 30 minutes. None of the 38 neighbors who heard her cries for help assisted in any way or even called the police. When interviewed, the witnesses said they were afraid to get involved. Such studies suggest that if people have enough time to examine the possible consequences of an altruistic action, then they are less likely to act in a helpful way if there is significant personal risk. Studies of situations that demand immediate responses, such as one in which someone has a heart attack in a bustling city environment, are far more likely to elicit a majority of altruistic responses from bystanders than do ones in which people have time to think about the consequences of their involvement.

Contemporary evolutionary theory has become an unexpected source of support for the survival value of altruism and for its pragmatic importance. Philosophers such as Badcock (1986), Slavin and

Kriegman (1992), and Trivers (1985) point out that the "every man for himself" interpretation of Darwin's survival of the fittest principle has been oversimplified. The more sophisticated interpretations point out that the survival of the species depends on a combination of self-interest and mutual cooperation. Kin altruism is a form of altruism that occurs among relatives who share genetic material. Altruistic acts aid mutual perpetuation of the shared genetic material and thus are also egoistic. Even among unrelated individuals, altruism can benefit the altruist by longer term, sometimes indirect reciprocal payments and exchanges, thus aiding survival of the species (reciprocal altruism). Evolutionary biology is thus developing its own terminology for what has been rediscovered by psychoanalysis, game theory, philosophy, ethics, political science, and religious studies, to name some of the many different fields that have begun to pay attention to the meaning of altruism.

Shapiro and Gabbard (1994) note that altruistic behavior and motivation have historically been regarded as a defensive reaction formation to sadism. Their research suggests that, in human beings, altruism is an independently motivated, nondefensive system that cannot be distinguished from selfish motives. Instead, self-oriented and altruistic motivations are equal and essential partners.

In applying the human altruistic response to the pragmatic demands of healthy communities, one must understand various complex cultural, social, intrapsychic, and biological determinants of the altruistic response. Shapiro and Gabbard list a variety of limitations on altruism, which emphasize intrapsychic factors. These limitations need to be addressed directly by anyone proposing to use this concept to improve the health, peacefulness, and cooperativeness of members of complex communities. Such limiting factors include:

1. The observer's ability to achieve an accurate understanding of the victim's needs (empathy).
2. The observer's ability to achieve a balance between self-interest and concern for others. Pathologically narcissistic leaders will have very serious problems in this regard, as is illustrated by extremists like Osama bin Laden and Adolf Hitler.
3. The observer's assessment of the cost-benefit ratio specific to the altruistic action.

To these we add two social influences on altruism:

4. Violent individual and community mindsets, as we define them, can provide young people with a defective social model for collaborative living. Currently, by using a loophole that will enable the state to draw interest on funds temporarily dispersed to nursing homes, the Kansas Legislature is examining a way to enable the state to obtain millions of dollars in funds it does not deserve. Political and legal experts are quoted as saying, "As long as it is legal, they aren't going to oppose it. After all, the state could use the money." The House Speaker said, "I think we would get beat up a bit if we decided not to pursue it" (*Topeka Capital Journal*, Feb. 27, 2000). Sanctioning unethical, manipulative behavior to produce undeserved financial gains, especially if covering budgetary ineptitudes, is an extraordinarily poor example to young people.
5. The extent of the numbing effect of subtle and not so subtle actual violence on individuals, so that the existence of neediness of others is denied, rationalized, or avoided.

Thus the altruistic response can be limited by unconscious and conscious factors, personality distortions, social and cultural mores and attitudes, and other influences. A person proposing to use this approach to create a healthy community must address all these issues.

Initial efforts of the HCI group were focused on building working alliances with a select group of community leaders. As these relationships were being built, the HCI group learned about the impediments to making change (e.g., transference toward those who are different or less fortunate, confronting denial about the plight of people living a short distance away, the challenges of transforming into actual behavior the narcissistically gratifying intention to help others, and so on) as well as issues of violence in Topeka. As with any psychoanalytic process, emphasis was placed on looking past the symptom to the underlying causes. The HCI *diagnostic process* is described in greater detail in a subsequent section. The HCI *treatment strategy* has focused on strengthening existing community stabilizing systems; it is a strategy that can loosely be compared to enhancing the analysand's ego strength and/or supporting developmental capacities. Finally, and most problematically, the HCI group looked at our own inhibitions or countertransference regarding taking action and making change.

## The Community's Presenting Problem

Most psychoanalysts would agree that a patient presenting with expectations of failure, absence of cohesive identity, aggressive acting out, and tolerance of unacceptable behavior would benefit from treatment. All of these problems existed in Topeka in the Spring of 2000. Essentially, the "presenting problems" stemmed from an extreme conflict between the mayor and the city council; for example, female members of the council felt so unsafe that they requested a security guard during closed sessions. On another occasion, the city came close to losing millions in federal grants because of a long conflict over a minor city ordinance. The local media had pounced on the struggle and reported blow by blow the insults and subterfuge. Several of these public servants pushed agendas benefiting a circumscribed constituency but not the city as a whole.

A "shrink" was called in to help break up the fighting (Twemlow, 2000; Twemlow and Sacco, 2003). Several group meetings followed individual meetings with the mayor and each of the council members. In spite of political and religious objections to psychiatric consultation, the "psychiatric diagnosis" and treatment occurred with the full participation of all members of the city council and the mayor, since no one wanted to be labeled as unreasonable, a gambit that is not uncommon in municipalities. There was a temporary amelioration of the conflict.

But the calm waters were soon troubled again. Topekans were appalled by the conflict but did little to act on their dissatisfaction; instead they passively watched the spectacle. After all, someone else's problems can divert attention from worries about one's own. There was a generalized sense that no one was in control and that the community was fragmenting anxiously on many levels. In addition, U.S. Department of Justice crime statistics ranking Topeka fifth in the nation among similar-sized cities for crime had just been released. What might be called "community coping mechanisms" were limited or diminished in effectiveness. The populace seemed passively dependent on others to punish convicted criminals rather than trying to prevent or resolve the problem.

The hateful conflict between the mayor and the city council, coupled with the alarming crime statistics, had a third comrade in divisiveness. At the time the HCI was formed, one did not need to look far to see that spread across Topeka's neighborhoods, racial/ethnic groups, and socioeconomic classes were deep divisions that consistently prevented sharing of resources and cooperating to reach mutually defined goals. There were numerous examples where stakeholders failed as collaborators and succeeded as adversaries.

In April 2000 Mayor Joan Wagnon and Stuart W. Twemlow convened the Healthy Community Initiative. The HCI group considered the conflicts between the mayor and city council, as well as the crime statistics, to be symptoms of underlying difficulties. However, the community at large did not share this depth of understanding and focused on short-term solutions such as replacing the mayor and city council and locking up criminals. The problems in leadership and with crime were largely ego syntonic and did not have the value of a clinical symptom for the citizens.

### Community Health Perspective Underlying Topeka's HCI: Stabilizing Systems and Healthy Capacities

> *The City Government can initiate change, but maintaining progress is up to the neighborhood and community.*
>
> —HCI Member

The Healthy Community Initiative placed primary emphasis on Topeka's *stabilizing systems* and *healthy capacities* (an approach unique among community improvement efforts being developed around the United States). Overreliance on methods of enforcement and a passive, hostile dependence on the city government had proved insufficient at best and counterproductive at worst for sustaining a vibrant community. Topeka had developed a character style of hammering at its problems with little foresight or genuine hope. The HCI effort aimed at engaging the roots of community functioning and spoke to the substrate of community cohesion, where the majority of citizens could become invested in solving the problems of others in the town. Surely this was a task greater than a few psychoanalysts could muster. Topekans of all colors and stripes would need to become involved. The psychoanalytic contribution was to identify a means by which both the conscious and the unconscious compromises impeding change could be identified and the community's repertoire for solving problems enhanced. Could the psychoanalyst's appreciation of developmental capacities, transference enactments, unconscious conflict, object relations, and narcissism improve the community's ego strength?

For the sake of discussion at HCI meetings, the investment in community stabilizing systems was compared to the strength of character that parents try to instill in their children. For example, courage and fairness, moral fortitude and charity, empathy and personal accountability, industriousness and civic duty, and many other capacities would be attributes of good character. Just as parents prepare their children for life's challenges by encouraging development of such capacities, communities need to develop and maintain the systems and capacities that form the base for that community's "character."[1] Courage and fairness, moral fortitude and charity, empathy and personal accountability, industriousness and civic duty are all characteristics that help stabilize a community so that the people, groups, and enterprises within can operate optimally. The four stabilizing systems deemed essential for process-oriented maintenance of Topeka's community health are described in Table 1.

The HCI membership was designed to maximize an awareness of our community's stabilizing systems and healthy capacities. HCI members were chosen not as representatives, in the typical democratic sense, of various groups or constituencies. Rather, HCI members were chosen by virtue of their professional and personal commitment to enhancing the stabilizing systems within Topeka. Certainly this is not the only way to conceive of community stabilizing

---

1. At the time, Topeka was participating in the City of Character Program, which promotes a character word each month to heighten people's awareness of desirable traits. Examples include orderliness, forgiveness, and responsibility. Thus, for us to use the word "character" in this report had some validity for Topekans. For psychoanalysts, use of the word "character" to describe objectives for psychoanalytic interventions in the community is more complicated. It may, however, provide a springboard for the purposes of our discussion.

---

**Table 1.** *Description of Community Stabilizing Systems.*

---

1. **Law Enforcement and Justice:** A community-stabilizing system supporting the healthy capacities for courage, fairness, peace keeping, safety, reparation, restitution, and so on.

2. **Religious Community:** A community-stabilizing system supporting healthy capacities for moral fortitude, charity, humility, spirituality, tolerance, altruism, mercy, generosity, and so on.

3. **Education:** A community-stabilizing system supporting the healthy capacities for industriousness, civic duty, integrity, achievement, enrichment, socialization, artistry, and so on.

4. **Social Services:** A community stabilizing system supporting the healthy capacities for empathy, personal accountability, self-expression, public health, social convention, and so on.

---

systems (CSS). Nor should these CSS be understood to represent all that a community requires to be successful. Of note is the purposeful exclusion of policy makers, politicians, and businessmen owing to the solution-oriented, rather than process-oriented, strategies intrinsic to each of these groups. Politicians have to produce quick results, or they will not be reelected. An example of political shortsightedness was President George W. Bush's decision to deny future federal support for research on stem cells and to keep only existing lines intact. This political compromise punts to future leaders the ethical and political dilemmas of what to do when, or if, the research yields significant results. Similarly, business people are geared toward gaining any competitive advantage. The value of change is determined by the bottom line, which is derived through goal setting and quick, effective decision making. Does this mean that the participation of politicians and businessmen is unimportant to a healthy community? Absolutely not. Their greatest contribution occurs at the implementation and fundraising phase of the project. One model for integration of CSS with community agencies is depicted in Figure 1.

Given the HCI perspective, when the stabilizing systems break down (or, from a psychoanalytic point of view, when the community ego strengths break down) leaders shaping policy or spending

**Figure 1.** *Interaction of Community Stabilizing Systems (CSS) in a Safe, Connected Community.*

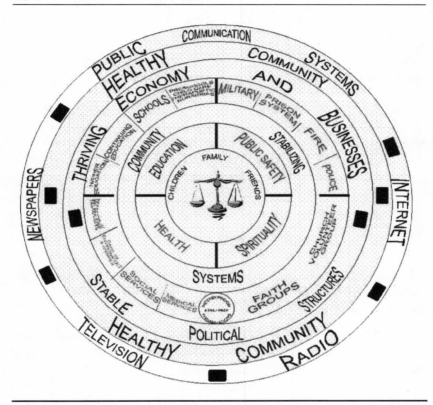

money to help make a community more cohesive, safe, moral, and productive have less and less influence over the problems. As happened in Topeka, without some degree of stability community members were pulled toward passivity, indifference, or demandingness. Leaders were pressured *to do! to fix! to spend!* Every special interest demanded immediate results. This call for action tended to be without the benefit of a clear understanding of basic needs or desired outcomes. The demand for a quick fix obscured the community's vision for the future. A vicious cycle began, and it was easy to imagine how the trio of hate, violence, and divisiveness took root.

### Healthy Community Initiative Basic Assumptions

*(1)  When these four stabilizing systems are supporting the community's general health, the stage is set for economic prosperity and effective political action.*

John Dugan (1999), former Topeka Planning Director, echoed this assertion when he wrote:

> Without a stable residential and institutional base, desired commercial, social, and infrastructure services are slow to follow if not impossible. . . . Recognizing that neighborhoods come in all shapes and sizes, different policies or strategies are needed because of their conditions, character, and values. When these micro-policies are balanced and coordinated with community-wide objectives for the City as a whole, all passengers on the boat move forward at full and deliberate speed [p. 1].

*(2)  People working within each of the stabilizing groups will see the blind spots in the programs or interventions sponsored by the other stabilizing groups.*

For example, members from law enforcement are particularly adept at setting limits on violence and enforcing the law; from the social services, at primary prevention of antisocial behavioral problems; from education, at helping youth become contributing citizens; from the faith community, at helping families find a moral compass. Given these different strengths, partnerships can be formed in which the police and mental health providers work together to help families and children involved in a violent incident. Educators and faith leaders can be recruited to follow up and further heal wounds. The point is that, once the power of the stabilizing systems can be recognized and harnessed, there are endless opportunities to forge partnerships between agencies, as well as helping, ultimately, citizens learn how to help themselves much more effectively.

*(3)  Relationships built on trust and understanding yield solutions with much greater staying power and effectiveness.*

Such trust-based relationships contrast with agreements cobbled together through quid pro quo arrangements, or plans spelled out by outside experts. In the case of quid pro quo, resources and power are held in abeyance or doled out to gain an advantage. The risk is that turf can become more important than collaboration. With experts, the advice may operate as scaffolding but be of little use if the people in need cannot own the plan (Dugan, 1999).[2]

To bring the example closer to home, in the absence of trusting relationships Cops might see Shrinks as quick to excuse antisocial behavior; and Shrinks might see Cops as quick to judge antisocial behavior (see the Marans and the Osofsky and Osofsky chapters, this volume). Consequently representatives from these two community-stabilizing systems may start to talk past each other, essentially setting at odds such healthy capacities as courage, fairness, safety, and reparation (law enforcement and justice) against empathy, personal accountability, public health, and social convention (social services). When representatives from one stabilizing system develop trusting relationships and open communication with representatives from another stabilizing system—as we have worked hard to do in the HCI group—then it becomes much easier to help solve each other's problems. Efforts to provide for safety and reparation can work in concert with efforts to ensure personal accountability and public health.

*(4) Credit for HCI accomplishments must go to those in the community who become involved and who ultimately are responsible for ongoing efforts.*

---

2. Dugan (1998) wrote about relationships as follows: "By their nature, volunteer neighborhood organizations are rarely equipped as specialized implementers. However, they are critical partners for neighborhood development in the role of community conveners and consensus builders (e.g., tax incentives, TIF). As representative of the neighborhood they must define a vision for the area—what they want to see in the future—before enlisting the help of specialized implementers. Without a neighborhood's clear direction or planning, specialized implementers are apt not to follow. Because of the need to rely more on local solutions to community development problems, it is imperative that nonprofit, private, and public entities be equipped to provide results. The local government offers unique tools for development, including eminent domain, grants, etc. to entice an otherwise reluctant private market to respond. In addition, data collection can be more readily and evenly performed by local government to be shared with neighborhood partners. If any partners in this mutually beneficial equation are poorly equipped, they all suffer."

We hope to empower community members to solve their own problems, an effort that is akin to helping an analysand take over self-analysis as the process terminates. Over time this means that the presence and influence of HCI should fade into the background. We have viewed ourselves in this mission more as catalysts for change than as the actual agents for change. As a group, HCI will not seek political affiliation, economic gain, public acclaim, or personal notoriety. HCI members are volunteers bonded by a dedication to the community rather than self-enhancing needs.

### Investing Time to Develop a Process

HCI has not been interested in building a better mousetrap or usurping the efforts of other Topeka groups. To do so would increase competition for finite resources and add to the existing problem that the left hand did not know what the right hand was doing. For example, in response to the spate of school shootings a few years ago, three different antiviolence youth groups scheduled events on the same weekend to initiate local prevention efforts. Their efforts, although well intentioned, were uncoordinated. In essence, the groups were competing with each other for funding and community involvement to accomplish the same goals. Rather than adding a fourth, overlapping entity, the HCI emphasis was on enhancing the stabilizing systems and healthy capacities that already existed. This was a new kind of strategy, aimed at developing partnerships and clearing away the doubts and excuses that interfered with Topekans' helping themselves.

This new strategy, with its different emphasis, operated under a timeline familiar to psychoanalysts. The HCI group discovered, as we tried to identify core problems in Topeka, that the underlying causes were complicated and overlapping. Like any neurotic symptom, the so-called fixations, regressions, condensations, and displacements were overdetermined. Repeatedly we returned to concerns about violence and crime, quality of life for our children, and the implications of Topeka's lack of identity and community pride. We discussed how a sense of entitlement, civic passivity, and a lack of accountability hobbled those in need. For example, some neighborhood improvement organizations suffer from poor organization and lack of vision. They seem to feel entitled to government funds and exude an attitude that the city has a duty to solve their neighborhood problems by producing more and more resources. This attitude and inertia stand in contrast to the attitudes of self-initiated groups that produce results for their neighborhood and generate their own momentum.

## Community Mindsets

As part of the ongoing "diagnostic" process we next assessed mindsets of Topeka leaders and residents. A violent and fragmented community creates in its members a way of thinking that distorts attitudes and even the perception of reality. Table 2 lists some of these distortions when compared to an altruistic mindset as defined earlier. A key issue in the violent mindset is a narrow self-centeredness that rarely looks at the good of the community as a whole or at the needs of others.

Topeka tended to weigh in under the violent mindset category. Creativity and thinking styles, especially among community leaders, tended toward antiintellectual, short-term, stopgap solutions rather than toward strategies requiring reflection, abstract thinking, and future planning. The conflict between the mayor and the city council, for example, resulted in leaders' becoming confused and wasting energy over insignificant problems (e.g., one council meeting was consumed by hot debate over whether or not to place a single stop sign in a residential neighborhood). Regressed power dynamics revolving around bully-victim-bystander roles led to oversimplified strategies.

Several times our level of concern about specific incidents or issues threatened to spur us to premature action, for example, the rocketing homicide rate, and reports of citizens killed in drive-by-shooting crossfire. This experience could be compared to the urge arising within a clinical psychoanalytic context to provide symptom relief in lieu of developing an analytic understanding. Discipline and perseverance were required of the HCI group (as of the analytic dyad in a clinical process) to establish a broad view of Topeka's functioning and to not overreact to dramatic and frightening incidents. Discipline and perseverance were also needed to cultivate an appreciation of the roles of the four stabilizing systems within the community.

**Table 2.** *Community Mindsets.*

|  | *Violent Mindset* | *Altruistic Mindset* |
|---|---|---|
| Thought Patterns | Reactive<br>Narrow Range of<br>Response Options<br>Perseverative | Proactive<br>Wide Range of<br>Response Options |
| Ruthlessness | High | Low |
| Economic Prosperity | Variable | High |
| Inner Peace | Low | High |
| Outer Peace | Low | High |
| Power Struggles | Fixed Bully-Victim-<br>Bystander dynamics<br>with unstable<br>political<br>structures | Stable political<br>structures, fewer<br>power struggles, and<br>more helpful<br>bystanders |
| Greed | High | Low |
| Envy | High | Low |
| Contempt | High | Low |
| Materialism | High | Low |
| Narcissism | High | Low |
| Creativity | Low | High |

We realized that singular efforts to address problems such as crime resulting from drug trafficking were doomed to failure. Increased interdiction by law enforcement might remove many of the offenders in the short term, but it would not help prevent the psychosocial problems contributing to children becoming addicts in the future. More antidrug education programs in schools would reinforce messages received by children in stable homes but not necessarily touch those kids from chaotic situations where drug use might have a multigenerational legacy. Spiritual outreach and social service intervention could offer succor and healing to some, but many more might not have the wherewithal to avail themselves of such aid. Thus, programs developed within any one of the four stabilizing systems might have some effect but would undoubtedly fall short of a comprehensive plan.

This strategy of developing a "community-mindedness," for lack of a better term, would have been short-circuited had we succumbed to our urges to do, to fix, to spend. Instead, the HCI adopted a disciplined approach of trying to assess just how the community functioned and how functional or dysfunctional the community was, how the community became dysfunctional and how the community's dysfunction served it. Drug use and its accompanying criminal behavioral symptoms, including domestic violence, were identified as the final common pathway of a whole host of problems relevant to the community stabilizing systems of law enforcement, social services, religion, and education. Thus, rather than pointing to drug abuse as the problem undermining Topeka, the HCI group developed a different kind of "diagnostic formulation" summarized in Table 3 that will sound familiar to psychoanalysts; since it focuses on causes, rather than results (symptoms), of conflict.

Appreciation of the degree of fragmentation, tolerance of unacceptable behaviors, expectation of failure, and apathy invited the inference that Topeka lacked a coherent narrative. This threshold is familiar to psychoanalysts, who specialize in using interpretation to help analysands retell their personal stories.

## The Power of Shared Experiences (or Knowledge by Itself Is Insufficient)

At the very beginning the HCI group had many ideas but not much personal experience living in high-crime neighborhoods. For the most part, the members of HCI interacted with people from those neighborhoods only when they came to the courts, clinics, schools, or places of worship. We were poised to offer intellectual solutions for problems we had not experienced first hand. The psychological distance between those of us living in more affluent neighborhoods than our fellow Topekans who lived under more alarming conditions greatly diminished when we took "the Trolley ride." Prior to boarding the trolley, the HCI group had seen maps high-

---

**Table 3.** *HCI Consensus Regarding Underlying Causes of Topeka's Problems.*

---

*Fragmentation*—geographic, economic, social, religious (e.g., collapsed dialogue among faiths), administrative (City Council conflict resulting in micromanagement without due acknowledgment of the big picture).

*Tolerance of the Unacceptable*—lack of community concern regarding prevention of violent crime, lack of concerted community action against hateful antigay picketers, neglect of children and inadequate parenting.

*Expectation of Failure*—government (electing officials, then daring them to succeed), business and community growth (stagnant downtown), common civility (disrespectful speech toward one another both publicly and privately).

*Apathy/Poor Attitude*—lack of follow-through to correct identified problems (e.g., many proposed solutions but sparse implementation), cultural blandness, lack of involvement in addressing others' problems, negativism among influential people.

---

lighting "Intensive Care" neighborhoods, needing emergency attention.[3] In East Topeka, for example, risk factors included a 32% poverty rate; very high violent crime; median residential property value of $12,447; house ownership rate of 30%; and median residential sale price change in the previous year of 22%. Thus armed with information and good intentions, we pulled up in front of a crack house. A resident living nearby described how the drug trade had systematically undermined the neighborhood. Across the street a widow regularly pried bullets from drive-by shootings out of the

---

3. Dugan (1999) suggests a creative classification of needy neighborhoods based on a medical care model: *Intensive care*—High risk factors, e.g., fewer owner-occupied homes, and many vacant lots and boarded-up houses, high violent crime rate, low home market value, no business investment. *At risk*—More owner-occupied homes, lower violent crime risk factors. *Outpatient*—Generally stable, but with areas of housing neglect that do not encourage a sense of community or interaction. *Healthy*—Low in risk factors and people feel safe and act that way; for example, children use front yards and play in the park.

porch trellis for her morning glories. Irresponsible landlords repeatedly allowed the most scurrilous tenants to take up residence at this crack house. If forced to evict owing to pressure from the police or the neighbors, these same landlords simply rented to a different batch of drug users. Through collaboration with a local program, "Safe Streets," homeowners of the Holliday Park neighborhood were making some headway, but there was a great deal left to do.

Onward the trolley drove through the Intensive Care and At Risk neighborhoods of Hi-Crest, East Topeka, and Old Town. One by one, neighborhood representatives took turns recounting the crime and blight that had diminished their sense of safety. We stopped at many abandoned, boarded-up houses to hear the stories of their deterioration. Mayor Wagnon described how existing housing codes prevented demolition of many such sites. HCI members were shocked that it was not easier to offer help, whether in cleaning up code violations or directing police to obvious criminals.

Slowly, layers of denial and projection were peeled away. These were parts of our city that we drove by every day, but that *we had managed not to see*. Yet here we were with our fellow Topekans hearing about daily experiences that diverged radically from our own. We began to feel what they felt. Every psychoanalyst knows that the experience shared with the analysand is the sum and substance of an analytic process. Analysts carefully monitor the nature and depth of exchanges, both verbal and nonverbal, between their patients and themselves. Whether these subversive phenomena are described as a manifestation of infantile neurosis, projective identification, selfobject transference, or an intersubjective phenomenon, psychoanalysts thrive on them. The subversion of one's habitual way of viewing problems clears the way for change. The subversion of one's habitual way of viewing neighbors clears the way for imagining a different community experience.

We cruised down a modest street not far from Monroe School, National Historic Site in which the Brown versus Board of Education Supreme Court Case was adjuticated. The story of this neighborhood accords with the groundbreaking achievement of Brown. The community police officers recounted the sting operation that closed the open-air drug market on this block a year earlier. Prior to that time residents were afraid to leave their home. Their fear kept them shuttered in their homes, and yards were littered with heaps of trash. On our stop there, we saw neatly mowed lawns and children playing out front. The residents had reclaimed their homes with evident pride. Children happily chased the trolley, and their parents waved to the community police officers. After what we had experienced so far on the ride, it was a relief to see that neighborhoods could turn around. Thankfully we were to see more of the same in Hi-Crest, but in Old Town the news was not so good. Many prostitutes were hanging out on the corners as we drove by.

The uncanniest moment of our trip occurred when we pulled up in front of a lovely gray Cape Cod cottage. In the small front yard, a middle-aged woman tended to her petunias and marigolds. A man sat nearby talking on a cell phone. They could have been any one of us. In the driveway was a late-model SUV. The woman who lived across the street was on the trolley with us and was eager to take the microphone. She spoke into the trolley's public address system and described the parade of shady characters who came to this home at all hours to buy drugs. The police chief took his turn and listed the legal technicalities that had hampered efforts by the police to close down this drug operation. So there we sat on the Topeka Trolley, the PA system broadcasting law enforcement efforts to arrest this seemingly average middle-class couple, who relaxed in their yard on a summer's evening. Not more than 10 yards from them, we looked at each other. They did not wave as the children near Monroe School had, but neither did they turn away. We drove on.

In another alarming story, this time as we spent time in East Topeka, a very angry and frustrated resident described how code violations regarding junk cars in yards, as well as drug trafficking, burglary, and physical assault, were common in his neighborhood. Several area thugs threatened arson to those who dared confront them. To try to increase his family's sense of safety, the resident had added so many outdoor lights that his yard was ablaze each night. Next door, were the charred remains of a house. It was clearly uninhabitable, but the city could not tear it down because the damage did not meet building code criteria for demolition. An older woman had died in the blaze, suspected to be arson, because she could not escape. She had nailed her backdoor shut to prevent robberies.

The story of this Topeka Trolley ride provides a window on the shared experience of the HCI members. We were shocked, saddened, angered. There was no doubt that help was needed.

Even more of an impression was created by our collective self-realization that we had been so blind to the plight of our fellow

Topekans. Our blindness made us complicit. One HCI member from a prominent Topeka family stated that he obviously did not know the town where he had grown up. The police chief later shared that he was "shocked" at how little we knew about our own city. Surely our lack of knowledge about our own "home town" indicated that the community stabilizing systems were not working well together.

Our shared experience of witnessing the effects of a deterioration spurred by loss of hope, as well as the renewal possible when relationships were formed, galvanized the HCI group. The discomfort we experienced when removing our personal blinders highlighted the challenges facing HCI efforts to strengthen the substrate of community cohesion. If such community traits as courage and fairness, moral fortitude and charity, empathy and personal accountability, and industriousness and civic duty were to take root in the neighborhoods seen on the trolley ride, all Topekans had to help. The city could do only so much to promote community health. We had to find a way to help others understand the shared experience that we had had on the trolley ride.

## Building a Community Mandate

As the HCI members reflected on the trolley ride, our task shifted from identifying underlying causes of Topeka's problems to enlisting the help of the community at large. We had learned a difficult lesson about countertransference, denial, and projection when we had to acknowledge the degree to which we had overlooked the problems in the At Risk and Intensive Care neighborhoods. Could it be that policy makers and others with power did not react to problems because the community as a whole did not see those problems? Although we had seen and heard personal accounts of Topeka's problems, we were well aware of a lack of consensual community urgency. At the same time, Mayor Wagnon noted: "Every time there is a headline about violence, people look to me and ask, 'What are we going to do about it?' There is a tremendous sense of unease in the community and schools." Would the entire community need to become fed up with crime before a lasting and effective change could be achieved?

Topeka had a history of generating potential solutions without sustained effort at implementation. HCI felt it imperative for the community health of Topeka that any intervention strategy involve the population as a whole, not merely physically, mentally, or socially at-risk individuals. Given that the behaviors negatively affecting health and development occur among people in an array of contexts, the city had to consider the largest possible set of potential issues underlying the problems and address those problems through a collaborative, multipronged approach. Knowledge (either about problems or potential solutions) was necessary but insufficient to create behavior change. Further, a single intervention addressing a single risk factor was unlikely to produce significant results. How do we get those living in Healthy neighborhoods to help out those in Intensive Care ones?

Given the growing conviction within the HCI group that many of Topeka's problems were attitudinal, we began to explore how we might take a baseline measure. With the assistance of Steve Pickard, an epidemiologist, several specific questions were included in the annual Kansas State Department of Health and Environment survey questionnaire interview about Topekans' perceptions of Topeka, summarized in Table 4.

Our hope is that the survey questions will be administered annually to provide a longitudinal reading to measure change. It is a complicated matter to assess perceptions of community members regarding the community, much less to interpret the findings. Pickard shared a set of positive predictors for community health distilled from research by the Kansas Department of Health and Environment and the Centers for Disease Control that we could use as a yardstick. State and county agencies around the country regularly conduct comparable epidemiological studies and a wealth of data is available to projects like the HCI (see Table 5).

## Group Process and Group Outcomes

The HCI's long evolution into a work group was complicated by the fact that it was very different from the goal-directed process familiar to most community leaders. First and foremost, we cultivated an awareness that HCI members were just as accountable and responsible for Topeka's problems as were the people living in the worst neighborhoods. The clinical comparison can be made to helping an analytic patient realize that relationship troubles are not simply personality conflicts with other people, who can then be

**Table 4.** *Structured Interview for Anonymous Telephone Survey.*

1. *How would you rate your community as a place to live?*
   *Excellent*
   *Very Good*
   *Fair*
   *Poor*

2. *How long have you lived in the community in which you live now?* _____

3. *During the past 5 years, have you been active in a coalition or civic group that attempted to address one or more community problems?*
   *Yes*
   *No*

   *Rate your community on each of the following questions as Excellent (5), Very Good (4), Good (3), Fair (2), or Poor (1):*

a. *Willingness of citizens to become involved in community issues*
   1. . . 2. . . 3. . . 4. . . 5

b. *Availability of effective leadership for solving community problems*
   1. . . 2. . . 3. . . 4. . . 5

c. *Cooperation and communication between community organizations (including government, civic organizations, and social agencies).*
   1. . . 2. . . 3. . . 4. . . 5

d. *People sharing a sense of belonging to the community*
   1. . . 2. . . 3. . . 4. . . 5

e. *Past history of success at problem solving*   1. . . 2. . . 3. . . 4. . . 5

f. *Community decision making shared among community members and among community organizations*   1. . . 2. . . 3. . . 4. . . 5

g. *Community investment of financial resources in community problem solving*   1. . . 2. . . 3. . . 4. . . 5

h. *People available in the community with skills to solve community problems*   1. . . 2. . . 3. . . 4. . . 5

i. *Shared values and vision among community citizens*
   1. . . 2. . . 3. . . 4. . . 5

j. *Self-honesty and ability to learn from mistakes*   1. . . 2. . . 3. . . 4. . . 5

---

**Table 5.** *Predictors of "Community Capacity"*
*(Derived from ongoing research by CDC and KDHE).*

---

*Strong Predictors of Community Capacity*—past history of success at problem solving; cooperation, and communication among community organizations (including government, civic organizations, and social agencies); self-honesty and ability to learn from mistakes.

*Good Predictors of Community Capacity*—availability of effective leadership for solving community problems; community decision making shared among community members and among community organizations.

*Moderate Predictors of Community Capacity*—shared values and vision among community citizens.

*Not Predictive of Community Capacity*—community investment of financial resources; community problem solving; people sharing a sense of belonging to the community.

---

objectified and externalized; relationship problems also have an intrapsychic template with many subjective facets, some of which can be consciously owned and some which, unconsciously disowned. Achieving this awareness was a challenge. For example, it took a full year to relinquish the urge to follow Robert's Rules of Order in favor of a slower paced, more reflective discussion. This transition involved clearly thinking through the problems (including resistances to acknowledging pain and frustrating complexities), as well as getting to know each other (not just as leaders solving community problems, but as citizen-participants accountable for the community's well-being). Full collaboration required us to step out of our professional roles. This move was facilitated by the gradual and heartfelt use of first names (rather than Mayor, Doctor, Chief, or Reverend, Father, or Rabbi), wearing casual rather than work clothes or uniforms, and, finally, meeting in each other's homes rather than at our work places.

We took our cues on encouraging personal familiarity with each other from the intersubjective school of psychoanalysis. There the value of appreciating the subjective experience of both analysand and analyst is fully recognized, and psychological encumbrances stemming from objectification or categorization by either member of the dyad are addressed through a measure of self-disclosure and subsequent analysis. The analyst is not simply the expert making observations from the outside, but an involved participant. In a similar fashion, we wanted to avoid having HCI members speak from within a particular role and thereby be less than fully immersed in the very human problems confronting Topeka.

We knew we were making progress when the CSS representatives began to relinquish the role of consultants, gathered to solve problems, and started to recognize their own participation in the perpetuation of problems. It was then relatively simple to tap into their sense of obligation to become involved in solving problems both within their own CSS, as well as across CSS. HCI members had to absorb the issues and become intensely and personally motivated to solve them: they needed to become committed social activists. We banked on this strategy as a means of preventing our recommendations from ending up in a forgotten filing cabinet drawer.

These goals were partially achieved. The trolley ride had been a major motivational impetus. We felt that we had achieved some insight into the communities we visited, though we were far from fully understanding their deep-seated problems. As well, we had arrived at a better understanding of each other's biases and priorities. After all this work, we took a poll of members and laid out five projects we felt were necessary to strengthen the Topeka community so that it could be safer and more creative.

## Five Projects for a Healthy Topeka

### 1. Support Successful Community Interventions

"Safe Streets," a program that had been in operation for several years, was the brainchild of a Lutheran minister and social activist who, through his intense commitment to the project, had obtained city and outside funding to hire a dedicated staff and to develop training procedures and interventions. The program was highly successful and was welcomed by the people it served. Interventions involved working with neighbors or landlords and tenants who were in conflict; helping individuals and neighborhoods reduce problems with gangs, violence, drugs trafficking, and prostitution; and connecting networks of helping individuals. One of the program's shortcomings was that it responded only when individuals or neighborhood representatives called for an intervention. This pattern maximized participation and positive outcomes, but little prevention or outreach was incorporated into the model.

In line with the HCI objective of mobilizing existing resources, we decided that it was desirable to extend the Safe Streets initiative into new areas, particularly prevention, education, and policy coordination. In other words, HCI would help build on to Safe Streets' existing partnerships with the city government, law enforcement, and education. We explored how we could procure use of the city television channel to broadcast programming relevant to the Safe Streets mission, particularly with regard to training natural community leaders and promoting the Safe Streets' Youth Citizens Academy.

### 2. Care of Children

A Topeka Police Department officer informed the HCI group of a survey on the prevalence and corresponding reporting rate for domestic violence. Worrying statistics suggested that less than 10% of all domestic violence was actually reported to the police and only a small percentage of reported cases were prosecuted because the family courts were unable to handle the increased caseload. Clearly, family safety and family conflict put enormous pressure on the functioning of all the community stabilizing systems and needed to be directly addressed. The Yale Child Study Center's Child Development-Community Policing program was identified as an immediate aid (Marans, this volume). Efforts to bring this program to Topeka continue as of this writing. Other local community efforts included reinforcement from local businesses for outstanding community service by children, access to parenting skills through churches, social agencies, and schools, and the encouragement of all Topeka's public schools to have an effective violence prevention program in place within three years.

### 3. Neighborhood Organizations

Federal funding for Topeka's Neighborhood Improvement Associations (NIAs) resulted in unintentional and heated infighting over how this money was to be spent. The NIA leaders often promoted themselves as having the interest of the neighborhood at heart, but later emerged wielding personal axes to grind or extreme religious or political opinions. With this kind of leader at the helm, the NIAs typically degenerated into self-centered groups attempting to use money for idiosyncratic and highly personal goals, often to the accompaniment of much complaining and fighting. In contrast, volunteer community service or neighborhood watch groups, self-initiated in the absence of government funding, were much more proactive, collaborative, and altruistic.

Given this observation about the distinctions between groups on the dole versus self-initiated projects, the HCI group planned several new interventions aimed at selecting and training natural helpers and leaders within neighborhoods. Previous research (Patterson et al., 1992) has characterized natural helpers as those who do not seek notoriety or accolades for their work, but receptively listen and facilitate the creation of solutions by clarifying problems, rather than carving out a leadership role for themselves. The analogy with the psychoanalyst is obvious. In a study of natural helpers in a small Midwest community, the typical profile was of a middle-aged housewife with no particular education in psychotherapy, or helping for that matter, but who offered an open mind and a receptive ear. The HCI group reasoned that in most communities, specifically in Topeka, natural helpers have only to be discovered and cultivated. This became a primary goal for HCI.

Specific interventions that could be embraced by a motivated natural helper might include the adoption of sister institutions across town to share in charitable activities, school projects, performing arts, and civic tasks. For example, children in affluent neighborhoods could collect old bicycles for children in Intensive-Care neighborhoods. Youngsters in "At-Risk" neighborhood schools could challenge comparable schools in other parts of Topeka to see who could have the greatest number of consecutive peaceful school days. In partnership with schools or houses of worship, this sort of outreach could also be extended to other communities for the mutual enrichment of all. Another idea would be to encourage local business promotion of cultural arts exchange from one neighborhood to another. For example, shopping centers in different parts of town might be the sites for sharing community stories, traditions, and myths, which often become diluted and even ruined by the fragmentation that occurs in unhealthy and self-centered communities.

Neighborhood projects suitable for natural-helper leaders could include the coordination of such complex cross-neighborhood projects as the sharing of community beautification activities, or the care of the elderly or terminally ill. Opportunities for such involvement already exist in the ongoing programs of many churches, temples, and parent-teacher organizations, as well as in nationally organized projects like Habitat for Humanity. The HCI narrowed its focus to how we could help coordinate and increase support for the implementation and evaluation of such programs and at the same time handle other emerging community problems; for example, identifying and rehabilitating vacant houses.

### 4. The Community Self-Image

City governments often focus on fostering a healthy public image as a substitute for community help and as enticement for potential investors, and Topeka was no different. There had been a number of focal efforts to improve Topeka's image under the auspices of highly motivated, goal-directed community volunteer organizations, such as the Junior League, but those efforts had had little direct effect on Topekans and others. After much discussion, the HCI group concluded that positive affirmations and vigorous marketing would do little to stem deeper problems in Topeka's "self-esteem." Instead, we looked to identify a shared experience that could unite the community in an affirming manner since Topeka had a rich and fascinating history.[4] A theater performance where

---

4. Topeka, the capital of Kansas, has a population of approximately 125,000 people with 50,000 more in the surrounding county. Eighty-two percent of the population is Caucasian. Topeka is rich in history. Lutie Lytle, who in 1897 became the second African-American woman admitted to the practice of law, called Topeka home. The Santa Fe Railroad was founded in Topeka. A Topeka dentist professing that his services "didn't hurt a bit!" created Alfred E. Newman, the smiling icon of *Mad Magazine*. Charles Curtis, the only Native American to serve as vice president (under Herbert Hoover) was born in Topeka. The first million-dollar high school was built there in 1931. Alf Landon, Republican presidential candidate who opposed FDR, lived in Topeka where he raised his daughter, former Senator Nancy Kassebaum Baker. In 1954 the United States Supreme Court

the community reviews its own history to create a narrative seemed more likely to help. The REVELS (1998) is a national group that employs volunteers to create a locally relevant script and large-scale community celebration and thus was an immediate creative option for Topeka.

## 5. Mobilizing Community Spirit

The HCI group discussed how different religious faiths, although occasionally in opposition to one another, had the potential to work together to provide reflection and a deepening perspective on our community problems that would complement initiatives by goal-directed people focused on the bottom line. For example, community religions leaders were interested in organizing public-safety neighborhood forums based on values rather than crime statistics. A mosaic of peace was discussed, including assessment of housing needs, crime, drug abuse, and collaboration in addressing these issues. A plan was formulated to organize teams of worshipers to make door-to-door visits in the areas around their places of worship to learn about their neighbors. Thus each quarter, or on specific religious holidays, congregants will become involved in demonstrating that such values as charity, humility, spirituality, tolerance, altruism, mercy, and generosity belong in the neighborhood.

---

decision in the Brown versus Topeka Board of Education changed the face of civil rights forever. The Menninger family founded the first psychoanalytic institute west of the Mississippi in the 1940s. Famed stripper Gypsy Rose Lee gave her first performance there, and Carrie Nation, the temperance crusader, lived in this town. Jazz great Coleman Hawkins lived in Topeka as a youth, as did poets Langston Hughes and Gwendolyn Brooks. Topeka hosts the only municipally funded university in the United States: Washburn University's Law School counts Senator Bob Dole among its graduates. In 2000 the Kansas Board of Education voted to remove the study of evolution from school science curricula, a decision that has since been repealed. Recently a female state representative opined that the 19th Amendment, which gave women the right to vote, was unnecessary. In this woman's opinion, if families were functioning optimally, women would stay home and not vote. Finally—regrettably—Topeka is home to a cult that travels the nation to picket against homosexuality (their hateful definition of homosexuality is broadly conceived and encompasses any person or issue they dislike). Topeka is midwestern in the best and worst sense of the term and its story would create exciting community theater.

## Taking Stock After the 18 Months

After 18 months of activity, the core HCI group had consolidated to about 10 members. Members with personal agendas had by then learned that the group was not going to be a conduit for their specific projects. Those who were frustrated by the lack of action dropped out. A number who clearly had political motives for joining were able to bow out without loss of face since it was clear that the group would not be used to elect any member to office or to support any specific political agenda.

The group, through developmental process and attrition, was distilled down to members committed to the community-as-a-whole and to each other; a process we feel is essential to the development of effective community interventions. This core group of HCI members selected the most interesting of the five projects detailed earlier and began to construct means for attracting stakeholders to address their goals. Additionally, they planned to attend City Council meetings on a regular basis. On reflection, it seems remarkable that the HCI group was able to sustain its selfless and altruistic mission. Even those with a clear political agenda, like Mayor Wagnon, did not try to derail the HCI process in favor of quick fixes. The core group now spent significant time exploring grant and funding resources and planning how different communities stabilizing systems could assist each other in bringing about changes. Then the unexpected happened.

Significant, and in some cases dramatic, shifts in leadership occurred within the HCI group as well as in significant sectors of Topeka. First, Mayor Wagnon, who had strongly supported HCI, was defeated during the primary race for reelection, despite efforts to rescue her image and to promote what was good for the city as a whole. Her defeat was punctuated by the placement of an extremely derogatory effigy outside her City Hall office, an act allegedly perpetrated by two prominent and politically active citizens. That hateful act cast an intimidating pall over the subsequent general election. The populace was outraged, but the council and mayoral political candidates would not touch on the issues of hate, violence, and divisiveness embodied in the act. The HCI group met with the new mayoral candidates, who had been supported by groups and individuals seeking to oust Mayor Wagnon. Both candidates superficially supported our initiative but without pledging active commitment. In a second leadership disruption, Stuart Twemlow, cofounder with Mayor Wagnon of HCI, decided on a job change that would take him out of Topeka. Leadership was transferred to Sallye Wilkinson, who, owing to organizational restructuring at her place of employment, was undergoing a major career transition of her own. Concurrently, the leadership of the Topeka Police Department, as well as several major private-sector and municipal entities in Topeka, were in flux. It was not clear who would emerge to lead on many levels of Topeka's functioning.

With so much internal and external change, the core HCI group became divided. One subgroup felt that Wagnon's political defeat nullified the initiative's purpose and that Twemlow's HCI strategies were irrelevant because, as one member expressed it, he had "left and is no longer part of the community." Nonetheless, just as Mark Twain had observed that news of his death was premature, Twemlow remained very involved in HCI through teleconferences, as well as with the community through regular family visits and his leadership in rolling out a "Peaceful Schools" program involving a large number of Topeka's public schools. Clearly some of the pitfalls familiar to readers of Bion (1952) were operational within the HCI group dynamics. The other subgroup, more committed and invested in the altruistic goals and projects of HCI, wished to continue and in fact did so despite the vicissitudes of leadership. We feel that the HCI continued because it was based on a long-term process oriented toward realistic assessment of what needed to be worked through and implemented.

Much like clinical psychoanalysis, the psychoanalytic community process exemplified by HCI involves understanding, however slowly, what can and cannot be achieved and accepting less than what was unrealistically wished for but more than what was unrealistically feared. The HCI process has demonstrated how neighbors making the effort to appraise the strengths and weakness of a community can be transformed into stakeholders willing to engage in a "community working through" of problems. As was often the refrain in HCI meetings: city government can initiate change, but maintaining progress is up to the neighborhood and community.

At the time this chapter was written (2003), participation by representatives from the CSS of education and the religious community had faded. Representatives from law enforcement and social services, however, continued to work actively to increase and formalize partnerships between these two community-stabilizing systems. This is a picture familiar to psychoanalysts accustomed to the waxing and waning of hope and motivation during advances and regressions in analysis. The work of Topeka's Healthy Community Initiative is ongoing and will be reported on as its effects result in useful community partnerships, social institutions, or, conversely, important lessons drawn from any shortcomings.

## References

Badcock, C. R. (1986), *The Problem of Altruism*. Oxford, UK: Bezel, Blackwell.

Bion, W. R. (1952), Group Dynamics: A re-view. *Internat. J. Psycho-Anal.*, 33:235–247.

Bracher, M. (1992), Psychoanalysis and social change. *Humanity & Soc.*, 6:461–479.

Clotfelter, C. (1980), Explaining unselfish behavior: Crime and the helpful bystander. *Urban Econ.*, 8:196–212.

Dugan, J. (1999), Healthy Community: Explanation of Health Map. Produced for the Topeka-Shawnee County Metropolitan Planning Department, Re: Work Session #2. September 23. Unpublished ms.

Freud, S. (1921), Group psychology and the analysis of the ego. *Standard Edition*, 18:69–143. London: Hogarth Press, 1955.

Ginsberg, H. J. (1977), Altruism in children: The significance of non-verbal behavior. *J. Commun.*, 27:82–86.

Menninger, K., Mayman, M. & Pruyser, P. (1963), *The Vital Balance*. New York: Viking Press.

Milgram, S. & Hollander, P. (1964), Murder they heard. *Nation*, 198:602–604.

Patterson, S., Memmott, J. L., Brennan, E. M. & Germain, C. B. (1992), Patterns of natural helping in rural areas: Implications for social work research. *Soc. Work Res. & Abstr.*, 28:22–28.

Revels Inc. (1998), *The Revels Newsletter*. Cambridge, MA, Spring/Summer.

Shapiro, Y. & Gabbard, G. (1994), A reconsideration of altruism from an evolutionary and psychodynamic perspective. *Ethics & Behavior*, 4:23–42.

Slavin, M. & Kriegman, D. (1992), *The Adaptive Design of the Human Psyche*. New York: Guilford Press.

Trivers, R. L. (1985), *Social Evolution*. Boston: Addison-Wesley.

Twemlow, S. W. (2000), Working with a mayor and city council. *Amer. Psychoanal.*, 34:18–19.

—————— & Sacco, F. C. (2003), The management of power in municipalities: Psychoanalytically informed negotiation. *Negotiation J.*, 19:369–388.

# 7

# A Retired Psychoanalyst Volunteers to Promote School-Based Mental Health

William L. Granatir

I first began working as a volunteer in the inner-city schools of Washington, DC at the age of 76 after a long career as a psychoanalyst. Five years later I found myself a moving force behind a citywide program promoted by a coalition of stakeholders and community leaders and the director of a new Department of Mental Health. This personal memoir captures my experience in an inner-city school and, I hope, illuminates a sense of how psychoanalytic clinical skills can be brought to bear in an environment that might otherwise be considered daunting. I hope by this account to provide a concrete idea of how one may roll up one's sleeves, as it were, to help children in difficult situations.

It is easy to describe my motivation for becoming a volunteer in schools at age 76. A year before I had decided that I was too old to commit to a new psychoanalytic or potentially long therapy. My psychoanalytic/psychotherapy practice had dwindled to a few patients. I was determined to retire at 77.

My volunteer work began in 1992. I was greatly disturbed by news reports about the violence that besieged children in the District of Columbia; the myriad cruelties visited on the local young people, including that caused by failing city institutions such as the child protection agencies. Washington had become a war zone. I wanted to see if I could offer psychiatric consultation or some other kind of service to school children who were traumatized and not operating at optimal levels. Thus I gladly responded when invited to join a program then being sponsored by the District of Columbia Hospital Association.

An old man, and a white, middle-class professional, I approached the idea of volunteering in the inner city with some trepidation and humility. I would experience a different culture in a needy, mostly African-American community with which I had had little contact or experience. I did not know how I would be greeted. From my clinical experience, however, I had learned from many reports from adults how a limited, brief contact in childhood or adolescence with a benevolent or admired teacher, counselor, or summer camp counselor had had a profound effect on their development. I knew how these contacts with older people, with accompanying elements of transference idealization, could be incorporated as building blocks in an ego-ideal system toward which these children could aspire. Thus, I was encouraged to try to offer some help. My personal experience growing up as a Jew—as a member of a minority and despised group—in the 1920s and 30s was also a help.

I did not have formal training as a child psychiatrist. After completing my psychiatric residency in April 1948, I obtained a position as director of an adult and child guidance clinic at the Washington Institute of Mental Hygiene, a community clinic financed by the United Way, which used a sliding fee scale for service. The work I did with children was supervised by the three child psychiatrists residing in the city at that time. There were no child fellowships in this area; with a growing family and my other commitments, no possibility existed for me to pursue formal training in child psychiatry. When, in the spring of 1950, a psychiatrist trained in child psychiatry visited me to apply for a position at the clinic, I asked the Board to hire him to replace me. I then concentrated on my training as a psychoanalyst and teacher.

I was assigned by the Hospital Association program to visit an elementary school in Northeast Washington two mornings a week. The principal and the school counselor welcomed me. I began by attending what was called the Breakfast Club, which met at 8 o'clock in the morning. I sat at the tables with the children. The younger children were curious and responsive to me and would permit me to help them open their cereal and juice boxes, they would talk with me. But the older children—10 years and older—looked at me with suspicion and did not engage in any conversation with me. The principal also was at the Breakfast Club. He would appear later at certain times during the day when there were special events, but very frequently he was absent from his office during school hours. I thought he must have had some other activity outside of school, perhaps some other business. He was very affable in his conversations with me and with others, but he was not helpful in organizing how I could be useful in the school.

The guidance counselor, a pleasant person who seemed to be overworked, was of more practical help. We had a number of discussions about troubled children in the school. She referred some children to me for assessment, some of whom I referred to outside clinical facilities after consultation with their parents. Then she referred four boys in the fifth and sixth grades who were troublemakers, disrespectful, overactive, and creating problems in their classes. I began to work with them twice weekly. We met in the library for an hour. These were very restless children. They could not sit still for more than two minutes and shouted obscenities at me. They would run around the library and snatch books from the shelves, which I had difficulty getting them to put back. We would sometimes read a little bit together. I helped them with some of their words. Only one of the four was able to read at all well. I gave them projects to do, with paper, coloring books, and art materials, and asked them to draw while I attempted to engage them individually in conversation.

Gradually, over a period of time, they began to tell me more about their experiences although it was often very difficult to sustain any kind of orderly discussion. They had a series of jokes about a white man, an Asian man, and a black man. In these the black man always came out to be the loser or abused. They also were eager to tell me about their sexual knowledge or experience, and two of them, only 10 years old, not only showed a good deal of knowledge about sex but claimed that they had had sexual intercourse.

I saw these boys as attractive, full of life and energy. In another environment, with proper emotional support, they might have been playing baseball, accepting rules, and trusting in the adults around them. Instead they were unruly, undisciplined, untrusting, and indifferent, if not hostile, to school assignments and teachers. As well, they disliked themselves. The oldest and most unruly boy was intriguing, partly because he was talented at drawing what was going on in his mind.

One day a policemen's band was presenting a kind of rock concert in the assembly hall. While the band played, I observed from the rear. All the children got up and danced in place. The boy I am referring to gradually moved toward me from virtually the opposite end of the auditorium. Dancing by himself, he moved closer and closer to me (smiling and doing his dance) until he was right in front of me. I realized that some bond had been established. After that, I was more comfortable paying more attention to him. It so happened that in the following year, when I transferred to a junior high school, he was also transferred to the same school. Although I did not work with him intimately, I did see him once in a while; he would come and tell me about his progress and his desire to become an architect. He also showed me two of his art projects. Clearly he had responded to and appreciated the attention I had paid him. I have long wondered what lasting effect the little I had offered may have had.

To get more information about these boys' behavior in class, I consulted their teachers. They did not appear to be very interested in talking with me. These were disturbing children. Their teachers would have preferred, I suspect, to have some way of eliminating these boys from their classrooms. The teachers were not sympathetic or interested in understanding the boys' behavior or their backgrounds. They had a very difficult task coping with a class of children that included a number of overactive boys. They wanted me to do something other than see the boys in a group—to give them medicine to calm them down or to get them out of the way.

By the spring of the year, the boys calmed down considerably in their sessions with me. There were periods when we could sit and talk about family relationships, friendships, and other personal values. They would sometimes make drawings when I asked them to. The counselor also reported that there was some improvement in their behavior in the classroom. The counselor also confided to me that she was ill with a peptic ulcer, partly as a result of stress, since she had another business that she was operating after school. I was not satisfied with either the school or my work in that school that year.

### Work in a Junior High School—Age 78

The following year I moved as a volunteer to a junior high school after reading an interview in the newspaper with the principal, who said that she needed help. She welcomed me. This was a large inner-city junior high school with three counselors and two attendance officers. There was one white counselor, who had been a gym teacher, and two African-American counselors. I spent some time sitting in classrooms to get to know the school, the teachers, and the atmosphere. I met with the counselors individually. I offered to set up a conference at which all the counselors and I might be able to meet on a regular basis and discuss some of the troublesome children. They told me that they never met together. The two attendance officers were more sensitive than the others to the needs of the children and the traumatized families from which they came. I had more contact with the two attendance officers, particularly with the woman counselor, with whom I became quite friendly. She had been a young mother, and I knew she was the grandmother of an infant. The other counselors treated this staff member, who had only a bachelor's degree and was not an accredited counselor, with passive aggressive contempt. I do not know how much our relationship and my encouragement helped, but the following year she attended college on weekends and in two or three years obtained a master's degree in psychology. I assisted her in writing her master's thesis, which was a personal history and memoir.

In January of my first year at the junior high school, I formed two groups, of eight girls and eight boys each. Different counselors at the facility had referred the students to me. All were troubled children. The boys were reported to be the most difficult and troublesome in the school. These children who were referred to me were also supposed to have problems with unresolved loss and grief. By this time I had joined with Bruce Sklarew, who had originated the School-Based Mourning Project. I had also attended training sessions with Dottie Ward-Wimmer, an experienced grief counselor and trainer at the William Wendt Center for Grief and Healing. I learned a great deal from her.

### Experience with the Girls' Group

I met with the two groups of students at this school two mornings a week for one hour each. The girls were seventh and eighth graders.

They formed a very good group; they bonded with each other and shared life experiences and feelings. They were very open in communicating about themselves. They would also frequently make drawings as we spoke. These pictures would give me clues to aspects of their unconsious. The girls did not seem to pay very much attention to me or expect very much of me; their group interaction was with each other. Occasionally I would make a comment or observation or ask a question, but it was not essentially necessary for me to be very active in this group. When, on a few occasions, I spoke in their inner-city slang, they laughed, and one girl said, "He can talk like us."

All these girls had issues of loss in their lives. One had a mother sick with cancer who was being cared for at home by an elderly grandmother. This girl also had an older sister, who was in an institution in the West because of her violent behavior.

Another, Allison, was a tall, thin, somewhat depressed girl who would not exactly disturb the class but would walk out of the room whenever she was displeased by anything happening in class. This behavior offended her teachers as well as the counselors. She had been with her single mother in a homeless shelter from the age of two or three until, when Allison was four or five, her mother was able to rehabilitate herself, forming an attachment with a man with whom she had a set of twins. Allison greatly resented that her mother expected her to spend a lot of time and attention caring for these younger siblings, and she complained regularly about her difficult relationship with her mother.

A third girl, Dorothy, said her mother was ill with a bad heart and was on welfare, and her father was in jail. She had been accused of taking money from someone, but the theft had never been proven. Dorothy once confided to me, "I don't know why it's so important to me, but I just *have* to have designer jeans."

A fourth girl, Georgia, was the youngest of six children. Her mother was depressed because her husband had died suddenly of a heart attack a year before, and a son had been killed—the poor woman had not been able to overcome her grief. Georgia also seemed somewhat depressed. She was living alone with her mother. She found the atmosphere very downbeat and was critical of her mother for being so sad all the time. This girl had three older sisters, all of whom were accomplished: one was a social worker; one was a Pentecostal minister; the third a teacher. One older brother was also a minister, and one was in jail. Her next older brother, with whom she had been closest, had been killed at the age of 18 in a drug gang conflict just around the corner from where the family lived. Georgia was an extremely well-built and beautiful young girl. She wore tight clothes and attracted a lot of attention from the boys, especially the older ones. One day she was apprehended in the school for carrying a knife. She said she carried this weapon to protect herself at the bus stop, where people sometimes accosted her.

Finally, there was Eva, a sparkling, attractive girl, not quite 15, in the eighth grade, who drew a great deal of attention in the halls. She was always surrounded by a group of boys and girls. She was a disturbance to teachers and counselors, who worried because she was defiant. Teachers reported that Eva was disobedient and combative. She was disrespectful with her teacher and told the group the teacher was "stupid anyway." Eva always dressed in straight shifts that seemed to be suspended from her prominent breasts, as, flanked by her friends, she walked proudly down the hall. She also had a serious boyfriend that everybody seemed to know about; he was an outstanding student in the ninth grade.

In the second year of the group, Allison confided that her putative grandfather had raped her when she was nine years old. She also said that, when she was four, her mother's boyfriend had molested her. She had been troubled by this experience ever since it had happened to her. The group was very sympathetic to her as she described what had happened, and then three of the other girls said family members had raped them also. None of these girls had ever shared knowledge about this experience with anyone. After the discussion, Allison told her mother about the incident, and the two spoke intimately. Allison's mother revealed that the same person, too, had raped her when *she* was a child. The mother called me the next day. She came in to talk with me about the experience. She did not believe that Allison had been molested when she was four, as Allison had also reported to the group, but she was going to contact this man, with whom she was still friendly, and inquire about the incident. Allison and her mother grew to be very close as the result of this intimate exchange. Allison shared her resentments with her mother, and her mother, in turn, was understanding and promised to make some arrangements to take better care of the twins to help relieve Allison of this extra burden of responsibility. Allison was very articulate in describing her feelings about the rape. She said that her grandfather had taken her confidence as a woman away from her, had destroyed her confidence in her sexuality. She doubted that she would ever be able to trust any man in a relaxed and loving relationship.

The other three girls who had been raped also described their experiences. Only one felt that she could talk to her mother about the rape; the others said they did not know anyone whom they could trust to discuss it with.

Georgia became increasingly provocative. She was no longer depressed. She was well aware of her attractiveness and that so many people took notice of her. Wearing her tight dresses, she walked with a sashay. She said people commented on her way of walking but that she could not help it; that was just the way she was. She said that her mother told her that she, too, walked that way when she was younger. Once Georgia revealed to the group that she was frequently visited by a man at the bus stop, who often gave her $20 bills. When I asked her what he was expecting in return for the money, she shrugged her shoulders and said, "Nothing. If he ever tried to act funny or do anything to me, I have an uncle who would kill him." I asked her what direction she thought she might be heading; if she thought she would end up like her older sisters or like her brothers, one of whom had been murdered and another incarcerated. She shrugged and said, smiling, "I guess I haven't decided yet."

In the winter of the group's second year, after the Christmas holidays, Eva confided to the group that she had missed her period and thought she was pregnant. The girls were very excited about this information. They all thought highly of her boyfriend, Lee, and a couple of the girls thought that she should have the baby. One of the girls said that Eva didn't have to worry about taking care of it—she could take care of the baby—and that welfare would provide support as well. Most of the girls in the group, however, supported the idea that she should seek advice from her mother. When Eva returned to the group after talking with her mother, she was in a state of great distress. She said her mother was insisting she have an abortion, because she did not want Eva to have the same difficulty in life that she had had by having a child at such a young age.

There was a considerable conflict between Eva and her mother. Her mother and grandmother came to the school requesting an interview with me. In this meeting I made some suggestions to them about how they might present the problem to Eva. The girl was adamant that she did not want to have an abortion, but her mother and grandmother prevailed on her and they arranged for her to undergo this procedure. She was depressed afterward.

Lee had been informed about the pregnancy. He said he was willing to take the consequences and help her raise the child, but, from what I was able to observe and from a conversation I had with him at his request, I think that he was relieved by the outcome. He had scholarly ambitions for himself that would have been interrupted had the pregnancy continued. Lee and Eva evidently continued to be intimate. Eva recovered from her depression, and her anger diminished by the end of the school year when I left.

In this group I was a facilitator and observer of the group process. I rarely made interpretative comments, although I sometimes asked questions. Frequently the group members interacted with each other entirely on their own, almost seeming to ignore my presence. I felt that, on the whole, the experience for these girls was a positive one. But, I cannot claim any great therapeutic advances. I did learn from them about their culture and experience. I had no experience using the instruments of evaluation necessary to make an objective evaluation of the effect the group experience might have had on their lives.

### Experience with the Boys' Group

The experience I had with the boys was entirely different. They were more aggressive, more disturbed in their behavior—more angry, defiant and difficult. During my volunteer work in the junior high school, a school counselor referred to me a group of eight boys whom I saw for an hour twice a week. They were considered to be very troubled and constituted problems for the school. Nelson was a large 13-year-old seventh grader who was quite immature. He was unable to read and did not talk or participate very much in the group discussions. Frequently, he lay on the floor and crawled around. But one day he sat on top of the table around which we were assembled, and, to my surprise, he took my hand. It was the first time he had approached me in any personal way. He squeezed so hard I thought he might break bones. I looked at him and said, "You know that you are hurting me, Nelson." He said, "OK, Doc, you're a psychiatrist; tell me what is going on in my mind." I said to him, "I can't tell you what is going on in *your* mind, but I can tell you what is going on in *my* mind." He said, "OK, tell me that." And I replied, "I think you would like so much to get close to me that it scares you."

He dropped my hand, grabbed a cookie, and ran out of the room. Now, I don't think this interpretation particularly helped him to understand himself, but I know that it relieved me and helped me to sustain my equanimity, particularly since this episode was taking place in the presence of the other boys with whom I was developing a sense of trust. Of course, the qualities I have mentioned (empathy, psychological awareness of mental processes, acceptance of difference and being neither noncritical nor judgmental) are not exclusive to psychoanalysts; other professionals, like lawyers and reporters, have these qualities. Poets have these qualities, and many other nonprofessional people also. Perhaps the experience of psychoanalytic observation, inquiry, and avoidance of critical judgment helped to refine these qualities, which, after all, are essentially personal.

Another interpretive intervention that reflects how I thought about the boys took place with Larry, another boy in the same group. This eighth grader was 15 years old, a leader of a group of boys who were considered troublemakers. I was standing in the hall one day waiting for someone to open our meeting room when Larry appeared. I asked him what he was doing in the hall since students were forbidden to be there during class time. I happened to know that his English teacher was giving an exam in his class that day. So I asked, "Larry, how come you're not taking the English exam?" He said, "Oh, I didn't feel like it." I responded, "Well, you know what I think? I think you'd rather get a zero for not taking the exam than take the test and fail, because you're embarrassed that you're not reading well." Larry left me, ran over to a group of the lockers, and broke into one that belonged to his friend Nelson, to whom he was mentor. He removed a jacket from the locker and started tossing it in the air. At that point the other students came out of their classes, and the hall filled with people. He and Nelson started fighting with each other over the jacket. When I told Larry that the vice-principal was very likely to come around and he would get into trouble, the boys stopped.

He started to walk toward me, and I said, "I think I have an idea about what made you run over and break into that locker." He asked, "What?" I said, "You didn't like what I said to you about the English test. It made you feel bad and angry with me. You went over to the locker instead of telling me about your annoyance." He responded, "Well, you know what I think? I think all you psychiatrists are full of shit!" I do not propose that such interpretative observations are useful, nor do I make them very often, but these examples certainly illustrate what was going on in *my* mind.

The boys never really formed a group responsive to each other, although they were respectful toward each other even while competing for attention. They sometimes shared their thoughts and feelings but remained mostly aloof. These angry and difficult boys, with the exception of one or two, did not behave with hostility in the group setting. Most handled themselves in a manner according to the rules of group behavior. We started each session with a greeting to each other, and we ended each session by standing for a minute holding hands in a circle, which I thought was a quieting time before they reentered the junior high school atmosphere. I brought cookies, and sometimes fruit, to each session.

Larry was a tall, self-confident, and attractive 15-year-old boy. He was admired by the other members of the group and by practically everybody else in the school. He led a group of boys who stood near a fence at recess and did not play the games in which the other boys were involved. When Larry was 13, his father had been stabbed to death outside the apartment house in which they lived. Larry ran down to the street and sat with his father as he bled to death while waiting for an ambulance. When the ambulance did arrive, his father was dead. He related these facts to me in a cold manner, without any affect; he wore a very grim expression. He said he would never discuss it again. And he didn't.

This boy's manner was mostly genial, charming, and witty. Larry was very successful with girls. He also had a lot of money—at one point he showed me a large wad of bills. He said he made money selling marijuana and shooting craps after school. He had a reputation for being an exceptional crapshooter. Though Larry was failing in mathematics in school, he knew enough to excel at figuring out the odds for the street games. He lived in the same apartment building as Nelson, to whom he was mentor and protector. Nelson also helped him sell marijuana.

Larry would not reveal very much about his private life or feelings, but one day gathered the attention of all in the group as he described in exquisite detail his lovemaking with his girlfriend. While the other boys sat there with wide eyes, he described how he had brought her to a state of ecstatic submission to him. Everybody sat spellbound, obviously envious as he painstakingly narrated the tale of his prowess.

Nelson was something of a mystery to me. I knew that he lived alone with his mother, who was an addict. He was very much concerned that, if the Department of Family Welfare found out about him, he would be moved to a foster home, and he did not wish this to happen. As I have mentioned, he spent a great deal of the group time on the floor, sometimes crawling around; only rarely did he sit up in a chair or talk to other group participants.

Martin was an interesting boy of 15, also in the eighth grade. He was referred to the group because of his defiant behavior and disrespect toward teachers. He also had a loss in his life: his father was in prison. He lived alone with his mother. Martin had a weekend job, sweeping at a McDonald's. He disliked his job intensely. He was very envious of Larry, who was such a success. Martin's ambition was to make a lot of money. One day he asked if he could see me privately because he had a problem he didn't wish to share with the group. He told me he had a girlfriend for whom he cared a great deal; she was also 15. Although she was ready for sexual intercourse, he was not. We discussed his anxiety and his concerns. We talked about his views about sex, his lack of confidence and his anxiety, his values and thoughts about responsibility. I saw him twice individually. On the weekend after the second time we met he came into the room early, and, beaming, threw his arms around me and kissed me on the cheek. Nothing was said between us, except I asked him if he had worn a condom and he said yes. The matter was not discussed again.

Jamal was a 15-year-old boy, also in the eighth grade, who had been arrested and was awaiting trial for attempting to hold up a 7-11 store. He'd had an accomplice, and a gun was involved, but it was unclear to me who had been carrying it. Jamal was very depressed and seldom spoke. He sat in the group meetings with his head in his hands and his shirt pulled up over his head. Jamal made only two comments that I recall, one in the form of a drawing of his apartment building with his address printed across the top of the sheet. Written on the drawing's façade was "No Love. No Love." The other comment he made grew out of a discussion in which the boys in the group speculated on what life would be like for them at 18 and what they would do after high school graduation. Jamal told the group, "My mother says I won't live to be 18."

Because this boy was so depressed, I spoke to a gym teacher to ask him whether he would pay some attention to Jamal if I could arrange with the principal to permit him to go to the gym once daily. The gym teacher said, "I'm not a psychotherapist." I replied, "I'm not asking you to be a psychotherapist, only that you pay him some attention. Teach him some moves in shooting baskets or some exercise or something like that." He said he would give it a try. The principal accepted the idea. Jamal said he was willing, and he went to the gym every day. I thought the contact, plus the activity and exercise, might make him feel better. It did seem to work, but eventually he went to trial over the summer recess and was sentenced to three months in jail. When he returned to school, he did not rejoin the group.

Eugene was a tall, thin eighth grader—bright, witty, and a fairly good student. He told me that he had been confined at Oak Hill (the youth detention facility for the District of Columbia) for 6 months for car theft. He said he was very good at stealing automobiles. He sat in the room, listening to everybody else talk, occasionally making comments, but mostly drawing pictures on the paper I had provided and eating cookies. Once I said to Eugene that although he had been coming to the group for some time, I didn't know very much about him and I didn't really know what he was thinking or feeling. "Why do you come to the group?" I asked. He looked at me, smiled, and said, "For the cookies." Once I thought he was frankly hungry, and asked him if he had breakfast. With a grin he replied, "Sure. My mother makes me breakfast every day. Ham and eggs, pancakes and sausage, waffles. The works." We both laughed.

On another occasion I mentioned to him that I thought I could tell something about his thoughts and feelings from the pictures he drew. A fairly good draughtsman, he drew violent pictures featuring tanks, cannons, and many meticulously rendered guns and also explicitly sexual illustrations. When I confronted Eugene about his not sharing any of his thoughts or feelings other than through his drawings, he said, "I don't tell anybody about myself."

Another boy, Michael, said, "Oh, you can trust Dr. Granatir. He won't tell anything that you share with him." Eugene then said, "OK, here's a question for you, Doc. If there was a confrontation between a group of skinheads standing on one side of Pennsylvania Avenue, with guns, and a group of African Americans on the other side, and you were there, what side would you join?" I responded that I am opposed to violence of any kind, but I also oppose what skinheads seem to believe in. I would be on the side of the African Americans. Apparently he found this comment acceptable, and there was no further discussion about it. After the second year of our group work, when I attended the class graduation ceremonies, Eugene came over to me to say goodbye. He was wearing a black silk suit, looking very sharp. We shook hands and said goodbye to each other.

Michael, my defender, was an interesting young boy. He was in the seventh grade, aged 13, when he asked one of the counselors if he could see me because he was having suicidal thoughts. When I saw him he did appear to be depressed. He said he was feeling suicidal; his parents had been arguing violently and were about to separate. I called his parents to invite them to come to the school. I saw them together once and then saw each of them alone. There was a long history of hostility and disagreement between them. When I saw the father alone, he was obviously depressed. He was a policeman on probation for some incident in which he was accused of misconduct. Michael's mother had a very good position in a government office in the city. She was considerably younger than her husband and quite attractive. She said she wanted a different life for herself, that she did not want to live with her husband any longer. I referred them for marriage counseling. The mother subsequently moved into another apartment alone. Michael remained with his father but would visit with the mother on weekends.

He did not mind very much traveling back and forth between his mother's residence and that of his father. I referred his father to a private clinic or therapist for treatment, but I don't know if he acted on my referral.

Because I did not have time to see Michael individually, I invited him to join us in our group. He fairly quickly got over his depression.

In our second year, by which time Michael was almost 14, I noticed that on Tuesdays he was alert in the group, but on Thursdays he seemed to be very sleepy. When I asked him about this, he said that on Wednesdays he went to New York. I also had observed that he wore brand-new Nike sneakers, and more than once he had shown me a second pair he kept in his book bag. Little by little Michael confided to me that he was flying to New York on Wednesday nights with his maternal uncle. They would rent two cars and sell marijuana in New York City. Then they would return on the last plane, so he did not get very much sleep on Wednesdays. He told me that he had 10 pairs of brand new Nike sneakers, each costing about $100. I asked him whether his parents knew about it, and he said, "Of course they do. I line the sneakers up next to my bed, but they never ask me about it." Nor was he questioned about where he was on Wednesday nights. Perhaps because he frequently slept in one or the other of his parents' apartments and not at a scheduled time, he was apparently not missed when he went to New York.

As time went on, Michael told me more and more about his continuing New York operation. After a few weeks, I asked to see him individually to discuss this information since it was information he could not share with the group. When he described driving the car that his uncle rented for him and told me about the sophisticated selection of guns they each had, I told him that I felt I could not continue to see him, either individually or otherwise. While I would keep the information confidential, I felt that, if I continued to see him, I would be condoning his behavior, and that he was a danger not only to himself but also to others. I also felt threatened by the possibility that if his uncle found out what Michael had shared with me I myself might be in some danger. He said, "Oh, I'll never tell my uncle, and anyway, he would never want to harm you." But all the same I felt I could not work with him anymore.

I was troubled about what my responsibility was. In my private practice, protecting the confidentiality of what my patients told me was a serious issue to which I was firmly committed. My case notes, for example, contained no names; my notebooks were coded with a private code. If I were to inform Michael's parents, or inform authorities about his activities, I would lose credibility in the school community. Probably I would not be able to continue this volunteer work. I also feared I would be placing myself in personal danger.

When I presented the facts about this case to a group of professionals, opinions were divided. Most of them felt I had behaved properly by not revealing to anyone the information that Michael had confided to me. One psychologist felt that I had a moral responsibility to inform the police about it. But I felt I could not do that and thus violate my professional responsibility to maintain confidentiality.

I did not see Michael again on a regular basis although I did speak with him a couple of times quietly after that. He said he was going to quit drug trafficking after he had amassed $100,000, a sum he thought would be sufficient to finance college educations for himself and his girlfriend. He was just 14 at this time and had about $10,000 in his bank account.

In the early winter of the second year of our group, the boys asked me if I knew anything about rap. I told them I didn't, but, if they told me what recordings I should get, I would buy them and learn about the music. They did, and I brought tapes and a tape player to listen to this music with them. These rap songs were very popular with the boys—the lyrics were full of anger and hatred toward society. I could not understand much of the speech or many of the words, but rapping along with the performer, they explained it to me. They really did unite in this activity and get a great kick out of listening to the music. I thought that rapping gave them an opportunity to express their feelings. It gave me an opportunity to know them better, to understand their anger, and it was a source for discussion with them. Unfortunately, however, not too long before the spring break, the vice principal one day rushed into the room to get some papers without knocking. When he saw and heard what we were doing, he became furious. He ordered the youngsters to leave the room and reprimanded me sharply, asserting, "You shouldn't be working with these boys. They're not going anywhere!" I replied that these boys had been referred to me by his counselors, that I had been working with them for some time, that I would not abandon them, and that I would continue meeting with them through the year. I told him that these boys had been telling me about their anger, and I did not think that there was anything wrong with my listening to them and helping if I could.

Here is how the vice principal responded. Just before the school vacation, when the principal was recovering from a heart attack and the vice principal was in charge, he transferred the boys he considered the most difficult and destructive students to another school, essentially breaking up the group. The remaining three participants—Michael, Julian, and Douglas, new to the group—continued for the rest of that year.

I learned a lot from these boys. I learned about their culture, their defiance, their disaffection from society, and their anger about so many things: their sense was that there was no one whom they could trust or turn to for support, that poverty was indifferent and cruel. I do not know what they might have learned from me. I have no illusions that the group experience changed anything in their lives or in their attitudes or behavior. I felt a great deal of sympathy for their feelings of hopelessness and rage. I felt helpless to offer them any significant support that could benefit their ultimate outcome. Knowing society's chronic neglect of them and their own antisocial attitudes and alienation, I feared for these young boys.

At the end of the school year, the principal of this school retired. The vice principal was promoted to his position and did not invite me back in the fall. I then concentrated instead on the School Consultation Program, which I had started with the assistance of Bruce Sklarew and Mary Ellen Bradshaw, the pediatrician responsible for school health. I directed a group of 12 professionals, older social workers and psychologists who volunteered to consult with counselors and principals once a week. The schools were selected by Diane Powell, the Director of Student Intervention of DC Public Schools. Some of the consultants developed warm relationships and went on to provide valuable help to principals and other counselors. These counselors broadened their perspectives about the children and initiated the process of making referrals and assessments and interviewing parents. On the whole, however, I did not think the program was very effective, and I looked for other methods to create significant change and provide better services.

## Joining the School-Based Mental Health Assistance Movement— Age 79

In the spring of 1997 an article appeared in *Psychiatric News*, a publication of the American Psychiatric Association, about a school-based health and mental health program in Dallas, Texas. The program consisted of 10 community clinics, each serving 20 schools by having staff go to the schools as well as by seeing other children referred to them. Thus some 200 schools were receiving mental health services. It emerged that the program had been established in 1993 with the assistance of Marc Weist, Director of the Center for School-Based Mental Health Assistance in the Department of Psychiatry of the University of Maryland in Baltimore. The Center was financed by the Health Resources Administration, a division of the federal Department of Health and Human Services, which also finances a similar center in the Department of Psychology at the University of Southern California. The Dallas Psychoanalytic Society and an association of hospitals in Dallas assisted in the development of this service and continue to serve in its operation. The chair of the service was shared by Jenni Jennings and Glenn Pearson, who were housed in the Department of Public Schools.

I was very impressed by the description of this program. I had been dissatisfied with the consultation program I had been operating in 12 schools with volunteer consultants. After reading this article, I realized that the program in Dallas must be a model one. I went to Baltimore to meet Weist and his staff, from whom I learned that there were 33 cities with school-based programs, no two exactly alike. I also obtained a description of the Dallas program and attended the second conference on school-based mental health held in New Orleans, which was jointly sponsored by the centers in Baltimore and California. I learned a great deal from the centers' publications and from the people I met at the conference. I felt it was imperative to try to establish a similar service in Washington. Two committees of the American Psychoanalytic Association, Psychoanalysis Community and the Liaison Committee to Schools, provided inspiration and support to me.

It was inspiring to attend the second annual conference of the Center for School-Based Mental Health in New Orleans in September 1997. The people from different cities and centers were enthusiastic about what was becoming a national movement to help children in our schools. The problems of youth who were not learning to read, who were behind grade in school, who were not prepared to learn, and who could not behave or follow rules persisted in schools throughout the country, particularly in poverty-stricken, inner-city areas. The many people attempting new methods to help these young people in school were enthusiastic and supportive. Of particular interest was the Dallas program, which was declared to be an exemplary model. I was determined to try to emulate it.

Helping me design a volunteer program was Richard Fritsch, a psychoanalyst and member of the Washington Psychoanalytic Society, as well as a professor in the Department of Professional Psychology at George Washington University. I used contacts I had with the Residency Training Department of St. Elizabeth's Hospital and with Aminah Moore, Chief Social Service Worker at the Northwest Family Center of the then-Commission for Mental Health Services for the District of Columbia. David Joseph, Director of the Residency Training program at St. Elizabeth's Hospital, and Kalman Kolansky, Chairman of Training in Child Psychiatry, had been supportive of the consultative program since 1995 and had encouraged residents to work under my supervision as consultants in the schools. Joseph and Kolansky are psychoanalysts. The Northwest Family Center had students from various universities doing internship-consultation service in 14 schools. Aminah Moore and I had collaborated on designing school consultation. Richard Fritsch and I thought we might connect these various departments into a partnership if we could find a school in which we could launch a pilot.

Fortuitously, I was introduced to Sheila Holt in the spring of 1998. Holt is an extremely intelligent, enthusiastic, affable person with a love for and understanding of children. As teacher and counselor she has worked at the Miner Elementary School in DC for 28 years. Sheila seemed to know almost all the children in the school, their parents' backgrounds, and the family issues that might have contributed to their vulnerability. Out of an unused bathroom she had created a playroom. Her office, filled with files and piles of papers, had shelves with toys and games she could use when she interviewed students or did play therapy. Sheila would lend her office to various interns with whom she had arrangements to supply some "enhancement" services to help children in the school. When I met her I knew this was the school where we should start the pilot program. Holt was enthusiastic when I described what I had in mind. The principal was soon won over, as well, by the idea.

Richard Fritsch and I wrote a description of a pilot project that was accepted by the staff of the Northwest Family Center, St. Elizabeth's Residency Training Department and by the department of George Washington University. Services were supplied by volunteer trainees—third-year students from George Washington's Department of Professional Psychology and fourth-year psychiatry residents at St. Elizabeth's.

## Supervising a Pilot Elementary School Project—Age 80

We began the pilot at Miner in September 1998. One of our key objectives was to form an interdisciplinary team of professionals to discuss, plan, and evaluate the project. In addition, the team would provide training opportunities for the volunteers to learn about the youth culture in the public schools, the problems of students living in poverty, the school culture and the difficulties teachers had teaching these children. The pilot project has other features that make it unusual: the project has been entirely volunteer operated, without funds—a weakness as well as a strength. There is not another clinical service similar to it in this area; the director is a retired psychoanalyst in his 80s who works as a volunteer.

Miner is an old school consisting of two buildings connected by a hallway-bridge. It is located in a dangerous neighborhood in Northeast Washington, plagued by the violent interplay of drug gangs and other street criminals. The students are all African American, all poor; almost all receive free breakfast and lunch. Outside the school, in a small, grass-covered triangle-island, is a granite slab paid for by contributions from students. It is inscribed:

Save The Children
Stop The Violence
We Care
We Love
We Remember Them All

Sixty percent of Miner's student body live with single mothers. Although there has been some improvement in the last two years, over 40% are behind in reading and math. Many children exhibit behavior problems and attention deficits. Teaching in this school, as well as in other schools in Washington, can be extremely arduous and frustrating. About 20% of the students are in or are about to be evaluated for Special Education services.

Our treatment team consisted of a social worker from the Northwest Family Center, four third-year George Washington graduate students who were to be supervised by university staff members, two fourth-year St. Elizabeth's residents (taking an elective course to work with us under my supervision), and two hearing-impaired graduate students in social work from Gallaudet University who came to our meetings with interpreters.

We have had other volunteers working with us, usually for an academic year: a graduate student studying at Howard University; a student intern from the University of the District of Columbia, a counselor in training at Washington's Trinity College, and a student intern in social work from Bowie State College in Maryland.

The team meets regularly on Tuesday mornings for one and a half hours. In the first year we met in an unused classroom, but later we were not so fortunate. One year we met in the basement of a nearby church, other years we met, sitting knee to knee, in Ms. Holt's office. We would discuss referrals, usually from teachers, sometimes from parents. Teachers were invited to give information about the child being referred and the reason for referral. Parents were invited to tell their stories. We would assign cases for psychological testing or clinical assessment by the psychiatric residents, or for individual or group therapy. Sheila Holt would share information she had about the child and family. She would also get permission slips signed by parents. The Northwest Family Center social worker would register the child for Medicaid reimbursement if a staff member of the mental health commission conducted the treatment.

The person assigned to see a child was responsible for calling on the parent to come to the school for an interview. These visits have often been difficult to accomplish. Once the permission document was signed, however, we would permit the student to begin the assigned treatment even if the parent had not appeared for a consultation; in these cases the staff member continued to try to reach a responsible adult by phone.

Space has been a problem. A schedule for use of the playroom is posted on the door and in Holt's office. Some students may use her office when she can make it available. At times there is a small space in the nurses' unit that may be turned to our purposes. One year a student conducted a group in an unused stairwell. We strive for consistency both in the therapist and in the use of space. Usually the student therapists come for one academic year and spend three to six hours each at Miner in addition to the team meeting on Tuesdays. This lack of continuity is a program weakness since therapists change each year. However, two of the psychiatrists volunteered for a second year, some of the George Washington students have come for two years, and one student—now graduated—volunteered for four years.

The great weakness of the pilot project at Miner is that I was not successful in obtaining a satisfactory program evaluation. We have assembled a great deal of anecdotal data supplied by our student therapists, noting improvement in behavior and other anecdotal evidence. But anecdotes are not considered evidence. The instruments purchased at the recommendation of an evaluator with whom we contracted proved too complicated for the student therapists and teachers to complete, so that we do not have compelling evidence that the interventions made a measurable difference in the lives or behavior of our clients.

## Serving as a Change Agent for School-Based Mental Health—Age 82

I continued to cast about for ways to further implement better school-based services for District children. In 1999, I became a founding member, with Mary Gardiner Jones, of a Coalition for School-Based Mental Health. The coalition has been chaired by Jones, who is a long-time community activist and President of the Mental Health Association of DC. Our monthly meetings have been attended by representatives of numerous community organizations, stakeholders, interested people (in both the public and private spheres), and DC public school system officials.

Momentum grew when, in the winter of 2000, Dennis Jones was recruited from Indianapolis to be the Receiver for Mental Health Services. Jones had a vision for developing a new Department of Mental Health for Washington. He also was aware of and endorsed the principle of school-based mental health.

Early in 1999 I applied to the Substance Abuse and Mental Health Administration (SAMHSA), an agency of the Health and

Human Services, for a one-year, Community Action-Systems Change Grant of $150,000. I cited the pilot project as following the "exemplary practice" of the one originated in Dallas. As I am a board member of the Washington Psychoanalytic Foundation, the application named this foundation as fiscal agent. Two board members had made contributions to the foundation for use by the pilot project, which enabled me to make the application. The application was approved but not funded. Encouraged by the changing climate of opinion toward our initiative, we reapplied the following year. This time our application was approved with funding, which began in December 2000.

As project director, I opened an office, hired staff, and proceeded to contact community groups and school officials to lobby for their support of our school-based mental health project. At the same time, Dennis Jones was preparing to establish a new Department of Mental Health responsible directly to Mayor Anthony Williams; he was also securing liaisons with other agencies responsible for serving DC young people. The coalition was also active in this process, which was a complex one. Eventually it was accomplished in the summer of 2001.

Martha Knisley, a strong supporter of school-based mental health assistance, was appointed director of the new department. She wrote a letter of commitment in support of my application to the Substance Abuse and Mental Health Administration for a second grant of $150,000. Her letter was cosigned by Paul Vance, the city's Superintendent of Public Schools. In this letter, Knisley and Vance committed to inaugurating the new program in a cluster of 17 schools and promised to establish school-based mental health assistance throughout the entire system within five years. The efforts of the coalition and the work of staff and myself can therefore be considered successful.

Knisley appropriated one million dollars for year 2002, and a total of three million dollars to be disbursed in 2003–2004. A cluster of 17 schools in Northeast Washington, including Miner (although it was not geographically in the original cluster) has been staffed. Vance selected schools that are poor performers; the cluster consists of a high school and the elementary and middle schools that feed into it. Olga Acousta organized and supervised this program.

The grant funds for the School-Based Mental Health Project were exhausted by the end of 2001. In 2002 we applied for a Phase Two grant from SAMHSA to continue community action activity, which was not funded.

### Reflections of a Psychoanalyst Serving in City Schools—Age 86

Psychiatrists, mental health workers, and mental health services are not highly regarded in the inner city of the District of Columbia. People have long memories of neglect and remember inadequate, humiliating or, inappropriate experiences, outpatient as well as inpatient, that too often masqueraded as treatment at St. Elizabeth's Hospital. Although the hospital somehow enjoyed a grand reputation nationally among the medical and psychiatric community, it was in fact a "snake pit" until sometime in the 60s, when psychotropic medications were introduced. Patients were sent home to the city and outpatient-care without adequate preparation, supervision, or treatment. After long stays in the hospital, they were often left with regression and dependency, unprepared for life on their own. Racial segregation reigned at the hospital until the 1960s, and children were not separated from adults until 1970, after a staff psychiatrist and I, as a consultant, initiated a ward for children without official permission.

Washingtonians familiar with St. Elizabeth's during this era and its woeful history are thus understandably suspicious of psychiatrists. They fear the possible stigma attached to a mental illness diagnosis. Such information might be attached to a child's school record, where it will remain for the duration of his schooling; it might even negatively influence future education or employment. Our reassurances that school-based intervention and assistance will be kept confidential and excluded from school records are met with skepticism.

After I made a presentation to a group of parents about the proposed school-based mental health program to be established in a local high school, one mother came up to me and demanded to know, "What are you going to do to our children?" I replied, "We are not going to do anything but talk with them and help them with their feelings." She persisted, "But what are you going to DO?!" The woman then walked away with a look of contempt and disgust.

Following a talk about the new mental health service, which included reassurances about the pivotal issue of confidentiality, an executive of a community organization, caustically asserted, "Confidentiality is not always confidential. Do you know what I am saying? You *are* from the city, aren't you? If somebody from the city government wants information about a child or his family that is in the school, how will you keep them from getting it? *Do you know what I am saying?*" She added, "These are the questions you will be asked, and you must be ready to answer." In this light it becomes all too clear that the question, "Are you planning to bring St. Elizabeth's hospital into our schools?" is loaded with apprehensive significance.

Poor people, however undereducated or inarticulate, will not suffer condescension, real or perceived, from middle-class professionals. They often suspect that we do not respect or "have a clue" to their feelings. Poor people also often feel that they are being told what's good for them and that they are not included sufficiently in the planning for what is needed. They resent being told what they need. In addition, they have had much experience with the introduction of services that they supported and were enthusiastic about, only to see the funds withdrawn after a year or two. They wonder if they will again be betrayed: "So how can you promise that this service you are talking about will be a continuing one? Where is the budget for it? Is it in place now? How can we be sure you will fulfill your promise?"

These questions and suspicions cause people to spurn close involvement with the schools and to regard them with a measure of mistrust. Some parents recall vividly their own unpleasant experiences with school personnel as children or as adult parents. Many are mistrustful of school and government organizations in general. Such memories interfere with their willingness to come to school even to discuss their children's difficulties. Some parents are embarrassed about their inability to read. And many parents—and teachers —are scarred with a sense of hopelessness and despair.

Another factor making it difficult to involve parents in the educational process of their offspring is that many are single parents who hold two jobs. These people are too tired and overwhelmed to be able to pay the attention to their children's education. Such conditions are unlikely to beset more affluent breadwinners in middle-class communities, where involvement with and enthusiasm in parent-teacher associations are the norm and where monetary contributions to provide special services in the schools can be quite bountiful.

My experience with the pilot project at Miner confirmed and provided more evidence for what I had been learning about children living in the inner city. About 18% to 20% of them have been referred for special education. These percentages are much too high to be accounted for by genetic learning disabilities. In many schools, 60% and more of the children are being raised by single mothers, many of whom work and leave their children to be supervised by caretakers. In some schools, at least 40% of the student population read below basic literacy standards. Colbert King, writing on adult illiteracy in the District for *The Washington Post* (August 28, 2002), stated that in one high school 64% of students were reading below grade level. He estimated that 37% of adults are functionally illiterate, reading at third grade level.

I think it is fair to conclude that many parents are unable to provide sufficient support to their children for reading and other academic work; nor can they provide consistent emotional and psychological support for their children to develop comfortable self-esteem and an interest in learning. Moreover, many kids are subjected to traumatic neglect, if not abuse. Violence is always around. Often kindergartners come to school unprepared for learning, undisciplined, and with serious anxiety and depression, which are frequently expressed in disorderly behavior. They lack expectable social skills and trust in adults. I think that many who are misbehaving, not learning, and frequently truant could be diagnosed, if given a thorough examination, as suffering from posttraumatic stress disorder, although a pervasive tendency exists to diagnose—and sometimes misdiagnose—overactive children as suffering from ADHD, and to medicate them.

### Principals, Counselors, and Teachers Have Different Reactions to Mental Health Assistance

Over the course of 10 years of volunteer work, I have met with many principals, counselors, and teachers in 12 elementary and junior high schools. (Keep in mind that I make no claim to characterize accurately the attitudes of any group of people. My remarks here are merely my impressions.)

Principals are like executives of a large corporation. They are responsible for the "products" of the organization—in the first instance its performance, both academic and behavioral, as measured by test results; they are also reponsible for the success or failure of the teachers, for the safety and condition of the building, for maintaining relations with parents and the community, and for monitoring the health and welfare of the students. They must check on whether the children are properly dressed, whether they have had appropriate vaccinations and medical examinations, and whether they seem properly nourished. All the principals I have met have a closet of used clothing to give to kids in need. Most inner-city children are fed breakfast and lunch paid for by federal programs. The lunchrooms must be supervised to assure that all the requirements of a food service establishment are met. Some of these tasks may be delegated, but the ultimate responsibility is with the principal. Then there are forms, records, and reports to be executed, demanding tasks themselves. Principals work long hours, often from early morning until late into the evening. Their position is very taxing.

Some principals seem to me to operate as dukes or duchesses, conscious of their absolute power and demanding complete loyalty and obedience from their subordinates. Some know how to delegate responsibility to competent staff and seem to have a smooth operating team. One can feel the sense of order and security upon walking into such a school. Some pay attention to every detail. Such persons appear to be overburdened by the demands of their position, and, like others so overinvolved in the minutiae of their jobs, they are not truly in control, They are critical, judgmental, and regarded coldly by their staffs.

Some principals are like overlords. They delegate everything to assistant principals and other staff. In my observation, these principals are more likely to be men; frequently they are charming. They often operate out of private offices where they meet with staff members, parents, and others by appointment. Such principals will make an appearance when groups of faculty, parents, or community leaders need to be addressed, but they seem to me to be distant to their staff and not knowledgeable about the children. In contrast to these principals, I have met a few who seemed to know every child in the school, especially those with problems, who knew the stories and conditions of the families, who were aware of and supportive of the work of the counselors, who had a personal acquaintance with all the administrative as well as the custodial janitorial staff; they were deservedly loved.

Principals are aware that many students have emotional, developmental, or mental problems. They remark to me, for example, as a psychiatrist, or to other mental health professionals I have introduced to them, how glad they are to have help for these individual children. Their understanding is, however, superficial. They are impatient with the time it takes to help such children to grow or to change. They show little compassion for the economic or emotional difficulties of the youngsters, or their families. They urgently want someone to "fix it" or at least get the trouble-making child out of the school.

For example, once when I was operating a consultation program in a group of 12 schools, I assigned a senior resident psychiatrist at St. Elizabeth's Hospital to a school in southeast Washington. This was a large elementary school of 530 children, all African-American, all living in poverty, all in supplemental nutrition programs. Seventy-five percent were children of single mothers; many of these children lived with three generations of women without a male in the family. The principal, his assistant, and the counselors were experienced, intelligent, and efficient. I was impressed with the school staff and was pleased to introduce a capable resident to consult in the school.

Within a short time, however, the resident reported to me his frustration about the kids who had been referred to him for assessment. They were, in his opinion, too disturbed for him to make a positive contribution as a consultant. I arranged for him and me to meet with the principal and his assistant. As we began the meeting, the principal said to me, "I think I know why you arranged this meeting, Dr. Granatir. You are finding the children referred to Dr. M too disturbed to work with. So are we." We arranged for the resident to make clinical assessments of some of these students so that the principal could have the necessary grounds to request referral of these children to another special school. This was not the objective of the consultation program, as the principal knew, but we agreed to the request.

Some teachers with whom I have spoken have expressed frustration and anxiety about the difficulties of their task. Older teachers with years of experience express concern for the children, who seem to be different from those they taught in past decades, when more children came from intact families, respected the authority of teachers, and were capable of paying attention and following instructions. "When most of your time and energy is spent in just keeping order, " one said, "It is impossible to teach. Yet we are held responsible for whether or not the children learn."

Younger teachers seem to me to be much angrier than the older ones. Many teachers seem to feel under attack by the students, parents, and the school system. The rate of attrition of teachers leaving the profession is high. What many want from a mental health professional is that the child be diagnosed with ADHD and given some medicine, or, that the professional "fix it" in some other manner. Many teachers become angry because they are expected to understand the developmental and emotional difficulties of the children. Managing the classroom is very difficult. In addition to being inattentive, disrespectful of authority, and angry, the children do not sit still and they get into fights with other children. Many children do not do homework. In too many instances it is questionable that a responsible parent is even at home to supervise homework, much less any other activities of the children.

If a child has not learned to read by age eight in the third grade, all his subsequent educational achievement is compromised. Even second-grade teachers of seven-year-old children complain of disorder. Even in kindergarten or first grade, children with emotional and developmental disorders can be recognized, although typically it is in fourth grade, at about age 10, that serious personality disorders become manifest. One sensitive and aware boy of 10 wrote to the school counselor, "Dear Ms. Holt: will you help me? From kindergarten through grade 3 I did not get into any trouble. Now in fourth grade I am having trouble with my feelings. I feel angry. Will you help me?" This was an unusual child.

My experience with school counselors is mixed. Many counselors have little psychological understanding. They have been trained only as educational counselors. They define their roles as keeping track of educational achievement, meeting with parents occasionally, keeping track of attendance, and assisting principals with testing and other administrative tasks. On the other hand, many counselors have sought and obtained further education in disciplines like psychology and social work. They are interested in helping the children and their families to resolve some of their problems. These counselors appreciate and welcome consultation and advice from a mental health professional. They interview parents and make referrals to clinics when indicated.

In some middle and high schools staff have formed small groups to meet in their offices to discuss their problems. Some schools have social workers and even a school psychologist as part of the regular staff (as distinct from the specialists in the special education team). In such schools the counselors and the professional staff can work as a team to provide sophisticated assistance and guidance to the young people and their parents. On the other hand, some teachers and counselors seem to look with resentment at mental health professionals as more privileged than they, as potentially supercilious or accusatory. I have observed that the relationship between the counselors and social workers with the principals is frequently tense. Often the principal does not wish to be burdened by the kind of information that a social worker, psychologist, or counselor may be able to provide and about which the principal has little power to do anything or to correct. A feeling of helplessness is not well tolerated by anyone, but I think that principals have less tolerance for it than others.

All these administrative professionals would greatly benefit from training in psychological development, the effects of neglect and abuse on such development, and the lack of emotional and educational support for children in many families. Such education could improve the decisions being made, particularly disciplinary ones. It is unconstructive to suspend children who misbehave but who have no one at home to monitor them. Children sent home for a few days to wander on the streets or spend their days watching television are certain to get into trouble. Yet few schools have instituted "in-school suspension" or other disciplinary programs that would be much more helpful.

The school environment could be greatly enhanced. Also, the manner in which children are spoken to could be improved to instill more self-respect. Metal-detection screening, locked doors, and other measures to provide security in these days of violence and danger may be necessary, but some schools have the quality of a jail instead of being a pleasant place to come to learn.

However, looking back, I must confess that the high school I attended in Philadelphia from 1929 to 1932, which offered a special academic program for interested students, was not such a pleasant place either. We students were not treated with much respect. The teaching was not so great. But there was order, the students behaved, and we were supported by our families to do homework assignments. Sometimes we were even inspired.

When I was first invited to contribute to this volume, I wondered what I did know and what I could offer, as a psychoanalyst, from the work I had been doing to develop and promote school-based assistance for children in public schools. I thought that any sensitive, intelligent, empathic person would be able to accomplish as much as I have or more. But on further consideration I can see how my experience as a psychoanalyst contributes to the way I behave in this community-based work. First of all, and probably most important, as an experienced analyst, I am a listener. I am experienced in listening with undivided attention; I am observant of projective mechanisms and less defensive in the face of receiving projections than the average person would be. Also, as a psychoanalyst I have an attitude of curiosity, inquiry, and acceptance of the differences among people. I observe behavior and speech patterns and think about the origin of some of these habits without necessarily trying to make interpretations. I observe what I can about mental processes in myself, a continuing process that might be called self-analysis.

# ❖ 8 ❖

## The Uses of Aggression
### *Healing the Wounds of War in a Community Context*

Martha Bragin

*Man is not born free. He cannot be free. He is incapable of being free. For only by being in chains can he be and remain "human." What constitutes these chains? Man has a bundle of rights and privileges that society owes him. In African belief, even death does not free him.*

—Okot P'Bitek

Neither war nor state or community violence happens to individuals. Even at their most contained, such violence is a catastrophe that happens to communities. Usually wars devastate whole nations and sometimes regions of the world. A clinician who wants to be of use in these situations is thrown into a quandary: Do I care for people exclusively one at a time? Is it possible to be of use across culture and class to societies that view their problems collectively? Is there a way to apply psychodynamic principles on a community scale?

The usual answer has been to work with communities on their practical needs, on one hand, and for trauma specialists to provide psychotherapy to individuals and small groups on the other. However, clinicians who are sufficiently well trained to address all the needs of those affected by large-scale disaster, clinicians who are willing to remain in affected communities long enough to make a real difference, are in short supply. The comings and goings of well-intentioned but not always culturally competent or adequately trained clinicians have caused worry in some circles that the best interests of affected persons, especially children, are not being served (Save the Children 1999). In fact, Graca Machel (1996), author of a special report to the Secretary General of the United Nations on the situation of children in areas of armed conflict, was so concerned about this problem that she included a recommendation that no new mental health programs for children be established. The question remains: how can a healing process be offered to individual members of communities in a way that is clinically sound and culturally competent and does not expose people unnecessarily to the swooping in of outsiders who open up wounds and do not stay long enough to see them closed again?

The two programs for community reintegration discussed here were designed to contain within themselves the means for interpretation, reparation, and integration of the aggression aroused by war and communal violence. The idea was to embed the psychological portions of treatment into social activity in such a way that they would be sustainable. The first program, designed in Angola, informed the second, which was designed in the United States. These programs in their entirety were very complex, having been designed to address the economic as well as the psychosocial effects of exposure to violence. I concentrate here on the aspects that are specifically germane to the study of psychosocial assistance, leaving out (except insofar as they are relevant) such essential, but separate, considerations as provision of health services and direct economic assistance.

The first of these programs was aimed at the psychosocial and economic rehabilitation of an area of Angola that had just been freed from armed conflict by United Nations peacekeeping forces. First, it demonstrated the usefulness of clinical interpretation when it is difficult to establish engagement with survivors of extreme situations. Second, it exemplifies the ways that a community social work program can adapt and make use of psychodynamic approaches while retaining practical cultural relevance. The second program was designed to reduce recidivism among juvenile offenders in New York City. It illustrates the way in which some of the same clinical principles apply to the developed world as to the developing one.

In both programs, psychodynamic theory informed the way basic social services were constructed and provided. Both programs were collaborative efforts involving colleagues from many disciplines and from varied cultural backgrounds; this integration was as true for the clinicians working with law enforcement personnel in Brooklyn as it was for the clinicians working with local professionals and traditional healers in Angola (see Bragin, 1998). The factor that bound this diversity into an effective force was the designers' recognition of the power of internal aggression and its accompanying guilt, and the need to interpret it, contain it, and find ways to make reparation for it.

## Some Definitions

To avoid confusion, it may be useful here to clarify some terms as they are used in this chapter, especially as some of these terms carry different meanings for different schools of thought.

### Making Connections: Linking and Containing

*Linking.* According to Bion (1962), people are connected to one another by one of three possible links: love (L), hate (H), and knowing (K). The most pressing clinical quandary facing the therapist is how to establish a K-link with the client, to help him or her begin to digest the terrible experience. To do this, the therapist must convey that she has the capacity to understand and tolerate the awareness of terrible, unacceptable events in the world as well as parts of the psyche.

### The Container and the Contained

This phrase was coined by Bion (1961), who described the container and the contained as "models of abstract representations of psycho-analytic realizations" (p. 90). An infant must project its intolerably bad feelings, representative of the presence of the aggressive drive, into a good breast. These projected, intolerably bad feelings are the contained, while the "good breast," or mother or therapist, is the container. That is, the therapist actually takes the feelings inside of himself or herself and experiences them. The goal of treatment is, then, to feed the experience back to the patient in small increments that can be emotionally absorbed.

*Mourning and Aggression:* The subjects of grief, loss, and mourning are not often integrated into the literature about extreme experience although the loss of close comrades and loved ones is a significant part of what survivors have experienced. Aggression plays a part in the experience of loss in all children and in complications of grief and mourning in adults.

Bowlby (1980) addressed the role of anger and hatred in normal mourning (p. 28). He pointed out that Freud (1913) initially took the position that there is a role for ambivalence in all mourning. However, Freud (1917) modified this position and came to believe that unresolved ambivalence toward the object is what turns mourning to melancholia, that is, converts a normal and resolvable process to a pathological and unresolvable one. Durkheim reported the use of direct expressions of anger in West African rituals of death (in Bowlby, 1980, p. 29). Freud frequently relied on studies of what is now called the developing world to support some of his early observations about aggression, including the conclusion that all relationships contain ambivalent characteristics and that many peoples have rituals designed to contain these features, especially around issues of grief and mourning.

### The Manic Defense

Klein (1935) discussed effects of early aggressive fantasies on normal development and thus their relationship to the psyche of the mature person. The period when objects begin to be understood as "whole" instead of as "part" she called the "depressive position." Because objects are understood as whole, they can be loved. Before discussing the problem of the actual loss of a loved object, however, Klein first explored the consequence of the phantasied loss of such an object through the destruction wrought by the infant's own sadistic fantasies, which, Klein maintained, are at a "zenith" when this position is achieved (p. 262):

A little child who believes when its mother disappears that it has eaten her up and destroyed her (whether from motives of love or hate) is tormented by anxiety both for her and for the good mother which it has absorbed into itself [p. 266].

In order to prevent persecution by objects both cruel and bad, and good and perfect, the child makes a series of restorative maneuvers, attempting to be really very good, and restore what its own sadism has destroyed. However, when the ego integrates whole objects it can be distressed by the disaster created by its sadism. This distress is related not only to its past but to its present as well since at this early stage of development sadism is at its height [p. 269].

Early aggressive fantasy remains even after whole objects have been integrated and object constancy has been achieved. To ward off excessive anxiety about these fantasies, and to avoid a slip into melancholia, the ego in the depressive position employs what Klein called "the manic defense." This defense is characterized by

the utilization of the sense of omnipotence for the purpose of controlling and mastering objects. . . . This is necessary for two reasons: (a) in order to deny the dread of them which is being experienced, and (b) so that the mechanism (acquired in the previous—the depressive—position) of making reparation to the object may be carried through.

The manic defense calls forth fits of action to protect a person from experiencing the pain of having destroyed loved objects [pp. 277–278].

All this inner fantasy, however, is repressed as it comes into modulating contact with an external reality that is more or less able to absorb the infant's demands and provide regular care and communication. In a context like this, the ego gains maturity and becomes able to keep early aggressive fantasy from the conscious mind. What remains is the desire to retain the good object within oneself, and with oneself, and so not to fall prey to melancholia if the object is lost.

*Reparation*

Because the child intensely loves the mother, despite violent fantasies toward her, the child desires to make certain that these violent acts in fantasy do no damage. This desire gives rise to "a profound urge to make sacrifices" (Klein, 1937, p. 311) and to do good acts in order to repair any harm that may have been done. In reparation lies the opportunity to identify with the goodness of the nurturing milk in the mother's breast, as well as to be forgiven for violent or aggressive feelings.

Klein (1927) asserted, and Winnicott (1939, 1964) elucidated in his writings on delinquent adolescents, that guilty feelings come from aggression toward those we love, and that guilt inhibits creative action. The capacity to repair the aggressive harm done to loved ones in fantasy frees that aggressive energy, which can then be used by the libido for creative purposes. However, external reality sometimes duplicates images that have been both imagined and repressed, bringing these fantasies back to the conscious mind and, with them, a pressing need for reparation. This is why the dismissal, however well meaning, of a survivor's sense of guilt undermines the treatment process; it dismisses along with it the need for reparation. Yet survivors feel this need profoundly. Manic reparative attempts may characterize a survivor's first contact with the return of repressed images of early aggressive fantasy. Opportunity for reparation must become an intrinsic part of any ongoing treatment if the survivor is to become able to bear and work through the sequelae of extreme experience.

## Angola: A Provincial Town Recovers from Conflict

*Background*

Angola is a mineral-rich country, possessing large quantities of gold, oil, and diamonds. It has fertile soil that can easily grow enough to feed its people and has produced some of the best coffee in the world. It has a seacoast lined with natural ports and oceans teeming with fish. Endowed with such wealth, Angola enjoyed great prosperity before the European conquest in 1483 (Antsee, 1996; Hare, 1998). Since then, however, it has seen mostly misery. During the colonial period it suffered more intensively from the slave trade than did any other single area in Africa; over four million people were taken from Angolan ports (Antsee, 1996; Hare, 1998). Repeated uprisings over hundreds of years failed to regain autonomy from a harsh colonial rule. A new struggle was mounted in 1961, and in 1975 Angola regained its independence as part of the "Revolution of the Carnations," the emancipation of Portugal's colonies that finally ended its colonial wars.

But the troubles still did not cease. The ideological preoccupations of the Cold War were very intense at that time, and a global contest arose for the political allegiance of this wealthy new country, whose elected leadership was avowedly socialist. The United States and the apartheid government of South Africa supported a rebel faction called UNITA (the National Union for the Total Independence of Angola), whose goal was the government's defeat. In response, the Soviet Union and Cuba supported the new government, first with arms and then with troops, training, and skilled personnel. Superimposed on Angola's intrinsic prosperity, therefore, have been centuries of tragedy and strife, and Angolans in the 21st century have decades of war, and very little peace, to look back on (Anstee, 1996; Hare, 1998).

On two occasions after the fall of the Soviet Union, the Angolan government signed peace accords with the rebel forces, and the armies were demobilized. However, in both cases the peace measures failed when the rebels refused to abide by electoral results, and war was eventually resumed. But after the second accord, with the support of the United Nations, the government began to rebuild the social services and economic infrastructure that the areas formerly under rebel control needed for parity with the rest of the country. This effort could not be pursued once the rebels took up arms again and fighting resumed in earnest. The program I describe here was a casualty of the war.

### The Problems to Be Addressed

In 1997, the Angolan government's Child Development Institute invited an international aid agency to work in one of the areas newly returned to government control. Its task was twofold: (1) to assist in economic development; and (2) to encourage the psychosocial reintegration necessary to make such development possible. The targeted area included the communities where the majority of recently demobilized excombatants were living, and it was difficult for the assessment team to get there from the provincial capital. Bandits who attacked, robbed, and often killed those in passage preyed on the roads regularly. Further, the road was still not free of landmines.

Seeds and tools had been distributed to all the families of former soldiers, and land was available; but the land mines were a serious problem here too, threatening agriculture as well as personal safety and drastically limiting how much food could be produced even in Angola's rich soil. Where enough land had been demined to allow for the production of surplus food, the farmers could not get their goods to town reliably because of the dangers on the roads. These difficulties made clear some of the issues that the program would have to address.

The community was deeply demoralized in spirit. Fighting in the area had destroyed many houses and other buildings. This compounded the difficulty of reintegrating an area where victims and perpetrators were now living side by side and where bitterness persisted against those who were thought to have gratuitously perpetuated a destructive and costly war. Furthermore, many of the demobilized were illiterate, in contrast with the rest of the population, which had been the beneficiary of government literacy programs. The resulting sense of inferiority compounded the political antagonism. The Angolan government had moved rapidly to put essential services into place. There were child-care centers, schools, and health centers, but they lacked supplies, and attendance was difficult because of the perils of the roads.

The situation was so discouraging that the provincial authorities were unable to find international nongovernmental organizations to work with them as partners in the area. The international agency I am discussing here had been told by other respected organizations that it was too dangerous to enter the area, that commerce and therefore economic development were impossible, and that the people there were so angry and so desperate that they were not willing to engage in any form of psychosocial work. Nonetheless, this organization decided it would make an attempt in conjunction with provincial government leaders and other committed Angolan professionals.

The tradition of international relief agencies is to hold community meetings and focus-group discussions to develop a preliminary needs assessment, and we followed this procedure. But the focus on economic recovery (to let people know that we were interested in meeting their basic needs) failed; as we had been warned, the people would not cooperate in such a discussion. The meeting took on a very angry tone of blame and fault-finding, and all efforts to focus attention on economic needs, or even practical problems, was ineffective.

The psychosocial team, standing apart from the conflict over economics as it developed, was watching the affect in the crowd. We noticed that, in spite of the angry voices and their apparent boredom with the discussion, many of the young men were playing attentively with their babies as the argument progressed.

### Early Interpretation in the Engagement Process

Wessels (1999) points out that, when outsiders come to a community in conflict, it is extremely important to be aware of the impact that even their mere presence may have, so we consulted with an Angolan psychologist colleague as to how best to manage the rancorous tone of the meeting. His considered opinion was that it would be unwise for us to leave without attempting to address the crowd's discontent. Therefore, after some discussion and continued observation of the baby-tending fathers, we decided to focus on concerns for the children, which seemed to be universal.

The psychologist advised us to use the traditional African call-and-response style, so that we would hear to what extent the participants were engaged, and to use hand and body gestures, to give the audience a sense of us even though we could not speak the local language. With the guidance of others on the psychosocial team, I made some initial interpretations to the large assembly to get people's attention, while the psychologist translated with great care. Addressing the crowd, the speaker said that, although leaders had signed peace agreements, the people did not yet have peace in their hearts; they still felt a great deal of anger for the unburied dead, for the time lost, and for the difficulty of daily life. The people agreed in a chorus. This was the first indication of concord since the meeting had begun

I began to identify for them, and help them to identify, their negative emotions; I asked if these were internal experiences that people had had. People responded affirmatively each time. Wars, I said, can feel like a nightmare come true—as though the worst thing that ever came into your mind had gotten out and started walking around. Yes, said an older woman from the back, but then you realize that it is your neighbor's nightmare and you are stuck inside of it. And then you feel dirty afterwards, just for having been a part of it all? Yes, this is true, said the group, which was now listening hard, united in its interest and responses. It is hard, I went on, to build anything with such bad feelings, when the spirits of the unburied dead are awake and destructive in our hearts and our minds, and even on our roadways.

The adults were now listening intently. We made similar efforts to engage other groups—the children, the young men, the disabled—until everyone had pledged to help create a program to rebuild the community. I acknowledged and affirmed repeatedly that the process would be difficult and that they would become discouraged. They responded that life had been difficult and that they had been discouraged for a very long time. The community members spontaneously sang and then divided into groups for further work.

A direct appeal to the negative emotions of the community members enabled them to move to a psychic space in which they could get beyond their rage and talk genuinely about the needs of their children. Talk about peace would not have enabled such a move; it was premature. However pressing their material needs—and their needs were pressing—they could not address them effectively until this psychological space for addressing their negative emotions had been created.

(I have said before, and want to reiterate here, that, although this is a dramatic story, that kind of dramatic swooping in and making an intervention is worthless by itself. I offer the story only to show how a dialogue began with a war-devastated people. It is also an example on the community scale of the clinical principle that one must connect to distressed people on a feeling level, before any sort of practical work can be attempted. Kernberg [personal communication, November 1996] told me early in my work on this study to link not with the material and the obvious, but with the angry and guilty part of the personality that has remained denied. The course of this meeting bears out that advice. The interventions that I made there—which were, in fact, interpretations of internal aggression—were not curative in themselves, but they allowed the people involved to begin to engage in a process by which local people could address local issues in their own way, together and over time.)

As the assessment proceeded, we came to feel that further space had to be made for the community as a whole to mourn its losses and to cleanse those who felt dirty from exposure to violence, whether as victim, perpetrator, or, often, both. Ceremonial assistance was provided as needed for those who had committed acts of violence, and larger community ceremonies were held for those who had been subjected to them. Traditional healers were involved in the planning, so that they could prepare public burials and symbolic cleansings for the community as a whole.

### Theoretical Considerations: Healing Community Violence

There are sequelae of violence for communities as well as for individuals, although they manifest themselves differently. When the communities include both the victims and the perpetrators of the extreme and random violence that characterizes war and occupation, the manifestations can be very dangerous. Most individuals, as we know, want to move forward and forget, but without intervention many are unable to do so, and this inability has community consequences. Although there are some identifiable aftereffects of violence (injuries, losses, poverty, etc.), most people cannot identify clearly how the war affected them. They may feel tired, hopeless, incompetent, listless. They may act violently, and even highly motivated people may find themselves unable to face the day without alcohol. They cannot cope well with their children, who may become disrespectful to their exhausted elders and inattentive at school. Some children are so overwhelmed by the aggression that violence excites that they cannot live at home any longer, and they take to the streets, seeking danger and excitement. Their depleted parents cannot stop them. Thus a pervasive sense of powerlessness and eternal poverty can corrode the structure and fabric of a community (Bragin, Tekle, and Zerai, 1999).

This Angolan community had many such troubled adolescents because of the large population of recently demobilized excombatants and the extra burden that the rebel policy of abduction and impressment of children placed on the community's young people. Much of the banditry on the roads in this community was practiced by young excombatants, and one important facet of the program in Angola was a group project for containing it. That project illustrates one way that the theory presented in this study was put to practical use in the community.

Troubled adolescents often turn to banditry following war when peace fails to bring prosperity and they cannot envision a meaningful future or reliable ways to provide for themselves. The violence of this banditry escalates when the perpetrators have become desensitized to violence during the conduct of war. The young former soldiers in Angola were particularly at risk, as they had been kidnapped as children and involved in programs deliberately designed to accustom them to extreme brutality. For these young people, the normal internal taboos against violence had never been properly instilled, and they would have to be established from scratch by the community.

It was clear from our problems getting to the target area that the violence that these youngsters acted out in their road banditry was a very powerful force in perpetuating the hopelessness and dependency of the community. It created a negative climate for the development of business, commerce, and economic growth, and it also made difficult the distribution of food, the provision of health care, and the access to education necessary to meet even basic needs. For those reasons, the agency concentrated on designing an integrated program for containing the banditry. Such a program would enable the growth of enterprise, as well as contain, channel, and, over time, repair the damage inflicted on the bandits by the violence in which they lived.

The program aimed at weakening the roots of violence (p'Bitek, 1985) in these war-bred youngsters. By creating conditions that would allow them to use fantasized violence to give genuine help to the community, we wanted to provide them constructive opportunities for dealing with their violence. We also wanted to give them opportunities to engage in the repair not only of their community and themselves, but also of the people whom they loved (Winnicott, 1984).

### The Safety and Security Organization: Violence and Reparation

One important priority was the restoration of safe travel to the region. Guided by what we already knew about the causes of banditry and the reparative value of positive actions, the psychosocial team supervised the formation of integrated youth safety teams. These teams included, but were not limited to, demobilized young soldiers and partisans from both sides of the conflict. We made strong efforts to include the young people who appeared particularly hard to reach in other ways.

A focus group of these young people was asked to fantasize actively about the dangers that might befall the psychosocial team on the road, especially if it were carrying supplies, such as seeds or medicines, into the community. We asked them to imagine the dangers as they applied specifically to us, and later to their workers, rather than to travelers in general. Thus, they would understand ever more clearly that violence is real and personal. We encouraged them to pay careful attention to such fantasies and to describe them exactly—their doing so helped us to discover to what degree the participants had the capacity to symbolize violence and to what degree they could develop that capacity. Once they had imagined all the terrible things that could happen to us, we asked them to fantasize about what it would take to protect us from such harm. The group then formed an action plan that would protect the workers, the transported goods, and, eventually, all community commerce from the kind of threats they themselves had posed.

After this session, we divided the group in two, carefully ensuring that each half contained representatives of all factions and both sexes. Young people who had previously had to carry weapons were now asked to accompany the psychosocial team in carrying medicines and emergency food supplies to the community. Other members of the group guarded them. This arrangement was intended to help the former child soldiers to repair their damaged sense of themselves. It allowed them to see themselves not only as bringers of harm, but also as capable of good. This reparative activity was designed also to help the young people begin to develop appropriate bonds to the community and its law (Winnicott, 1939) and to discourage them from returning to violence.

On the basis of our experience with the focus group, we planned an extensive organization for maintaining safety and security on the roads, which would use affected youngsters both to secure the roads and to deliver needed supplies. In this way they could freely fantasize violence while protecting others from it and being protected themselves; at the same time, they could perform reparative activity to address their terrifying unconscious guilt. By this means, multiple community-based organizations could reach large numbers of youngsters.

## Community Demining and the Manic Defense

Another vital priority was the removal of land mines. To have fresh food, communities must be able to farm, but land mines in the area made farming impossible. There are not enough professional demining teams, and the wait for one can be very long. This leaves communities helpless and vulnerable in the meantime. Therefore, community demining efforts are widespread today. They have been used successfully in parts of Cambodia, and they were in effect in another province of Angola at the time that this program was being designed.

There were practical reasons to propose such an activity here. But it also struck us as the perfect job for some young desperados who were satisfied with only the most extreme reparative efforts. (Only volunteers were considered for this program; while some of those who applied were child soldiers, rape victims and widows also offered to help. This is further demonstration of the universality of Klein's [1935] vision of the place of violence in the human psyche.)

The demining project illustrates on a community level a process that is well known in the literature regarding individual veterans. A manic defense may be called forth against overwhelming anxiety, sometimes owing to the belief that one is responsible for the death and destruction that is happening all around. The manic defense may also be a response to inhibited mourning and as such calls forth a feeling of invulnerability; its primary feature is the denial of death or danger (Klein, 1935, 1940). Certain members of this Angolan community felt themselves beyond the pale. They were soothed by, rather than terrified of, the opportunity to clear mines. That work would allow them to contain their anxiety with dangerous tasks and at the same make reparation to the community for their real or imagined role in the violence and suffering of their times.

(This Kleinian view that ordinary reparation is sometimes not enough is supported in the African literature on survivors. Dawes and Honwana [1996] and Monteiro [1996] point out that some people feel so overwhelmed by guilt that they cannot accept or participate in traditional healing, and not a few of them commit suicide. The community demining plan was a radical solution, but sometimes radical solutions are called for. Obviously, the demining would have been strictly supervised, and all possible safety precautions enlisted. No one under 18 was allowed to volunteer for this project.)

The demining program included a discussion group to be led by a healer who was in consultation with the technical team. This was intended as a way to allow group members to process difficult material that might otherwise remain hidden.

To be successful, psychosocial reintegration programs such as these must continue over a fairly long term. This stipulation is based on Keilson's concept of sequential traumatization (i.e., that the transition from war to peace poses its own problems), the "best practices" model of the Save the Children Federation, and the view that developing the capacity for concern in young people affected by war cannot take place overnight (Winnicott, 1984). I have advocated in assessment reports to international relief agencies, on the basis of my own experience over time, that programs for young people returning to civilian life must be maintained for a minimum of 36 months, as must programs for at-risk children and their families. When sustaining programs over the long term is possible, the participation of demobilized soldiers in such programs can lead to positive social development and adjustment, especially if staff is consistent and alert in providing special support and training to the leaders who emerge from the groups of participants.

### Summary

The goal of this project was to create a climate of peace and stability (not merely the absence of war) for all the people of the region. Achieving this goal would make possible economic development and prosperity, and a democratic civic structure without threat of violence. We had to address specifically and immediately the issues of the various populations—the underage demobilized, the orphans, the disabled, and so forth—in this war-torn community. However, we also had to address the reintegration of the affected communities as a whole, so that, over time, their structures would be able to develop normally. The focus of this project and all its component parts was step-by-step recovery and reintegration. It aimed at strengthening the capacity to imagine, and ultimately plan for, a better future for the children. To this end, all the program components, including the economic ones, were designed with the idea of harnessing (as opposed to denying or suppressing) aggression and creating opportunities for reparation among community members.

Obviously, communities affected by war are likely to need economic assistance and (possibly desperately need) material aid. The question is always how to design that aid in such a way that it does not increase the community's collective sense of powerlessness, and perpetuate the need for outside intervention. A well-designed program can also promote the psychosocial goals of channeling the rage and hatred that have been stirred up by war into constructive outlets.

## United States: Juvenile Offenders Return to the Community

> Oh, Mother! We can't stop the violence
> Because the war is not over
> Until we hear peace and love in the silence.
> But I smell gunpowder, Haiti's gunpowder,
> Brooklyn's gunpowder, Zaire's gunpowder . . .
> —Wycliffe Jean, Haitian-American Hip Hop Artist

### Background

The problem of chronic recidivism in the juvenile justice system is the subject of an enormous literature. Any program designed to intervene in this process could certainly have been the basis of a study of its own. The program described here is offered not as any definitive solution, but to demonstrate that the theory propounded here is as applicable to social work practice in the United States as it is to application abroad. I am including here, therefore, only a schematic discussion of the aspects of the program that are related to the matter of recovery from experiences of extreme violence. I am not attempting any sort of thorough analysis of the recidivism situation or even of the program itself.

The rate of recidivism in the juvenile justice system has been estimated at upward of 86% nationwide (Altshuler, Armstrong, and Mackenzie, 1999). Altshuler (1999) found that the key to reducing

it was the establishment of specific and intensive programs for helping young graduates of the juvenile justice system with their psychosocial reintegration into the community. Jones (1997) pointed
out that the juvenile boot camp model that was popular in the
United States at the time, had, in fact, not had a significant effect
on decreasing recidivism in this population.

It has been asserted (Garbarino, Kostelny, and Dubrow, 1991)
that the psychological situation of children from poor neighborhoods in United States cities who have been recruited by adults into
the world of drug dealing and crime is in many ways not unlike
that of youngsters recruited into guerrilla armies in the developing
world. On the strength of that assertion, I was asked by an employer,
the Children's Aid Society, to design and develop an aftercare program for one group of such youngsters. These youth were being
released into aftercare following six months of incarceration in a
boot-camp-model prison. This particular program, which was run
by an enlightened former colonel of the United States army, had
been cited as the only one of its kind to reduce recidivism significantly (Mackenzie et al., 1997).

The goal of the program was to keep these youngsters from
returning to criminal behavior. We made a careful assessment of
the root causes of their acting out and then tried to create a comprehensive collaborative program that could address those issues.

### The Problem to Be Addressed

The psychodynamic, social, and economic roots of criminal recidivism in young people had to be identified if we were to address them
therapeutically. To summarize simply: the youngsters in this population were exclusively African-American, Afro-Caribbean, and Latino
males between the ages of 13 and 17. Most were 14 or 15 years old.
Their parents all had a high-school education or less. (We considered
these significant factors. White and Asian young people, and young
people with educated parents, appear to receive differential treatment
in the judicial process; they tend to be assigned to residential treatment or to psychotherapy and community service while living at
home—that is, they do not enter the juvenile justice system.)

These youngsters had histories of extreme psychosocial stress.
Almost all had been beaten by their parents, and quite a few had

suffered sufficient abuse to warrant removal from the home. Most had seen someone die by accident, murder, or suicide. Most had suffered the loss of a parent or caretaker before the age of two. They had also experienced another traumatic loss just before commission of the crime for which they were incarcerated. Most had crack-addicted mothers earlier in their lives. A significant minority had fathers who had been incarcerated.

I hypothesized that the youngsters' ubiquitous school difficulties, and their acting-out behavior, had to do with a conjunction of three factors: difficulty with symbolization, the unmanageable intrusion into consciousness of aggressive fantasy, and the real-life experience that success and happiness were impossible to attain. Interestingly, all these children had enjoyed their experience away at the boot camp. Predictability, safety, and community had been offered there, along with goals that they could learn to achieve. The world at home was not full of such supports, especially for those children (78%) who had been raised for some portion of their lives by drug-addicted caregivers.

Klein (1934) and Winnicott (1939) made similar points: when "good-enough" maternal care is not available (be it through drug addiction, loss, or cruelty and abuse) to children whose sadism is at its zenith, these children may not be able to learn to manage their normal early anxiety or to integrate the management of aggressive impulses into the personality as a whole. This issue certainly applies to these inner-city children as it did to the children impressed into combat in Angola. The punishments meted out to them by parents, peers, and authorities are often similar to the ones expected by the cruel and heartless superegos they construct in such harsh circumstances, leading them to expect that their worst fantasies are realizable in the external world. The actions that they take to relieve anxiety often provoke incarceration, which symbolically becomes both punishment and containment.

Of these recidivist youngsters, 97% had suffered as well actual sights of violent death and disintegration. In some cases, the distress caused by these experiences elicited a manic defense, the same defense that worked for the desperate Angolans who turned to community demining for relief of their rage and guilt. Children such as these inner-city youngsters, however, are often without such constructive outlets. Some numb themselves with drugs, but many find themselves fighting in the streets or committing what have some-times been called "senseless acts of violence" (Garbarino, Kostelny, and Dubron, 1991). Klein (1930) commented on the inhibition of learning and the problems with symbol formation in those who do not adequately integrate early anxieties. However, the children she wrote about were still very young, and Winnicott (1939) offered the salutary and contrasting reminder that such youngsters who commit criminal acts still believe that there is something to gain from society.

Our program was designed, therefore, to help the youngsters to understand their behavior symbolically and to allow them to per-form symbolic acts of sufficient reparative power to allow them to feel worthy of a good life. At the same time, the program would allow them to build a community of relationships in which they could learn to tolerate their fantasies and to feel hopeful about cre-ating a future. For this promise to be realized, they would need to develop both concretely useful skills and the supports that would allow them to think through and moderate the violent propensities of their own murderous superegos.

## Description of the Program

The Children's Aid Society, in collaboration with public and pri-vate partners, participated in the construction of a comprehensive program to address these issues within the context of the existing juvenile justice system. It included both school and after-school activities, including recreation and cultural enrichment. It involved clinical assessment of child and family and also referral for indi-vidual treatment, although referral was not always accepted. It attempted to provide an experience that would permit and facili-tate the integration of psychic trauma and create the conditions nec-essary to allow these youngsters to continue to develop.

The youngsters were serving 18-month sentences. The first six months had been spent at the Youth Leadership Academy, a locked facility with a school on the premises. On release, the boys spent another six months at the day-detention facility, during which time they lived at home. The detention facility itself was an attractive and homey brownstone building staffed by corrections officials. There was a school on the premises that operated from 9 A.M. to 2 P.M. on school days and offered high school courses as well as the Virtual Enterprise program described here. The house was located in the heart of an African American community in Brooklyn, across the street from a respected church whose pastor and members played a supportive role in the program. (See Tully, 1999, for a discussion of how important the participation of churches has been historically.)

The school day focused on an instructional curriculum entitled "Virtual Enterprise," a mock business in which the children learned computer literacy and other business skills. Instruction was available at all levels, as the Virtual Enterprise needed employees of all levels of expertise, so that the youngsters could participate at their own levels whatever their intellectual capacity. After school hours, the business was transformed from a virtual enterprise, with virtual contacts at schools and programs all over the world, into a real one, a program that they named Tasty Treats. Each youngster was an equal shareholder in this endeavor, and each could make a contribution and stand to share in the profits.

There was an industrial kitchen on the first floor, as well as a lunchroom. The boys produced baked goods there under the supervision of a "sergeant" (one of the guards) and a Children's Aid Society after-school worker. The business part of the program was conducted in classrooms designed to look like business offices, with an after-school "technical teacher" from the Children's Aid Society providing instruction and guidance. Volunteer entrepreneurs from baking businesses in the community came and supplied recipes, guidance, and encouragement. The CAS onsite clinical director, a Latino who is a social worker expert in the treatment of adolescents and a psychoanalyst as well, directed the program. I also attended weekly to lead initial group meetings and discussions of such issues as the rules of the business. A volunteer poet and expert in juvenile justice issues came once a week to assist in the development of advertising copy. As in all the programs described in this study, it appears to have been critical that staff be consistent throughout the program's life.

The youngsters made a good product, proving to themselves that they could create something good. Their Tasty Treats were much appreciated at the schools, shelters, and day care centers to which they delivered. The boys discovered that other people knew they could create good things, too.

The Tasty Treats members had a hand sign to use if they saw one another, or any of the staff, on the street. They also had weekly shareholders' meetings, at which they addressed each other as "shareholder." At these meetings they discussed both practical questions and feelings about their enterprise. Tasty Treats did, indeed, generate money, and the distribution of dividends became an important topic for the youngsters. Immediate gratification versus long-term investment was a topic that came up frequently at meetings. With it came discussion of what was fantasy and what was realistic, and the difference between the apparent and the genuine. There were also practical questions: whether there should be equal reward for all jobs, from mind work to technical work to cleanup, or whether some jobs should be more highly rewarded than others. They discussed the nature of sales and whether or not street hustling was the same thing.

The shareholders discussed how forgiving they should be of absence, sickness, or just plain goofing off. They reminded one another that when one person goofed off, the whole group suffered; but that, on the other hand, they themselves all knew what it felt like to be too "stressed out" to show up for work. Such discussions opened the way for investigation of such important philosophical and psychological questions as "good-enoughness." The participants started out wanting to make very strict rules, and, when they could not keep them, they felt the need to punish themselves severely. One goal of the group was to develop realistic standards that they could meet as individuals yet still manage to fulfill the needs of the group as a whole; these concerns mirror the questions I raised earlier about the role of individuals in a collective society that I have raised in the case reviews above.

The Tasty Treats participants also tackled their aggressive fantasies at these group meetings. They imagined and discussed violent and cutthroat business tactics, and then they visualized the severe punitive measures appropriate for those who commit such misdeeds. They were living illustrations of the contentions of both Klein (1927, 1934) and Winnicott (1964) that young delinquents' superegos are not lacking in firmness, but are rather too harsh and punitive. The punishments these young men thought of for fellow workers who missed a day, came habitually late, or just "ate too much product" were cruel, often to the point of being torturous. It was very apparent that such superegos as theirs might lead them to seek out real punishment. No matter how terrible that punishment was, it would still be a relief compared with their expectations. The group leaders' role was to help them to modify those raging super-egos toward greater compatibility with real life, and to help them produce a set of rules and regulations that was both clear and for-giving. Endurance and predictability on the part of the workers again proved essential, as Winnicott (1971) has discussed.

As the young men prepared to move out of the program and into the community, each had to "break in" new shareholders. Leaving, therefore, involved not only saying goodbye, but also becoming a mentor to others who were beginning the process: another form of reparation. The sergeants at this program were reluctant to insti-tute too formal a termination process. They wanted to develop a situation in which the youngsters could remain part of the program as mentors to new arrivals, and where the staff could continue to serve them as mentors throughout their lives.

Frequent community meetings had accompanied the entire six-month process, where community values as taught at the boot camp (self-discipline, self-esteem, self-worth, and affiliation) were dis-cussed among the youngsters in terms of their own life experiences. These issues were reaffirmed at termination. In the meetings and in the psychosocial assessment process, serious issues came up with regard to early trauma, abuse, disappointment, and loss. The Tasty Treats program gave the youngsters a way to concretize reparation and channel aggression sufficiently for them to begin to tolerate their internal experiences without acting on them.

While I do not believe that six months is an adequate time for youngsters to internalize changes like these characterologically, I do think that the design of the program illustrates how the psy-chodynamic principles informing this study can be used within sus-tainable community mental health and social work programs in the United States. I also think that such an approach could be tested and extended to longer term models.

## Discussion

War, as well as state, community, and individual violence, affects the lives of hundreds of thousands of people every year. The effects cannot be treated one person at a time. Furthermore, these effects are more than individual; the fabric of a society is influenced by them as much as the people are. When suffering affects a society as a whole, especially a communal society, so must the means of repair. Yet the boundary between the one and the many is not absolute, and, as has often been said, the political can be very personal, as when one sees one's child killed by enemy soldiers or one encounters the torturer's knife. Therefore, it is important to be mindful of the affects of the aggregate suffering of individuals while attending to the needs of the group as a whole. The examples I have offered illustrate the possibility that effective group and community programs for psychosocial reintegration can, without resort to specific psychotherapy, improve the psychic experience of community members. And they can do this while attending to the critical task of recreating the fabric of community life necessary not only to mental health but to survival itself.

### References

Altshuler, D., Armstrong, T. & Mackenzie, D. (1999), Do they measure up? Reintegration, supervised release, and intensive aftercare: A comparative analysis of juvenile correctional programs. *Juv. Just. Bull.*

Antsee, M. (1996), *Orphan of the Cold War.* New York: St. Martin's Press.

Apprey, M. (1993), Dreams of urgent/voluntary errands and transgenerational haunting in transsexualism. In: *Intersubjectivity, Projective Identification and Otherness,* ed. M. Apprey & H. Stein. Pittsburgh, PA: Duquesne University Press, pp. 102–131.

Bion, W. R. (1957), Attacks on linking. In: *Melanie Klein Today, Vol. 1,* ed. E. Spillius. London: Routledge, 1988, pp. 87–101.

———— (1961), A theory of thinking. In: *Melanie Klein Today, Vol. 1,* ed. E. Spillius. London: Routledge, 1988, pp. 160–178.

———— (1962), *Learning from Experience.* Northvale, NJ: Aronson.

Bragin, M., Tekle, T., & Zerai, W. (1999). Children in Eritrea affected by the border conflict: A psychosocial needs assessment. Asmara: MOLHW and UNICEF.

Children's Aid Society (1998), *Collaboration Between the New York State Office of Children and Family Services and the Sergeant Henry Johnson Youth Leadership Academy and the Children's Aid Society: The Development of a Role for the*

*Private Sector in a Public Program*. New York: Children's Aid Society.

Dawes, A. & Honwana, A. (1996), Children, culture and mental health: Intervention in conditions of war. Keynote address at Rebuilding Hope: Congress on Children, War, and Persecution, Maputo, Mozambique.

Freud, S. (1913), Totem and taboo. *Standard Edition*, 13: 1–162. London: Hogarth Press, 1955.

Freud, S. (1916). Resistance and repression. *Standard Edition*, 15:286–303. London: Hogarth Press, 1957.

Freud, S. (1917). Mourning and melancholia. *Standard Edition*, 14: 237–259. London: Hogarth Press, 1957.

Garbarino, J., Kostelny, K. & Dubrow, N. (1991), *No Place To Be a Child*. Lexington, MA: Lexington.

Hare, P. (1998), *Angola's Last Best Chance for Peace*. Washington, DC: United States Institute of Peace Press.

Jones, M. (1997), Is less better? Boot camp regular probation and re-arrest in North Carolina. *Amer. J. Crim. Justice*. Reprint made available by United States Department of Justice Office of Juvenile Justice and Delinquency Prevention.

Klein, M. (1927), Criminal tendencies in normal children. In: *The Writings of Melanie Klein, Vol. 1*. New York: Free Press, 1975, pp. 170–186.

——— (1930), The importance of symbol formation in the development of the ego. In: *The Writings of Melanie Klein, Vol. 1*. New York: Free Press, 1975, pp. 219–233.

——— (1934), On criminality. In: *The Writings of Melanie Klein, Vol. 1*. New York: Free Press, 1975, pp. 258–262.

——— (1935), A contribution to the pathogenesis of manic depressive states. In: *The Writings of Melanie Klein, Vol. 1*. New York: Free Press, 1975, pp. 262–290.

——— (1937), Love, guilt and reparation. In: *The Writings of Melanie Klein, Vol. 1*. New York: Free Press, 1975, pp. 306–344.

——— (1940), Mourning and its relation to the manic depressive states. In: *The Writings of Melanie Klein, Vol. 1*. New York: Free Press, 1975, pp. 344–370.

Mackenzie, D., Souryal, C., Sealock, M. & Bin Kashem, M. (1997), Outcome study of the Sergeant Henry Johnson Youth Leadership Academy (Y.L.A.). Washington, DC: National Institute of Justice, Office of Justice Programs, U.S. Department of Justice.

Monteiro, C. (1996), Cultural issues in the treatment of trauma and loss: Honoring differences. Prepared for the Christian Children's Fund, Richmond, VA, July 31.

p'Bitek, O. (1985), The sociality of self. In: *African Philosophy*, ed. C. Eze. Oxford: Blackwell Press, pp. 73–74.

Tully, M. (1999), Lifting our voices: African-American cultural responses to trauma and loss. In: *Honoring Differences: Cultural Issues in the Treatment of Trauma and Loss,* ed. K. Nader, N. Dubrow & H. Stamm. Philadelphia: Brunner/Mazel, pp. 23–49.

Ulman, R. & Brothers, D. (1988), *The Shattered Self*. Hillsdale, NJ: The Analytic Press.

UNICEF (2000), The state of the world's children. New York: UNICEF.

Wessels, M. (1999), Culture, power, and community: Intercultural approaches to psychosocial assistance and healing. In: *Honoring Differences: Cultural Issues in the Treatment of Trauma and Loss*, ed. K. Nader, N. Dubrow & H. Stamm. Philadelphia: Brunner/Mazel, pp. 98–121.

Winnicott, C., ed. (1984), *Deprivation and Delinquency*. London: Tavistock/Routledge.

Winnicott, D. W. (1939), Aggression and its roots: Aggression. In: *Deprivation and Delinquency,* ed. C. Winnicott. London: Tavistock/Routledge, 1984, pp. 84–92.

——— (1964), Aggression and its roots: Roots of aggression. In: *Deprivation and Delinquency*, ed. C. Winnicott. London: Tavistock/Routledge, 1984, pp. 92–100.

# ❖ 9 ❖

# The School-Based Mourning Project
## A Preventive Intervention in the Cycle of Inner-City Violence

Bruce Sklarew • Janice Krupnick

Dottie Ward-Wimmer • Carol B. Napoli

## Background

Freud's (1917) elaboration of the work of mourning is still the basis of this work. Elvin Semrad, a gutsy psychoanalyst at Harvard's Massachusetts Mental Health Center, asked bereft patients suffering loss, "Where in your body do you feel the pain?" It was a powerful way to facilitate mourning. Semrad spoke of "the sorrow that is the vitamin of human growth," and that "it is a necessary condition of human healing to be able to bear what has to be borne, to be able to think what has to be thought." He often asked his residents, "How many times have you read 'Mourning and Melancholia'?" Semrad's framework helped patients acknowledge, bear, work through, and put into perspective painful feelings and experiences. Our resistance to grieving, taught Semrad, derives from avoidance defenses, including denial, projection, and distortion, to avoid feeling the emptiness. When faced with these formidable, relatively unyielding defenses in hospitalized patients, Semrad's stance was to investigate, investigate, and do more investigating of the details about the facts, memories, affects, and fantasies about loss

(Adler, 1997). Semrad's tenacity taught us that these vulnerable patients could face emotional pain, sadness, anger, shame, and guilt, at least for those moments during an interview when they could communicate lucidly and would not fall into psychosis. The difficulty of investigation with borderline and psychotic patients resembles that of therapy with bereaved and traumatized children in that both use primitive defenses and have fragile ego organization.

## Loss in the Inner City

One author (B.S.) has worked part-time for over 30 years assessing, treating, and supervising the treatment of inner-city children and adolescents at the Northwest Family Center of the DC Commission on Mental Health Services. There it was observed over the years that most of these children had lost their fathers through abandonment, imprisonment, or death and were unable to confront and mourn their losses. In the past 10 years, however, clinicians began to hear, at an accelerating rate, similar stories about the mothers. They may have been institutionalized at St. Elizabeth's (Psychiatric) Hospital or incarcerated. Others drifted into drug or alcohol addiction, homelessness, prostitution, depression, or illness from AIDS, or they may even have been killed as a result of violence. The emergence of the crack epidemic resulted in mothers addicted to crack and living outside the home. They returned for replenishment and nurturance to the home of their own mothers, aunts, or great aunts, where their own children live. A child's continuing hope for reunion was raised with the mother's return but was dashed when the mother left once again.

These families no longer seemed to have relatives in the South, as they had had for generations. No longer did the children visit aunts and grandmothers in the summer or in times of crisis for a rural respite. Many of the older generation who had not migrated to the North in the decades after World War II were ill or had died. Not only were many inner-city youth losing their mothers and fathers, some were losing siblings and peers as well through violence, including both homicide and suicide. These children were at high risk because they had experienced multiple losses, often through trauma, and at various developmental stages.

Pynoos and Nader (1990) speak of a three-part mourning process: revisiting the traumatic moment in all its complexity; dealing with the loss itself; and confronting changes in living circumstances such as reduced income and a shift in housing. This ideal process of mourning, however, is often undermined if the loss is traumatic and unexpected. A traumatic loss is more difficult to mourn than is a nontraumatic death. The mourning process can also be undermined by other factors. Caretakers who might console bereaved children or act as models for mourning hobble beneath the weight of their own unmourned losses, developmental traumas, and sexual and physical abuse. E. Furman (1974), A. Freud (1931–1944), and Bowlby (1980) emphasized that consequent psychopathology may depend on the availability of adequate supportive and replacement objects. Environmental impediments such as lack of safety, poverty, and loss of community add to an already overstressed family system. For example, a mother, ambivalent about allowing her child's participation in a grief group said, "Grief is a weakness, and we just don't talk about it. I need to keep myself together." This view suggests that allowing children to grieve threatens the already fragile caretakers, thereby threatening the family's homeostasis. Sometimes lost fathers, considered to be ne'er-do-wells and deserters, often are not talked about after they die or are imprisoned. As a result, mourning is subverted. Instead, children and other family members use denial, avoidance, suppression, and isolation to cope with their losses instead of dealing with their grief directly.

Minimal clinical contact with lower-class white families led to the question of how race and social class interact to influence the ability to mourn effectively. One of us (B.S.) approached this issue with the late Charles Pinderhughes (personal communications, 1995), one of the first African-American psychoanalysts. Pinderhughes elaborated that over thousands of years, African cultures had developed rituals around mourning and loss. Fewer than 150 years ago, during slavery, not only were families dissolved, but efforts to annihilate these millennia-old traditions forced African Americans to start anew.

### Observational Origin of the DC School-Based Mourning Project

Attuned to the devastating effects of cumulative unmourned losses for decades, we contemplated an intervention. The impetus to action was an observation that occurred in one-way mirror supervised sessions with three psychology interns. Evaluating very recalcitrant, acting-out adolescents, we were surprised that three of these teenagers, spontaneously and with poignant affect, began talking about the fatal shootings of peers. One death was of a good friend who had been killed a year before; the other two had acquaintances who had died more recently. We realized that some of the intensity of their affect had been displaced from earlier losses of parents and caretakers, which are often more difficult to articulate than are peer losses. This observation led to the idea of forming mourning groups in which, in the company of their peers, adolescents might experience safety, containment, and empathy. Talking about their recent losses in this setting might allow them to initiate the mourning of their earlier parental or caretaker losses.

Later, we decided to focus on children and preadolescents in order to counter the developmental arrest that results from traumas and unmourned losses at an early age and to counter the regressive pull at pubescence, which is particularly intense for those with developmental disturbances. This project is predicated on the idea that once children reach adolescence, they are more likely than younger children to deal with the overwhelming and unbearable emptiness and threatening abyss of helplessness and depression by acting out sexually or aggressively or by self-medicating with drugs. Moreover, the capacity to learn is compromised. For example, one boy whose friend was shot said, "I feel so sad that I am about to cry, and then I get mad and beat people up and start messing stuff up. I want to kill the person who did it." Another said, "The sadness tries to get out but it can't." A suicidal 15-year-old who, within one year, had lost his great grandfather, father, and a series of aunts, uncles, and cousins, explained that the "sadness comes out as anger. Anger makes the sadness go away. Feeling it [the anger] usually works; doing something [acting out the anger] always works." When the adolescent cannot bear sadness from losses, depression, and suicidal thoughts, acting out can result.

### Violence

Underlying much violence are feelings of shame, humiliation, helplessness, and hopelessness, and finally, a provocative "dissing" (Gilligan, 1996). A perpetrator of violence is usually the victim of physical, mental, or sexual abuse who has turned from the passive, vulnerable position to identifying with the aggressor. The victim then becomes the active perpetrator, often enjoying some of the destructiveness of the hatred. A cycle of retaliatory violence is set in motion. The victims and their friends take the shame and humiliation they have endured and turn it back on their "prey."

Certainly there are many causes of the violence that exists in the inner city. Combined with a toxic history of slavery and segregation, which has already instilled a sense of degradation and humiliation in African American communities, other causes of high rates of violence include the availability of guns, drugs, poverty, the rich–poor gap, abuse, neglectful parenting, losses, inadequate models for identification, and racial discrimination. Noshpitz sees slavery and the ensuing traumatic history as building up an

> inner hater, inner enemy, inner destroyer. This is portable; they carry it with them everywhere. Few youths escape its effects and overcome the pressure of the self-destructive moiety, but that is exceptional. Most simply hate themselves (albeit largely unconsciously); when they are dissed or insulted, they have extreme reactions not only to the external threat but to the even more painful inner gout of derisive self-devaluation [Noshpitz, personal communicaion, 1996].

Maurice Apprey (1999) delineates how human suffering is absorbed by the victimized group and is subsequently reenacted by future generations.

A prominent African-American psychiatrist recently acknowledged (personal communication, 1998) that he and many friends experience fears of being lynched when walking in white areas. Cohen (1996) has pointed out, "A paranoid stance can develop: the world is a dangerous place and no one is to be trusted. The behavior resulting from this paranoid stance can then provoke others to act in kind." In addition, the absorption of self-hatred and self-destructiveness can be projected onto others, leading to further attacks. Noshpitz (personal communication, 1996) described an incident in an inpatient drug rehabilitation center where a 19-year-old drug addict being interviewed bolted away and tried to choke to death a newly arrived female patient. When the scene quieted down, Noshpitz learned that, years before, the woman had announced that she had AIDS and had challenged, "Are any of you guys man enough to fuck me?" This man did and contracted AIDS. Now, not acknowledging his own self-destructiveness, he attacked her as though she were responsible for his AIDS.

Newspaper articles refer to adolescents planning their own funerals in exquisite detail. Sixty percent of inner-city children say they do not expect to make it to old age, a symptom of posttraumatic stress disorder termed foreshortened future. One in 21 African-American men will be murdered. Deborah Prothrow Stith (1991) ironically suggests how violence is destroying our young population at an ever-increasing rate. Maybe we should erect a black marble slab and start compiling the names of all whose lives are wasted by violence. Covering the slab would not take long. Every day more than 60 Americans die in homicides—about 450 a week, about 1900 a month, 23,000 a year, 46,000 in two years.

In two years we would have a solemn memorial covered with names, just like the Vietnam Memorial in Washington, DC. Mourners could come and weep. Mothers and fathers could express their anguish. Children could find a legacy, small but powerful, as they trace their fingers over the names of the fathers taken from them. Only this memorial would be different. Very soon the names would spill over, and we would need another memorial and another and another to report the names of the endless streams of fatalities.

This inner-city war is most insidious. In contrast to normal warfare, in which the community coheres and acts as a group to fight the other, inner-city wars are fought within the community itself. While every war is terrible and involves victimization, there is the expectation that some day it will be over. This expectation is in striking contrast to the hopelessness in the inner city where the war continues, generation after generation (Cohen, 1996). Many adolescents committed to prison or residential placement are fathers or fathers-to-be perpetuating the cycle of loss and the potential for violence in their children's lives. Punitive prison conditions precipitate retaliatory violence, thus creating a breeding ground for even further crime.

## Origin of the Project

This bleak picture of the inner city is the context for the origin of the School-Based Mourning Project. Under the auspices of the Northwest Family Center of the DC Commission on Mental Health

Services, this psychoanalytically informed, school-based mourning group project was developed to provide and evaluate an intervention for high-risk, bereaved elementary school children in low-income, inner-city DC public schools. It was developed to help children who had been subjected to multiple losses and traumas, the devastating effects of poverty, and often-chaotic family environments to mourn the death of a parent or significant caregiver. The project was designed for children who would not otherwise have access to mental health services. In 1994, the project received two small grants, primarily for the research and training aspects. Training was provided by clinicians from the St. Francis Center in Washington, DC (renamed the Wendt Center for Loss and Healing), known for its innovative methods of helping inner-city children deal with trauma and loss, and by Robert Pynoos of UCLA, an international expert on the effects of loss and trauma on children in South Central LA and throughout the world (with UNICEF).

Our undertaking was designed as a school-based project conducted during regular school hours because we knew that substantial attrition would occur if the groups met in clinics or after school. For a year and a half, we had difficulty obtaining the cooperation of the principals, counselors, and teachers. Many of the school staff were wary of the project; they were themselves depressed and overburdened or did not have the resources to help identify children and select the control groups. Next, we struggled with obtaining parental or guardian permission to allow children to participate in this clinical/research project. Our unsuccessful approaches included sending letters home with the children and asking the principal to write letters that explained the project. It was not until we hired a master's degree student who traveled into the most troubled areas of DC that we were able to obtain developmental histories and permissions.

A female African-American Muslim wearing a white headdress, this student, Wanda Guy, received cooperation in almost all cases. After 18 months with little to show for our efforts, we suddenly had 19 groups in elementary schools and 15 the next year. Some groups operated in conjunction with a federally funded pupil-personnel program in Southeast Washington led by Frances Howell that provided play therapy in high-risk elementary public schools.

When presenting the project to school personnel and family members, we realized that some words were confusing or taboo. Not comprehending "mourning," they were more comfortable with our conducting "grief" groups. Instead of saying "control groups," we had "wait list" groups. We spoke of "evaluations" not "research" on the African-American population.

## The Intervention Model

An innovative model designed for working with inner-city children who have experienced multiple and traumatic losses due to death, divorce, abandonment, incarceration, or illness is described in a manual written in 1999 by another author (D.W.W.). Ward-Wimmer is a nurse and play-therapist supervisor who focuses on grief work. Ten years ago she discovered that traditional therapy approaches failed to work in the inner city; therefore, she set out to learn the language and culture of children who came mostly from single- or no-parent families and who were dealing with multiple and often violent deaths.

Ward-Wimmer learned that the children's tools for mourning were minimal. Even when death was due to illness, the children were excluded from "knowing" what was going on and thus had little or no opportunity for anticipatory grieving. These children had scant understanding about the nature of the losses and were, therefore, left to "fill in the gaps" with fantasy explanations. They had no language for exploring the phenomenon of death or their feelings around it. Grief often was not allowed to continue, and most felt they were expected to "get over it." Feelings about one-self were slow to be recognized and were most often couched in bravado or insults lest the teller become or even appear vulnerable. Ward-Wimmer also found that chaos was prevalent and fairly well tolerated. In fact, the children seemed comfortable carrying on con-versations while simultaneously appearing to be doing two (or more) things at once. It appeared that because their pain was so great and their coping skills so minimal, these youngsters could not tolerate listening attentively to others. They needed to regress to their most familiar chaotic and deflecting behavior style of verbal provoca-tion, "mouthing."

Ward-Wimmer began to incorporate several innovative approaches in her grief groups with inner-city youth. In one instance, carrying a bag of various instruments, she marched into a group of previ-ously resistant teens. Rules were forgotten, and everyone was talking at once. It sounded more like a playground than what "should" be going on in a professionally led grief group. Her acceptance and awareness prevailed, and the session turned from a circle of participants unwilling or unable to voice their feelings into an interactive group singing about the deceased. The meeting ended with a discussion of what it was like when the youngsters heard the news of the death.

Ward-Wimmer's unique approach is informed by the work of various contributors. Grieving a loss is especially difficult for children because the process can invoke feelings of helplessness and guilt at times when they are developmentally unable to understand them cognitively (Zambelli and DeRosa, 1992) or to bear the pain. The frequency and circumstances of losses and the lack of accessible primary support systems increase the potential for a complicated mourning process because one is unable to resolve one grief experience before having to face another (Nader and Pynoos, 1991).

Unresolved issues of childhood grief will ultimately resurface later in life if they are not fully worked through (Wolfelt, 1991). Children often regrieve previous losses as new coping and cognitive abilities emerge (Kubler-Ross, 1969). Depression, addiction, and poor school performance have all been associated with the experience of complicated grief.

The child's developmental level and cognitive capacity influences his or her perception of the event(s) (Furman, 1974). In general, the preverbal child experiences separation as abandonment—the mother leaves, the baby cries. The child aged approximately three to seven years is a literal thinker and views death as an extension of this life elsewhere: Grandma goes to heaven just as though she were going to Pittsburgh. An 8- to 12-year-old is better able to understand death but is most often concerned with the impact of the loss on himself or herself. Some of the questions this group of children ask are, Who will take care of me? Will we have to move? Will I die? Did I cause it?

Children grieve differently from adults. Because most people do not realize this difference, adults often assume that the process for children should proceed as their own does. While the core process is the same, a child's grief is usually expressed in *brief* episodes of overt sadness layered between apparently happy, normal behavior. Children are often seen crying one moment at a funeral and in the next moment playing happily. Some children do not cry at funerals because the adults around them are so overwhelmed with grief that the children do not feel safe enough to "let it go" as well. Also, children's grief is often acted out in irritability, hyperactivity, hostility, insomnia, or impairment in schoolwork. An adult observing this behavior may incorrectly conclude that the child does not understand the event, is not affected by it, or is not mourning or adapting in his or her own way. But the child, on some level, understands quite well yet is able to tolerate feelings of loss for only brief periods of time. Often only a third of a therapy session focuses directly on the grief.

Ward-Wimmer's model uses such projective techniques as drawing, drama, clay, games, stories, and musical instruments and provides children a safe place to express difficult feelings. She adjusts her approval to the child's developmental level and ability to tolerate difficult feelings. Her self-described gestaltlike approach is compatible with a psychodynamic one. Structure is integral to her work. Each group has a ritual for beginning and ending the session and invites nonverbal expression of feelings. For example, musical instruments may provide a child "another voice" to express varied feelings: happiness, sadness, anger, fear. In one activity, the children are encouraged to select an instrument that they would have chosen for the funerals of those who have died.

In another technique, Ward-Wimmer places paper in balloons with such charged questions as, "How are you similar to or different from the person who died?" and "What did the person do that made you mad?" In another activity, the children decorate "memory boxes" to store items that remind them of the person who died. Opening or closing the box allows the child to maintain control over the grieving. In another projective technique, children mold clay into objects toward which they may express both aggressive and loving feelings to act out, or they describe traumatic events and alternate outcomes. A child may mold an image, for example, of a loved one and the murderer. After speaking to the murderer, the child pulverizes the clay. When there is intense ambivalence about a lost parent, as in cases of sexual or physical abuse, the child removes a piece of clay that represents the aspect that they loved; this piece can be preserved in a safe place, thus not destroying the whole person. "Moving day" allows children to act out traumatic and helpless situations followed by more empowering ones. This technique evokes issues of deprivation and loss. A toy moving truck is presented and the children are told that they can take with them only 10 things or people. Then the truck breaks down and a smaller truck is presented so their limit becomes five, then three. One 10-year-old boy chose video games, his girlfriend, and her clothes!

## The Mourning Groups

The therapists in the first year of the project included 22-year-old master's degree students, psychology interns, experienced therapists, staff members at the Commission on Mental Health Services outpatient clinics, one retired psychoanalyst, and another very experienced child analyst. An early phase of the project included 73 inner-city school children, almost all of whom were African American. Residing in low-income areas of Washington, DC, each, since the age of the three, had experienced the loss of a parent or significant caretaker through death, abandonment, or incarceration. Many of these 7- to 15-year-olds had endured multiple losses, sometimes through violence. Of the 73 children, 43 had been randomly assigned to the experimental groups. They participated in 12-session weekly loss groups; 30 control subjects had pre- and posttreatment evaluation only. On the basis of this pilot project, we obtained a significant grant from George Soros's Project for Death in America.

In the initial stage the children became highly involved and very connected to the cotherapists.Working during school hours, the groups had minimal attrition. Some weekly groups were short term; others lasted most of the school year, depending on practicalities. Most of the children did significant mourning work and began to deal with their multiple traumas and deprivations.

One group initiated unusual funeral rituals as a form of mourning. We were challenged by some significant discipline problems with children who were acting out in this less structured situation. In the third year of the project, we conducted six grief groups starting in October 1998 and ending in May 1999. Thirty-six children (grouped by age, eight to 13 years old) were seen in two inner-city DC elementary schools. Each group comprised five or six children. The losses of parents or caretakers included ten by homicide, five by suicide, eight from cancer, three from heart attacks, two from AIDS, and three from incarceration. Other deaths were from diabetes, sickle cell anemia, kidney failure, and strokes. Sixteen of the 36 children had experienced multiple losses. Attrition was limited to four children who moved out of the school area. One-third of the children had been in a grief group the previous year. Each group had three leaders, at least one being an experienced therapist. Sheila Hill, an enlightened school counselor/social worker, coordinated many volunteers and a school-based mental health clinic and functioned as a key liaison with principals, teachers, and parents or surrogates.

## Results

The children eagerly participated in the groups, often coming early and only reluctantly returning to classes. As might be expected in this disadvantaged population, some of the children evidenced insatiable hunger for all types of supplies including attention, nurturance, art materials, and food—often requesting or sneaking second or third portions.

Although they used various defensive operations, the children began to believe to various degrees that mourning work and any other feelings and fantasies were acceptable; they learned to express feelings that they did not consciously know, had avoided, or had been previously afraid to discuss with others. They were encouraged to voice concerns about their vulnerability to death and other worries, fears about the loss of other family members, and whether they felt responsible for causing another's death or not intervening to prevent it. They expressed sadness and remorse as well as anger and revenge fantasies, and attempts were made to relate these difficult-to-bear fantasies to present destructive and self-destructive behavior.

The children were gradually able to bear and voice uncomfortable thoughts and feelings about their losses. Many of them evidenced a heightened capacity for empathy and compassion. Parents reported that their children showed an increased ability for concentration and a decreased tendency to act out aggressive impulses. We learned that children with developmental delays and behavioral limitations and who also lived in chaotic surroundings nevertheless could engage in useful mourning work.

This preventive project addresses the underlying sense of hopelessness and depression subsequent to the multiple deaths and losses endured by children. The grief groups had a positive impact on many children. One 13-year-old, an identical twin repeating sixth grade while his twin was promoted, participated in a grief group. His father had been murdered by an unknown assailant. This child was tall, handsome, and hyperactive and had an incipient phallic-narcissistic character. He frequently had been disciplined by the principals and suspended. Twice he bolted from the group when he saw a white, middle-aged coleader. He eventually engaged in the group with significant mourning work and received an award for excellence when he graduated. He said, "This group kept the blade from my throat." It is clear that grief and loss feelings, left unaddressed, can later translate into violence, poor school performance, and premature sexual acting out. Clearly, we believe that intervention at the elementary school age is an appropriate and effective prevention.

All the children were administered the Reynolds Manifest Anxiety Scale, The Child Depression Inventory Scale, a hopelessness scale, the Draw-a-Person test, and a new unstandardized test developed by Ward-Wimmer. These tests and the parental Achenbach Child Behavior Checklist were administered before and after the groups were completed.

The Draw-a-Person test provided the most significant and encouraging results. The psychologists scored the drawings according to the well-recognized and validated Koppitz method and were kept blind to whether the children were in the experimental or control group and whether the drawing was from the beginning or the end of the group. They did not know any of the children, nor did they participate in any of the groups. There was very high interscorer reliability. The children who participated in groups had a significant increase in developmental indicators on their pre- and postgroup drawings ($p < .009$), while there were no significant changes for the children in the control group. The projective Draw-a-Person test is nonverbal and relatively culture free. (More extensive test results will be reported by the research director, Janice Krupnick, in a later communication.)

Although we are optimistic about the work accomplished with these children, they continue to be at high risk to be retraumatized with abuse and multiple losses. Forty-five minutes per week of grief groups for seven months a year is significant but hardly sufficient. We would like to continue to work with the same children throughout their elementary years so that they can approach adolescence less likely to act out the underlying depression that results from unmourned losses and emotional and environmental deprivations.

## Future Directions

Many ideas have surfaced to extend the project and evaluate findings in a systematic way.

1.  Work with children should continue throughout their elementary school years (K to 6) with longer term follow-up through high school. We would also like to evaluate the effectiveness of twice weekly groups.
2.  Training and intervention groups should be extended beyond the approximately 200 mental health professionals and graduate students already sensitized to the complexity of mourning in the inner city. The in-school counselors are often poorly trained and unprepared to deal with the multitude of problems; many are burdened with depression themselves. They would benefit immensely from specialized training and supervision. In another extension of this project, all school personnel in a given school could be trained in issues of loss and trauma as well as in child development. Included in this training group would be guards, janitors, cafeteria workers, bus drivers, and some volunteers. Children might feel freer to talk in a casual circumstance to one of this array of adults rather than those they would see as authorities in a more formal setting. This scenario would be the equivalent of adults talking to their hairdressers or bartenders. The trainers might begin by shadowing the school workers and spending a day with them to learn about their experiences in the school.
3.  Much effort is needed to gain the participation of overwhelmed parents and parental surrogates who resist and mistrust joining groups that could inform them about mourning. In a pilot study, by defining these groups as focus groups in which we sought their expertise, we paid each person $20 per session, thereby gaining their cooperation in discussing their children's and their own difficulties. We also plan to enlist selected parent aides in groups in which their children are not participating. A psychology intern,

Andrea Lurier, conducted extensive and revealing home interviews that facilitated parental and guardian participation.

4. From a chance meeting of the DC Medical Examiner with an author (B.S.), a psychoanalyst, Recover, a joint project with the Wendt Center has evolved. Specially trained grief counselors meet the 1500 families who come to the DC morgue to identify the deceased. Mourning begins at this acute stage of grief, and the same counselor continues at a centrally located office for longer term work with children and adults. The adults are assisted in helping children to deal with the loss.

We hope that the School-Based Mourning Groups will evolve into efficient and effective programs so that more children can start working from the inside, hopefully to plan their futures instead of their funerals.

This approach to mourning has far-ranging consequences. It suggests a way to bear frustration and conflict rather than act them out and to adapt eventually to the multiple demands of their internal and external world.

Barbara Brown, Martha Gibbons, William Granatir, Sheila Hill, Francis Howell, Andrea Lurier, Diane Powell, Robert Washington, and volunteer group leaders contributed greatly to this project. We are grateful for the support of the Kenworth-Swift Foundation, The AB Foundation for Medical Research, The American Psychiatric Foundation, George Soros's Project on Death in America, and the Kimsey Foundation.

## References

Adler, G. (1997), Elvin Semrad's contributions to the everyday practice of psychotherapy. *Harvard Rev. Psychiat.*, 5:104–107.

Bowlby, J. (1980), *Attachment and Loss, Vol. 3.* New York: Basic Books.

Cohen, D. (1996), Praeger Lecture, George Washington University, Department of Psychiatry.

Freud, A. (1937–1944), *The Writings of Anna Freud, Vol. 3.* Madison, CT: International Universities Press, 1974.

Freud, S. (1917), Mourning and melancholia. *Standard Edition*, 14:243–58. London: Hogarth Press, 1957.

Furman, E. (1974), *A Child's Parent Dies*. New Haven, CT: Yale University Press.

Gilligan, J. (1996), *Violence*. New York: Putnam.

Krupnick, J. & Solomon, F. (1987), Death of a parent or sibling in childhood. In: *The Psychology of Separation Through the Life Span*, ed. J. Bloom-Feshbach & S. Bloom-Feshbach. San Francisco: Jossey-Bass.

Kubler-Ross, E. (1969), *On Death and Dying*. New York: Macmillan.

Nader, K. & Pynoos, R. S. (1991), Play and drawing techniques as tools for interviewing traumatized children. In: *Play, Diagnosis and Assessment*, ed. C. Schaeffer, K., Gitlan & A. Sandergund. New York: Wiley, pp. 375–389.

Noshpitz, J. (1996), Self-destructiveness in adolescence. *Amer. J. Psychother.*, 48:330–346.

Pynoos, R. S. & Nader, K. (1990), Children's exposure to violence and traumatic death. *Psychiatric Ann.*, 20:334–344.

Stith, D. P. (1991), *Deadly Consequences: How Violence Is Destroying Our Teenage Population and a Plan to Begin Solving the Problem*. New York: HarperCollins.

Ward-Wimmer, D., Napoli, C. & Brophy, S. (1999), *Three-Dimensional Brief: A Model for Facilitating Brief Groups for Inner-City Children*. Washington, DC: William Wendt Center for Loss & Healing.

Wolfelt, A. D. (1991), Ten common myths about children and grief. *Healing the Bereaved Child*. Ft. Collins, CO: Companion Press.

Zambelli, G. C. & De Rosa, A. P. (1992), Bereavement support groups for school-age children: Theory, intervention, and case examples. *Amer. J. Orthopsychiatry*, 62:484–493.

# ❖ 10 ❖

# Psychoanalytic Responses to Violent Trauma
## *The Child Development-Community Policing Partnership*

Steven Marans

Although circumstances have shifted—from the consulting room, to the Hampstead war nurseries, to pediatric wards, to the care of Holocaust survivors, to the best interests of children in custody and placement disputes—child psychoanalytic inquiry and practice have always been based on, first, taking the perspective of the child. At its best, the field of child psychoanalysis has developed theories that articulate clinical and naturalistic findings that derive from multiple points of observation. Direct clinical work has not been the only beneficiary of the decades of this work. In addition to developing the conceptual tools for conducting the psychoanalytic treatment of children, child analysts like Donald Cohen, Anna Freud, Hansi Kennedy, George Moran, Sally Provence, John Schowalter, Al Solnit, Stuart Twemlow, and others have devoted much of their work to conveying a psychoanalytic appreciation of children's experiences to those other professionals whose work affects children's care and the course of the children's development.

The task of child analysts has been to bring complex formulations about the inner and outer life of children into a language of observations that can be recognized by anyone who can bear to see and revisit life through the eyes of a child. Anna Freud (1968) set the standard for the child analyst's role of consultant/collaborator with two essential goals: (1) to appreciate the complexity of children's experience of their lives and (2) to describe the implications of that experience in ways that are accessible to those professionals whose handling and decisions have a potential bearing on the trajectory of a child's development. Anna Freud taught her students to attend, to listen, to observe, and to apply a psychoanalytic perspective to the clinical and extraclinical interventions that aim to maximize developmental potential.

Since Freud's (1926) earliest work, trauma has been a central and enduring concern of psychoanalytic inquiry. In recent years, the problems of childhood have gained increased clinical and conceptual focus while the general public has become more aware of the vast numbers of children who are exposed to the violence associated with war and domestic and neighborhood disputes. Children living in urban centers afflicted with high rates of violence are especially vulnerable to the psychic trauma that occurs when the "actual danger" (Freud, 1926) is in the form of gunfire, wounding, or death. Traditional clinical services alone are unequal to the task of responding to the numbers of children whose development may be compromised as a result of their acute and chronic experiences of violence in their homes, on the streets of their neighborhoods, and at school.

In Anna Freud's tradition of involving ourselves with other professionals concerned about children (child-care workers, teachers, pediatricians, social workers, and lawyers), under the leadership of Donald J. Cohen, a child analyst and the director of the Child Study Center until his death in October 2001, child analysts and analytically oriented faculty members at the Child Study Center recognized the central role played by a group whose professional relationship with children has not always been appreciated: the police. As the profession with the most immediate and frequent contact with children and families exposed to and involved in violence, police officers can have a profound impact on the ways children experience their increasingly unsafe, disorganized world.

The collaboration between child analysts and police, the Yale Child Development-Community Policing (CD-CP) program,[1] is

---

1. The Child Development-Community Policing model, developed at the Yale Child Study Center, is being replicated around the United States under the auspices of the United States Department of Justice.

based on the application of psychoanalytic concepts that provide a frame of reference for extending the observations and interventions of police officers and analytically informed clinicians in responding to the needs of children who have been exposed to, or involved in, violent events. Prior to the inception of the CD-CP program, police contact with mental health professionals generally was limited to delivering psychotic or suicidal patients to the hospital Emergency Service. Similarly, official responsibilities and options regarding children were restricted to such acts as arresting juvenile offenders and referring abused and neglected children to social services. Police did not refer for clinical services the numerous children they encountered on the scenes of violent crimes or exposed to family violence. The goal of the CD-CP program is to expand the role and options available to police officers through training and consultation and to introduce a new partnership in which psychoanalytic principles are conveyed and applied.

A major result of the New Haven Department of Police Service-Child Study Center collaboration is the expansion of our clinical field of observation. Since 1991, clinical contact has been initiated on the scene by officers and child analysts and analytically oriented clinicians, sometimes only moments after shootings, stabbings, beatings, and other scenes involving the potential for psychological trauma. As a result, we have had an opportunity to learn more about a child's experience of violence and overwhelming danger. In addition, this close and immediate contact has afforded us the chance to respond to the various reactions of parents, professionals, and the larger community in ways that help to mediate the overwhelming anxiety/trauma that often accompanies involvement in such events. While the core of the CD-CP program remains the police–mental health partnership, domestic violence advocates, juvenile probation officers, child protective services, and education personnel have become part of the work that has developed in New Haven and elsewhere during the past decade. In this time period, the CD-CP program has been implemented in numerous communities around the country, and the number is growing. Current CD-CP sites include Chelsea, MA, Madison, Guilford, Stamford, and Bridgeport, CT, Baltimore, MD, Charlotte, NC, Nashville, TN, Pinellas County, FL, and Spokane, WA.

In 1998, President Bill Clinton, Attorney General Janet Reno, and Deputy Attorney General Eric Holder established the National Center for Children Exposed to Violence (NCCEV) at the Yale Child

Study Center. Based on the CD-CP model of collaborative responses to violent traumatization, the NCCEV was charged with providing (1) consultation, training, and technical assistance to other communities implementing similar models of response; (2) increased public and professional awareness about issues of childhood trauma and violence exposure; and (3) a web-based resource center for information regarding diagnostic, treatment, and systemic issues related to childhood trauma and violence exposure.

### The Context of Community Policing

Until the last decade, standard police practice in the United States could be characterized as primarily reactive. Officers patrolled in squad cars and were dispatched by central headquarters to one complaint or crime scene after another. They were generally not known by members of the communities in which they worked. In the absence of establishing a continuous, personal presence in the neighborhoods, police were often viewed as ineffective or as intruders in the neighborhoods where they responded to criminal activity. They frequently arrived too late and left too soon. Within this system, police themselves often felt dissatisfied. In spite of their difficult and often dangerous work, they felt that there was little they could do to make a lasting difference. They repeatedly came back to the same neighborhoods, hangouts, and homes to deal with recurrent illegal activities and the tragic aftermaths.

Criminal justice experts have recognized the limitations of the standard model (Goldstein, 1977; Kelling and Moore, 1989; Brown, 1990; Bureau of Justice Assistance, 1994). In many cities in the United States and around the world, police practices are being reorganized around an innovative philosophy, often referred to as community-based or problem-oriented policing. Community-based policing puts officers in neighborhoods where they walk beats, develop relationships, and try to prevent rather than simply respond to one crisis after another. In the New Haven model of community policing, police have increasingly been recruited from the racially and ethnically diverse communities they patrol. When these officers are placed in neighborhoods and work from small substations rather than central headquarters, they observe and experience the lives of children and families much more acutely. They learn who are involved in criminal activities, where and with whom trouble is likely to occur, and why things are heating up. They see and often know the many victims of violence—not only those who have been shot, stabbed, or beaten and their assailants, but the many child witnesses who observe the events in horror or run for safety. As they have become a more established and personal presence, the police place greater emphasis on devising strategies to prevent or interrupt crime and on developing problem-solving relationships with members of the neighborhoods in which they work. Officers who walk the beat understand the rhythms and underlying dynamics within their communities. This day-by-day engagement brings with it additional personal burdens. As officers become closer to and invested in the people who either ask for or require their interventions, they also run an increased risk of being overwhelmed by the problems they confront.

This vulnerability to seeing and feeling too much is especially pronounced in officers' engagements with children at risk. They find it particularly difficult to see children caught in the spiral of inner-city violence, the children who are witnesses to family battles and street crime and who then move from being victim to active perpetrator. On the beat, police officers begin to feel the pain and frustration that go with a sense of impotence, and they naturally wish to have the competence and authority to intervene more effectively.

## Police and the Psychoanalytic Perspective on Children

In contrast to police officers, mental health professionals are equipped to respond to children's psychological distress. However, the acutely traumatized children who are most in need of clinical service rarely are seen in existing outpatient clinics until months or years later, if at all, when chronic symptoms or maladaptive behavior brings them to the attention of parents, teachers, or the juvenile courts. Lost are valuable opportunities to intervene at the moment when professional contact could provide both immediate stabilization and bridges to a variety of ongoing services. To be effective in their new roles within communities, officers need to be provided with a framework for understanding children and families, and they need new partners who can help them deal with the challenges and tragedies they encounter.

In the CD-CP program, psychoanalytic theories about development—the ego and superego mediation of instinctual life; the interaction between conflict and defense; the concept of developmental lines and phases; the interaction between significant environmental factors and psychic reality (A. Freud, 1936, 1965)—provide a shared frame of reference. Similarly, the program follows a model of consultation, pioneered by Anna Freud and adapted by Al Solnit and others, that relies on a process of learning about the perspectives and experiences of the other professional with whom one is working to consider the developmental implications of shared observations and actions. Psychoanalytic clinicians in the CD-CP program have learned that, to be useful to police officers, they first must see the clinical phenomena from the officers' point of view. They have been able to do so through the institution of fellowships for clinicians and supervisory officers. In the Police Fellowship, clinicians move into police settings—whether in ride-alongs in squad cars, joining police at crime scenes, or sitting in on discussions of case investigations—and learning about their tasks, demands, and professional needs. At the same time, through the Clinical Fellowship, officers become familiar with mental health settings and psychoanalytic perspectives by observing clinical activities and consultations. Also, a 24-hour consultation service and weekly case conference provide ongoing opportunities for applying developmental concepts in the field. Where each of these components serves as a basis for the continued development of the collaboration, the seminars attended by senior police officers, Child Study Center analysts, and analytically informed clinicians provide the shared conceptual framework that guides observations, discussions, and interventions.

### Seminars on Child Development, Human Functioning, and Policing

The central task of the seminars is to engage officers in the examination of (1) basic human needs; (2) capacities for self-regulation and mastery; (3) phase-specific sources of danger/anxiety; (4) the link between behavior and underlying psychic processes (i.e., the relationship between anxiety and defenses); and, (5) individual variation in potential life adaptations. Proceeding along a developmental sequence, the seminars also highlight the ways in which phenomena originating in an earlier phase of development may be observed in various forms throughout the life cycle. Seminar leaders use scenarios encountered in police work, films and videotapes about children, and cases initiated through the Consultation Service to demonstrate that a greater understanding of human functioning does not mean inaction or decreased vigilance with regard to personal safety. Rather, by helping the informed officers understand the complexities of human development, the goal of the seminars is to help the police to discover new ways of observing and formulating responses to children. In addition, the officers have the opportunity to establish a realistic appreciation of the impact they can have on the lives of children and families with whom they interact.

Typically, the following first meeting, in which seminar members introduce themselves and talk about their expectations of the course, discussions begin about early development. The topic of infancy is introduced by the supervisory officer, who coleads the seminar with an analyst who describes the following scene: "You have responded to a complaint of breach of the peace and arrive at an apartment where music is blaring. You are greeted by an angry young mother, an apartment that is disordered and dirty, and three children under the age of four in similar disarray. Diaper changes for two of the children appear long overdue. What is your reaction?" The officers often begin the discussion by expressing their feelings of despair and anger about a scene that is all too familiar.

As the instructors probe the nature of these reactions, the class begins to identify concerns about the babies, who are unable to fend for themselves; about the children's physical discomfort; and about the notion that the mother is overwhelmed. What emerges from the discussion is the group's awareness of an infant's physical and emotional needs and the role of the mother in mediating and responding to those needs. The seminar leaders ask, "And what happens to the infant if those basic needs aren't met?" The answers are usually that the baby will be overwhelmed with pain, discomfort, and despair because it is not yet equipped to feed, clothe, comfort itself or satisfy the demands of its feelings on its own. The leaders ask for more details, and the class responds by identifying the child's lack of abilities—the absence of verbal language, motoric maturation, and coordination; underdeveloped cognitive processes for problem solving; and, finally, the utter reliance of the infant on the mother for the experience of physical and emotional well-being.

Attention then turns to the young mother. "How," the leaders ask, "do we understand her apparent insensitivity or incompetence?" The discussion must first address her surly response to the officers and their consequent indignation. Here the concepts of displacement and externalization are introduced. The seminar leaders expand the discussion to a young woman apparently unable to look after her children, let alone herself. They ask, "How might she feel about herself?" The answers vary: "Like a failure?" "Maybe she just doesn't care!" The seminar leaders ask, "Given either of those possibilities, how might she feel when two police officers come to her door?" "Like we're going to tell her off, tell her what she should be doing, how she should behave." "And who are you to her at that moment? Who tells *you* you're not getting it right, messing up? Parents? teachers? a critical boss or colleague?" In one session, an officer jumped in and offered, "Right, and then when she feels criticized, she takes on an obnoxious attitude and treats us like dirt." Another officer added, "As though she already knows you are."

In this particular discussion, the clinical coleader suggested that perhaps from the moment of their arrival, the officers represent something very familiar to the young woman: "Before you open your mouth, you may be the critical voice, the presentation of authority, the voice that agrees with her own self-criticism and assessment of incompetence. How does it feel to be criticized? What is it like to feel inadequate and to have someone, by their very presence on your doorstep, point it out to you? Is it possible that her surly and combative response serves a defensive function that is triggered by you but is not about you personally?" The discussion goes on, often ending with some greater appreciation for the complexity of the scene and the interaction but with the residual wish to do something concrete for the babies. That wish is either to implore the woman to be a more attentive mother or, to remove the children so that they can have a better home.

The Robertsons' film *John (1969)* is shown in the following session. In the discussion that follows, seminar members describe the 17-month-old's efforts to soothe himself in the midst of a nine-day separation from his parents. They note John's attempts to reach out to the child-care nurses, cuddly toys, and the observer—and his utter despair when these efforts fail. The discussion also compares

John to the other children who have spent their entire lives in the residential nursery. Seminar members often observe that, while seeming unfazed by the limited attention and multiple changes of nursing staff, in contrast to John, these children appear dominated by aggressive, driven, and need-satisfying behavior. Slowly and often painfully, as the discussion continues, the simple solution of removal from care when parenting seems inadequate fades. The idea that removal always represents rescue is replaced by a growing appreciation for the complexity of the child–parent relationship. There is a recognition of the developmental significance of continuity of care and the impact of disrupting it. In addition, seminar members have a fuller understanding of the balance between the child's needs and capacities as well as the distress that follows when needs are not met.

The link between these processes and overt behavior *and* the observer's responses and overt behavior is pursued as the seminar moves into the next session, in which the hallmarks of the toddler phase are introduced. Using videotapes of normal children engaged in imaginative play, officers are able to consider children's use of fantasy, identifications, and burgeoning cognitive and physical resources to achieve aim-inhibited sources of pleasure and mastery. Failures to negotiate oedipal conflicts over competition, envy, love, and hate, along with the often unstable, overstimulating home situations, are explored in discussions of latency-age children who come to the attention of police because of their antisocial activities. Similarly, puberty is discussed in the context of the intensification of struggles over sexual and aggressive urges.

Seminar leaders introduce phases of development by asking officers to describe the most salient aspects—either observed or assumed to play a part—of a given period of life. As the discussion evolves, officers often invoke their own memories as a vehicle for understanding the behaviors they observe and encounter on the street and as a way of becoming conscious of the complicated identifications that these interactions may evoke. For example, when discussing puberty and early adolescence, officers initially describe their concerns about the provocative, tough, drug-involved, pregnant youngsters and the frustration the officers experience when logic and warnings about consequences seem to have no impact on behavior. As they begin to talk about their own experiences of this phase of development, however, the frustration and angry dismissal of these children is substantially altered. Officers often describe memories from their own lives or recollections of children whom they have met over the course of their work which they have not been able to forget. The accounts speak to the vulnerability, anxiety, and loneliness so common in this period of development and the various means used to defend against these feelings. Stories of fighting, social isolation, school difficulties, and losses alternate with the ones about best friends, first girlfriends and boyfriends, team sports, and the like. Each of the discussions inevitably focuses on concern about body image, group acceptance, struggles with parents, losses, and the overreaching experience of embarrassment and urgency in the competing wishes for competent, independent functioning and feelings of utter inadequacy and the embarrassing wish to remain a small child.

John Singleton's (1991) film, *Boyz N the Hood*, and Michael King's (1998) Emmy award-winning film *Bangin'* are used as the text for the seminars that deal with adolescence. Both films provide rich opportunities for seminar participants to discuss the challenges, hopes, and dilemmas inherent in adolescence. In the discussion of Singleton's film, issues of race and the socioeconomics of the inner-city are interwoven with perspectives on the internal and external worlds of two brothers in the film—one becomes a gun-toting drug dealer, the other a high school football star bound for college until he is shot dead by gang members. King's documentary looks at the impact of violence on young people as both victims and perpetrators. Through interviews with incarcerated adolescent violent offenders, officers and clinicians are afforded insight into the experiences and thoughts of children with whom contact typically would have been limited to times of arrest or brief emergency-room or court-ordered evaluations.

As the seminars come to an end, officers increasingly refer to their responses to the scenes of violence and suffering they confront on a daily basis. Sealing over, "getting used to it," and distancing themselves as best they can, or displacing their frustration onto citizens or their own family members, viewing the world dichotomously—"us versus them"—and heightening their sense of vigilance to danger are all themes that commonly emerge in the discussions. These reponses are discussed in terms of the defensive functions they serve against unwanted feelings of fear, inadequacy, sadness, despair, and anger. As a result of these discussions, officers become more aware that the nature of their work makes it especially difficult, but absolutely necessary, for them to be able to recognize and distinguish between internal responses and external reactions.

## Changes in Police Responses

Regardless of the setting, the aim of the discussions for officers and clinicians alike is to "place ourselves in the position of children of different ages, of different developmental phases, and of different backgrounds" (Goldstein, Freud, and Solnit, 1979, p. 137). For the officers, the opportunity to reflect on what they observe, to have a framework for ordering what might have otherwise been too overwhelming to notice, and to have colleagues with whom to share the burden of responding—at any hour—has led to dramatic changes in police practices regarding children. These changes are reflected in the officers' regularly referring children who have witnessed and experienced violence as well as, increasingly, children who have committed serious violent offenses.

Incorporating developmental perspectives, the changes are also apparent in standards of police practice that go beyond making referrals for children victimized or involved in violence. These standards include, for example, consideration of how parents are treated when issued a warrant or put under arrest. In one typical seminar discussion, an officer described a high-speed chase involving a man and five-year-old boy on a motorcycle. When he finally stopped the man, the officer began screaming at him about his endangering the young boy. In reporting the scene, the officer described the panic he felt that accompanied his fantasy of the motorcycle crashing and killing the boy. What bothered him the most, after this incident, however, was that, as he yelled at the man, the boy began to cry and shouted at him to stop being mean to his father. The officer pointed out that, while he had justified his tirade as in the boy's best interest, he had completely left out any consideration of the boy's identification with or admiration of the father, regardless of whatever anxiety he might have felt about father's reckless behavior. In addition, the officer's wish for the boy to view the police in a positive light had, in fact, been undermined by his own intense emotional reaction of fear followed by anger. In retrospect, the officer decided that taking the father aside and discussing the danger and his concerns for the boy's safety, in addition to issuing a ticket, might have served the boy's and his own professional interests far more effectively.

Similarly, officers have become more attentive to the humiliation and potential for dangerous confrontation when they deal with adolescents—especially juvenile offenders—in a harsh manner. As officers have become regular fixtures in the neighborhoods, they have replaced anonymous responses to the groups of kids on the streets with interactions that are informed by familiarity and relationships with individuals. From the seminars to the streets, this contact is enhanced by officers' increased appreciation of the upheaval of adolescent development, often compounded by the despair and feelings of impotence associated with severe social adversity. As a result, wholesale condemnation, frustration, and anger are no longer the only responses to the provocative—and, at times, illegal—behavior with which adolescents confront the police. The recognition of displacements and counterreactions that are so often associated with police–adolescent interactions on the street has also led to a more judicious and strategic use of authority when it is based on new relationships that replace stereotypic responses of the past. In turn, police imposition of authority (e.g., clearing a street corner known for drug activity, keeping public noise down, picking up truant students, etc.) is more frequently now met with compliance rather than an immediate escalation to violent confrontation and arrest.

Where the application of developmental principles has affected police approaches to typical interactions with youth on the streets and in schools, it has also led to interventions that are anything but standard in the traditional approach to law enforcement. Following the shooting death of a 17-year-old gang member, there was good reason for concern about retaliation and further bloodshed. In the days that followed the death, grieving gang members congregated on the corner where the shooting had taken place. Efforts at increased presence and containment took the form of police, neighborhood-based probation officers, and clinicians spending time on the corner listening to gang members express their grief.

As one senior police officer put it, "We could show our concern for their trauma by being with them, lending an adult ear to their misery. Alternatively, we could put more officers on the street, show them who's boss, and, with a show of force, sweep them off the corner as often as necessary. We could then offer them an additional enemy and wait for them to explode." At that crucial moment, however, the police did not assume the role of enemy. They did not serve as the target for displaced rage or, in confrontation, offer an easy antidote to sadness and helplessness. Rather than turning passive into active "payback" in blood, gang members became active, discreetly assisting the police to make a swift arrest in the shooting. As one gang member, the brother of the victim, put it to a neighborhood officer, "You were there for us. That helped—and we were there for you."

Where arrests continue to be an essential tool for police, a new look at the range of prevention measures has been added to the repertoire of law enforcement. In New Haven, arrests of juvenile offenders involved in drug dealing, assault, or murder are often accompanied by requests for consultation from psychoanalytically oriented clinicians. In many situations, the officer's concern about the psychological status of a young offender may lead to questions about whether jail or hospitalization is the more appropriate, immediate disposition. In the context of collaboration, questions about what the child needs have expanded to what the officer has to offer the child, the family, and the community beyond the arrest and detention.

Since 1995, juvenile probation officers and corrections personnel in the juvenile detention center have been trained as part of the CD-CP program. Juvenile offenders are now provided a continuity of interventions from arrest, to detention, to adjudication, to treatment planning and implementation that had never previously existed. The program provides child psychiatric coverage for the detention center and makes available on-call clinical services for youngsters involved in the probation programs.

## CD-CP Responses to Trauma

As police officers and others have found a forum for reflecting on what they have observed and as they have found partners in responding, they no longer need simply to turn away from the traumatogenic events they were unable to prevent. Instead, the police are able to consider the children's unfolding experiences and needs long after they have left the crime scene. While officers have an opportunity to expand their knowledge and repertoire of interventions, the collaboration with the police provides clinicians with a new setting to increase their understanding of the impact of violence and trauma. Discussions about referrals from the CD-CP Consultation Service, frequently emphasize the extent to which children describe the violent events they have witnessed in terms of developmental phase-specific anxieties that are aroused. By following the unfolding stories of the children exposed to violence, clinicians in the program are able to see more clearly what constitutes the specific dangers that overwhelm the individual child, which aspects and meanings of the event are experienced as "traumatizing." Clinicians, generally, assume that traumatization is related to the "facts" about violence that has been witnessed. These assumptions may have little to do with the child's actual experience of the event or the meaning that is attributed by the child in its aftermath. And little attention may be paid to learning about the child so as to begin to appreciate what an experience of violence might be for the child in the context of his or her life—history, family constellation, developmental phase, defense configuration and the like—and therefore which interventions might be most useful. As Anna Freud (1965) pointed out:

> Traumatic events should not be taken at their face value but should be translated into their specific meaning for the given child. Attributes such as heroism or cowardice, generosity or greed, rationality or irrationality have to be understood differently in different individuals, and judged in the light of their genetic roots, their phase and age-adequateness, etc. [p. 139].

Consideration of the child's perspective has led to a lessening of the additionally traumatizing effects of how the police react to a child's situation in the wake of exposure to violence. Sgt. G described Lisa, a seven-year-old girl who had witnessed a beloved neighbor bleed to death after being fatally stabbed by another woman living nearby. Believing he was protecting her from the gore of the crime scene, Sgt. G had Lisa wait on the porch while officers conducted their investigation inside the house. Haunted by the intent gaze, a mixture of despair and rage, that Lisa fixed on him, he finally invited her into the apartment as the officers were leaving. The next day Sgt. G returned to the house and spoke with Lisa and her grandmother. He realized that his attempt at being helpful had backfired because he had not considered what Lisa was experiencing and what she needed and from whom.

As Sgt. G explained in the case conference, "Especially in the midst of so much blood and terror, what she needed was to be close to her grandmother, the most stable figure in her life, not to be stranded alone with images of the scene." Both Lisa and her grandmother eagerly accepted his offer of a referral for clinical services. Lisa's treatment revealed the extent to which frightening themes and fantasies involving extremes in love and hate dominated her inner life. Her ambivalence and uncertainty about relationships were heightened by her experience of growing up with a heroin-addicted mother who dropped in and out of her life, and by concerns about her aging grandmother's fragile health. Internalized as well as external conflicts were boldly underlined by her confusion of loyalties in the stabbing. While she mourned the death of one beloved and idealized maternal substitute, she anxiously told her therapist about the love letters she was writing to the assailant, now in jail on murder charges. Even this dangerous woman seemed safer and more available than her inconsistent, but absent mother.

Nine-year-old Mike witnessed the shooting death of an idolized teenage neighbor, John. The older boy had squarely beaten an opponent in a game of one-on-one basketball and was then accused of cheating. The two teenagers got into a shoving match that culminated in John's challenger pulling out a gun and shooting John twice in the chest. John died almost immediately. Mike was the only witness to the murder, and the police needed to interview him. Mike was understandably distressed by the death of his friend, and the police decided to interview him later that day. Rather than see him at police headquarters downtown, the investigating officer asked the boy and his mother where they would be most comfortable and if they would like a referral to a CD-CP therapist. At their request, Mike and his mother were seen by the therapist immediately after the police interview.

In the acute phase of the intervention, the therapist invited the boy to draw pictures. He drew picture after picture in which the shooter and gun grew larger and larger while the boy and his teenage friend shrank to mere dots on the page. Over the next days, Mike had recurring nightmares and was irritable at home and school; he fought with his younger brother and peers. Despite Mike's father having abandoned them when Mike was three years old, mother described an unremarkable developmental history prior to the shooting. He did fairly well in school. His mother's only concern was that Mike spent too much time away from home, hours on his own or watching the older boys play basketball on the courts where the shooting had taken place. She worried that Mike would fall under the influence of the drug dealers that were part of their public housing landscape.

During the course of the twice-weekly psychotherapy that continued for eight months after the shooting, Mike's drawings and accompanying narratives grew more elaborate. In them he revealed the central role that John had played in his inner life as a realization of a dimly remembered and highly idealized father—strong, competent, and interested in Mike. Mike described how John's attention—letting him hang out at the basketball court and occasionally teaching him some shots—had been an important contrast to his mother's nagging and worries about his safety, which made him feel like a baby. In this context, as Mike repeatedly returned to depicting the moment that John was shot, his sense of disbelief turning to grief and then to rage and guilt. As he described the enduring image of watching John fall to the ground with an expression of surprise, Mike could now put into words what constituted the essence of his traumatic moment. The figure of strength and competence with whom he so desperately identified now seemed like a helpless baby. Mike again felt abandoned and helpless. Recognizing the link between the past and the present, associated with his longings for a father and friend who had abandoned him, Mike and his therapist could begin to make sense of the irritability and fighting that enabled Mike to reestablish power, express rage, and defend against "babyish" feelings and connect with longings for a father and friend who had abandoned him. Increasingly, Mike was alerted to those situations in which his sense of competence felt under attack—whether the joking of friends, teasing of a younger brother, or the concerns and expectations of his mother—and gave rise to angry counterattacks. His irritability and fighting diminished and eventually stopped, as did the nightmares that captured his terror and robbed him of the safety of sleep. While Mike ended his treatment with a good resolution of his posttraumatic adaptation, both his life setting and his history make Mike vulnerable to a dangerous future. How will the shooting and all its meanings be organized and represented in the developmental phases to come?

Children referred to the CD-CP program by police give child analysts the opportunity to learn more about the ways trauma is defined for each child by a convergence of current and past experience. A child's experience of overwhelming anxiety derives from the realization of nodal, phase-specific fantasies, concerns, and conflicts regarding aggressive and sadistic wishes, fears of object loss, invasion of bodily integrity and damage, or guilt and shame associated with loss of control and infantile feelings of helplessness (Marans, 1994; Marans et al., 1996; Marans and Adelman, 1997). Moreover, the psychoanalytic understanding of development and psychic functioning guide the process of appreciating the child's and family's experience of potentially traumatic events.

### Psychoanalytic Perspectives on Violence and Trauma

The psychoanalytic understanding of trauma in families, of the impact of witnessing violence in the inner city, and of the multiple pathways that can lead children from being traumatized into becoming aggressive is an important complement to other approaches to understanding children in this era of violence (Marans and Cohen, 1993; Marans, Berkman, and Cohen, 1996; Murphy, 2002). Psychoanalytic theories stand alongside sociological, political, economic, and other "explanatory" systems. In this area of research, contemporary psychoanalysts play a special role in underlining the complexity of these various relationships, the role of individual differences among children and families, and the distance between outer displays and internal experiences.

Anna Freud and Dorothy Burlingham (1943) demonstrated that during the blitz, children responded as much to their parents' affects and to disruptions in parenting as to the actual dangers of bombing (Hellman, 1962, 1983). These observations have been repeated wherever children are studied during warfare, for instance, in Israel during the missile attacks in the Gulf War when child analysts worked with children and families evacuated from their homes, and in the midst of natural catastrophes (Laor, 1996, 2001, 2002). When children are provided an interpretive frame, when they and their families can see their exposure and suffering within a community and a shared set of beliefs, the experience of trauma is given a context and is transmuted. However, unlike British families during World War II or Israeli families that endured a series of wars since the founding of the nation, children exposed to violence in the inner cities of the United States often have little in the way of community, ideology, or, sometimes, cohesive family structure on which to rely for mutative support and amelioration of trauma. It is in those circumstances that police officers, properly equipped and supported by acute clinical intervention, may be the first best source of stability and containment available to children and their families. Psychoanalytic understanding of the nature of trauma and of the importance of intellectual, interpretive, and psychosocial mediation of experiences guides all efforts to help children caught in war and otherwise experiencing or witnessing violence.

Through acute and long-term involvement with children overwhelmed by their exposure to violence, child analysts have an opportunity to extend the field of observation and inquiry into the long-term impact of trauma. Here there is an important convergence of psychoanalytic understanding of individual differences in the processing and meaning of events, biological theories of brain functioning, and developmental theories about critical stages in development. There is thus a confluence between what the brain perceives and what the mind understands. That which is traumatic represents the conspiracy of both when the protective barriers give away; presumably psychological structures as well as biological structures are overwhelmed (van der Kolk et al., 1985; Burges Watson, Hoffman, and Wilson, 1988; Pynoos and Nader, 1989; Pynoos, Steinberg, and Wraith, 1995). One model of the neurophysiological mediation of stress and trauma proposes that, when an individual is unable to anticipate or defend against an experience of overwhelming danger, the central regulation of the noradranergic system—which mediates heart rate, respiration, and startle reflexes—is compromised (Southwick et al., 1993; Perry, 1994; Yehuda, 1998, 2000).

In the work with the New Haven Department of Police Service, child analysts have had the advantage of observing children and adults within minutes of exposure to acute episodes of violence. This proximity and timing of involvement has allowed these clinicians to follow patients' responses from their acute to longer term adaptations. Regardless of their premorbid or previolence-exposure functioning, each child and adult seen has presented with a range of acute symptoms involving dysregulation of affect, attention, memory, and such bodily functions as sleep. Subsequently, each has shown a marked exacerbation or introduction of increased anxiety and new symptomatic behavior.

Integrating physiologic and psychoanalytic models is extremely useful for understanding the acute presentation of trauma. In the acute phase, a person's attempts to process, anticipate, and regulate levels of excitation through typical patterns of mentation and defense may be seen in increased motor agitation at one end of the spectrum, and withdrawal, isolation, and numbing at the other end. Subsequent hypervigilance, symptom formation, and a propensity for dysregulation of basic ego functions—generalized or restimulated by traumatic reminders—may thus reflect alterations in central neuroregulatory capacities as well as attempts to mediate somatopsychic experiences through the reintroduction of ideational representation, signal anxiety, and subsequent defensive responses in the service of restitution and ego reorganization.

Short-term distress, as in brief separations, leads to adaptive coping, structure formation, and healthy defenses. These reactions prime a child's psychological "immune" system, allowing him or her to accommodate to the experiential "viruses" of the real world. Persistent distress, as in repeated exposure to violence in the home, in school, or on the streets, predispose the child to fail to develop the ability to feel safe and secure with others or when alone; to enjoy reciprocity, and to be able to tolerate normal frustrations. What constitutes a normal, "immunizing dose" and what overwhelms the mental adaptive immune system remain crucial questions for those studying children living in psychosocial adversity. These questions represent potential areas of collaboration among child psychoanalysts, child psychiatrists, social workers, and developmental psychologists. The Child Development-Community Policing program offers a vantage point for addressing these questions.

## Post 9/11

In the midst of its ongoing activities, the National Center for Children Exposed to Violence (NCCEV) was mobilized within moments after the news of the attacks on the World Trade Center and the Pentagon. In the hours, days, and weeks that followed, psychoanalysts and analytically informed faculty members responded immediately to requests for consultations with colleagues in New York and lower Fairfield County, CT, as well as providing direct services to children and families in affected neighborhoods in New York City. In addition, NCCEV faculty met with members of Congress and their families, as well as advising members of the U.S. Departments of Justice and Education in addressing the psychological needs of children and families directly affected by the attacks and those affected across the country. Interviews with print and broadcast media were another outlet for disseminating psychoanalytically informed views about the psychological effects of the terrorist attacks on children and families and ways of ameliorating their impact.

In the aftermath of 9/11, the NCCEV published guidelines for parents, mental health professionals, primary healthcare providers, and clergy about how to understand stress, trauma, and bereavement and about how to talk with children about their concerns about the attacks and subsequent threats. They wrote also guides for mental health workers, primary health care providers, and clergy about stress, trauma, and bereavement in the aftermath of 9/11. These materials were posted on the NCCEV website (http://www.nccev.org) and disseminated on linked websites around the country. They were also distributed by the U.S. Departments of Justice and Defense, through all members of the U.S. Senate and House of Representatives, and through a range of professional organizations, including the Academy of Pediatrics. The NCCEV, in conjunction with the Departments of Psychiatry at Yale and the University of Connecticut, have delivered training and direct services throughout the state of Connecticut and are working with the governor's office and commissioner of mental health to develop comprehensive mental responses to possible subsequent crises.

On behalf of the U.S. Department of Education and the New York City Board of Education, I, along with child analyst Robert Pynoos and his colleague from Los Angeles, Marlene Wong, consulted with school, mental health, and disaster officials about coordinated responses to children throughout the New York City school system. In collaboration with the Mental Health Partnership in New York City, the NCCEV has continued to consult with and provide school system-wide training for developing school-based crisis response and mental health service delivery approaches. All this work has derived from the extensive experience gained, in New Haven and around the country, in responding collaboratively to thousands of children who were affected by violence and disaster during the past decade, whether at home, in their neighborhoods, or in school.

## Conclusions

Regardless of the setting, child analysts have been most successful in applying psychoanalytic knowledge when they have invited collaborators to observe the world from first of all the perspective of children. Similarly, when analysts have been able to provide a common language and a conceptual framework that helps collaborators from other fields to organize and increase their range of observations, partnerships between analysts and others grow. Anna Freud exemplified these approaches to applied psychoanalysis. She was not content simply to observe and learn about the inner workings of children's minds or about the paths of children's development. What, she might have asked, can we learn about the unfolding lives of children so that we can support their optimal development and do the least amount of harm to them? And who must see what we have learned? And with whom must we work to apply what we have learned and intervene when children's development is threatened by environmental factors that may all too often reach traumatic proportions?

Anna Freud and later child analysts have been devoted to the notion that a greater understanding of development and of children's perspectives can inform the ways in which children are treated—in a psychoanalytic treatment, a custody dispute, a hospitalization, a routine pediatric exam, the classroom, and the home. Both in and out of the consulting room, their work reflects an interest in the special populations of children who have endured special, significant environmental factors that shaped internal experience and adaptations in daily life. In considering the role of the environment in children's development Anna Freud (1968) suggested "that every single aspect of the child's personality is affected adversely unless definite sources of supply and support are made available to him has been proved beyond doubt by analytic work carried with the children of severely disturbed parents, concentration camp and disinstitutionalized children, orphaned children, handicapped children, etc." (p. 116). She discussed the dilemma that often confronts analysts when their assessment indicates that the damage to a child's development is "caused and maintained by active, ongoing influences lodged in the environment" (p. 115). She pointed out that whether these negative influences disregard and frustrate or actively oppose the normal course of development, the child victim is in need of therapeutic help. However, "in neither case is the type of help clearly indicated, nor the therapist's role in the process clearly circumscribed" (p. 115).

Our ability to make psychoanalytic findings about the inner lives of children accessible to nonanalysts has determined the extent to which psychoanalytic ideas have helped to shape policies and practices that affect the lives of children in many circumstances and settings. The pioneering work of Anna Freud and those who would follow introduced a model for the roles played by child analysts outside clinical hours—as consultants, teachers, and partners— translating and applying psychoanalytic principles of development to a variety of settings. These roles have been an especially important complement to direct clinical work, particularly in those cases and situations in which the type of therapeutic help, the role of the therapist, or the needs of the child could not be adequately defined or addressed in the consulting room alone. Without the opportunity to learn from children in the clinical setting, we would have few opportunities to help others consider what children need. Without venturing beyond the consulting room, child analysts might have few occasions to be heard or to learn more about those exigent circumstances in children's lives that so often undermine developmental potential and immobilize the efforts of adult caregivers to intervene on their behalf.

In the Child Development-Community Policing program and in the work of the National Center for Children Exposed to Violence, child analysts and analytically informed colleagues have found a new setting in which psychoanalytic principles of development can be applied, explored, and expanded. Through these programs, the fields of observation have been increased by collaborations requiring the development of a common language in which to extend the observations, concerns, and approaches of disparate professionals who deal with the children at greatest risk for developmental psychopathology.

For many of the children and families seen through the CD-CP services, the chronic symptoms and adaptations that immobilize progressive development may, fortuitously, no longer be the only outcome of their exposure to violence. When the significance of their exposure is first recognized by police officers, children and families no longer need to be alone in their struggle with the immediate effects of trauma. When partners from various social services share a developmental perspective, interventions can be comprehensive and driven by the specific needs of the children and families they serve. For the professionals involved, the availability of immediate consultation, access to acute situations, and a broader scope of information and intervention options have decreased their burdens. Police officers and mental health professionals in particular are able to become active in the immediate aftermath of violence and tragedy rather than being overwhelmed by it. For so many of the children and families seen, the police and mental health response may offer a rare experience of feeling regarded and feeling that one's experiences of tragedy, fear, and trauma are recognized as exceptional no matter how frequently they may be part of one's life. In many of the situations requiring acute response, police, seen as representatives of the larger social order, are viewed not simply as providing too little, too late but as benign figures of authority who are able to play a role in reestablishing a semblance of stability in the midst of the emotional chaos.

In weekly case conferences, child analysts and other analytically informed investigators and clinicians, police, and other partners are able to explore the effects of exposure to violence on children, their families, and the professionals who become involved with them. In turn, all involved are in a better position to assess short- and longer-term psychotherapeutic, policing, social service, probation, medical, and educational interventions that may offer the best hope for ameliorating the impact of violence and trauma. To help children and their families return to the optimal paths of development and functioning, CD-CP partners continuously attempt to learn more about the implications of our respective interventions, as well as the potential benefits and limitations of our coordinated efforts. Whether responding to children who have witnessed the deadly outcome of a domestic dispute between parents, or to a neighborhood that has seen young men die in a shootout, or to a school community that has witnessed the death of classmates and teachers at the hands of fellow students, or to a city and country stunned by the destruction and loss of life resulting from a terrorist attack—a mutual psychoanalytic stance is mobilized and informs the background for response.

This work is supported by the U.S. Department of Justice, which established the National Center for Children Exposed to Violence at the Yale Child Study Center in 1999.

### References

Brown, L. P. (1990), Neighborhood-oriented policing. *Amer. J. Police*, 9(3).

Bureau of Justice Assistance (1994), *Understanding Community Policing: A Framework for Action*. Washington, DC: The Bureau.

Burges Watson, I., Hoffman, L. & Wilson, G. (1988), The neuropsychiatry of post-traumatic stress disorder. *Brit. J. Psychiat.*, 152:164–173.

Freud, A. (1936), *The Ego and the Mechanisms of Defense*. New York: International Universities Press, 1966.

———— & Burlingham, D. T. (1943), *War and Children*. New York: Medical War Books.

———— (1965), *Normality and Pathology in Childhood: Assessments of Development*. New York: International Universities Press.

———— (1968), Indications and contraindications for child analysis. *The Writings of Anna Freud, Vol. 7*. New York: International Universities Press, pp. 110–123.

Freud, S. (1926), Inhibitions, symptoms and anxiety. *Standard Edition*, 20:77–174. London: Hogarth Press, 1959.

Goldstein, H. (1977). *Policing a Free Society*. Cambridge, MA: Ballinger.

Goldstein, J., Freud, A. & Solnit, A. J. (1979), *Before the Best Interests of the Child*. New York: Free Press.

Hellman, I. (1962). Hampstead nursery followup studies: I. Sudden separation and its effect followed over twenty years. *The Psychoanalytic Study of the Child*, 17:159–174. New Haven, CT: Yale University Press.

———— (1983), Work in the Hampstead war nurseries. *Internat. J. Psycho-Anal.*, 64:435–439.

Kelling, G. L. & Moore, M. H. (1989), *The Evolving Strategy of Policing.* Washington, DC: U.S. Dept. of Justice, Office of Justice Programs, National Institute of Justice.

King, M. (1998), *Bangin'* [videorecording]. Boston, MA: Boston Productions, Inc.

Laor, N., Wolmer, L., Mayes, L. C., Golomb, A., Silverberg, D. S., Weizman, R. & Cohen, D. J. (1996), Israeli preschoolers under Scud missile attacks: A developmental perspective on risk-modifying factors. *Arch. Gen. Psychiat.*, 53:416–423.

——— Wolmer, L. & Cohen, D. J. (2001), Mothers' functioning and children's symptoms 5 years after a SCUD missile attack. *Amer. J. Psychiat.*, 158:1020–1026.

——— Wolmer, L., Kora, M., Yucel, D., Spirman, S. & Yazgan, Y. (2002), Posttraumatic, dissociative and grief symptoms in Turkish children exposed to the 1999 earthquakes. *J. Nerv. Ment. Dis.*, 190:824–832.

Marans, S. (1994), Community violence and children's development: Collaborative interventions. In: *Children and Violence*, ed. C. Chiland & J. G. Young. Northvale, NJ: Aronson, pp. 109–124.

——— & Adelman, A. (1997), Experiencing violence in a developmental context. In: *Children in a Violent Society*, ed. J. D. Osofsky. New York: Guilford Press, pp. 202–222.

——— & Cohen, D. J. (1993), Children and inner-city violence: Strategies for intervention. In: *The Psychological Effects of War and Violence on Children*, ed. L. A. Leavitt & N. A. Fox. Hillsdale, NJ: Lawrence Erlbaum Associates, pp. 281–301.

——— Berkman, M. & Cohen, D. (1996), Child development and adaptation to catastrophic circumstances. In: *Minefields in Their Hearts: The Mental Health of Children in War and Communal Violence*, ed. R. J. Apfel & B. Simon. New Haven, CT: Yale University Press, pp. 104–127.

Murphy, R. A. (2002), Mental health, juvenile justice, and law enforcement responses to youth psychopathology. In: *Handbook of Serious Emotional Disturbance in Children and Adolescents*, ed. D. Marsh & M. Fristad. New York: Wiley.

Perry, B. D. (1994), Neurobiological sequelae of childhood trauma: PTSD in children. In: *Catecholamine Function in Posttraumatic Stress Disorder: Emerging Concepts*, ed. M. M. Murburg. Washington, DC: American Psychiatric Press, pp. 233–255.

Pynoos, R. S. & Nader, K. (1989), Children's memory and proximity to violence. *J. Amer. Acad. Child Adolesc. Psychiat.*, 28:236–241.

—— Steinberg, A. M. & Wraith, R. (1995), A developmental model of childhood traumatic stress. In: *Developmental Psychopathology, Vol. 2: Risk, Disorder, and Adaptation*, ed. D. Cicchetti & D. J. Cohen. New York: Wiley, pp. 72–95.

Robertson, J. & Robertson, J. (1969), *John, Seventeen Months, in Residential Nursery for Nine Days*. New York: Distributed by New York University Film Library.

Singleton, J. (1991), *Boyz N the Hood* [videorecording]. Culver City, CA: Columbia Pictures.

Solnit, A. J., Adnopoz, J., Saxe, L., Gardner, J. & Fallon, T. (1997), Evaluating systems of care for children: Utility of the clinical case conference. *Amer. J. Orthopsychiat.*, 67:554–567.

Southwick, S. M., Krystal, J. H., Morgan, C., Johnson, D., Nagy, L. M., Nicolaou, A., Heninger, G. R. & Charney, D. S. (1993), Abnormal noradrenergic function in posttraumatic stress disorder. *Arch. Gen. Psychiat.*, 50:266–274.

Van der Kolk, B., Greenberg, M., Boyd, H. & Krystal, J. (1985); Inescapable shock, neurotransmitters, and addiction to trauma: Toward a psychobiology of post traumatic stress. *Biol. Psychiat.*, 20:314–325.

Yehuda, R. (2002). Posttraumatic stress disorder. *N. Engl. J. Med.*, 346:108–114.

—— McFarlane, A. C. & Shalev, A. Y. (1998), Predicting the development of posttraumatic stress disorder from the acute response to a traumatic event. *Biol. Psychiat.*, 44:1305–1313.

# ❖ 11 ❖

# Children's Exposure to Community Violence
## *Psychoanalytic Perspectives on Evaluation and Treatment*

Howard J. Osofsky  •  Joy D. Osofsky

## The Nature of the Problem

Children's exposure to community violence in the United States is a problem of such significance that it has been characterized as a "public health epidemic" (Rosenberg, O'Carroll, and Powell, 1992; Finkelhor and Dzuiba-Leatherman, 1994; Flannery and Huff, 1998). We have been alerted in a different and more alarming way than ever before to the severity of this problem as a result of the terrorist attacks in New York City and Washington, DC on September 11, 2001, with the resultant death and sequellae for the survivors and witnesses in those cities and throughout the country and the world. In many ways, this tragedy serves as a reminder that many children, especially impoverished, inner-city children, grow up in an environment where they experience terror chronically most days of their lives.

Our decade of experience with a community-based program, the Violence Intervention Program (VIP), addressing the needs of these children and families, is described later in this chapter. Although related in part to transient, age-related demographic changes, children's exposure to violence has declined slightly in recent years; still, the homicide rate is more than double that reported in 1950, according to the National Summary of Injury Mortality Data (Centers for Disease Control and Prevention, 1996). The United States has the highest level of violence exposure of any developed country in the world. Homicide is the third leading cause of death for children 5 to 14 years of age, the second leading cause of death for those ages 15–24; it has been the leading cause of death for African-American youth for more than a decade (Dahlberg and Potter, 2001). It is crucial that we understand what such levels of exposure may mean for children in our country.

While exposure to community violence occurs less frequently for children who do not live in lower socioeconomic neighborhoods, those children are often exposed to violence repeatedly in their homes and in the media (Huesmann and Eron, 1986; Murray, 1997). Exposure to both media violence and family violence crosses socio-economic and cultural boundaries; it occurs in all groups in our society. Its effects are often less visible, or even hidden, in higher socioeconomic groups than in lower strata but, nonetheless, such violence has a significant impact on children during their development and influences their later relationship experiences.

### Community Violence Exposure

Community violence exposure, whether isolated, frequent, or, at times, almost continuous, includes frequent and continual exposure to the use of guns, knives, drugs, and random violence. It is now unusual in urban elementary schools *not* to find children who have been exposed to such negative events. The children who were interviewed as part of the VIP program in New Orleans as well as in other studies lucidly told stories of witnessing violence, including shootings and beatings, as if they were ordinary, everyday events (Bell and Jenkins, 1993; Marans and Cohen, 1993; Groves and Zuckerman, 1997; Jenkins and Bell, 1997; Osofsky, 1997).

In a survey of sixth, eighth, and tenth graders in New Haven, CT in 1992, 40% reported having witnessed at least one violent crime in the past year (Marans and Cohen, 1993). Very few of these inner-city children were able to avoid being exposed to violence and almost all eighth graders knew someone who had been killed in a violent incident. In a study involving 500 children at three elementary schools on the south side of Chicago in 1993, one in four had witnessed a shooting and one third had seen a stabbing (Bell and Jenkins, 1993). In another study, surveying 200 Chicago high school students in 1993, almost two-thirds had seen a shooting and close to one-half had seen a stabbing (Jenkins and Bell, 1997). Three out of five of those who had witnessed a shooting or stabbing indicated that the incident had resulted in a death. Over one-fourth of these high school students reported that they had themselves been victims of severe violence.

Even very young children are exposed to high levels of violence. In a 1993 survey of parents whose children attended a pediatric clinic at a public hospital in Boston in 1993, reports indicated that one of every 10 children under the age of six years had witnessed a shooting or stabbing (Groves et al., 1993). In a 1997 study, African-American third- and fifth-grade children living in a high-violence area of New Orleans were asked to draw pictures of "what happens" in their neighborhoods. They drew in graphic detail pictures of shootings, drug deals, stabbings, fighting, and funerals and reported being afraid of the violence and of something happening to them. Children living with domestic and community violence commonly draw similar pictures (Lewis, Osofsky, and Moore, 1997).

In 1993, an extensive interview study of exposure to violence was conducted with 165 mothers of children, ages 6–10, living in a low-income neighborhood in Washington, DC (Richters and Martinez, 1993). According to police statistics, this neighborhood was characterized as having a moderate level of violence: there might be an occasional murder or violent incident, but violence was not a regular event. Concurrently, another study gathered similar interview data on 53 African-American mothers of children, ages 9–12, in a low-income neighborhood in New Orleans (Osofsky et al., 1993). According to police statistics, this neighborhood had a high level of violence; a murder or more than one violent incident occurred on a regular basis. Some differences in violence exposure were noted to be likely owed, to a considerable extent, to differences in the levels of violence in the two neighborhoods being sampled. The data from both studies, however, clearly showed that children frequently are victims of and witnesses to significant amounts of violence. Fifty-one percent of the New Orleans fifth-graders and 32% of the Washington, DC children had been victims of violence, ranging from being chased or beaten to having a gun held to the head.

While specific rates of exposure to community violence vary depending on the definition of exposure and the nature of the sample, children of all ages are being exposed to community violence at an alarming rate. Such exposure has been linked to high rates of posttraumatic stress symptoms, depressive symptoms, serious behavioral problems and antisocial behavior, and decreased school performance. Overstreet (2000) has suggested that repeated exposure to community violence may influence children to become numbed, demonstrating uncaring behavior toward others and desensitization to aggression. Such children may themselves show increased aggression, acting out, and subsequent antisocial behavior. The problem of children's exposure to community violence is significant. Without intervention efforts, it may increase with age shifts in coming years. It is clear that major efforts need to be undertaken to decrease violence exposure and to mitigate the effects of this exposure when it occurs.

## Impact on Children in School

Exposure to violence is not limited to homes and neighborhoods. For many of our young people, schools, which should be safe havens, are instead sites of violence that affect students' ability to concentrate and be successful in school. The Centers for Disease Control and Prevention in Atlanta, in their recent Surveillance Summaries, reported survey results from a nationally representative sample of students in grades 9–12 for selected risk behaviors both at school and outside of school (Centers for Disease Control and Prevention, 1998). The survey covered the following categories: carried a weapon, carried a gun, participated in a physical fight, injured in a physical fight, threatened or injured on school property, in a physical fight on school property, and having had property stolen or deliberately damaged on school property. The study found alarmingly high incidences of these disturbing behaviors in schools throughout the country.

Students living in inner-city environments commonly provide vivid descriptions of the violence they see and experience, sometimes on a daily basis. A 1994 poll of high school students indicated that 30% of white students and 70% of African-American students knew someone who had been shot within the last five years; 19% of white students and 37% of African-American students identified violence as the biggest problem at school; and 5% of white students and 27% of African-American students reported worrying about shootings at school (Chira, 1994). A Harris poll of 2000 teenagers from around the country indicated that one in eight, and almost two in five from inner cities, said that they carried a weapon to protect themselves. In addition, one in nine, and one in three living in high violence areas, said they had stayed away from school for fear of violence (Appelbone, 1996). This poll was carried out before the many school shootings that have received widespread media exposure and national concern in the past two years. Despite the previously noted data indicating that the overall incidence of violence exposure has been decreasing slightly (although this trend may be transient), national surveys demonstrate increased concern and fears about violence in school, especially among older children (*Time Magazine*, 2000). Thus, in some school and home environments that should be safe for children, they are being exposed to violence.

### Clinical Impact of Children's Exposure to Violence

Both the short and longer term sequelae of violence exposure are significant for children (Osofsky, 1997). Li and colleagues (1998), in a study of 349 low-income African-American urban children (ages 9–15), found that those who had witnessed or were victims of violence showed symptoms of posttraumatic stress disorder similar to those of soldiers coming back from war. The symptoms increased according to the number of violent acts the child had witnessed or experienced. Hill and colleagues (1996) focused on the sociopolitical issues related to violence exposure as well as the importance of support for children by the family, teachers, and community in effective prevention and intervention efforts. This work is consistent with the findings of the VIP program indicating the importance of a broad base of support both for violence prevention and for effective intervention efforts with children exposed to violence (Osofsky, 1997).

Gorman-Smith and Tolan (1998) found that children's exposure to community violence was related to subsequent symptoms of depression and anxiety as well as to aggressive behaviors as reported by the children, their parents, and teachers. In this study, having a mother present in the home seemed to be a major factor in mitigating the relationship between exposure to community violence and subsequent depressive symptoms in the children. Other studies have reported specific symptoms linked to the children's ages, the type and frequency of violence exposure, the relationship to the perpetrators and other victims, and the quality of available supports and services (Marans and Cohen, 1993; Pynoos, 1993). Adding complexity to the children's exposure, in our experience, parents are also often traumatized themselves. Their needs and vulnerability may contribute to their feeling less secure about protecting their children from subsequent violence exposure. Clearly, it is very important for mental health professionals to be attuned to the needs of the parents when working with their traumatized children. For successful outcomes, a supportive community network can be crucial.

In considering the impact on the community at large, and specifically on the school system, it is important to consider that students directly affected need a great deal of understanding by sensitive staff. Further, especially when there has been a shooting or other violent act in or near a school, all the students are, to varying degrees, victims and require an emotionally available and informed staff. In supporting the staff, it is important to recognize that exposure to violence and trauma can lead to feelings of helplessness, hopelessness, and vulnerability not only in the children but also in the adults supporting them. Some children may react with anger and aggression that can lead to behavior and discipline problems in school. Others may withdraw and become depressed, which, while not drawing as much attention as the children's reactions do, can greatly affect their ability to concentrate, their self-esteem, and, consequently, their performance.

Beyond the psychological and behavioral consequences of exposure to violence that may affect children in school, they may come to believe that violence is an acceptable behavior. Children learn violence from what they observe and may conclude that fighting and violent behavior are acceptable inside and outside the classroom. They do not learn to communicate feelings and to negotiate, and may be easily pressured by peers. They may believe that aggressive behaviors lead to attention and respect. Bullying and intimidating behaviors may be other consequences. All these issues need to be understood and addressed for children exposed to violence.

## Conceptualizing Violence Prevention and Intervention Programs from a Psychoanalytic Perspective

Psychoanalysis has been described as more than therapy. It is a method for learning about the mind and also as a theory, a way of understanding the processes of normal, everyday mental functioning through the stages of normal development from infancy to old age. Conceptually, it can be viewed as a psychological, metapsychological, and developmental theory (Stern, 1997). Psychoanalysis seeks to explain how the human mind works. It contributes insight into whatever the human mind produces (American Psychoanalytic Association Website: www.ApsaA.org). The psychoanalytic perspective helps therapists to understand people's strengths and weaknesses and their overall life situations, all extremely important components for effective early intervention.

Psychoanalytic theory may be most helpful and relevant for work with children exposed to violence. Freud's original formulation of childhood trauma centered on the breaching of a stimulus barrier. Later, however, Freud (1926) provided more elaborate developmental definition; he defined a traumatic situation as one in which external and internal real and imagined dangers converge. The experience of external threat accrues from the perceived magnitude of the threat, the unavailability or ineffectiveness of protective actions by self or others, and the felt extreme physical helplessness—all these factors cannot be avoided and are literally out of one's control. The experience of internal threat involves an inability to tolerate one's affective and physiological reactions as well as a sense of impending catastrophic personal consequences. Subjective appraisals of the situation will influence the experience of internal and external threats as well as how the situation is addressed and the internal responses are managed. Especially relevant to a child's exposure to violence, the appraisals and the child's ability to cope will vary with the developmental level of the child, the degree of maturation, previous experiences, and reliance on parents or other caregivers.

On the basis of his psychoanalytically grounded work with traumatized children, Pynoos (1994) stated that the developmental impact on the child may be overlooked if one focuses primarily on posttraumatic symptom reactions. Often the necessary developmental expectations have failed to evolve, so that the child's ability to appraise and respond appropriately to external dangers may be jeopardized. For example, the child may fail to show typical alarm reactions (Krystal, 1978), protective reactions, and ability to resist coercion. He or she may not be able to trust relationships or may fail to show the protective emotions to avoid harm. The child may not have developed a belief in a socially modulated world and may be resigned to having to surrender to unavoidable danger. All these factors point to a failure in normal developmental processes that would ordinarily protect a child both internally and externally from traumatization.

Exposure to a traumatic event may be particularly challenging for a child (Pynoos et al., 1993) because this new and frightening inner model of the world has to be imposed on an inner model that is already undergoing constant revision. For children born into poverty and living under circumstances of chronic violence exposure, their view of themselves and the world around them may be marked by fragmentation, insecurity, inconsistencies, and, at times, chaos.

Developmental factors that influence children's reactions to violence include their appraisal of the threat, the intrapsychic meaning they attribute to the event, prior experiences and supports, their emotional and cognitive means of coping, their capacity to tolerate strong affects, and their ability to adjust to other changes in their life, including losses and grieving. In developing a model to understand the effect of violence exposure on children's development, it is important to take into account biological givens, the children's early experiences, and their current relationship experiences. Both intrapsychic and interpersonal development must be included in the model if we are to understand the development of children born into high-risk environments (Osofsky, 1993).

For a child who does not receive responsive and reciprocal caregiving in the earliest relationship, and who does have the opportunity to experience shared affect states and affect attunement, the outcomes will likely be negative. Without necessary sensitivity to the developmental and emotional needs of the child, there may be a derailment of the normal developmental process, and even a polarization of affect, "the splitting of affect," that is characteristic of borderline pathology (Osofsky, 2000). If the child has difficulty nuancing and modulating early affective experience, resultant responses may lead to increased aggression, anxiety, or depression. Shame related to problems with self-esteem and self-concept may play a role in this process for young children and contribute to an increase in both aggression and withdrawal (Gilligan, 1996).

At least moderate consistency in the development of relationships across generations is assumed by most developmental and psychoanalytic theories. However, for children coming from families where stress and violence characterize their lives, inconsistencies are common. These inconsistencies, which are also contributed to by the stresses of poverty, can lead to marked instability in their lives. Observations of children growing up in poverty—in the inner cities, where sustained and unremitting actual trauma, including physical and sexual abuse, neglect, and violence occur with some regularity—suggest negative behavioral and affective outcomes that likely affect the children's psychic structure (Marans, 1995; Marans and Adelman, 1997; Osofsky, 1997). These children display a range of problem behaviors, including impulsive and acting-out behaviors rather than verbalization, verbal and physical aggression, and little frustration tolerance or future orientation. In such children, object relations are primitive, reflecting, at best, ambivalent interactions with others. Adults are frequently experienced as interchangeable. Many researchers have commented, consistent with our observations, that such children lack the ability for basic trust (Garbarino et al., 1992; Pynoos, Sternberg, and Wraith, 1995). Their defenses are rigid and archaic, interfering with adaptive functioning.

With much exposure to violence, the trauma is often continuous and may overwhelm the child and produce a state of chronic strain (Sandler, 1967), and difficulties with ego organization. Careful follow-up studies are needed to understand the later development of these children. We need to know, for example, how young children who experience abuse or violence, or who observe the death of a parent, friend, or sibling, later subsequently deal with concepts of identity, intimacy, and sexuality. Our observations of very young children exposed to violence reveal negative affective interaction experiences and significant affect dysregulation. Without intervention, these children appear to be at high risk for developing later psychopathology such as conduct disorder, antisocial personality disorder, and, in some cases, borderline personality organization. With psychoanalytically informed interventions, including, when appropriate, brief treatment, positive gains are striking. The gains will, we hope, be long lasting and help the children to master their developmental milestones. This is an area we will be addressing over time.

Healthy intrapsychic and interpersonal development are facilitated by positive experiences of affect attunement (Stern, 1985), empathy (Kohut, 1977), and the ability to think symbolically and internalize positive relationship experiences. Children who grow up in the midst of chronic community and family violence frequently lack the facilitating environment necessary for the nuancing of affects leading to a well-modulated affective experience and thus for healthy ego development (Osofsky, 1993). Primitive defenses and reactions may emerge early in the lives of these children in an attempt to control extreme anxiety and impulses. Early adverse experiences may derail the normal developmental trajectories of infants and young children, compromise their ability to regulate affects, and lead to early behavioral and relationship problems. Further, these early experiences tend to be linked with feelings both of shame and of humiliation (Gilligan, 1996) and with resultant anxiety and problems with impulse control. These, in turn, can contribute to a general alienation of those around them and a reverberating cycle of anger and rejection. Here, too, long-term prospective studies are needed for us to understand outcomes for infants and children raised in violent environments, especially children with poor early relationship experiences. However, based on our current knowledge about early development and retrospective information (Fonagy and Target, 1996) as well as our clinical experience, it is likely that such children, especially those who do not receive effective interventions and support, will find it difficult to develop a healthy sense of self and a capacity for later relationships.

Under such circumstances, helpers (therapists, analysts, teachers, counselors) may react like rescuers, feeling that, if they "take the child home," they will be able to save him or her from a terrible family and environment. Some of this reaction is endemic to work of this type. However, it may also result from frustration and feelings of helplessness when working with this group of people so much in need. It can be discouraging, even depressing, to work with children whose families will not cooperate, sometimes because they cannot, and whose teachers are continually angry at them because of frustration and stress. The mental health caregivers may take on the helplessness and hopelessness of the people they are helping. At the same time, feelings of anger, of victimization, of being the abuser, or the neglecter may emerge. It is crucial to be aware of the countertransference feelings and to be able to obtain feedback and support (Osofsky and Fenichel, 1996).

It is within such a context that the Violence Intervention Program for Children and Families (VIP) originated. In addition to a systems approach to early prevention and intervention, we incorporated a relationship-based perspective to promote change and growth in all individuals involved in the children's lives.

## The Violence Intervention Program

The Violence Intervention Program for Children and Families (VIP) was initiated by the Department of Psychiatry at Louisiana State University Health Sciences Center in 1992 as a direct response to the crisis of rising violence in New Orleans (paralleling that in the United States as a whole) and the fact that ever-increasing numbers of children were being exposed to violence as victims or witnesses.

The philosophy guiding the VIP is a systems approach designed to work with the whole community to solve the problem of violence among our youth. The project aims to decrease violence through a combination of early intervention, counseling, and services to victims, as well as education and prevention forums directed to the needs of police, school administrators and teachers, parents, and children. A vital component of the program is a mutually respectful collaborative involvement with the police department. Mental health professionals are available for ride-alongs to help in violent episodes. The police act as mentors around issues of community safety; the program educates police officers about childhood emotional development, the effects of violence on children and families, and helpful interventions that have led to heightened officer sensitivity when dealing with violent incidents. Over time, VIP has expanded evaluation and treatment services for children who have been exposed to and traumatized by violence. Concurrent with the treatment services for children are parenting groups providing both education and support. Evaluation of the effectiveness of our work has been built into our intervention program from its inception so that we will be able to learn about what works and what does not and determine the changes that are needed to make the program more effective.

Education and evaluation of the police have been ongoing since 1995, with over 800 police officers receiving training in the year 2000. Evaluation of the effectiveness of education provided for police indicates increased sensitivity over the years to the needs of traumatized children as well as more knowledge about and use of resources for referral. The majority of police officers surveyed believe that witnessing community and domestic violence has a negative impact on children. The majority of officers also reported that even very young children are affected by exposure to violence. They report that the education provided them over the years will enable them to talk to the children at the scene of violence and refer them for consultation or counseling by distributing the Hotline cards; they are sure they are now less likely to do nothing for the children at the scene.

In 1995, approximately 100 children and families were referred to our clinic for consultation, therapy, or parental guidance related to exposure to violence. In 1996, as our program expanded, referrals more than doubled to at least 250 children. Since 1998, over 500 traumatized children and families have been seen each year, and more than 3000 direct clinical services are being provided annually to the children and families. Sixty percent of the calls are for children ages 12 and younger; some children are only 1–4 years of age. The number is continuing to grow, not so much because more children are witnessing violence, but, rather, because of increased referrals through police officers, greater knowledge about and respect for the program in the community, and greater recognition of the importance of prevention and early intervention.

By developing the VIP program as a multidisciplinary effort, we have worked to find ways to build relationships among community, police, mental health professionals, and schools to address issues of prevention and services for referred children; these children witness violence and suffer from symptoms related to their exposure such as nightmares, disruptive behavior in school, and, in the most extreme cases, posttraumatic stress disorder. We have employed psychoanalytically informed approaches to understanding children's needs, developing educational programs, and providing clinical care. We continue to problem solve with police to improve interactions and refine strategies for talking with child witnesses when violent incidents, such as homicides, are being investigated.

Toward this end, the police have collaboratively worked with VIP to develop the COPS for Kids program. COPS for Kids was conceived by community police officers initially in three public housing developments, and ultimately in five, as a way to keep children and teenagers off the streets in the summer. Summer in many areas of inner cities is often a time when nonviolent juvenile crime, such as break-ins, petty theft, and the like, increases dramatically. With the cooperation and collaboration of the New Orleans school system, the New Orleans Police Foundation, LSU Extension, VIP at LSU Health Sciences Center, and others in the community, the police developed this program for these children and adolescents.

During the mornings, educational programs, including mentoring and tutoring, were made available. In the afternoons, the youngsters went on field trips to the zoo, parks, the aquarium, and area businesses. Many of the young people involved in the program had never before traveled out of their neighborhoods. Police officers who worked in the program often even obtained licenses so that they could drive the school buses to transport the children. They and the other staff obviously served as role models for the children. The VIP program scheduled classes in violence prevention, conflict resolution, and building empathy and negotiation skills. The staff of VIP also offered counseling to individuals or groups of children when needed. An important byproduct of this counseling and mentoring program for young people living in public housing was a marked increase in the adolescents' (and their families') trust of police officers and a dramatic fall in juvenile crime. Through VIP, we also work with parents to enhance their strengths and sense of competence and help them find ways to protect their children and keep them safe. Further, we work to build strengths within the school system and the community at large to help parents and children alike.

## Countertransference Issues in Working with Traumatized Children and Families

In this work, mental health professionals are dealing with very difficult situations, which expectably can elicit very strong and complex emotions in the treaters. Parents are dealing with their grief resulting from the tragic loss of a child or other family member or with their own victimization. Assaulted children may have been brutalized emotionally as well as physically. Children exposed to violence may have witnessed the killing or serious injury of parents, siblings, other relatives or friends. Their wounds, on many levels, can be great and their suffering intense. This suffering can elicit strong countertransferential feelings in the therapists (Osofsky and Fenichel, 1996). Further, the teachers, childcare providers, health care and social service workers, and the police officers called to the scene of the violence may be suffering. The other professionals may also have witnessed the violence. At the very least, they all deal with the aftermath. They all must cope with the resultant and ongoing psychological effects, for example, the disruptive, aggressive, inattentive, and withdrawn behavior typical of traumatized children.

The term "burnout" has become familiar throughout the helping professions as a way to describe a practitioner's reduced effectiveness, often accompanied by feelings of helplessness, hopelessness, frustration, anger, or cynicism. Parents, friends, teachers, police officers, and other members of the community may have similar, if at times unrecognized, feelings. Likewise, countertransference reactions, which occur frequently when one is working with traumatized children and families, can interfere with the therapist's ability to understand the patient and be available; the countertransference can adversely affect the therapeutic technique. Being aware of these reactions can help us to understand the inner world of victimized children so that we can offer sensitive and effective therapeutic interventions.

Many helpers deal with countertransference issues on a daily basis in work with traumatized children—the police officers who see young children at the scene of a violent incident, school teachers, parents and other supportive persons, mental health professionals who try to help the children and families. Especially early on in their experience, therapists and others may feel a desire to rush in and "make it all better." Given the limitations of this approach or, at times, the enormity of the trauma, therapists may feel frustration, anger, and a wish to distance themselves from their discomfort, at times leading to premature termination of treatment. In the VIP program, problems with countertransference reactions seem to occur most often in the following situations: (1) in acute crisis situations, such as when police must confront the senseless killing of a young child; (2) when parents at home or teachers at school need to cope with unruly, disruptive, and aggressive children on a daily basis; and (3) with new trainees whose first reactions are often to "rescue" the children because they feel that they can help them much more than their parents or teachers can.

We strongly believe that early interventions at the time of and immediately after exposure to violence significantly reduce negative outcomes. Indeed, we find that the longer the interval from the violence exposure to the referral for therapy, the more intransigent are the symptoms. The kind of work we advocate, however, will quickly "burn out" a staff without adequate time-out, support, and respite from the work. Teachers who work in the classroom every day with children who are traumatized by violence exposure and whose behavior is problematic, and who are falling behind educationally, need to be aware of and have the support to deal with their frustrations as well as countertransference feelings. Nader (1994) recommends the following guidelines for professionals working with traumatized young children and their families: (1) be willing to hear anything; (2) recognize the phasic nature of trauma recovery; and (3) recognize the need for occasional "time-outs" in therapy from direct focus on the trauma.

## Conclusion

Children's exposure to community violence represents a major problem in our country. As exemplified by the Violence Intervention Program, the effective preventive intervention models presented here draw on a psychoanalytic underpinning and have been conceptualized from a systems perspective and psychoanalytic orientation. The programs are designed to prevent or reduce the risk following violence exposure. They address mental health problems following exposure, comorbid conditions, interference with normal developmental progression, academic performance, family functioning, and prevention of subsequent behavioral and conduct disturbances. Ultimately, the programs will also allow the children a fuller range of comfortable options in their future adult roles.

A number of programs, such as VIP, work with police officers, educators and parents to increase their sensitivity and responsiveness to traumatized children and to inform them about appropriate and available referral sources, as well as to provide evaluation and treatment services for identified children. A psychoanalytic underpinning helps with this work in important ways. From a therapeutic perspective, the mental health professionals are better able to understand and work with the children's strengths and weaknesses and overall life situation. From a systems approach, a psychoanalytic perspective allows for a fuller conceptualization of a chaotic environment or social situation—such as, at times, the inner city schools or neighborhoods where we work—and an enhanced ability to work in a reflective and collaborative manner with diverse professionals and community service agencies. The approach of psychoanalytically grounded professionals increases the depth of the programmatic interventions. Further, and of much importance, a psychoanalytic approach greatly increases understanding of transference and countertransference issues, allowing for more flexibility than otherwise and for effective problem-solving strategies.

On the basis of our experience in the VIP, we recognize the value of understanding children exposed to community violence in terms of their developmental phases and within a social context. We must address the intrapsychic conflicts and disturbance within each child, the trauma that has been experienced, and the chaotic and distressing environments that frequently are important components of the child's life experience. We have learned through our program, which has been ongoing for nine years, that early intervention with traumatized children is effective and very likely prevents later, more serious difficulties. We have seen impressive therapeutic successes in young children who have experienced very serious traumas. In contrast, in the many referrals of children who were traumatized years earlier, dysfunctional behaviors and symptoms generally have been more severe and difficult to ameliorate. We, like others who work in this area (Marans and Adelman, 1997; Murphy, Pynoos, and James, 1997), firmly believe that children exposed to community violence need thoughtful support and early clinical intervention. When difficulties are unrecognized and left untreated, the prognosis is considerably more guarded. Without appropriate intervention, there is a great likelihood of increased psychopathology, impaired developmental progress, and a distorted view of the world that may seriously affect the child's development and contribute to the cycle of violence.

## References

American Psychoanalytic Association Website Home Page (2001), Retrieved from http://www.apsaa.org.

Appelbone, P. (1996), Crime fear is seen forcing change in youth behavior. *The New York Times*, p. A6, January 12.

Bell, C. C. & Jenkins, E. J. (1993), Community violence and children on Chicago's southside. *Psychiatry*, 56:46–54.

——— & ——— (1997), Exposure and response to community violence among children and adolescents. In: *Children in a Violent Society*, ed. J. D. Osofsky. New York: Guilford, pp. 9–31.

Centers for Disease Control and Prevention (1996), *National Summary of Injury Mortality Data, 1987–1994*. Atlanta, GA: National Center for Injury Prevention and Control.

——— (1998), *CDC Surveillance Summaries*, 47 (No. SS-3). Atlanta, GA: August 14.

Chira, S. (1994), Teenagers in a poll report worry and distrust of adults. *The New York Times*, p. 1, July 10.

Dahlberg, L. L. & Potter, L. B. (2001), Youth violence: Developmental pathways and prevention challenges. *Amer. J. Prev. Med.*, 20:3–14.

Finkelhor, D. & Dziuba-Leatherman, J. (1994), Victimization of children. *Amer. Psychol.*, 49:173–183.

Flannery, D. & Huff, C. R. (1998), *Youth Violence: Prevention, Intervention, and Social Policy*. Washington, DC: American Psychiatric Press.

Fonagy, P. & Target, M. (1996), Predictors of outcome in child psychoanalysis: A retrospective study of 763 cases at the Anna Freud Centre. *J. Amer. Psychoanal. Assn.*, 44:27–77.

Freud, S. (1926), Inhibitions, symptoms, and anxiety. *Standard Edition*, 20:77–175. London: Hogarth Press, 1959.

Garbarino, J., Dubrow, N., Kostelny, K. & Pardo, C. (1992), *Children in Danger: Coping with the Consequence of Community Violence*. San Francisco, CA: Jossey-Bass.

Gilligan, J. (1996), *Violence: Our Deadly Epidemic and Its Causes*. New York: Plenum Press.

Gorman-Smith, D. & Tolan, P. (1998). The role of exposure to community violence and developmental problems among inner-city youth. *Develop. & Psychopathol.*, 10:99–114.

Groves, B. M. & Zuckerman, B. (1997), Interventions with parents and caregivers of children who are exposed to violence. In: *Children in a Violent Society*, ed. J. D. Osofsky. New York: Guilford, pp. 183–201.

———— Zuckerman, B., Marans, S. & Cohen, D. (1993), Silent victims: Children who witness violence. *J. Amer. Med. Assn.*, 269:262–264.

Hill, H. M., Levermore, M., Twaite, J. & Jones, L. (1996), Exposure to community violence and social support as predictors of anxiety and social and emotional behavior among African-American children. *J. Child & Family Stud.*, 5:399–414.

Huessman, L. R. & Eron, L. D. (1986), *Television and the Aggressive Child: A Cross-National Comparison*. Hillsdale, NJ: Lawrence Erlbaum Associates.

Jenkins, E. J. & Bell, C. C. (1997), Violent cities, violent streets: Children draw their neighborhoods. In: *Children in a Violent Society*, ed. J. D. Osofsky. New York: Guilford Press, pp. 277–299.

Kohut, H. (1977), *The Restoration of the Self*. New York: International Universities Press.

———— (1978), Trauma and affects. *The Psychoanalytic Study of the Child*, 33:81–116. New Haven, CT: Yale University Press.

Li, X., Howard, D., Stanton, B., Rachuba, L. & Cross, S. (1998), Distress symptoms among urban African-American children and adolescents: A psychometric evaluation of the Checklist of Children's Distress Symptoms. *Arch. Pediat. & Adolesc. Med.*, 152:569–577.

Marans, S. (1995), *The Police–Mental Health Partnership*. New Haven, CT: Yale University Press.

———— & Adelman, A. (1997), Experiencing violence in developmental context. In: *Children in a Violent Society*, ed. J. D. Osofsky. New York: Guilford Press, pp. 202–222.

———— & Cohen, D. (1993), Children and inner-city violence: Strategies for intervention. In: *Psychological Effects of War and Violence on Children*, ed. L. Leavitt & N. Fox. Hillsdale, NJ: Lawrence Erlbaum Associates, pp. 281–302.

Morse, J. (2000), Looking for trouble: More and more schools are trying to spot the potential killers in their midst. But what about the innocents? *Time*, 155:50, April 24.

Murphy, L., Pynoos, R. S. & James, C. B. (1997), The trauma/grief-focused group psychotherapy module of an elementary school-based violence prevention/intervention program. In: *Children in a Violent Society,* ed. J. D. Osofsky. New York: Guilford Press, pp. 223–255.

Murray, J. (1997), Media violence and youth. In: *Children in a Violent Society,* ed. J. D. Osofsky. New York: Guilford Press, pp. 72–96.

Nader, K. (1994), Countertransference in the treatment of acutely traumatized children. In: *Countertransference in the Treatment of PTSD,* ed. J. P. Wilson & J. D. Lindy. New York: Guilford Press, pp. 179–205.

Osofsky, J. D. (1993), Applied psychoanalysis: How research with infants and adolescents at high psychosocial risk informs psychoanalysis. *J. Amer. Psychoanal. Assn.,* 41:193–207.

——— (1997), *Children in a Violent Society.* New York: Guilford Press.

——— (2000), Early developmental issues for understanding borderline personality organization. In: *Handbook of Borderline Personality Disorder,* ed. O. Kernberg, B. Dulz & U. Sachsse. New York: Schattauer.

——— & Fenichel, E. (1996), *Islands of Safety: Assessing and Treating Young Victims of Violence.* Washington, DC: Zero to Three/National Center for Infants, Toddlers, and Families.

——— Wewers, S., Hann, D. M. & Fick, A. C. (1993), Chronic community violence: What is happening to our children? *Psychiatry,* 56:36–45.

Overstreet, S. (2000), Exposure to community violence: Defining the problem and understanding the consequences. *J. Child & Fam. Stud.,* 9:7–25.

Pynoos, R. (1993), Traumatic stress and developmental psychopathology in children and adolescents. In: *American Psychiatric Press Review of Psychiatry,* ed. J. M. Oldham, M. B. Riba & A. Tasman. Washington, DC: American Psychiatric Press, pp. 205–238.

——— & Giller, E. (1994), *Posttraumatic Stress Disorder: A Clinical Review.* New York: Sedran Press.

——— Nader, K., Black, D., Kaplan, T., Hendriks, J., Gordon, R., Wraith, R., Green, A. & Herman, J. (1993), The impact of trauma on children and adolescents. In: *International Handbook of Traumatic Stress Syndrome,* ed. J. P. Wilson & B. Raphael. New York: Plenum Press, pp. 535–657.

——— Sternberg, A. M. & Wraith, R. (1995), A developmental model of childhood traumatic stress. In: *Manual of Developmental*

*Psychopathology: Risk, Disorder, and Adaptation*, ed. D. Cicchetti & D. J. Cohen. New York: Wiley, pp. 72–95.

Richters, J. E. (1993), Community violence and children's development: Toward a research agenda for the 1990's. *Psychiatry*, 56:3–6.

———— & Martinez, P. (1993), The NIMH community violence project: I. Children as victims of and witnesses to violence. *Psychiatry*, 56:7–21.

Rosenberg, M. L., O'Carroll, P. & Powell, K. (1992), Let's be clear: Violence is a public health problem. *J. Amer. Med. Assn.*, 267:3071–3072.

Sandler, J. (1967), Trauma, strain and development. In: *Psychic Trauma*, ed. S. S. Furst. New York: International University Press, pp. 154–173.

Stern, D. (1985). *The Interpersonal World of the Infant.* New York: Basic Books

———— (1997), How far is empirical research relevant to psychoanalytic theory and practice? The example of research in infancy. A discussion with Daniel Stern and Andre Green. The Psychoanalysis Unit, University College London, November.

# ❖ 12 ❖

## Early Mental Health Intervention and Prevention
### *The Implications for Government and the Wider Community*

Peter Fonagy  ◆  Anna Higgitt

### The General Relationship Between Policy and Developmental Research

Historically, psychoanalysts have shrunk from involvement with public policy. The nature of a psychoanalyst's commitment to an individual, the intensely personal nature of the interaction, which sustains the 'no holds barred' study of subjectivity, is experienced by most analysts as incompatible with a commitment to populations, institutions, organizations, and other faceless systems. This attitude, of course, is illogical. As citizens, we are all too painfully aware that institutions consist of all of us as individuals, and that government policy that affects particular populations affects everyone individually. Thus the study of subjectivity is essential to an understanding of populations, government policy, and public initiative. The absence of this perspective is, to our mind, responsible for the general failure of economists to anticipate changes that depend on an appreciation of the irrational rather than the rational person.

Psychoanalysis, as a discipline committed to the study of unconscious processes, arguably has a better understanding of irrational aspects of behavior than almost any other discipline. Nowhere is this conclusion more self-evident than in the study of early development. Psychoanalytic developmental theory has two sources of inspiration. The original psychoanalytic interest in discovering the residues of childhood experience projected onto the screen of adult personality as templates of relationships organizing memories, or even as bodily experiences, has recently been coupled with a second source of inspiration: psychoanalytically oriented behavioral observations of infants and young children. Both these lines of knowledge have contributed to increasing concern with the formative aspects of early experience. While psychoanalytic theory has, since its inception, claimed that the first years of life contain both risk and protection for later psychological disturbance, it was not until some of the greatest figures in the field (Rene Spitz, Peter Wolff, Robert Emde, Daniel Stern) succeeded in translating some very general principles of early relationship experience into behavioral observations that psychoanalytically informed initiatives to prevent later psychological disturbance could begin. Psychoanalysts, perhaps the first to provide serious developmental models to be used in prevention-intervention, and government policy, were soon joined by other developmental specialists. It is both gratifying and instructive to observe that in this context, psychoanalytic ideas, far from being rejected or the subject of ridicule, were warmly embraced by mainstream researchers and policy makers.

Naturally, the relationship between policy and developmental research is far from simple. In most areas researchers are not of a single mind about policy matters—there are different bodies of knowledge, a broad range of beliefs and values, and different criteria for the hardness of data. For example, among the growing number of mental health professionals who currently believe that relatively more resources should be allocated to prevention as opposed to treatment, there are still sharp differences of opinion about the types of prevention activities to be recommended to policy makers. Some would argue for programs focused on those at risk (Coie et al., 1993); others seek to build and maintain psychological wellness across the population from early on (Cowen, 2000).

Prevention of suboptimal mental health is far broader than intervention to prevent mental illness because there is significant interdependency between physical, social, and cognitive development as well as psychological functioning (Cicchetti et al., 2000).

The policy justification for prevention can be summarized as follows:

- The majority of people do not receive mental health input from even the best designed services until they have longstanding and serious problems that are resistant to change and are very costly in both time and resources.
- Even those interventions with the best evidence base (pharmacotherapy, psychotherapy) are far less than 100% effective, arguably because they are used so late in the evolution of a disorder.
- Systems resources are insufficient to meet all demands, and therefore often only subtherapeutic doses of an intervention of known effectiveness may be offered.
- Even highly effective mental health treatment services rarely make a serious impact on the population-prevalence of the disorder.

An acute issue concerning the nature of evidence in prevention science has to do with the view that observational evidence is an inadequate basis for the formulation of health policy. The argument goes as follows: evidence is required that an intervention is effective before it can be recommended for implementation as part of a prevention program. The only acceptable evidence for this is a randomized, controlled trial. Yet, for years, critics of the dietary fat/plasma cholesterol theory of the aetiology of coronary heart disease claimed that there was no evidence that reducing cholesterol would benefit patients or indeed that it might be harmful. This opinion flew in the face of a wealth of observational evidence from observational studies. With the advent of the 4S and WOSCOPS studies[1] showing the effectiveness of statins in lowering plasma cholesterol and reducing primary and secondary occurrence of coronary heart disease, most critics of the preventive benefits of statins have been cholesterol converted. How many have died in the service of their commitment to science? The randomized controlled trial (RCT) is the best tool we have for evaluating medical interventions for our patients. But the further upstream we go in our search for causes of disorder, the less applicable is the RCT. An RCT to improve the social capital is beyond our grasp. We must, therefore, rely on observational evidence and judgment to formulate public

---

1. Scandinavian Simvastatin Survival Study; West of Scotland Coronary Prevention Study.

health policies. These formulations should not take place in the absence of evidence, but we must not be paralyzed into inaction while we wait for the evidence to be absolutely unimpeachable.

Prevention that aims to reduce inequalities in morbidity within a society may need to be quite different from an intervention that reduces morbidity as a whole. Many prevention-interventions increase inequalities rather than decrease them, because it is the most socially excluded who are least likely to benefit from those interventions.

## The Role of Early Experience in Shaping Neural Organization

### Context

The past two decades have seen a sharper focus on the earliest years of life for the promotion of optimal development in our children. There have been legislative changes to ensure that both parents can have paid leave at the time of the birth of their child. These and other measures indicate a government-level recognition of the importance of parents' spending time with their child. Even the British Government has invested £452 million (including £15 million for research) over three years to deliver Sure Start (a national program aimed at improving services for young children). Initiatives such as these have been backed by studies of behavioral outcomes and early intervention in various at-risk populations. These include studies of: (1) the effects of prenatal nutrition and exposure to toxic substances on brain and behavior development (e.g., Morgan and Gibson, 1991); (2) the strong influence of the quality of nutrition and stimulation on brain development in early life (Grantham-McGregor et al., 1991; VanPelt et al., 1994); (3) the effects of maternal depression in pregnancy and infancy on the later cognitive and emotional functioning of children (e.g., Goodman and Gotlib, 1999); and (4) the effects of early interventions for improving the cognitive, academic, and social functioning of children from disadvantaged backgrounds (e.g., Campbell and Ramey, 1994) and in children with a variety of genetic brain developmental disorders such as childhood autism (e.g., Dawson and Osterling, 1997).

Media interest has been almost overwhelming. A White House Conference in 1997, a special edition of *Newsweek* (1997), and a certain triumphalism on the part of pressure groups (e.g., Families at Work), have suggested to the scientific community that a target might have been overshot. For example, Bruer (1999) argued that the media have been misguided in promoting what he called the myth that the first three years of a baby's life can determine the child's long-range outcome. Let us consider some persuasive and robust findings from neuroscience that are undoubtedly relevant to early developmental interventions.

### Early Brain Growth and Synaptogenesis

Early in a child's life, the brain produces trillions more synapses than are found in adulthood. In humans, rapid synapse formation begins in the first postnatal months and reaches highest densities at about three months in the sensory cortex and two- to three-and-a-half years in the frontal cortex (Huttenlocher and Dabholkar, 1997). These, and other growth spurts have been linked to the acquisition of capacities essential to human function (Diamond and Goldman-Rakic, 1989). The proliferation of synapses is followed by the selective elimination of synapses, presumably in the natural process of neural net formation (Rumelhart and McClelland, 1986). Put simply, neuroscience and developmental science have clearly demonstrated that early life is a time of truly remarkable growth in both the brain and behavior. Still very little is known though about how early experiences (e.g., parenting) actually influence neural organization (e.g., the rate or patterns of synaptic formation or pruning).

It is known that experience plays a role in selecting and establishing preferentially active synapses through some kind of neural competitive process (Edelman, 1987). Once a specific pattern of neuronal groups is selected, exposure to the same or similar stimulus is likely to activate preferentially previously selected neuronal groups. In this way, developing neural patterns become stabilized (Edelman, 1989). It has been suggested that the predictability of caregiver behavior in early relationships may therefore be considered critical to the formation of neural networks for relationship representation (Schore, 1997). It is precisely such speculations that have given the premature application of neuroscience to prevention and early intervention work such a poor scientific name. What has been well established is the vulnerability of the visual system to a lack of early stimulation (Cynader, 1994) and the deleterious effects for cortical development of social deprivation in small mammals (e.g., dams not licking their newborn offspring) (Sapolsky, 1997).

### Sensitive Periods and the Long-Term Effects of Early Experience

It is known that sensitive periods of brain development exist (Knudsen, 1999)—that is, that there are specific times in development when certain experiences are needed for normal brain development. Developments when the brain is "ready" for certain types of information have been termed "experience expectant." It has been argued that the overproliferation of synapses in early postnatal life reflects the brain's readiness to receive expected information in this period, the subset of synapses being selectively retained depending on particular experience (Black et al., 1998).

*Effects of Early Stress.* Numerous studies have documented the negative effects of exposure to early stress. In particular, prenatal exposure to stress has been shown to have deleterious effects on the development of the offspring. For example, in response to stress, offspring of pregnant rats injected with adrenocorticotropin hormone (ACTH) showed increased basal levels of corticosterone and decreased levels (Fameli, Kitraki, and Stylianopoulou, 1994). The young of stressed mother monkeys manifested increased disturbed behavior (e.g., clinging to other monkeys) (Schneider, 1992). Multigenerational effects have been observed in the caregiving behavior of female offspring of rats stressed during pregnancy (Weinstock, Fride, and Hertzberg, 1988).

There are now numerous demonstrations of abnormal life-span stress responses in rat pups exposed to separation stress. In fact, as we gain in our understanding of how genes work, we discover that at least part of each gene is a control mechanism for the process of transcription, in other words this control mechanism determines whether a gene will be expressed. Internal and external experiences, hormones, stress, learning, and social interaction all alter the binding of transcription regulators (Kandel, 1998). For instance, rat pups separated from their mother in the first two weeks of life showed a permanent increase in the expression of genes controlling the secretion of CRF (corticotrophin releasing factor), a stress hormone (Plotsky and Meaney, 1993). However, this lifelong vulnerability to stress would be reversed if the mothers showed increased physical care of their pups once reunited (Liu et al., 1997). Similarly, it has been demonstrated that handling newborn rat pups once a day in the first three weeks of their life leads to improved function of the stress system throughout the life cycle (lower basal corticosterone concentration and faster physiological recovery in stressful situations) (Meaney et al., 1988). Clearly, then, the question for policy makers is simply to learn which aspects of the environment influence these control mechanisms in humans.

What is known about the influence of early postnatal stress in human development? Studies of early maltreatment have consistently confirmed the deleterious physiological consequences of maladaptive parenting both at the autonomic nervous system (ANS) (DeBellis et al., 1999) and the cortical level (Pollak et al., 1997). Children brought up in circumstances of family instability have an increased incidence of insulin-dependent diabetes (Hales, 1997) relative to children from stable families. Associations with physical illness such as these are explicable by the excessive involvement of the stress hormone (HPA) axis. The evidence, however, is better for nonhuman primates (Shively and Clarkson, 1994). We know that secure attachment relationships buffer the cortisol responses of behaviorally inhibited 18-month-olds to a novel situation (Nachmias et al., 1996). It is only inhibited toddlers who are insecurely attached who experience an increase in salivary cortisol to novel stimuli; they also show lower levels of coping competence (affective sharing, social referencing, inquisitive vocalization). The same group of researchers found that attachment security moderated the cortisol response of 15-month-olds to inoculation distress (Gunnar et al., 1996). These data suggest that, especially for temperamentally inhibited or fearful children, sensitive, responsive caretaking may be an important factor in modulation of the HPA axis.

One of the most profound long-term naturalistic studies of early deprivation occurred with Romanian orphanage children. They experienced significant deprivation until their adoption into homes in Europe, Canada, and the United States. About six years post-adoption the effects of early institutional rearing on cortisol levels and quality of attachment security were examined (Gunnar and Chisholm, 1999). Children who had experienced eight or more months of institutional rearing had significantly higher salivary cortisol compared with sex-, SES-, and age-matched controls and compared with children who had experienced four or fewer months of institutional life. Further, a significant positive correlation between evening cortisol levels and time in institution suggests that the longer the exposure to deprivation, the greater the effect on the HPA axis. Moreover, securely attached institutionalized children were more likely to show normal cortisol levels.

*Maternal Depression.* It has been argued that extreme circumstances, such as those of the studies of children in Eastern European orphanages, have little relevance to the concerns of typical parents (Bruer, 1999). In fact, even less extreme variations in early parenting related to the parent's own emotional well-being appear to have significant long-term effects on children's brain and emotional development. Evidence for this conclusion comes from studies of the effects of maternal depression. Children of mothers who experienced affective disorder in the early postnatal years are at risk of developing problems in self-regulation, difficulties in sleep regulation, mood disorders, academic difficulties, behavior problems, and problems in peer relationships (Coghill et al., 1986; Alpern and Lyons-Ruth, 1993; Goodman and Gotlib, 1999; Kurstjens and Wolke, 2001). Toddlers of depressed mothers have been found to display fewer positive affiliative behaviors toward their mothers and higher levels of hostile aggressive behavior (Dawson et al., 1999). By early childhood, children of depressed mothers have a 29% chance of developing a behavioral or emotional disorder as compared with 8% of children of medically ill parents (Hammen et al., 1990, 1999). The impact of early postnatal depression appears to be enduring, at least until middle childhood (Alpern and Lyons-Ruth, 1993; Civic and Holt, 2000).

The most likely mechanism mediating these effects is the mother's reduced ability to interact with her infant in a way that facilitates the infant's development. A metaanalysis of 46 observational studies looking at the association between depression and parenting behavior revealed that the link between depression and parenting appears strongest for negative maternal behavior (irritability and hostility) (Lovejoy et al., 2000). The evidence appears less strong in cases of disengagement from the child and least strong for a reduction in positive maternal behaviors. Current depression tended to be associated with the largest effects, particularly for negative maternal behavior, but a history of depression still had a significant impact on parenting behavior.

In any case, there is a neurophysiological level at which depressed mothers appear to affect their child. Studies have demonstrated reduced electrical brain activity over the left frontal scalp region in 14–15 month-old infants of depressed mothers (Dawson et al., 1997). Those atypical EEG patterns appear to be linearly related to the severity of maternal depression (Dawson et al., 1997) and were also observable in the interaction of 13–15 month-olds with a familiar experimenter (Dawson et al., 1999). It has been suggested that infants "imitate" the mother's depressed behavior, whereas other researchers have hypothesized that children fail to develop adequate means to regulate arousal and negative affect (Commings and Daries, 1994). There is substantial evidence to suggest that contingent responding to an infant's spontaneous expressions of intentionality might be crucial to the development of self-organization and self-regulation (Bahrick and Watson, 1985; Watson, 1995; Watson et al., 1996; Gergely and Watson, 1999). Causal statistical analyses indicated that a mother's insensitivity to her infant mediated the relation between maternal depression and abnormalities of infant frontal EEG activity (Dawson, Ashman, and Carver, 2000). These speculations about preventable influences should be qualified by pointing to the potentially toxic aspects of the prenatal (intrauterine) environment for these children as well as to the influence of genetic factors.

## Implications for Social Policy

The following may be assumed to be established facts in this complex field: (1) the prenatal and early postnatal years are a time during which remarkable growth occurs in both brain organization and behavioral development; (2) these years are likely to represent a "sensitive period" with respect to the effects of nutrition, exposure to toxins and possibly stress; (3) this period also seems to be a sensitive one with respect to the long-term beneficial effects of early intervention on brain and behavioral development for some genetically based disorders; and (4) evidence suggests that parental mental health during the first years of a child's life is a significant factor with respect to early brain activity and behavior and long-term behavioral outcome.

*Timing.* While prevention and early intervention efforts should not focus exclusively on the earliest years of development, such efforts should begin as early as possible. By efforts directed toward optimal prenatal and infant health and toddler development, the long-term negative consequences of factors having their greatest influences in early development and setting the stage for future development may be avoided or minimized. The increasing number of children in alternative care and the growing number of late-placed adoptions as a percentage of full adoptions (Howe, 1998; Quinton et al., 1998; Minty, 1999) face service providers with a key challenge: how best to serve children who come to adoption or fostering with a history of severe neglect or deprivation. We know that placement breakdowns are extremely likely with this group of children and that behavioral problems in the children contribute to these breakdowns (Quinton et al., 1998), but we know too little about what might be helpful for the adoptive or foster parents in meeting the child's needs.

The most powerful arguments for early intervention come from researchers into delinquency and criminality (e.g., Loeber and Farrington, 2000). The argument tends to run something like this: (1) The foundations for prosocial and, by implication, antisocial behavior are established in the first five years of life (Kochanska, Murray, and Coy, 1997; Kochanska and Murray, 2000). These foundations are likely to include numerous individual, relational and systemic processes by which intervention is thought to be effective (see Loeber et al., 2000, for a review). (2) Preschool children already engage in antisocial behavior and dealing with them has been an insoluble challenge for most juvenile justice authorities (Office of Juvenile Justice and Delinquency Prevention, 1998). (3) Early disruptive behavior in toddlers (2–3 years) increases the risk of a child's later delinquency (7–12 years) by 200%–300% (Loeber and Stouthamer-Loeber, 1998; Loeber et al., 2000). (4) Most juvenile justice resources are spent on adolescent offenders, not on child delinquents, and consequently are not in proportion to the risk of long-term, serious outcomes (Children's Secretariat, 1999). These arguments are extremely compelling both from a financial and from a public health (the good health of the average citizen) point of view.

*Prenatal Development.* Prevention efforts that promote healthy prenatal development should focus on heightened public awareness, outreach efforts, and intervention programs related to improving prenatal nutrition, reducing fetal exposure to toxins, and minimizing maternal stress and psychopathology in pregnancy. Prenatal screening should include a prenatal assessment of mental health so that appropriate psychological or medical interventions can begin at this time. Intervention programs for pregnant women suffering from alcohol and drug addiction are needed.

*Maternal Mental Health.* A brief assessment of mother's mental health should be included as part of regular well-baby clinics along with educational materials about infant nutrition and behavioral development. Health care workers need to be trained to respond to these needs or to involve graduate primary-care mental health workers. Specific efforts should be made to include the deprived areas, as evidence indicates that commonly preventive and early intervention initiatives increase rather than decrease inequalities in provision.

*Infant Health.* Continued efforts to identify psychopathology in infancy should be supported. Genetic and developmental disorders need to be identified early; additional public and professional education will be necessary to achieve this aim. Further, parents who seek help for their children should be strongly supported by government agencies through the provision of accessible services, nonstigmatizing aid programs, and the active addressing of barriers to service use.

*Cross Government Collaboration.* In the light of the multiple risk factors involved, ensuring normal brain development of children must entail collaboration by multiple agencies—not just health, but also social services, education, and judicial systems (crime prevention and police). Many of these considerations have had a major impact on government policies around the world.

## Types of Prevention Programs

### Relation-Based Early Family Interventions

Relation-based early family interventions are among the most effective early interventions, at least in terms of postintervention effect. In the Durlak and Wells (1997) metaanalysis, the effect size (ES) was .87, indicating that around 80% benefited significantly. A more recent metaanalysis by Kendrick and colleagues (2000) found 34 studies, of which 17 reported significant improvement in a standardized measure of the quality of home environment and 27 studies of which 21 reported significantly improved parenting outcomes.

Among the best-known programs are the Infant Health and Development Program (Brooks-Gunn et al., 1994) targeting low-birth-weight infants with three years of home visits, an educational program in specially designed preschools, and parent group meetings. During the intervention there were significant benefits to IQ and health status and a reduction in behavioral problems. Two years postintervention, only the heavier babies (2–2.5kg) showed continuing IQ benefits. The physical presence of a home visitor and educational supportive input are unlikely to benefit infants from high-risk families in the long run. Two large United States randomized controlled trials have yielded negative results (Villar et al., 1992; Oda, Heilbron and Taylor, 1995) and several studies found limited sustainability (Lally, Mangione, and Honig, 1988; Black et al., 1994).

By contrast, the Elmira Project (Olds, Henderson, Chamberlin, and Tatelbaum, 1986; Olds, Henderson, Tatelbaum, and Chamberlin, 1986) chose a high-risk population, made contact in the 25th week of pregnancy, visited for two years with decreasing frequency, and advised on parenting techniques, enhancement of social support, and basic education. Benefits included a reduction in emergency-room visits and verified child abuse and improved child management practices. While some of the benefits did not last, the IQ gains, reduction in child behavioral problems, and maternal employment remained robust (Olds, Henderson, and Kitzman, 1994; Olds, Henderson, and Tatelbaum, 1994). At 15 years (Olds et al., 1997) low socioeconomic status (SES) unmarried nurse-visited mothers made fewer social service claims and had fewer arrests or convictions. The program has been successfully replicated in Memphis, TN with a larger sample (Kitzman et al., 1997; Olds et al., 1998). Mothers participating in the program appeared to create more facilitative environments for their infants and made better use of community support than nonparticipants while also exhibiting high levels of perceived mastery. It seems that programs need to start early (during pregnancy) and to be of sufficient duration and intensity for effects to be substantial as well as sustained. In the Elmira Project, the mothers' engagement in adaptive activities may have been critical in protecting the children from future disadvantage.

Perhaps the most elegant and comprehensive study so far is the UCLA Family Development Project (Heinicke and Ponce, 1999). The basic assumption of the project is that, when a mother is provided with the experience of a stable, trustworthy relationship, then her own functioning; her relationships with her family of origin, her partner, and child; and the child's development will all improve. The intervention is carried out by professionals who focus on all aspects of the family's functioning and are guided by a general relationships process model of change and a specific, manualized set of interventions. The sample is a small but high-risk group ($n = 70$) but includes randomization.

The results are so far quite positive. Mothers report increased support from the family of origin (structural change); they encourage more task involvement and autonomy and less coercion in disciplining; and the children are more secure, autonomous, and task involved at 12 and 24 months. Children in the experimental group at 12 months were more likely to be coded secure in the strange situation (77% vs. 52%) (Heinicke et al., 1999). In particular, the number of disorganized classifications was reduced by almost two thirds. The intervention increased partner support, which was associated with a greater likelihood of secure attachment (Heinicke et al., 2000). At 24 months, the intervention made a significant positive impact on (1) the mother's responsiveness to the needs of her child and the related development of the child's attachment security; (2) the mother's encouragement of her child's autonomy and the related development of the child's autonomy; (3) the mother's encouragement of her child's task involvement and the related development of the child's task orientation (Heinicke et al., 2001); and (4) the mother's use of more appropriate means of controlling the child (less coercive).There was no measurable impact on depression and anxiety levels in the home-visited group.

Broadly speaking, mothers participating in the intervention benefit more than their infants did. They respond more effectively to their child's needs. These changes are, however, often not sufficiently focused to generate a detectable change in infant behavior or cognitive functioning. In thinking about the mechanism of change in the behavior of these mothers, we should not lose sight of such structural changes as the impact of these vulnerable young mothers' delaying their next pregnancy and entering productive employment.

Similar observations may be made in relation to many other studies in this group (e.g., Seitz, Rosenbaum, and Apfel, 1985).

This may partly explain why only a very small minority of home visitation programs is apparently effective. As we have seen, it appears that home visitors need to be able to engage with the family, which they can do only if supported by a firm psychosocial model of individual and family function. They need this support to bring about changes in family structure that can set the family on a course of a virtuous cycle. To be successful, the intervention needs to be multisystemic. Having the knowledge, skills and emotional resources to establish with a high-risk family a human relationship of sufficient strength to bring about such a reorganization of family structure is no minor task. What follows is an 'ideal' attachment-theory-based visitation program for high risk families.

An intensive, multisystemic family focus, such as the one promoted in the Heinecke study, may be key to a successful intervention. The overriding goals must be to give parents the skills and resources needed to address independently the inevitable difficulties of raising children and to empower those parents to cope with familial and extrafamilial problems. For example, assessment and intervention should explore the mother's role in various systems and consider the interrelationship among these systems. Specific attention should be given to strengthening the various systems, and an attempt should be made to promote appropriate and responsible behavior among all family members. Medications should be offered as part of the program when necessary.

Although effective home visitation should involve a number of techniques from a range of approaches, it needs to be far more than a mere amalgamation, and the focus on the interrelationship among systems should be retained. Interventions need to be individualized and highly flexible but also documented in treatment manuals. Weekly group supervision meetings with a doctoral-level supervisor are needed to ensure intervention fidelity, and supervision meetings may also include a medical consultant. The entire team needs to review goals with each family regularly to ensure a multisystemic focus. The intervention can generally be delivered by a Master's level professional with a caseload of 20 families. The visitor is a full-time generalist who directly provides most of the physical and mental health interventions, directs access to services, and coordinates the activities of these services to monitor quality control. The visitor is available to the family five days a week, but input is adjusted according to need.

### Attachment Interventions: Parent Sensitivity Training

It might be argued that the quality of the attachment relationship is a correlate of the risk for potential problems but does not constitute a risk itself. Insecure and even disorganized classifications are far too common within normal samples for insecure attachment classification to be other than a necessary, but not a sufficient, criterion for potential difficulty. Nevertheless, at least a proportion of those children who move from negativity, through conduct disorder, to delinquency and crime, likely do so because of harsh and abusive parenting, which in some way undermined their understanding of, or concern with, the mental states of those around them. Hence, an obvious target for prevention is the attachment relationship between parent and child. Parents can be helped to be more sensitive to their children. Even depressed young mothers can be assisted in improving their withdrawn or intrusive interaction style with young infants (e.g., Malphurs et al., 1996). The question is whether such improvements in sensitivity engender secure attachment. Fortunately, there are some persuasive studies in this area.

Dymphna van den Boom (1994, 1995) showed how effective relatively brief (three-session) personalized parent sensitivity training could be with infants preselected for difficult temperament. At 12 months, 62% of the intervention group were classified secure as opposed to 22% of controls; at 18 months, this discrepancy increased to 72% versus 26%. Large differences in mother–child interaction, still evident at 42 months, suggest that this approach may be of value in selective prevention. The data, if replicated, as Maria Bakermans-Kranenburg and her colleagues (1996) are attempting, suggest that well-timed focused early intervention may set up a virtuous cycle of protection rather than the various vicious cycles of vulnerability we are far more used to studying. Current evidence suggests that short, behaviorally focused interventions work better than do interventions focusing on the parents' history or relationship representation to enhance security of attachment in the strange situation (van Ijzendoorn, Juffer, and Duyvesteyn, 1995); the long-term significance of this finding, though, remains to be demonstrated. That we can bring about changes in test-taking behavior that improve IQ scores will not materially affect the intellectual capacity of the child.

The early caregiver–child relationship powerfully shapes the child's view of self, the social world in which he or she lives and his or her sense of worthiness, security, belonging, and being loved (Carlsson and Sroufe, 1995). As we have seen, the caregiver–child attachment relationship is shaped by many factors, including caregiver life history; readiness for parenthood; sensitivity to the developing child's needs; existing family climate; cooperation and support; chronic exposure to stressful environmental variables falling into three categories: (a) those which are largely fixed (e.g., child's physical attractiveness); (b) those which depend on macrosocial change (e.g., poverty), and (c) those which are amenable to intervention.

The last group of factors may be affected by policy changes of either a distal or a proximal kind. Examples of the former include improvements in living conditions and reductions of major environmental stresses (particularly during pregnancy and early childhood). Examples of effective infancy and early childhood programs to strengthen attachment relationships include the Infant–Family Resource program (Broussard, 1997) and a one-year toddler–parent psychotherapy program, in the Mount Hope Family Center, for depressed mothers (Cicchetti, Toth, and Rogosch, 1999). The latter program was designed to provide a corrective emotional experience for depressed mothers and to strengthen the mother–toddler relationship. Over the course of a year it succeeded in bringing the attachment security of the participating mother–infant dyads within the range of a normal control group. Three groups were included in the study: an intervention and a nonintervention group of mothers with major depressive disorders and a demographically matched control group of nondepressed mothers. The two depressed groups had comparable attachment security at the preintervention point; both were much less secure than the nondepressed group. At the end of the 45-session (one-year) program, the intervention group had attachment security levels similar to those of the controls, and both groups significantly exceeded the depressed controls in attachment security.

## Parent Training

This is an intervention that has grown out of treatment work with families with oppositionally defiant young children. As is well known, these parents appear to regulate their children's behavior through criticism and coercion. They fail to praise and are inconsistent in their reinforcements. By contrast, Kochanska (1997; Kochanska, and Askan, 1995; Kochanska et al., 1997) has demonstrated that parents of children who internalize the parents' value system have shared positive affects, promote autonomy, and engage in cooperative play with their children. Parent training has been thoroughly evaluated as a therapeutic intervention for conduct problems, but it is sufficiently easy to administer to be considered in the context of prevention.

Webster-Stratton (1996, 1998), extending her video-based parent training program to the school environment, explored the value of specific parent training as an addition to the traditional Head Start curriculum. The study assessed the effectiveness of a parenting program for 394 mothers, 264 in the intervention group and 130 in the control group. The sample was disadvantaged; over 50% were single parents, one fifth were teenage mothers, 45% had been physically or sexually abused as children, and 20% had recently been involved with child-protection services because of abuse or neglect of their children. The intervention, an abbreviated version of the basic program, lasted eight to nine weeks. Weekly parent group meetings led by family support workers (30% with Master's degrees) aimed to promote parental involvement in school activities. The teachers also received some special training, in addition to the Head Start curriculum, which promoted the teachers' classroom management skills.

In general, the program resulted in significantly larger behavior changes in children and parents alike in the experimental group, but the results were mixed. At posttreatment, externalizing behaviors on the Child Behavior Checklist (CBCL) decreased significantly for treatment as well as control groups. Only on the Eyberg Child Behavior Inventory (ECBI) was the decrease significantly larger for the intervention group. Not surprisingly, home observations of the mothers' behavior favored the intervention group. The impact on the children's behavior was marked. The children's social competence improved in the mothers' and in the teachers' reports. On the teachers' reports there was no effect on externalizing behavior. For both groups, there was a tendency for externalizing behavior to deteriorate. For both the intervention and the control group, externalizing behavior continued below baseline on the mothers' reports but was above baseline on the teachers' reports.

With regard to clinical significance, 69% of the mothers in the intervention condition and 52% in the control condition showed marked changes in their behavior. Correspondingly, in the experimental group, 73% of children above clinical cutoff showed a 30% reduction in noncompliant behaviors compared with 55% in the control group. However, these group differences were no longer significant at one-year follow up for either mothers or children. It is not clear whether the limited success of this implementation is due to the higher level of deprivation of the sample, the relatively abbreviated administration of the program, or the nonclinical setting. A similar large-scale preventive implementation of parent training also failed in the Worcester Public School system (Barkley et al., 2000).

A more successful preventive implementation of a parent training behavioral program was reported from the University of Queensland (Brisbane, Australia) by Sanders et al. (2000). Four groups of three-year-old children were recruited by an advertisement stressing maternal concern about the children's behavior. Three of the groups of about 75 parents each were offered 10–12 training sessions in 17 core child-management strategies in the usual group format; the fourth was a waiting list control. One of the groups received additional training in partner or social support and coping skills. Another group was given only training materials on management strategies and how to set and monitor behavioral change goals.

Practitioners with advanced mental health training implemented the enhanced and standard interventions. Parent-reported measures indicated that all three groups showed significant changes. Parent reports are known to be very open to bias in evaluations of parent training (parents judging the success of their own work). Clinician-observed ratings confirmed the superiority of the parent training program enhanced by coping skills training, but not the other two experimental groups. The key difference between this preventive trial and the previous ones was the recruitment of the sample. A major problem in prevention trials is client engagement, which is invariably difficult, given that the problem is (by definition) not yet there to be recognized by the family. Selection by advertisement identifies an atypical group who are sensitive to the children's problems.

### Preventing the Adverse Consequences of Maternal Depression

In light of the adverse consequences known to be associated with maternal depression (both ante- and postnatally), preventing these sequelae would seem a high priority. The risks to children probably arise from a range of sources, including genetic influences, altered parenting behavior, disrupted family functioning, and so on. (Dickstein et al., 1998). There have been surprisingly few studies to tackle this complex problem of prevention. The work of Tiffany Field and her colleagues (1996) on infant massage therapy, in which depressed mothers are taught to massage their infants, has had a remarkable impact on the child's sleep pattern and fussiness. Intervention also led to improvements in the quality of interaction between mother and baby. Lyons-Ruth, Connell, and Grunebaum (1990) constructed a home-visitation program for low-income depressed mothers. The intervention was similar to the high-quality, multisystemic intervention just described, which addressed maternal competence, modeling, selective reinforcement of appropriate parenting, reduction of social isolation, and the like. The infants benefited in cognitive development and an almost three-fold increase in security of attachment. Interestingly, the maternal symptoms of depression did not lift as a consequence of the intervention. The most comprehensive trials (Cooper et al., 2003; Murray et al., 2003) contrasted a cognitive behavioral intervention with psychotherapeutic intervention in mothers with depression. Both treatments were more effective than a control group.

### Kindergarten-Based Early Childhood Interventions

Two relatively common types of mental health promotion programs are targeted to young children. Interpersonal problem-solving programs have been influenced by Spivack and Shure's (1974) theory that problem-solving skills are an important part of adjustment. Programs vary in which specific skills are targeted, but they generally

attempt to instruct children in the use of cognitive strategies to identify interpersonal problems and develop effective means of resolving such difficulties. The effect size for these programs, based on
six studies for children aged two to seven, was 0.93. It should be
noted, however, that these approaches tended to increase competencies (ES = 1.11) rather than ameliorate problems (ES = 0.41).
Interpersonal-problem training did not significantly reduce malad-
justment. The increase in competencies was largely attributable to
improvements in problem-solving skills. It has been argued (Weissberg
and Bell, 1997) that this program is more effective when combined
with other program elements (e.g., social skills, negotiation skills,
assertiveness skills) under the broader rubric of social competence
training. Programs that coordinate the teaching of multiple competencies, such as self-control, stress management, responsible decision making and communication training, are underway (Consortium
on the School-Based Promotion of Social Competence, 1994).

The second category of programs offered affective education to
young children with the aim of increasing their awareness and
expression of feelings and their ability to understand the possible
causes of behavior. Affective education is likely to enhance children's capacity for understanding the role of mental states (feelings,
beliefs, wishes, and desires) in their own behavior as well as others'. This generic capacity has been termed "mentalizing" by cognitive developmentalists (Morton and Frith, 1995). Enhancement
of mentalizing could be at the core of prevention in early childhood.
It has been shown, for example, that understanding emotion at three
and a half years predicts a positive perception of social relations,
mature moral sensibility, and an understanding of complex emotions (Herrera and Dunn, cited in Dunn, 1996).

Affective education programs often combine stories, puppet play,
music, and exercises appropriate for the children's age; they range
from brief interventions to lesson plans lasting an entire school year.
These programs are particularly relevant to the treatment and prevention of conduct disorder (a category discussed in more detail
later). A significant number of trials (n = 46) have demonstrated
that affective education attempting to increase children's awareness
and expression of feelings and their ability to understand the possible causes of behavior is effective in reducing behavioral problems, as well as in enhancing competencies (Durlak and Wells, 1997).

Overall, 76% of children who had the benefit of the program were better off than were the untreated controls. The program was successful in reducing problems (ES = 0.85) but less successful in enhancing competencies (ES = 0.69). It would thus be appropriate to argue that such programs enhance children's resilience because they do not directly focus on problem behaviors. That these programs, like interpersonal problem-solving programs, were far less effective for older children suggests that a critical period exists for the acquisition of mental state attributions under the age of seven. Beyond that period, preventive initiatives using affective education are either insufficiently intensive or inappropriate.

### Developmental Programs for Disadvantaged Children

Developmental programs for disadvantaged children have become a significant additional pursuit for mental health professionals over the last decades.

*The Perry Pre-School Project.* The Perry Pre-School Project is perhaps the best documented of the studies aimed at disadvantaged children. The study's initial goal was to equip poor minority children for school entry (Schweinhart, Barnes, and Weikart, 1993). It targeted poor families from a high-risk group, had low attrition rates, and included a follow-up to age 27. The program included two and a half hours of special classes for 30 weeks and teacher home visits once a week. Most of the children participated for two years. Active learning and the facilitation of independence and self-esteem were the focus of the intervention. Problem-solving skills and task persistence were also strongly encouraged. The teachers were highly skilled and supervised and had a special brief to establish good home–school integration.

This high-scope intervention was contrasted with a behaviorist programmed learning approach and a child-centered nursery program. Until adolescence, the high-scope preschool group fared best and the programmed learning group worst (Schweinhart et al., 1985). At age 19, only 15% of children in the preschool project had been classified as mentally retarded, whereas 35% of the control group had been so labeled. The high rates in both groups underscore the profound need for such early intervention among this greatly disadvantaged population. While over half the control group had been arrested, only 31% of the preschool group had ever been detained. In the follow up to age 27, lifetime arrests in the preschool group were halved. While minor offenses and drug-related arrests accounted for much of this difference, recidivist crime was also reduced. Overall, 33% of the control group but less than 7% of the preschool group had been arrested more than five times. Similar improvements were observed for the lowering of teenage pregnancy rates, high school graduation, home ownership, and social benefits. Cost–benefit analysis revealed that the program saved United States taxpayers $7 for each dollar spent on welfare, social services, and legal and incarceration costs (Schweinhart, Barnes, and Weikart, 1993; Schweinhart and Weikart, 1993).

It should be noted that the sample was small ($n = 58$ and $n = 65$ in the preschool and control groups, respectively). Moreover, the program did not totally prevent delinquency: 30% of the preschool group had been arrested at least once. By age 19, the teen pregnancy rate was 68% in the preschool group. At age 27, 34% of the experimental group had not graduated from high school and 57% had been arrested. However, as other high-quality Head Start programs produced similar findings, and as the cost–benefit analysis showed substantial long-term savings (Karoly et al., 1998), the early intervention prevention movement received a substantial boost from this study.

*Sure Start.* What, if anything, has the slew of developmental programs taught us about rolling out expensive programs for the 21st century? The Labor government in England made an early commitment to tackle child poverty and reduce social exclusion as part of a cross-departmental spending review (see Glass, 1999). It was acknowledged that the issues of children's early years were broader than a single government department's responsibilities could address. The following were the major findings of the review:

1. The earliest years of life are the most important for a child's development.
2. Early development is more vulnerable to environmental influences than has been previously realized.
3. Multiple disadvantages for young children are a severe and growing problem, greatly increasing the chances of social exclusion later in life.

4. The quality of service provision for young children and their families is variable and uncoordinated.
5. The provision of a comprehensive and community-based program of early intervention and family support that builds on existing services not only could have positive and persistent effects on child development and family relationships but also could help to break the cycle of social exclusion.

Sure Start is a cross-government and wider program aimed at improving the health and well-being of families and children before and from birth so that children are ready to flourish when they start school. To accomplish this goal, local Sure Start programs are established to provide and improve services for families with children under four years of age. In addition, everyone involved in providing services for children received the benefit of effective practices learned from local programs. By 2004 there will be at least 500 Sure Start local programs in England. They will be concentrated in neighborhoods defined by the proportion of children living in poverty. The four main concerns of these programs will be: (1) ensuring easy access to family support, (2) advice on nutrition, (3) health services and (4) early learning. There will be local differences, but all programs are planned to offer outreach and home visits, support for families and parents, and encouragement of high quality play and learning activities. Also offered is primary and community information about health care, such as advice about family and child health and development, as well as support for children and parents with special needs, including help in gaining access to specialized services. The government invested £452m during the period 1999–2002, and the spending review in July 2000 announced an extra £580m for 2001–2004. In July 2001 a fifth wave of sites was announced; another 177 programs will bring the number of preschool children from disadvantaged areas involved in Sure Start to at least 300,000.

Among the specified targets are reducing the number of children reregistering with child protection after Sure Start support. All local Sure Start programs must have agreed to, and implemented in a culturally sensitive manner, ways of caring for and supporting mothers with postnatal depression. Another goal is a 10% reduction among women who smoke while pregnant (now known to be specifically associated with later conduct disorder). One hundred percent of families should be contacted by local programs within two months after children are born. Parenting support and information is to be available in all Sure Start areas. By 2004, we anticipate a reduction of five percentage points in the number of children with speech and language impairments requiring special intervention by the age of four. Each target has a delivery target associated with it. Thus, speech and language delivery targets identify access to high-quality playing and learning opportunities and well-equipped libraries. There are also employment targets for the families (e.g., a 12% reduction in the number of children under three years living in households where no one is working). Sure Start Plus pilots will pioneer special initiatives to support pregnant teenagers and teenaged parents under 18.

The guidance notes issued concerning the mental health needs of children recognize that schools may be better sites than mental health services to help children with mental health problems. The guidance notes identify such risk factors as learning difficulties, low self esteem, a child's academic failure, parents' marital conflict, inconsistent discipline, early loss in the family, discrimination, and poverty in the community. The notes consider factors that might promote resilience (but regrettably, the notes do not consider the accessibility of these factors to intervention).

Resilience factors for a child include a secure early relationship, being female, a high IQ, an easy temperament as an infant, good communication skills, humor, religious faith, and the capacity to reflect. Resilience factors in the family include at least one good relationship, clear firm discipline, support for education, support of long-term relationships, and the absence of discord. Resilience factors in the community include a wide supportive network, good housing, high standard of living, and the like. Characteristics of resilience-promoting schools are also discussed in the guidance notes, which emphasize early intervention and various models of good practice (e.g., Seattle Social Development Project—PATHS curriculum) mostly taken from the United States but also highlighting some United Kingdom–based initiatives. Of major importance in the notes, however, is the attention drawn to the core mental health aspect of the education.

An example of implementation is the Guidance on Promoting Speech and Language Development (Department for Education and

Skills, 2001). The guidance includes summaries of good practice, short descriptions of ongoing activities, and research summaries of evidence-based practice. The advice is specific: for example, about creating a toy library offering leaflets to accompany toys on loan to give ideas to a parent to talk about the toy while the child is playing with it. The guidance advice, however, does not tell workers what to advise parents to talk about with each toy. There is advice on how to read with children, support for increasing parental literacy, interaction training using behavioral principles, parent training for children's behavioral problems. The booklet is more informative than similar publications (Office of Juvenile Justice and Delinquency Prevention, 1998) but falls short of providing a manualized intervention. Such an intervention is particularly desirable given the recently reported RCT from the United Kingdom that formal speech therapy for children aged four through eight was no more effective than no treatment.

There are early indications that the Sure Start program is taking hold. A snapshot survey has shown that 90% of parents using Sure Start think that services for young children have improved significantly since the local programs began (MORI, 2001). The results also suggested that parents view their children as more confident and as having improved social skills, which, in turn, enable better interaction with adults and children. Parents also commented that they have increased confidence as parents in teaching, managing, and playing with their children. Of course, there is no information yet from parents who did not engage in the programs or from those who engaged but discontinued their engagement.

### Policy Implications

*Why Are Programs Successful?*

There is good evidence that effective programs have a number of features in common (Dryfoos, 1990). These features are (1) comprehensiveness, (2) system orientation, (3) relatively high intensity and long duration, (4) structured curriculum, (5) early commencement, (6) specific to particular risk factors, and (7) specific training.

*Comprehensiveness.* Successful programs contain multiple components because no single program component can prevent multiple high-risk behaviors. A package of coordinated collaborative strategies is necessary for successful outcome. For example, the Consortium of School-Based Promotion of Social Competence (Elias and Tobias, 1996) includes in its package (1) the teaching of families, (2) phasing in new competencies at developmentally appropriate times, (3) the provision of "booster shots" to reinforce learning, and (4) changes to the school environment consistent with the assumptions of the program. The studies that have shown the most dramatic outcomes for employment, delinquency, graduation rates, and so on contained an educational child care component as well as a parent-involvement component (e.g., Wasik et al., 1990; Schweinhart et al., 1993; Campbell and Ramey, 1994). It seems that effecting change in the behavior of parents toward their children requires an adult-focused component, whereas achieving change in children requires extensive interactional experience, which is most easily created through educational child-care settings. Outcomes for children will be achieved only if the program enables or motivates the parents to spend more time with their children in positive, nurturing, language-rich interactions. Programs involving a home-based intervention alone may have failed because, without support, information, and toys, they could not provide a suitable environment.

*System Orientation.* Interventions should be aimed at changing institutional environments as well as individuals. For example the Child Development Project (CDP) (Battistich et al., 1989) strives, over the course of the entire elementary school period, to engineer a total school environment that will promote wellness by enhancing children's sense of autonomy, competence, and relatedness. The program is designed around system changes that include having students set and uphold discipline standards, cooperative learning formats, buddy systems, and problem-solving and conflict-resolution strategies that embody democratic values and that emphasize the value of helping peers and others in the community. The CDP is built on the notion of partnerships among parents, teachers, and children and is designed to incorporate all facets of a child's life in a coherent, goal-oriented way. The results of the program are highly encouraging with benefits in some areas of academic attainment (reading comprehension) as well as major social benefits (e.g., dealing with conflict, peer competence, empathy and sensitivity to others, self-esteem and sense of community) (Battistich et al., 1995).

*High Intensity and Duration.* Some controversy surrounds the relationship of program intensity and program effectiveness. In one review intensity was defined as a combination of such variables as amount of contact per week, total duration, and resources available (Wasik and Karweit, 1994). Defined in this way, high-intensity programs appeared to have greater impact on academic outcomes, but no conclusions were drawn about such nonacademic outcomes as family functioning. In a similar review, intensity was defined as the number of hours of intervention received during a specific time period (Innocenti and White, 1993). Metaanalysis of 89 studies found no relationship between intensity of interventions and effect size. Further, an inverse relationship between intensity and effect size emerged when high-quality studies were looked at separately.

There are problems with both approaches to quantifying intensity. The first review (Wasik and Karweit, 1994) defines intensity in a subjective way and conflates program type with intensity. For example, combined center- and home-based approaches (e.g., Campbell and Ramey, 1995) are inevitably classed as intensive. By contrast, defining intensity in terms of number of hours of contact may privilege single-component programs delivered at relatively high frequency. The metaanalytic approach (Innocenti and Whre, 1993) may also conflate the impact of intensity on different outcome measures. It seems that the relationship between intensity and outcome should be specific to the program components and outcome measures in order for meaningful associations to result.

Successful programs are seldom brief. Short-term programs have, at best, time limited benefits, especially with at-risk groups. Multiyear programs (e.g., Seitz et al., 1985; Johnson and Walker, 1987) tend to affect on more risk factors and have more lasting effects than short-term approaches do. Programs such as Head Start offer only one-year preschool experience, which may be too short to have a lasting effect with multirisk families. For academic achievement, at least, program duration appears to be strongly related to outcome, with children who participate for at least four years showing significantly better results than those who participate for less time (Reynolds, 1994). It should be noted, however, that, even when disadvantaged children participate in long-term interventions, they tend to perform below age-appropriate grade level (Karweit, 1994). Preventive efforts need to be titrated to the severity of the disorders they are intended to prevent. In the past, because the net was cast too wide, inevitably in many cases the intervention was too weak to permit clinically and economically significant reductions of risk, and prevention was only partial. The prevention of serious disturbance needs to be a long-term and intensive enterprise.

*Structured Curriculum.* This review shows no clear indication of the "ideal curriculum" for preventive interventions. The Perry Pre-school Project (Schweinhart et al., 1993) found the high-scope cognitive approach to be superior to the Distar structured learning approach,[2] but the latter group included more high-risk children (single parents and boys) and on average they received less treatment. Other studies that experimentally compared different curricula yielded inconclusive findings (Karweit, 1989). The failure to identify a specific curriculum that works better than others may suggest that no curriculum is effective for all children and all are effective for some. Alternatively, we may conclude that different curricula actually possess the same key effective components. Most probably attempts at comparing curricula conflate such parameters as intensity, duration and timing, and the absence of clear differences are a consequence of such confounding.

Proactive interventions should be directed at risk and protective factors rather than at categorical problem behaviors. In this way, multiple adverse outcomes may be addressed within a single program. As was stated in the introduction, the perspective of developmental psychopathology creates a framework for focusing on the mediators or moderators along the developmental paths leading to mental disorders and social maladaptation (National Institute of Mental Health, 1995). Examples of this approach may be found in the Baltimore prevention research studies (e.g., Kellam et al., 1994) and the work of the Conduct Problems Prevention Group (described later). Prevention should be focused on specific risk or protective factors and be firmly rooted in empirically based formulations of the development of the disorder. For example, Durlak and Wells (1997) report that nondirective forms of counseling or group discussion had a relatively small impact on problems as well as competencies (ES = 0.25). The coherence of the approach might be more important than its content. In one study, for example, a teacher-

---

2. SRA Distar is a computer-based reading program.

directed academic model was contrasted with a child-initiated pre-school model and an with 'in-between' condition that combined the two (Marcon, 1992). On almost all measures the children in the "in-between" group performed less well than did the children exposed to either of the other two models.

*Early Commencement.* There is some agreement among studies that early commencement of preventive interventions is essential. Experimental studies (e.g., Larson, 1980) show that intervention during pregnancy is beneficial. A prevention strategy devised by Spivack and Shure (1974), involving the teaching of interpersonal problem-solving skills, was more effective with preschoolers than with older children (Shure and Spivack, 1988). Although early intervention is more effective than later, there is a need to sustain any improvements that may have been brought about (Cox, 1993b). Thus, the overall cost of prenatal intervention will be greater. The timing of interventions, however, is mostly conflated with duration (those which start earlier tend also to last longer). Reynolds (1994) attempted to untangle this conflation in a naturalistic study. He found that children who received at least four years of intervention, regardless of the age at which they entered the program, performed better on achievement tests and grade retention than did those whose intervention was of a shorter duration. On measures of social adjustment and parental involvement, however, those entering the program early fared better than those who entered later. In the Abecedarian program there was no effect of later (kindergarten to second grade) intervention (Campbell and Ramey, 1994). It is possible that the effect on both intellectual development and parent–child relationship is greater because of so-called sensitive periods, which may make subsequent attempts at prevention more challenging, if not impossible (Ramey, Yeates, and Short, 1984; Rutter, 1990).

*Specific Risk Factors.* The era of generic therapies is over. No treatment can be equally applicable without modification to every disorder. Similarly, it is unrealistic to hope that a generic preventive intervention will be able to reduce the risk for all psychological disorders. The Durlak and Wells (1997) metaanalysis showed a significant heterogeneity in the outcomes of primary-prevention programs. There were interactions between developmental level, type of program and target group. This finding suggests that the assumption of homogeneity ("one size fits all") implicitly held by some preventionists should be abandoned (Lorion, 1990). Prevention, as treatment, will need to be disorder, context, and objective specific. That is, we should address ourselves to those disorders for which longitudinal studies have given us sufficient clues about identifying "at risk" populations.

Further, while universal prevention is desirable, the very generality of such an approach militates against any particular individual's experiencing it as relevant to himself or herself. It may, indeed, be very difficult to modulate a program so that it is perceived to be of equal relevance to all groups (McGuire and Earls, 1991). For example, although in some studies boys appeared to derive greater benefit than girls from certain programs (Walker and Johnson, 1988), in others only girls appeared to benefit (Lally et al., 1988; Fuerst and Fuerst, 1993); and in yet others no gender differences were found (Reynolds, 1994). African-American children appear to derive greater benefit from the Head Start program than do Caucasian children (Lee, Brooks-Gunn, and Schnur, 1988). It is unclear which aspects of these programs interacted with the children's gender and ethnicity.

*Training.* There is little consistency in the literature on the qualifications required to perform preventive work. Most studies in the United Kingdom use health visitors who have a statutory obligation to visit young children and their carers. Preventive programs have added to this health visitor training by providing extra didactic seminars, backup consultation (Hewitt and Crawford, 1988), support groups and joint case work (Thompson and Bellenis, 1992), and a combination of didactic, supervisory, and mutual-support case discussions (Bellenis and Thompson, 1992). It is noteworthy that, despite the highly trained nature of this group of workers and their excellent integration with the statutory services, controlled evaluation studies have not yielded striking results either from the point of view of the caregivers or the children (Stevenson, Bailey, and Simpson, 1988) or from the point of view of reduced referral to secondary services[3] (Bellenis and Thompson, 1992; Thompson and Bellenis, 1992). Often the takeup rates are quite low, suggesting that many people who would use a preventive service choose not to do so (Stevenson et al., 1988).

---

3. Reduced referral may not always be a desirable outcome in any case.

Interestingly, although formal comparisons have not yet been made, the outcomes from volunteer-based schemes are more promising (Cox, 1993a). In such schemes, there is no expert helper and the distinction between befriender/volunteer and a befriended mother is not stressed (Pound and Mills, 1985). A controlled trial showed that these minimally trained volunteers were effective in bringing about improvements not only in the mothers' mental state but also to some degree (Cox, Pound, and Puckering, 1992), in mother–child relations as revealed by blind rating of video recordings.

Supportive interventions have their roots in nursing, social work, and community psychology. Through intervention, parents' (normally mothers') access to resources (housing, child-care, welfare benefits) is effectively facilitated (see Minde et al., 1983; Booth et al., 1987). Inevitably, the support role goes beyond bringing about an improvement in the caregiver's objective situation. An implicit aim of such interventions is the activation of the young mothers' attachment systems through the provision of a stable, safe, nonexploitative relationship with the home visitor (Minde et al., 1983). The provision of information concerning child development often is a subsidiary goal of prevention programs (e.g., Belsky, 1985; Pfannenstiel and Honig, 1995). Again, it is difficult to conceive of such information having an impact on a child's relation to the caregiver, and the implicit goal must include the enhancement of parental sensitivity to the child.

Recent studies have highlighted predictors of failure to intervene. At least two studies indicated that racial factors might be critical in undermining the formation of an effective therapeutic relationship in the context of a parent-training intervention (Orrell-Valente, 1999) on the child's behavior (Crijnen, Bengi-Arslan, and Verhulst, 2000). In one pertinent study of an evaluation of the Preparing for Drug Free Years Program and the Iowa Strengthening Families program only socioeconomic status (SES) was found to be a significant predictor of lack of engagement, which in our view reflected the lower level of educational attainment (Spoth, Goldberg, and Redmond, 1999). By contrast, a community treatment study that shared many features with the Spoth et al. study found that parental psychopathology and lower level of quality of life were the most important predictors of early drop out, and the influence of these factors was not explained by social disadvantage or by the severity of children's dysfunction (Kazdin, 2000). Parents' perception of the demandingness of the intervention seems to be critical to its success.

## Recent Concern About Integration

It is now generally recognized that the promotion of early intervention will not take place without extensive integrations at various levels of the social-care system. In a helpful policy document Knitzer (2000) identifies several levels at which integration can take place and, in fact, is already partially taking place.

1. There is a need for the integration of behavioral service teams into primary health care, child care, and Head Start settings. For example, the Starting Early, Starting Smart (Knitzer, 2000) program is a public–private initiative to link high-risk families to specialists and provides advocacy services, and in some cases therapy, for these children.
2. Provision of services needs to be located within other treatment delivery contexts to ensure that prevention services are offered where they are most clearly required. There are several good examples of building state-wide systems of behavioral support for young children and families in the United States. For example, the Children's Upstream Project (CUP) in Vermont provides prevention and treatment linking child health, substance abuse, mental health, domestic violence, and other agencies. This project may not seem relevant to some other countries, where health and social services are already well integrated (Australia, for example); nevertheless, the location of prevention services is an important issue to bear in mind in the design of new initiatives.
3. The integration of services has powerful training implications particularly in the call for increased early childhood competencies with multiproblem families among a wide range of workers. For example, by the use of manualized exercises encompassing inquiry, reflection, and respect, Project Relationship in Los Angeles aims to enhance the skills of those working in the field. These might appear at first sight to be trivial considerations from a policy point of view, yet the patchy success of prevention programs indicates that standardization of intervention procedures is a high priority.

4. An obvious but rarely practiced point for integrating services is bringing parenting issues to bear on work in substance use, mental health, and domestic violence agencies. Clients of these services are not often asked whether they have children. Service providers seldom have the opportunity to show concern about the risks these children face; and, even if they had those opportunities, they rarely have the skills and resources to do much beyond making a referral to another agency. This situation is, of course, less than ideal, for, as we know, the successful treatment of the parent's problem may not be the best or at least most cost-effective protection for the child. More immediate protection can be provided. For example, Rainbow House, a shelter in New York, and Exodus, a California residential program for substance users and their families, both provide positive parent training as part of their package.

Integration is widely perceived as a desirable goal, but it is not readily attainable. The experience of Sure Start in England has highlighted some of the problems that the combinations of initiatives at system and at program levels can face.

1. The requirement to share fiscal and planning responsibilities across different agencies can create tensions and in any case calls for administrative skills that the agencies concerned do not by definition have. Consequently, they feel threatened, which adds to local difficulties.
2. Plans for integrations inevitably draw attention to barriers related to different professional training and orientation, administrative procedures, and confidentiality requirements between systems.
3. Fragmentation and categorization of financing for different social services is currently pervasive. Moving toward more rational financing of social interventions would appear highly desirable from all points of view. However, program heads frequently argue against joint initiatives. They claim, with reason, that if funding is lost for one agency, the whole program may be put at risk.
4. There is a clear dialectic between the petrification generally created by a centralized governmental control system that issues initiatives, regardless of their local relevance, and the chaos that can ensue if each local group is asked to create a system relevant to its community's needs. Most of these groups have little

experience with major initiatives individually, let alone in combination with one another as the terms of federally issued dictates for local integration imply.

5. A further problem that can arise as a consequence of local control is the vulnerability it creates in local governmental financial constraints that in most countries tend to change faster and more dramatically than funding from federal or state sources.
6. Another problem is created by local innovation, which can risk national inequalities in service provision. This is an inevitable difficulty of locally led programs simply because of the individual differences in energy, intelligence and skill across regions.
7. An evidence base is a further problem, since local integrated initiatives do not have the resources to support studies of effectiveness. When such Demonstration Studies are funded (mostly nationally), they tend to "demonstrate and die" after the research funding has disappeared precisely because the local groups were insufficiently involved in the design and implementation of the trials.

None of these is a reason for not pursuing possibilities for better integration of service providers, policy makers, educators, social service and juvenile justice authorities, and researchers from the public health and psychological development fields. These points are simply an indication of the challenge that the task of prevention, unattainable solely within any of the traditional categories of service provision, actually represents. Considerable heartache seems inevitable along the road to a genuine policy of prevention.

### Principles of Intervention to Reduce Risks for Adverse Outcomes

Let us summarize some of the principles that, in the light of attachment research and theory, should govern the implementation of prevention programs aimed at reducing adverse developmental outcomes through early intervention.

1. Interventions need a strong theoretical framework that takes account of the transactional influences between the child and the social environment. We have known for three decades or longer (Thomas and Chess, 1977) that neither the child nor the

caregiver is appropriately considered to be either "cause" or "effect" of adverse outcomes. Each, being part of a human system, naturally affects the other, and interventions must take this into consideration. The theoretical framework must have strong systemic components.

2. It follows from the complexity and interactional character of psychosocial risk that early intervention aimed at a single protective factor is highly likely to be ineffective. Only comprehensive multiple-focus programs work.

3. Along the same lines, it is unlikely that "off the shelf" prevention programs are pertinent or attractive to every population, and it is clear that even universal early intervention should be specific to the population targeted.

4. Evidence, as well as common sense, suggests that prevention should be directed not just toward a reduction of negative outcomes, but also toward a promotion of competencies (skills) incompatible with the problem behavior targeted. Thus the reduction of negativity and coercion in parenting is ineffective without the promotion of playfulness in parenting. The United Kingdom Sure Start initiative has taken this concept on board, and toy libraries with instructions on "how to play with your child using this toy" are being established as part of early intervention.

5. Empowerment must be a key part of preventive initiatives, and interventions should try to capitalize on (build on the strength of) the individual, family, or group toward whom the intervention is being addressed. For example, in the Sure Start initiatives, a condition for establishing an initiative is user involvement in governance.

6. Interventions should target salient vulnerabilities at several levels of a system that generates adverse outcomes. For example, educational success (language competence) is causally related to social success, educational competence, and self-control through self-talk and is therefore likely to be a key target for early intervention.

7. Prevention should always be looked at in a developmental context, and the success or failure of an intervention must be judged against the appropriate developmental expectations for the outcome under consideration. For example, as we have learned that aggressive behavior in most children natually follows a downward path during middle childhood (e.g., Nagin and Tremblay,

2001) a program that achieves a reduction of aggression with development should not necessarily be considered to have been successful. However, because we also know that a predictable subgroup does not follow this path, a program that aims at this group (identified by parental and early childhood predictors) attaining a reduction is to be celebrated.

8. Acceptability is far more important for prevention than for treatment interventions, and barriers to prevention are even more of a challenge to service providers than to those engaged in the provision of treatment (Kazdin, Holland, and Crowley, 1997). Thus sensitivity to (sub)cultural attitudes is essential.

9. In an ideal world, prevention should aim only at fostering an intervention that can become self-sustaining.

10. Attempts should be made to provide comparison data, ideally by randomization—but, failing that, by multiple baseline design—to provide evidence of effectiveness relative to a control group for any new intervention or new application of an intervention of known effectiveness.

## The Dangers of Prevention

Finally, we should not assume that prevention initiatives are without risk. Any intervention that purports to be effective will inevitably carry a side effect. This is undoubtedly the case for prevention initiatives, too. First, it must be acknowledged that the effectiveness of most popular and well-disseminated programs has not yet been demonstrated (e.g., parenting books). Second, if ineffective programs are implemented, finding support for more effective interventions at a later stage could become more difficult. There is a real risk of building up immunity to prevention initiatives by implementing prevention programs in "subclinical doses" that have little effect on population levels of disorder. Third, the easiest interventions are usually the least effective. For example, educational approaches tend to have no discernable impact. Parent education and parent-support programs in general are far less effective than are structured, skill-based approaches that are a great deal harder to implement. Fourth, there are a number of counterproductive approaches that are likely to create more problems than they solve. For example, information-only models tend to create a demand for assistance without providing services to meet this demand. Involving youths with adults with antisocial norms or aggregating high-risk youths without experienced adult leadership is known to generate adverse outcomes. Less well known is that child-focused work without addressing family problems may lead to improvement in a child but at the cost of deterioration of family function. There are many other similar examples.

## Conclusions

The promise of primary preventive intervention is considerable. From the studies referred to here and others, we may conclude that early preventive interventions have the potential, in the short term, to improve children's health and welfare (including better nutrition and physical health and fewer feeding problems, low-birth-weight babies, and accident and emergency room visits, as well as a reduced potential for maltreatment). In the short term, parents can also expect to benefit in significant ways (including more educational and work opportunities, better use of services, improved social support, enhanced self-efficacy as a parent, and an improved relationship with both their children and their partners). In the long term, children may further benefit in critical ways behaviorally (less aggression, distractibility, delinquency), educationally (better attitudes to school, higher achievement), and in social functioning and attitudes (increased prosocial attitudes); parents can benefit in employment, education, and mental well-being. In general, caring and protective relationships are potent protective factors against adverse outcomes. "To hug is to buffer," is a conclusion that applies as much to society and community intervention as it does to families and individuals.

These conclusions should be qualified substantially in the following ways: (1) Outcomes are selective—no study achieved all these effects together. (2) Many of the studies reported unacceptable rates of refusal, which threatens generalizability. For example, even in the highly successful Rochester nurse home visitation program only 80% of the pregnant women invited to participate agreed to become involved (Olds, Henderson, Tatelbaum et al., 1986). Unfortunately, it is most likely those in greatest need who decline the invitation to take part. (3) Attrition is high in most studies, making

conclusions from long-term follow ups doubtful; the low self-per-
ceived risk of adverse outcome may account for the low uptake and
high rates of attrition observed in many prevention studies. For
example, three of the most influential studies, the Houston Parent-
Child Development Center Program (Johnson and Walker, 1987;
Johnson, 1990, 1991), the Parent-Child Interaction Training Project
(Strayhorn and Weidman, 1991) and the "I Can Problem Solve: An
Interpersonal Cognitive Problem-Solving Program" (Shure and
Spivack, 1982, 1988) had attrition rates of around 50%. (4) Results
are generally poorer with, what appear to be, higher risk samples.
(5) Theoretical models of prevention lag behind those underpinning
treatment interventions. (6) The heterogeneity of the studies does
not permit clear recommendations about "the" effective preventive
intervention program. (7) Many of the studies were carried out at
a time when social problems (violence, substance abuse, fear, and
despair) were relatively mild compared with the difficulties we are
facing currently (Takanishi and DeLeon, 1994). While broad-based
programs appeared to be more effective than narrowly focused ones,
there are also spectacular examples suggesting that programs that
attempt to do it all end up spreading resources thinly and achieving little (St. Pierre et al., 1994).

Developmental research is not a direct application of psychoanalytic ideas. Research inspired by psychoanalytic theory has led
investigators to explore young children's experience of the earliest
environments and to contemplate how these could be modified,
enriched, or buffered in order to reduce dramatically the risk of
psychological and physical disorder. Of course, the field of prevention has itself undergone development, and, just like the parent,
has to let go of the adolescent child. The psychoanalysts who have
initiated this field must accept that many developmental ideas,
beyond those rooted in psychoanalysis, have come to have an influence. Arguably the epistemology of this body of work is no longer
consistent with that of psychoanalysis (Green, 2000), although here
we would disagree. If psychoanalysis is to continue to be relevant
to the field of prevention, it has to prove itself de novo. The application of psychoanalytic ideas should not be simply from the
classical individual setting to the public arena, but modern psychoanalytic voices should struggle to make themselves heard in a multitude of rapidly evolving fields, including that of early prevention

intervention. Psychoanalysis is perhaps one of the richest sources of theoretical inspiration for social science. If we have one criticism about this body of knowledge, it is that there is a tendency of psychoanalytic theorists to "rest on their laurels" and assume that "ideas speak for themselves." Perhaps in an ideal world, ideas would do so. In reality, they do only if they are accompanied by a chorus of approval. The application of psychoanalytic ideas thus depends on our capacity to win the debate at the interface of individual and society. This debate can never be won for all time: it must be repeated again and again, year after year, if we are to ensure that the subjectivity of the individual is clearly and forcefully heard at the level of social policy.

## References

Alpern, L. & Lyons-Ruth, K. (1993), Preschool children at social risk: Chronicity and timing of maternal depressive symptoms and child behavior problems at school and at home. *Develop. & Psychopathol.*, 5:371–387.

Bahrick, L. R. & Watson, J. S. (1985), Detection of intermodal proprioceptive-visual contingency as a potential basis of self-perception in infancy. *Develop. Psychol.*, 21:963–973.

Bakermans-Kranenburg, M. J., Juffer, F. & van IJzendoorn, M. H. (1996), Intervention and infant security: Experiences with a focused, short-term intervention. Paper presented at World Association for Infant Mental Health, Sixth World Congress, Tampere, Finland, July.

Barkley, R. A., Shelton, T. L., Crosswait, C. C., Moorehouse, M., Fletcher, K., Barrett, S., Jenkins, L. & Metevia, L. (2000), Multimethod psycho-educational intervention for preschool children with disruptive behavior: Preliminary results at post-treatment. *J. Child Psychol. Psychiat.*, 41:319–332.

Battistich, V., Solomon, D., Kim, D. I., Watson, M. & Schaps, E. (1995). Schools as communities, poverty levels of student populations, and students' attitudes, motives and performance: A multi-level analysis. *Amer. Educ. Res. J.*, 32:627–658.

——— ——— Watson, M., Solomon, J. & Schaps, E. (1989), Effects of an elementary school program to enhance prosocial behavior and children's cognitive social problem solving skills and strategies. *J. Appl. Develop. Psychol.*, 10:147–169.

Bellenis, C. & Thompson, M. J. J. (1992), A joint assessment and treatment service for the under fives: Work with health visitors in a child guidance clinic. Part 2: Work done and outcome. *Newsletter Assn. Child Psychol. & Psychiatry*, 14:262–266.

Belsky, J. (1985), Experimenting with the family in the newborn period. *Child Develop.*, 56:376–391.

Black, J. E., Jones, T. A., Nelson, C. A. & Greenough, W. T. (1998), Neuronal plasticity and the developing brain. In: *Handbook of Child and Adolescent Psychiatry, Vol. 6*, ed. N. E. Alessi, J. T. Coyle, S. I. Harrison & S. Eith. New York: Wiley, pp. 31–53.

Black, M. M., Nair, P., Kight, C., Wachtel, R., Roby, P. & Schuler, M. (1994), Parenting and early development among children of drug-abusing women: Effects of home intervention. *Pediatrics*, 94:440–448.

Booth, C. L., Barnard, K. E., Mitchell, S. & Spieker, S. J. (1987), Successful intervention with multiproblem mothers: Effects on the mother–infant relationship. *Inf. Mental Health J.*, 8:288–306.

Brooks-Gunn, J., McCarton, C. M., Casey, P. H., McCormick, M. C., Bauer, C. R., Bernbaum, J. C., Tyson, J., Swanson, M., Bennett, F. C., Scott, D. T., Tonascia, J. & Meinert, C. L. (1994), Early intervention in low-birth-weight premature infants: Results through age 5 years from the infant health and development program. *J. Amer. Med. Assn.*, 272:1257–1262.

Broussard, E. B. (1997), Infant-family resource program. In: *Primary Prevention Works: Issues in Children's and Families' Lives, Vol. 6*, ed. G. W. Albee & T. P. Gulotta. Thousand Oaks, CA: Sage, pp. 239–267.

Bruer, J. T. (1999), *The Myth of the First Three Years*. New York: Free Press.

Campbell, F. A. & Ramey, C. T. (1994), Effects of early intervention on intellectual and academic achievement: A follow-up study of children from low income families. *Child Develop.*, 65:684–698.

———— & ———— (1995), Cognitive and school outcomes for high-risk African-American students at middle adolescence: Positive effects of early intervention. *Amer. Educ. Res. J.*, 32:743–772.

Carlsson, E. & Sroufe, L. A. (1995), Contribution of attachment theory to developmental psychopathology. In: *Developmental Psychopathology. Vol. 1*, ed. D. Cicchetti & D. J. Cohen. New York: Wiley, pp. 581–617.

Children's Secretariat (1999), *Early Years Study*. Toronto: Author.

Cicchetti, D., Rapaport, J., Sandler, I. & Weissberg, R. P. (2000), *The Promotion of Wellness in Children and Adolescents*. Washington, DC: Child Welfare League of America Press.

———— Toth, S. L. & Rogosch, F. A. (1999), The efficacy of toddler-parent psychotherapy to increase attachment security in offspring of depressed mothers. *Attach. & Human Develop.*, 1:34–66.

Civic, D. & Holt, V. L. (2000), Maternal depressive symptoms and child behavior problems in a nationally representative normal birthweight sample. *Maternal & Child Health J.*, 4:215–221.

Coghill, S. R., Caplan, H. L., Alexandra, H., Robson, K. & Kumar, R. (1986), Impact of maternal postnatal depression on cognitive development of young children. *Brit. Med. J.*, 292:1165–1167.

Coie, J. D., Watt, N. F., West, S. G., Hawkins, J. D., Arsanow, J. R., Markman, H. J., Ramey, S. L., Shure, M. B. & Long, B. (1993), The science of prevention: A conceptual framework and some directions for a national research program. *Amer. Psychol.*, 48:1013–1022.

Consortium on the School-Based Promotion of Social Competence. (1994), The school-based promotion of social competence: Theory, research, practice, and policy. In: *Stress, Risk, and Resilience in Children and Adolescents*, ed. R. J. Haggerty, L. R. Sherrod, N. Garmezy & M. Rutter. New York: Cambridge University Press, pp. 268–316.

Cooper, P. J., Murray, L., Wilson, A. & Romaniuk, H. (2003), Controlled trial of the short- and long-term effect of psychological treatment of postpartum depression: 1. Impact on maternal mood. *Brit. J. Psychiat.*, 182:412–419.

Cowen, E. L. (2000), Psychological wellness: Some hopes for the future. In: *The Promotion of Wellness in Children and Adolescents*, ed. D. Cicchetti, J. Rapaport, I. Sandler & R. P. Weissberg. Washingon, DC: Child Welfare League of America Press, pp. 477–503.

Cox, A. D. (1993a), Befriending young mothers. *Brit. J. Psychiat.*, 163:6–18.

———- (1993b), Preventive aspects of child psychiatry. *Arch. Dis. Childhood*, 68:691–701.

———— Pound, A. & Puckering, C. (1992), Newpin: A befriending scheme and therapeutic network for carers of young children.

In: *The Children Act 1989 and Family Support*, ed. J. Gibbons. London: HMSO, pp. 37–47.

Crijnen, A. A., Bengi-Arslan, L. & Verhulst, F. C. (2000), Teacher reported problem behavior in Turkish immigrant and Dutch children: A cross-cultural comparison. *Acta Psychiatrica Scandinavica*, 102:439–444.

Cummings, E. M. & Daries, P. T. (1994), Maternal depression and child development. *J. Child Psychol. & Psychiatry*, 35:73–112.

Cynader, M. S. (1994), Mechanisms of brain development and their role in health and wellbeing. *J. Amer. Acad. Arts & Sci.*, 123:155–165.

Dawson, G., Ashman, S. B. & Carver, L. J. (2000), The role of early experience in shaping behavioral and brain development and its implication for social policy. *Develop. & Psychopathol.*, 12:695–712.

——— Frey, K., Panagiotides, H., Yamada, E., Hessl, D. & Osterling, J. (1999), Infants of depressed mothers exhibit atypical frontal electrical brain activity during interactions with mother and with a familiar, nondepressed adult. *Child Develop.* 70:1058–1066.

——— ——— Self, J., Panagiotides, H., Hessl, D., Yamada, D. & Rinaldi, J. (1999), Frontal electrical brain activity in infants of depressed mothers: Relations to variations in infant behaviour. *Develop. & Psychopathol.*, 11:589–605.

——— & Osterling, J. (1997), Early intervention in autism: Effectiveness and common elements of current approaches. In: *The Effectiveness of Early Intervention: Second Generation Research*, ed. M. J. Guralnick. Baltimore, MD: Brookes, pp. 307–326.

——— Panagiotides, H., Grofer-Klinger, L. & Spieker, S. J. (1997), Infants of depressed and non-depressed mothers exhibit differences in frontal brain electrical activity during the expression of negative emotions. *Develop. Psychol.*, 33:650–656.

DeBellis, M. D., Keshavan, M. S., Clark, D. B., Casey, B. J., Giedd, J. N., Boring, A. M., Frustaci, K. & Ryan, N. D. (1999), A. E. Bennett Research Award: Developmental Traumatology. Part II: Brain Development. *Biolog. Psychiatry*, 45:1271–1284.

Department for Education and Skills. (2001), Sure Start: Promoting speech and language development, guidance for Sure Start Programs. Nottingham: DfES.

Diamond, A. & Goldman-Rakic, P. (1989), Comparison of human infants and rhesus monkeys on Piaget's A-not-B task: Evidence for dependence on dorsolateral prefrontal cortex. *Exper. Brain Res.*, 74:24–40.

Dickstein, S., Seifer, R., Hayden, L. C., Schiller, M., Sameroff, A. J., Keitner, G., Miller, V., Rasmussen, S., Matzko, M. & Magee, K. D. (1998), Levels of family assessment. II. Impact of maternal psychopathology on family functioning. *J. Fam. Psychol.*, 12:23–40.

Dryfoos, J. G. (1990), *Adolescents at Risk*. New York: Oxford University Press.

Dunn, J. (1996), The Emanuel Miller Memorial Lecture 1995. Children's relationships: Bridging the divide between cognitive and social development. *J. Child Psychol. & Psychiat.*, 37:507–518.

Durlak, J. A. & Wells, A. M. (1997), Primary prevention mental health programs for children and adolescents: A meta-analytic review. *Amer. J. Comm. Psychol.*, 25:115–152.

Edelman, G. M. (1987), *Neural Darwinism*. New York: Basic Books.

——— (1989), *The Remembered Present*. New York: Basic Books.

Elias, M. J. & Tobias, S. E. (1996), *Social Problem Solving*. New York: Guilford Press.

Fameli, M., Kitraki, E. & Stylianopoulou, F. (1994), Effects of hyperactivity on the maternal hypothalamic-pituitary-adrenal (HPA) axis during pregnancy on the development of the HPA axis and brain monoamines of the offspring. *Internat. J. Develop. Neurosci.*, 12:651–659.

Field, T., Grizzle, N., Scafidi, F., Abrams, S. & Richardson, S. (1996), Massage therapy for infants of depressed mothers. *Inf. Behav. & Develop.*, 11:109–114.

Fuerst, J. S. & Fuerst, D. (1993), Chicago experience with an early childhood program: The special case of the early child-parent center program. *Urban Ed.*, 28:69–96.

Gergely, G. & Watson, J. (1999), Early social-emotional development: Contingency perception and the social biofeedback model. In: *Early Social Cognition*, ed. P. Rochat. Hillsdale, NJ: Lawrence Erlbaum Associates, pp. 101–137.

Glass, N. (1999), Origins of the Sure Start programme. *Children & Soc.*, 13:257–264.

Goodman, S. H. & Gotlib, I. H. (1999), Risk for psychopathology in the children of depressed mothers: A developmental model for understanding mechanisms of transmission. *Psycholog. Rev.*, 106:458–490.

Grantham-McGregor, S. M., Powell, C. A., Walker, S. P. & Himes, J. H. (1991), Nutritional supplementation, psychological stimulation and mental development of stunted children: The Jamaican study. *Lancet*, 338:1–5.

Green, A. (2000), Science and science fiction in infant research. In: *Clinical and Observational Psychoanalytic Research*, ed. J. Sandler, A.-M. Sandler & R. Davies. London: Karnac Books, pp. 41–73.

Gunnar, M. R., Broderson, L., Nachmias, M., Buss, K. & Rigatuso, J. (1996), Stress reactivity and attachment security. *Develop. Psychobiol.*, 29:191–204.

——— & Chisholm, K. C. (1999), Effects of early institutional rearing and attachment quality on salivary cortisol levels in adopted Romanian children. Presented at the Society for Research in Child Development, Albuquerque, NM, April.

Hales, C. N. (1997), Non-insulin dependent diabetes mellitus. *Brit. Med. Bull.*, 53:109–122.

Hammen, C., Burge, D., Burney, E. & Adrian, C. (1990), Longitudinal study of diagnoses in children of women with unipolar and bipolar affective disorder. *Arch. Gen. Psychiatry*, 47:1112–1117.

——— Rudolph, K., Weisz, J., Rao, U. & Burge, D. (1999), The context of depression in clinic-referred youth: Neglected areas in treatment. *J. Amer. Acad. Child Adolesc. Psychiat.*, 38:64–71.

Heinicke, C. M. & Ponce, V. A. (1999), Relation-based early family intervention. In: *Rochester Symposium on Developmental Psychopathology, Vol. 9*, ed. D. Cicchetti & S. L. Toth. Rochester, NY: University of Rochester Press.

——— Fineman, N. R., Ruth, G., Recchia, S. L., Guthrie, D. & Rodning, C. (1999), Relationship-based intervention with at-risk mothers: Outcome in the first year of life. *Inf. Mental Health J.*, 20:349–374.

——— Fineman, N. R., Ponce, V. A. & Guthrie, D. (2001), Relation based intervention with at-risk mothers: Outcome in the second year of life. *Inf. Mental Health J.*, 22:431–462.

——— Goorsky, M., Moscov, S., Dudley, K., Gordon, J., Schneider, C. & Guthrie, D. (2000), Relationship-based intervention with at-risk mothers: Factors affecting variations in outcome. *Inf. Mental Health J.*, 21:133–155.

Hewitt, K. & Crawford, W. V. (1988), Resolving behavior problems in pre-school children. Evaluation of a workshop for health visitors. *Child Care, Health & Develop.*, 14:1–9.

Howe, D. (1998), *Patterns of Adoption.* Oxford: Blackwell Science.

Huttenlocher, P. R. & Dabholkar, A. S. (1997), Regional difference in synaptogenesis in human cerebral cortex. *J. Compar. Neurol.*, 387:167–178.

Innocenti, M. S. & White, K. R. (1993), Are more intensive early intervention programs more effective? A review of the literature. *Exceptionality*, 4:31–50.

Johnson, D. L. (1990), The Houston parent–child development center project: Disseminating a viable program for enhancing at-risk families. *Prev. Human Serv.*, 7:89–108.

———— (1991), Primary prevention of behavior problems in young children: The Houston Parent–Child Development Center. In: *Fourteen Ounces of Prevention: A Casebook for Practitioners*, ed. R. Price, E. L. Cowen, R. P. Lorion & J. Ramos-McKay. Washington, DC: American Psychological Association, pp. 44–52.

———— & Walker, T. (1987), Primary prevention of behavior problems in Mexican-American children. *Amer. J. Comm. Psychol.*, 15:375–385.

Kandel, E. R. (1998), A new intellectual framework for psychiatry. *Amer. J. Psychiatry*, 155:457–469.

Karoly, L. A., Greenwood, P. W., Everingham, S. S., Houbé, J., Kilburn, M. R., Rydell, C. P., Sanders, M. & Chiesa, J. (1998), *Investing in Our Children: What We Know and Don't Know About the Costs and Benefits of Early Childhood Interventions.* Santa Monica, CA: RAND Corp.

Karweit, N. L. (1989), Effective preschool programs for students at risk. In: *Effective Programs for Students at Risk*, ed. R. E. Slavin, N. L. Karweit & N. A. Madden. Needham, MA: Allyn & Bacon, pp. 75–102.

———— (1994), Can preschool alone prevent early learning failure? In: *Preventing Early School Failure*, ed. R. E. Slavin, N. L. Karweit & B. A. Wasik. Needham, MA: Allyn & Bacon, pp. 58–77.

Kazdin, A. (2000), Mental Health Services Research.

———— Holland, L. & Crowley, M. (1997), Family experience of barriers to treatment and premature termination from child therapy. *J. Consult. & Clin. Psychol.*, 65:453–463.

Kellam, S. G., Rebok, G. W., Ialongo, N. & Mayer, L. S. (1994), The course and malleability of aggressive behavior from early first grade into middle school: Results of a developmental epidemiologically-based preventive trial. *J. Child Psychol. & Child Psychiatr. & Allied Disc.*, 35:259–281.

Kendrick, D., Elkan, R., Hewitt, M., Dewey, M., Blair, M., Robinson, J., Williams, D. & Brummell, K. (2000), Does home visiting improve parenting and the quality of the home environment? A systematic review meta-analysis. *Arch. Dis. Child*, 82:443–451.

Kitzman, H., Olds, D., Henderson Jr., C. R., Hanks, C., Cole, R., Tatelbaum, R., Connochie, K. M., Sidora, K., Luckey, D. W., Shaver, D., Engelhardt, K., James, D. & Barnard, K. (1997), Effect of prenatal and infancy home visitation by nurses on pregnancy outcomes, childhood injuries, and repeated childbearing: A randomized controlled trial. *J. Amer. Med. Assn.*, 278:644–652.

Knitzer, J. (2000), *Promoting Resilience: Helping Young Children and Families Affected by Substance Abuse, Domestic Violence, and Depression in the Context of Welfare Reform* (Children and Welfare Reform Issue Brief no. 8). New York: National Center for Children in Poverty.

Knudsen, E. I. (1999), Early experience and critical periods. *Develop. Psychol.*, 26:398–408.

Kochanska, G. (1997), Mutually responsive orientation between mothers and their young children: Implications for early socialization. *Child Devel.*, 68:94–112.

——— & Aksan, N. (1995), Mother–child mutually positive affect, the quality of child compliance to requests and prohibitions, and maternal control as correlates of early internalization. *Child Devel.*, 66:236–254.

——— & Coy, K. C. (1997), Inhibitory control as a contributor to conscience in childhood: From toddler to early school age. *Child Devel.*, 68:263–277.

——— & Murray, K. T. (2000), Mother-child mutually responsive orientation and conscience development: From toddler to early school age. *Child Devel.*, 71:417–431.

Kurstjens, S. & Wolke, D. (2001), Effects of maternal depression on cognitive development of children over the first 7 years of life. *J. Child Psychol. & Psychiat.*, 42:623–636.

Lally, J. R., Mangione, P. L. & Honig, A. S. (1988), The Syracuse University Family Development Research Project: Long-range impact of an early intervention with low-income children and their families. In: *Annual Advances in Applied Developmental Psychology, Vol. 3*, ed. D. R. Powell. Norwood, NJ: Ablex, pp. 79–104.

Larson, C. P. (1980), Efficacy of prenatal and postpartum home visits on child health and development. *Pediatrics*, 66:191–197.

Lee, V. E., Brooks-Gunn, J. & Schnur, E. (1988), Does Head Start work? A 1-year follow-up comparison of disadvantaged children attending Head Start, no preschool, and other preschool programs. *Devel. Psychol.*, 24:210–222.

Liu, D., Diorio, J., Tannenbaum, B., Caldji, C., Francis, D., Freedman, A., Sharma, S., Pearson, D., Plotsky, P. M. & Meaney, M. J. (1997), Maternal care, hippocampal glucocorticoid receptors, and hypothalamic-pituitary-adrenal responses to stress. *Science*, 277:1659–1662.

Loeber, R., Burke, J. D., Lahey, B. B., Winters, A. & Zera, M. (2000), Oppositional defiant and conduct disorder: a review of the past 10 years, part I. *J. Amer. Acad. Child Adolesc. Psychiat.*, 39:1468–1484.

——— & Farrington, D. P. (2000), Young children who commit crime: Epidemiology, developmental origins, risk factors, early interventions, and policy implications. *Devel. Psychopathol.*, 12:737–762.

——— & Stouthamer-Loeber, M. (1998), Development of juvenile aggression and violence. Some common misconceptions and controversies. *Amer. Psychol.*, 53:242–259.

Lorion, R. P. (1990), Evaluation HIV risk-reduction efforts: Ten lessons from psychotherapy and prevention outcome strategies. *J. Comm. Psychol.*, 18:325–336.

Lovejoy, M. C., Graczyk, P. A., O'Hare, E. & Neuman, G. (2000), Maternal depression and parenting behavior: A meta-analytic review. *Clin. Psychol. Rev.*, 20:561–592.

Lyons-Ruth, K., Connell, D. B. & Grunebaum, H. U. (1990), Infants at social risk: Maternal depression and family support services as mediators of infant development and security of attachment. *Child Devel.*, 61:85–98.

Malphurs, J. E., Field, T. M., Larrain, C., Pickens, J. & Pelaez-Nogueras, M. (1996), Altering withdrawn and intrusive interaction behaviors of depressed mothers. *Inf. Mental Health J.*, 17:152–160.

Marcon, R. A. (1992), Differential effects of three preschool models on inner-city 4 year olds. *Early Childhood Res. Quart.*, 7:517–530.

McGuire, J. & Earls, F. (1991), Prevention of psychiatric disorders in early childhood. *J. Child Psychol. & Psychiatry*, 32:129–154.

Meaney, M. J., Aitken, D., Bhatnager, S., van Berkel, C. & Sapolsky, R. M. (1988), Effect of neonatal handling on age-related impairments associated with the hippocampus. *Science*, 239:766.

Minde, K., Shosenberg, N., Thompson, J. & Marton, P. (1983), Self-help groups in a premature nursery—Follow-up at one year. In: *Frontiers of Infant Psychiatry*, ed. J. D. Call, E. Galenson & R. L. Tyson. New York: Basic Books, pp. 264–272.

Minty, B. (1999), Annotation: Outcomes in longterm foster family case. *Child Psychol. Psychiatry*, 40:991–999.

Morgan, G. & Gibson, K. R. (1991), Nutritional and environmental interactions in brain development. In: *Brain Maturation and Cognitive Development*, ed. K. R. Gibson & A. C. Petersen. New York: Aldine de Bruyter, pp. 91–106.

MORI (Market and Opinion Research International Department for Education and Skills) (2001), The Impact of Sure Start: One Year On (result of a small qualitative study). http://www.surestart.gov.uk/_doc/0_B065B7.pdf.

Morton, J. & Frith, U. (1995), Causal modeling: A structural approach to developmental psychology. In: *Developmental Psychopathology, Vol. 1*, ed. D. Cicchetti & D. J. Cohen. New York: Wiley, pp. 357–390.

Murry, L., Cooper, P. J., Wilson, A. & Romaniuk, H. (2003), Controlled trial of the short- and long-term effect of psychological treatment of postpartum depression: 2. Impact on the mother–child relationship and child outcome. *Brit. J. Psychiatry*, 182:420–427.

Nachmias, M., Gunnar, M. R., Mangelsdorf, S., Parritz, R. H. & Buss, K. (1996), Behavioral inhibition and stress reactivity: Moderating role of attachment security. *Child Develop.*, 67:508–522.

Nagin, D. S. & Tremblay, R. E. (2001), Parental and early childhood predictors of persistent physical aggression in boys from kindergarten to high school. *Arch. Gen. Psychiatry*, 58:389–394.

National Institute of Mental Health (1995), *A Plan for Prevention Research for the National Institute of Mental Health: A Report to the National Advisory Mental Health Council*. Rockville, MD: National Institute of Mental Health.

*Newsweek* (1997), Your child: From birth to three. Spring/Summer.

Oda, D. S., Heilbron, D. & Taylor, H. J. (1995), A preventive child health program: The effect of telephone and home visits by public health nurses. *Amer. J. Pub. Health*, 85:854–855.

Office of Juvenile Justice and Delinquency Prevention (1998), Serious and violent juvenile offenders. *Juvenile Justice Bulletin*. Washington, DC: US Department of Justice, OJJDP.

Olds, D. L., Eckenrode, J., Henderson Jr., C. R., Kitzman, H., Powers, J., Cole, R., Sidora, K., Morris, P., Pettitt, L. M. & Luckey, D. (1997), Long-term effects of home visitation on maternal life course and child abuse and neglect: Fifteen-year follow-up of a randomized trial. *J. Amer. Med. Assn.*, 278:637–643.

————— Henderson Jr., J. R., Chamberlin, R. & Tatelbaum, R. (1986), Preventing child abuse and neglect: A randomized trial of nurse home visitation. *Pediatrics*, 78:65–78.

————— ————— & Kitzman, H. (1994), Does prenatal and infancy nurse home visitation have enduring effects on qualities of parental caregiving and child health from 25 to 50 months of life? *Pediatrics*, 93:89–98.

————— ————— ————— Eckenrode, J., Cole, R. & Tatelbaum, R. (1998), The promise of home visitation: Results of two randomized trials. *J. Comm. Psychol.*, 26:1–21.

————— ————— & Tatelbaum, R. (1994), Prevention of intellectual impairment in children of women who smoke cigarettes during pregnancy. *Pediatrics*, 93:228–233.

————— Henderson Jr., J. R., Tatelbaum, R. & Chamberlin, R. (1986), Improving the delivery of prenatal care and outcomes of pregnancy: A randomized trial of nurse home visitation. *Pediatrics*, 77:16–28.

Orrell-Valente, J. K., Pinderhughes, E. E., Valente, E., Laird, R. D. & the Conduct Problems Prevention Research Group (1999), If it's offered, will they come? Influences on parents' participation in a community-based conduct problems prevention program. *Amer. J. Comm. Psychol.*, 27:753–783.

Pfannenstiel, A. & Honig, A. S. (1995), Effects of a prenatal 'Information and Insights about Infants' program on the knowledge base of first-time low-education fathers one month postnatally. *Early Child Devel. & Care*, 111:87–105.

Plotsky, P. M. & Meaney, M. J. (1993), Early, postnatal experience alters hypothalamic corticotropin-releasing factor (CRF) mRNA, median eminence CRF content and stress-induced release in adult rats. *Brain Res. Molec. Brain Res.*, 18:195–200.

Pollak, S. D., Cicchetti, D., Klorman, R. & Brumaghim, J. T. (1997), Cognitive brain event-related potentials and emotion processing in maltreated children. *Child Devel.*, 68:773–787.

Pound, A. & Mills, M. (1985), A pilot evaluation of Newpin. *Newsletter of the Assn. Child Psychol. & Psychiat.*, 70:13–15.

Quinton, D., Rushton, A., Dance, C. & Mayes, D. (1998), *Joining New Families: A Study of Adoption and Fostering in Middle Childhood*. Chichester: Wiley.

Ramey, C. T., Yeates, K. O. & Short, E. J. (1984), The plasticity of intellectual development: Insights from preventive intervention. *Child Develop.*, 55:1913–1925.

Reynolds, A. J. (1994), Effects of a preschool plus follow-up intervention for children at risk. *Develop. Psychol.*, 30:787–804.

Rumelhart, D. E. & McClelland, J. L. (1986), *Parallel Distributed Processing*. Cambridge, MA: MIT Press.

Rutter, M. (1990), Psychosocial resilience and protective mechanisms. In: *Risk and Protective Factors in the Development of Psychopathology*, ed. J. Rolf, A. S. Masten, D. Cicchetti & S. Weintraub, New York: Cambridge University Press, pp. 181–214.

Sanders, M. R., Markie-Dadds, C., Tully, L. & Bor, B. (2000), The Triple P-Positive Parenting Program: A comparison of enhanced, standard, and self-directed behavioral family intervention for parents of children with early onset conduct problems. *J. Consult. Clin. Psychol.*, 68:624–640.

Sapolsky, R. M. (1997), The importance of a well-groomed child. *Science*, 277:1620–1621.

Schneider, M. L. (1992), Prenatal stress exposure alters postnatal behavioral expression under conditions of novelty challenge in rhesus monkey infants. *Develop. Psychobiol.*, 25:529–540.

Schore, A. (1997), Neurobiology and psychoanalysis. In: *The Neurobiological and Developmental Basis of Psychotherapeutic Intervention*, ed. E. A. M. Moscowitz, S. Ellman, C. Kaye & C. Monle. Northvale, NJ: Aronson.

Schweinhart, J. L., Barnes, H. & Weikart, D. P. (1993), *Significant Benefits: The High/Scope Perry School Study Through Age 27.* Ypsilanti, MI: High/Scope Press.

——— Berrueta-Clement, J. R., Barnett, W. S., Epstein, A. S. & Weikart, D. P. (1985), Effects of the Perry Preschool Program on youths through age 19: A summary. *Topics Early Childhood Sp. Ed.*, 5:26–35.

——— & Weikart, D. P. (1993), Success by empowerment: The High/Scope Perry Preschool Study through age 27. *Young Children*, 49:54–58.

Seitz, V., Rosenbaum, L. K. & Apfel, N. H. (1985), Effects of family support intervention: A ten-year follow-up. *Child Devel.*, 56:376–391.

Shively, C. A. & Clarkson, T. B. (1994), Social status and coronary artery atherosclerosis in female monkeys. *Arterioscler. & Thrombosis*, 14:721–726.

Shure, M. & Spivack, G. (1974), *Social Adjustment of Young Children.* San Francisco, CA: Jossey-Bass.

———— & ———— (1982), Interpersonal problem-solving in young children: A cognitive approach to prevention. *Amer. J. Comm. Psychol.*, 10:341–356.

———— & ———— (1988), Interpersonal cognitive problem-solving. In: *Fourteen Ounces of Prevention: A Casebook for Practitioners*, ed. R. Price, E. L. Cowen, R. P. Lorion & J. Ramos-McKay, Washington, DC: American Psychological Association, pp. 69–82.

Spoth, R., Goldberg, C. & Redmond, C. (1999), Engaging families in longitudinal preventive intervention research: Discrete time survival analysis of socioeconomic and social-emotional risk factors. *J. Consult. & Clin. Psychol.*, 67:157–163.

St. Pierre, R., Goodson, B., Layzer, J. & Bernstein, L. (1994), *National Evaluation of the Comprehensive Child Development Program: Report to Congress.* Cambridge, MA: ABT Associates.

Stevenson, J., Bailey, V. & Simpson, J. (1988), Feasible intervention in families with parenting difficulties: A primary prevention perspective on child abuse. In: *The Prediction and Prevention of Child Abuse and Neglect*, ed. K. Browne. Chichester: Wiley, pp. 121–138.

Strayhorn, J. M. & Weidman, C. S. (1991), Follow-up one year after parent-child interaction training: Effects on behavior of preschool children. *J. Amer. Acad. Child Adolesc. Psychiatry*, 30:138–143.

Takanishi, R. & DeLeon, R. H. (1994), A head start for the 21st century. *Amer. Psychol.*, 49:120–122.

Thomas, A. & Chess, S. (1977), *Temperament and Development.* New York: Brunner/Mazel.

Thompson, M. J. J. & Bellenis, C. (1992), A joint assessment and treatment service for the under fives. *Newsletter Assn. Child Psychol. Psychiatry*, 14:221–227.

van den Boom, D. C. (1994), The influence of temperament and mothering on attachment and exploration: An experimental manipulation of sensitive responsiveness among lower-class mothers with irritable infants. *Child Devel.*, 65:1449–1469.

——— (1995), Do first-year intervention effects endure? Follow-up during toddlerhood of a sample of Dutch irritable infants. *Child Devel.*, 66:1798–1816.

van Ijzendoorn, M. H., Juffer, F. & Duyvesteyn, M. G. C. (1995), Breaking the intergenerational cycle of insecure attachment: A review of the effects of attachment-based interventions on maternal sensitivity and infant security. *J. Child Psychol. & Psychiat.*, 36:225–248.

VanPelt, J., Corna, M. A., Uylings, H. B. M. & Lopes da Silva, P. H., eds. (1994), *The Self-Organizing Brain*. Amsterdam: Elsevier.

Villar, J., Farnot, U., Barros, F., Victora, C., Langer, A. & Belizan, J. M. (1992), A randomized trial of psychosocial support during high-risk pregnancies. *New Engl. J. Med.*, 327:1266–1271.

Walker, T. & Johnson, D. L. (1988), A follow-up evaluation of the Houston Parent-Child Development Center: Intelligence test results. *J. Genetic Psychol.*, 149:377–381.

Wasik, B. H. & Karweit, N. L. (1994), Off to a good start: Effects of birth to three interventions on early school success. In: *Preventing School Failure*, ed. R. E. Slavin, N. L. Karweit & B. A. Wasik. Needham, MA: Allyn & Bacon, pp. 13–57.

——— Ramey, C. T., Bryant, D. M. & Sparling, J. J. (1990), A longitudinal study of two early intervention strategies: Project CARE. *Child Devel.*, 61:1682–1696.

Watson, J. E., Kirby, R. S., Kelleher, K. J. & Bradley, R. H. (1996), Effects of poverty on home environment: An analysis of three-year outcome data for low birth weight premature infants. *J. Ped. Psychol.*, 21:419–431.

——— (1995), Self-orientation in early infancy: The general role of contingency and the specific case of reaching to the mouth. In: *The Self in Infancy*, ed. P. Rochat. Amsterdam: Elsevier, pp. 375–393.

Webster-Stratton, C. (1996), Preventing conduct problems in Head Start children: Strengthening parenting competencies. Presented at meeting of the American Public Health Association, New York.

———— (1998), Preventing conduct problems in Head Start children: Strengthening parenting competencies. *J. Consult. Clin. Psychol.*, 66:715–730.

Weinstock, M., Fride, E. & Hertzberg, R. (1988), Prenatal stress effects on functional development of the offspring. In: *Progress in Brain Research*, ed. G. J. Boer, M. G. P. Feenstra, M. Mirmiran, D. F. Swaab & F. VanHaaren, Amsterdam: Elsevier, pp. 319–331.

Weissberg, R. P. & Bell, D. N. (1997), A meta-analytic review of primary prevention programs for children and adolescents: Contributions and caveats. *Amer. J. Comm. Psychol.*, 25:207–214.

# Index

# THE VET HAS NINE LIVES

The second in the hilarious series by the author of *It's a Vet's Life*.

Now a partner in his uncle's Knightsbridge veterinary practice, Michael Morton is asked to do a country locum for a friend, Phil Brogan. But even before he starts, Michael is given a timely warning:

> 'Just remember that the animals of Craftly aren't doggies and pussies of Knightsbridge. You know, Michael, in London you've a chance of a bit of peace. Even a vet can disappear in the crowd. Not in Craftly; it's a community as concentrated as pure alcohol. A village is dynamite; and the vet needs nine lives . . .'

'Lots of laughs and lots of fascinating animal revelations (and a few human ones too).'                    SHE

'What Richard Gordon has done for doctors, Alex Duncan is doing for vets.'                    BOOKS AND BOOKMEN

Also in *Star* by Alex Duncan

# THE VET HAS
# NINE LIVES

Alex Duncan

**A STAR BOOK**
published by
WYNDHAM PUBLICATIONS

A Star Book
Published in 1976
by W. H. Allen & Co. Ltd.
A Howard & Wyndham Company
44 Hill Street, London W1X 8LB

First published in Great Britain by
Michael Joseph Ltd.
Star edition reprinted 1976

Printed in Great Britain by
Richard Clay (The Chaucer Press), Ltd., Bungay, Suffolk

ISBN 0 352 39879 5

# CHAPTER 1

How should I have known? How is one to take seriously a girl dressed in zipped fur boots, a g-string of velvet fig-leaves and a handknitted beige woollie? There she stood, bare booted legs tautly dug into the sheepskin hearthrug . . . my fiancée Julia.

'You needn't laugh, Michael.' She lifted the edge of her jersey to let the fire warm the naked small of her back. 'I mean it . . . I really mean it.'

'Of course you do, darling. But let's be reasonable . . .'

'Reasonable!' Her grey bushbaby eyes looked larger than ever. I couldn't see in them the slightest liking, let alone love for me.

'Well, we've had rotten luck about that house.'

'Yes, it's rotten luck that you're so slow. If you'd signed the lease the day it came instead of three weeks later the house would be ours, and the Development Company couldn't have done a thing about it.'

'Julia dear, I couldn't sign a lease without reading it.'

'You could have read it at night in bed . . . Oh, all right, don't tell me; you were up with Mr Topper's sick cat and Mrs Preston's poodle. But even a vet's entitled to some private life of his own.'

'Am I?'

'I'll give you time to find out.' Julia's voice had become disturbingly soft. 'Our wedding's off, and it'll stay off until we have a roof over our heads.'

'But we have a roof . . . two in fact.'

Julia did not seem interested in two roofs. She frowned at me, eyes bright with suppressed tears, and marched out of the room letting the heavy mahogany door slam shut.

At last it dawned on me that she'd been angry, really angry. But I still couldn't see why. Of course a house opposite my consulting rooms would have been convenient for us, but it wasn't much of a house or it wouldn't have stood empty for so long. In fact, looking at it on an icy February day, our Knightsbridge Mews wasn't much of a mews. It would take the millions of a Radiant Homes Development Company to make this corner of London even vaguely radiant.

My Uncle Simon came in, stripped off his white coat and flung it into the corner behind the settee. He could afford to fling things; having married Muriel he could be sure they'd be picked up. A bachelor like me had to do his own picking up.

Simon sat down and spread his hands over the fire. 'You'd better call on the Pipers this evening,' he said. 'Their monkey's still too sleepy for my liking. And while you're in Brook Street you might as well visit Lady Jane's fish . . . they've been eating each other.'

'What are *you* doing tonight?'

'Taking Muriel to a show. You don't mind, do you?'

'No, no. I may as well look after your patients while I can.'

'And what does that mean?'

My partner's relaxed smugness had helped me to a decision. 'You are going to be on your own for two or three months.'

'What!'

'*You* are going to work, partner. And I am going to do a locum for Phil Brogan in Surrey. I had an SOS from him. He's got undulant fever and he's hard up for someone reliable to keep his practice going. That's me.'

'Don't be an ass. What do you know about pigs? Anyway you can't just beetle off; we've got an agreement and . . .'

'That's just what I was thinking. According to our agreement I'm entitled to six weeks holiday. So I'm taking the six weeks I didn't have last year plus this year's holiday.'

'Look here, this is our busiest time. You can't leave me flat.'

'I'm leaving you sitting up, looking revoltingly fit.'

'Michael,' he shook his head, sadly. 'Lord Chequers has asked me down for some rough-shooting. I really think I ought to go . . . In our kind of practice one can't afford to neglect the social side.'

'The social side will keep.'

'And Julia?' Simon guessed, rather cleverly. 'She won't like starting married life in someone else's house. She didn't want to marry you while you live *here*, remember.'

'She won't marry me, and that's that.'

6

'You mean . . .'

'Yes, the house has fallen through, so the wedding's off.'

'Nonsense boy, you don't understand women. Talk to her.'

'What do you think I've been doing? I know Julia,' I told him. 'While I'm in London she won't marry me . . . not as long as she and I live in a couple of rooms in your house . . .'

'And she won't marry you while you're living in Phil Brogan's house either, so . . .'

'She's got to be on her own and think again.'

'Or stop thinking and find herself another boy friend. It's a risk.'

'I'm going to take it.'

Simon said nothing. I'd done it. And I tried my best to feel fed up with his gaunt mahogany room, with the draughty house, the down-at-heel Knightsbridge Mews, and with the small town-animals who made up the majority of our patients. What I needed were horses and hounds, pigs and cows; they were a *man's* animals.

'It's the cattle you've got to watch, Michael.' Phil Brogan raised himself on his elbows, found it too much of an effort and flopped back into his pillows. An elderly nurse was regarding me with hostility.

'Don't worry, Phil,' I said, chiefly to convince the nurse that I too had the patient's welfare at heart.

'Listen,' Phil persisted, 'I know what I'm saying. That outbreak of foot-and-mouth last year was hell. Out at all hours; no sleep; powerdiggers making mass-graves for all those fine beasts. The waste of it! . . . the stink of disinfectant. Couldn't get the stink out of my nose for weeks. Michael, you've got to be on the ball. One case of foot-and-mouth and before you know where you are you've got an epidemic on your hands.'

'Want to scare me off?'

'I'm not that sick. No, just remember that the animals in Craftly aren't doggies and pussies of Knightsbridge. You know, Michael, in London you've a chance of a bit of peace. Even a vet can disappear in the crowd. Not in Craftly; it's a community as concentrated as pure alcohol. A village is dynamite; and the vet needs nine lives.'

'Thanks for the warning.'

'Well, just don't ruin a promising career; yours *or* mine.'

7

'Any more sick cows about the place?'

'Don't think so. Primrose . . . the one that's given me my dose of fever was the last of that lot. You should find things pretty straightforward just now, that's as far as anything can be straightforward with Sir Roger about.'

'Sir Roger?'

'Coolcrow.'

'The racehorse owner?'

'And owner of Lady Beverley, six dachshunds, Member of Parliament – he doesn't yet own the House – chairman of this, that and the other company, one-fifth owner of the greyhound Kenwood.'

'The hound that belongs to a syndicate of M.P.s?'

'That's the one. Two of his masters are Labour, one's a Liberal, two are Conservatives. Clearly they *had* to call the poor beast Kenwood . . . A word of warning; any time you visit a Coolcrow animal take along a consultation chit and make sure you get it signed, either by the Coolcrows or by Cecil – their trainer.'

'What are those chits?'

'Just a confirmation that you've been consulted. Had them specially printed for people like the Coolcrows; saves arguments about my bill.'

'They're stingy?'

'No worse than most of my other animal-owners. Only, Sir Roger's a *politician* as well as a businessman.'

The nurse had come to stand over me like a figure of fate. 'Mr Morton, you're tiring the patient.' She gave Phil an absent-minded smile. 'Mustn't have you look worn-out when your wife comes in, must we?'

'My wife's seen worse,' said Phil, with a grin. 'That time when I slept with . . .'

The nurse drew herself up but wouldn't budge.

'With Mimi the prize sow . . . oh well, I'll tell you about it another day. We mustn't tire the staff, must we? . . . When are you moving down to Craftly?'

'Today.'

'Good . . . Finished your chores for the wedding?'

'There isn't going to be a wedding.'

'What have you done to Julia?'

'Didn't get the house she wanted. Radiant Homes Development Company pipped me at the post.'

8

'It *would* be Radiant Homes. That's one of Sir Roger's companies. Don't think you'll get any change out of him though.'

'I'm not going to try. We'll find another house *one* day.'

'Is Julia going to wait?'

Phil's question worried me as I left the hospital. It niggled at the back of my mind while I packed my bags and pursued me as I drove my bubble-car through the dripping lanes of Surrey.

Julia had always been liable to do the unexpected; anything could happen once I'd left her to her own devices. I imagined her back at the Purple Pigeon, the striptease joint in Soho where I'd found her. Of course it was true that Julia had been the star-turn and not a stripper, and that the Purple Pigeon was owned by an elder of the kirk with strict ideas about morals and 'art'. But all the same I hated the idea of my Julia back in the entertainment tangle.

I also had to admit that I hated the thought of Julia in West End restaurants with some fast-talking, fast-spending man. And there was the problem of Julia's peculiar aversion to wearing things that covered her legs. It was too easy to misunderstand a girl who mostly wore fig-leaves and fur boots. How would she manage without me? She'd been safe while I had been there to explain to casual visitors that her costume was due to something psychological dating back to her early childhood in India.

\* \* \*

The High Street of Craftly was deserted, presumably because people were at supper. I was hungry myself. I turned right past the doctor's house, bumped along a frozen farm-track and stopped the bubble in the yard. The windows of Phil's old farm house were dark. The bell, on the wire beside the door, gave a reluctant tinkle.

I waited, shivered, gave the bell another pull. No reply. Hands outstretched I made my way round the house, stumbling over a wheelbarrow and barking my shin on a ladder. But there was a light in the kitchen and the back door was open.

A pot of soup was simmering away on the Aga cooker, there was a nice smell of baking, and on the draining-board

I saw a perfect still life of onions, potatoes and five or six wood-pigeons. Suddenly I became aware of another still life . . . Mrs Pitt, the Brogans' char, laid out on the quarry-tiled floor.

My first thought was that she'd been murdered, but there was no blood about and I noticed that her formidable bosom was peacefully rising and falling. In fact her short, sturdy figure looked quite wrong in such a position. Perhaps she was drunk. Yet there was no suggestion of alcohol when I bent down to sniff. Poor Mrs Pitt had clearly been taken ill.

I dashed out, found the yard and the road and made for the brightly-lit house of Dr Eller.

Mrs Eller, unwilling to listen to me in the cold, insisted on my coming into the drawing-room.

She pushed a chair close to the fire. 'I'm glad you've come,' she said. 'Phil was so worried about his practice. How is he?'

'Getting on quite well. Mrs Eller, is the doctor in?'

'I'll call him.' She sat down opposite me, and picked up her knitting.

'Mrs Eller . . . I'm sorry to trouble the doctor, but Mrs Pitt is unconscious. I found her on the kitchen floor and . . .'

She lifted her benevolent old-lady's face. 'Do tell me, Mr Morton, how is Phil's sister . . . the one who's out in Kenya? Such a charming girl.'

'I don't know. Mrs Pitt is lying . . .'

'And Phil's mother?' Mrs Eller chattered on gathering momentum every second. 'She did enjoy our horticultural show last summer. You know she told me her daughter grew runner-beans fourteen inches long, and they were as tender as the little ones. Mine are . . .'

'Mrs Eller,' I almost shouted. 'Mrs Pitt is ill. She's lying . . .'

'Oh yes,' she smiled briskly, 'Mrs Pitt. Did you see any birds about the place . . . dead ones with feathers?'

'Birds?'

'Yes, a chicken or a duck.'

'Well, there were some wood-pigeons.'

'Then you've nothing to worry about.'

'Hadn't the doctor better see . . .'

'It'll be quite all right.' Mrs Eller shook her head, 'Londoners do worry so . . . but I'm sure you'll settle down nicely. Now, let me make you a cup of tea.'

'No thanks. I'd better get back.'

'Oh well, I expect you're hungry . . . I do hope Phil's sister is happy in Kenya.'

When I got back Mrs Pitt, looking rosy and pink, was taking a steak and kidney pie out of the oven.

'Fancy you coming in the back way, Mr Morton,' she greeted me. 'Could 'ave hurt yourself in the dark.'

'Are you all right?' I asked.

'Course I am.'

'Well, when I came in earlier . . .'

'Oh that,' she shrugged her shoulders. 'Now that wouldn't have happened in Wandsworth.'

'Wandsworth?'

'Where I come from. It never did happen in Wandsworth, 'cause there you don't have people barge in your kitchen with birds with all their feathers on. Feathers,' she shivered, 'they make me go funny all over; what I mean is dead birds what still have their feathers. Never could abide them. When Pitt was alive he always stripped them before he gave them to me for the pot, rotten though he was . . . God rest his soul . . . Now you forget all about them pigeons, Mr Morton, and make yourself at home. There's a nice fire in the dining-room . . . and I've put you in Mr and Mrs Brogan's bedroom. Don't hear no cows there. If you want anything . . .'

'I'm just going to make a telephone call.'

'Right you are . . . and the supper's ready when you are.'

I had decided that for my own peace of mind and my future with Julia I should take some positive action. It took me ten minutes to get through to Leamington Spa and another to make some little child understand that I wanted to speak to Colonel Hanley, the Colonel, the uncle with the moustache, Julia's father.

'Yes?' he enquired, cautiously.

'Michael speaking. Sir, about the wedding . . .'

'Wedding,' he cleared his throat. 'But I thought it was all settled.'

'It was, but . . .'

'Look here, I've made up my mind. I won't mate that bitch of ours just yet.'

'That's no way to talk. Your daughter . . .'

11

'Now don't try talking me into it, old man. I know as much about bitches as you do.'

'It's disgusting. If you think . . .'

'Well, I just got bothered because she was in heat. But I can handle Biddy. So let's leave it . . .'

'Sir,' I yelled, 'I'm not talking about your alsatian bitch, I'm trying to talk to you about Julia, *Julia* . . . your daughter.'

'Oh yes.' Colonel Hanley sounded rather less interested. 'She rang up the other day . . . think she said she wasn't getting married just yet. Independent little thing, Julia. Got that from her mother, you know. Never did know when her mother would suddenly take herself off . . . painting animals in the jungle usually. That big picture of the elephants . . . is that what you want to talk about? It's no use,' the Colonel's voice became hard, 'I'm not parting with it. I told Julia, if she wants a picture as a wedding present she'll have to be satisfied with the one of the snakes. Better give me a ring the day before the wedding.'

'Colonel, the wedding's off.'

'Well, I expect Julia knows best. Her mother always did.'

'Sir, Julia does *not* know best. I wanted to ask you whether you could ask her to go home. She'd be safer with you.'

'Safer? Has anything happened to her?'

'No, no. It's just . . . I'll be away from London for two or three months and I don't like the idea of Julia being on her own in London.'

'Why? The atmosphere? I shouldn't worry about it, my boy. Julia's got perfectly healthy lungs.'

I gave up. 'Good-bye, sir.'

'Good-bye, my boy. And don't forget to give me a ring the day before the wedding.'

I decided to have at least one bottle from Phil's wine-cellar with Mrs Pitt's steak-pie . . .

My hangover was fairly mild; what had awakened me was a fit of sneezing. I'd been breathing in Patty's fluff. Stealthily the black kitten had draped itself on my shoulder and now its face lay snuggled up against my nose. I moved. So did the kitten. It stretched all fours, its claws digging into the skin of my neck.

I picked off the cat and flung it to the other end of the

double eiderdown. Patty came back for more. Though my head was throbbing I considered it simpler to get up.

Outside my window a chilly looking sun cast a damp sheen over fields and parkland, but the village itself was wrapped in a haze like stale cigarette smoke. A little girl in blue school uniform stopped at the gate below, glanced at the house, and then leaped on to the narrow wall surrounding the yard.

I watched her take a few steps, clamber across an overhanging walnut-tree, and land with acrobatic skill on the other side. She spread her arms tight-rope walker fashion, displaying fingernails so long and bright red that for a moment I believed she'd cut her hands. Those hands fluttered in some kind of rhythm.

'I live dangerous . . . ly,' she sang to herself. 'I live dangerous- pom-pom.' Her feet in a pair of flat-heeled winkle-pickers performed a dance step on the uneven flints of the wall. 'I live dangerous -ch cha cha- dangerous-like cha cha . . .' One moment she looked like one of those possessed teenagers in Soho, grimly gyrating, blonde hair all over her face, the next she'd assumed the night-club languor of a cool cat.

Suddenly she turned and dropped into a clump of rhododendron on my side of the wall. A land-rover had drawn up in the yard. Its owner, a big weather-beaten fellow about forty saw me and waved.

I opened the window.

'Morning!' he called. 'Just wanted to make sure you'd arrived. Thornton's my name . . . Spring Farm, that's my farm the other side of the Parish hall. Got the pigeons all right, Mr Morton?'

'The pigeons?'

'Good, fat birds they are.'

I remembered Mrs Pitt out cold on the floor. 'Yes, so they are. Thanks.'

'Think nothing of it,' said Thornton, magnanimously. 'Maybe you'd like to do some shooting yourself. Any time you like. Just let me know.'

The moment the land-rover was out of the gate the child popped up from the bushes and came to stand beneath my window. She was older than I'd thought, probably about twelve.

13

'Just let me know,' she mimicked Farmer Thornton. 'Big guy. Wonder what *he* wants.'

'That's not very nice of you,' I told her. 'Who are you, anyway? And what do you think you're doing here?'

'Hasn't Mr Brogan told you about me?'

'No.'

'Oh well, I'm Tail.'

'Tail?'

'Short for Tailend. You see there were nine of us and I was the youngest. Now there's only Conny and I. My brother Dick's married, and John's married, and Bill's . . .'

'Yes, I see.' I was getting cold, but even when I made to shut the window Tail stood her ground.

'Conny and I,' she raised her voice, 'we have the piggery next to Thornton's farm . . . I'm going to be an actress.'

'Well, seeing you on the wall I thought you'd be all right in a circus.'

'Don't be silly,' Tail flashed her scarlet finger-nails in a gesture of disdain. 'You can't be an actress without knowing how to move. I might have to play a girl in a circus who's eaten by the lions, or a dancer in . . .'

'Aren't you going to be late for school?'

'School!' She fished about her raincoat pockets and brought out a bottle and a stained rag. 'Conny wants you,' she put some stuff from the bottle on the rag and began to take off the nail-varnish. 'Conny thinks Myrtle's sickening for something . . . she's our best sow . . . Myrtle is . . . I wonder what *he* wants.'

'If you mean Mr Thornton . . .'

'He gave you some pigeons, didn't he?' Tail stuffed bottle and rag back into her pocket. 'I think your breakfast's ready,' she said, gazing into the window below mine. 'It's kippers . . . byee!'

It was kippers, and while I ate them Mrs Pitt hovered beside the fire.

'What *I* say is, you can't blame the child,' she told me. 'A man what's done such a thing . . . well, you never know where you are with the likes of him.'

'What has he done, Mrs Pitt?'

'You wouldn't know, being a stranger here. But there isn't many in Craftly what don't have their own idea. It was

Tail's dad had the best dairy herd in the county. And now look at them. Pigs, nothing but pigs. And who is it what's got Roderick and Petunia? Farmer Thornton.'

'Who are they?'

'The bull and the cow, of course. Best animals in the county; and that goes back twenty years if it's a day. But Mr Thornton don't fool nobody. Roderick and Petunia . . . they're the spit image of that Ayrshire what belonged to Tail's dad. And Mr Thornton, he never knew *how* his cow got in with that Ayrshire bull. An accident it was, he said . . . and, if you please, *his* cow came to no harm.'

'That sounds like old history, Mrs Pitt,' I said.

'Old 'istory, maybe. But who's got the best herd *now*? And there's poor Miss Conny working her fingers to the bone . . . and what for? *Pigs* . . . Shall I make you another pot of tea, Mr Morton?'

'No thanks.' I picked up the paper. 'I don't want anything else.'

'Well, I'll be going then. It's my day at Tit House, so I've left you some cold pie in the larder . . . Oh dear, I nearly forgot. Miss Sabina said, would you come over to Tit House today because of the owl what's still got the tummy ache. It's awful, Mr Morton . . . drop, drop all over the house. I'm never without a cloth in my hand. It would never happen in Wandsworth . . . Now if you're sure there's nothing else you want . . .'

'Quite sure,' I told her, firmly.

A pig and an owl to visit. I thought there was time enough to read the local paper as well as the *Telegraph*.

There was news about the mystery buyer of the colt Princeling the Second. He wasn't a mystery any longer. Someone from the Russian Embassy had acquired him for the 'Russian People', with the intention of racing him at Ascot. The local paper surmised that the Russians still felt rather hurt at their defeat in the Grand National. There was a rumour that the English horse they'd acquired would be trained in Surrey and ridden by a jockey imported from Russia.

Dog racing. A few lines about Kenwood, that greyhound resident at Craftly, who had once again won a race against odds such as running from the outside trap against the champions Dalwood and Kingpin.

The Veterinary Investigation Department had issued a warning. It was printed in fat type. There was a suspected case of foot-and-mouth disease on a farm some fifteen miles from Craftly. Laboratory tests were being carried out.

By far the longest report was devoted to the village of Craftly's 'splendid fight' against the Radiant Homes Development Company. Apparently the Company had submitted plans for an estate of chalet-type bungalows on the north side of the parish boundary, on land owned by Sir Roger Coolcrow. The planning authorities, under fire from the Countrymen's Association, had refused building permission.

Radiant Homes Development Company had brought a case against its adversaries, the 'splendid fight' had raged for two years or more. Now the Minister of Housing and Local Government had given his verdict. It was in all our interests, he'd said, to preserve the natural beauty of our English countryside; at the same time it was impossible to disregard the needs of our age for more and better housing. He felt that, in the present circumstances, the proposed estate would not be in accordance with planning policy. However there would be nothing against building such an estate if the Development Company were to acquire additional land closer to the centre of the village. If such land were added to the present site the scheme would fall into the category 'filling in', thus conforming with filling-in policy.

The editorial comment made it clear that the village would resist being 'filled in' with all its might. The lands adjoining Sir Roger's development site were owned by Farmer Thornton, Miss Sabina Webb of Tit House fame, and Mr Jenkins, the market gardener. All three had firmly declared their intention of keeping every crumb of their soil to themselves. I couldn't help wondering what would have happened to those three if they had not given firm declarations.

I was with them all the way, and with the rest of the villagers who were pledged to fight Radiant Homes Development Company. If it hadn't been for that beastly Company, Julia would have been there to pour my tea and give me a hand in the surgery.

\*    \*    \*

16

After I had seen the last patient, a sheepdog with a cut paw, I phoned Julia. She was still staying with Muriel and Uncle Simon, but she told me she'd be moving to a room near the zoo at the week-end.

'I was hoping you'd come down to Craftly,' I told her.

She said, 'Not for two or three weeks, Michael . . . How's the work?'

'So far less than in London . . . much the same cases; cats, dogs and canaries.'

'Nothing unusual?'

'Well I'm going to see an owl with diarrhoea presently.'

'Put a hat on, darling.'

The long gravelled drive to Tit House was overgrown with interlaced trees. Their branches stooped viciously down to scratch the new paint of my bubble-car. Birds, chiefly tits, kept whirring past in agitated darts, and as I reached the door of the house dozens of them seemed to be flying in and out of the open windows.

Mrs Pitt, duster in hand, took me into a freezing drawing-room which looked as if it hadn't been cleaned for years. Dried bird-droppings lay like plaster-mouldings on writing-desk and oak-chests, tables and chairs.

Miss Sabina Webb appeared from behind a tallboy and silently shook my hand. Her thin little fingers had a grip like a vice. Her whole lean person reminded me of steel.

'Must get that owl fit,' she announced. A tit came flying in and disappeared into a shoebox on the desk. 'The bird's making the most frightful mess.'

'Your other birds don't?' I asked.

'They don't drop nearly so much.' She went to a perch, which had no doubt belonged to a parrot once, and lifted off a little barn-owl. The bird seemed perfectly tame. Though it dropped a large watery blob on the carpet the moment I started examining it I did not think it looked ill.

'You should keep her warm,' I told Miss Webb. 'And give her some olive-oil with a pinch of salt. If that doesn't do the trick I'll send Mrs Pitt over with medicine.'

'*Not* a chemical!'

'It's a herb-extract,' I assured her. Miss Webb had sounded quite fierce.

'I disapprove of chemicals most strongly,' she said. 'Dreadful stuff! That neighbour of mine, Thornton, uses chemical fertilisers . . . murders dozens of my birds every year.'

I saw that it would be futile to contradict her theories. 'You have no idea of the trouble I've had, Mr Morton. Certain societies whose job it is to protect birds have sent people down, but in the end they did nothing . . . *nothing* to stop Thornton's murdering. There are days when my problems are quite overwhelming; if Thornton doesn't kill with chemicals he's out and about shooting those lovely wood-pigeons with a gun. And there's Conny Crosby's cats . . . always in my grounds.'

'How large are your grounds, Miss Webb?'

'Almost one acre.'

'But that's hardly enough for . . . wildlife.'

'If people were less savage it would be quite sufficient,' Sabina Webb assured me. 'I proved it last year. We had a most successful season. Dr Schwertsteiger of Switzerland came to England specially to congratulate me on my venture.'

'Something connected with medicine?'

'It *is* medicine. Mine is the first lodge of the Beginner-Birdwatcher-Brotherhood of the Post-Skiing-Fracture-Fraternity. I work on Dr Schwersteiger's methods. You see, an increasing number of people go skiing every year. Naturally there are more and more who break bones. To alleviate the depressing effects of a limb imprisoned in plaster of paris Dr Schwersteiger starts his patients on bird-watching. The little feathered friends make our patients forget about their troubles. It really is wonderful to watch their improvement. We certainly do a worthwhile job here, Mr Morton.'

'No doubt,' I muttered.

'But I simply must get the owl fit. I can't have her dropping all over the place with the first patients due to arrive the day after tomorrow.'

Curiosity got the better of me. 'Do you shut the windows when you have patients in the house?'

'Certainly not. It's a combination of bird-watching and cold that has the beneficial effect. Dr Schwersteiger wouldn't have one without the other. Naturally, if anyone does catch pneumonia we do put an electric fire in his room . . . Oh, I meant to offer you a drink. You'll have one, won't you?'

18

Without waiting for my answer Sabina Webb opened a drawer and took out two wine-glasses and a bottle of whisky whose label was new to me. She filled the glasses to the brim.

'To a happy partnership,' she said, swallowing her whisky in one go.

'To the owl,' I said. The so-called whisky burnt my throat and rendered me speechless.

'Good stuff,' Miss Sabina gave a gentle belch. 'Made by a friend of mine in Acharacle. Most of it is exported, so you won't be able to get it at your wine-merchants. But if you would like a bottle or two . . .'

'No thanks,' I managed to get out. I picked up my hat and put it on.

'Now, now, Mr Morton!' Miss Sabina looked horrified. 'Don't you know? Birds simply loathe hats.'

I avoided a couple of blue-tits which were dashing about with manic joy and made for the door. 'Give her the olive oil and salt.'

'Yes, at once. Mustn't have the little one dropping things when the patients are here.'

'Miss Sabina thinks,' Tail giggled, 'that my sister and Thornton are lovers.'

'Miss Sabina isn't interested in anything but her birds,' Conny Crosby wiped a strand of mousy hair out of her eyes.

'Ah, but you don't know Miss Sabina,' said Tail.

'Go and play with a cat, child.'

Conny, leaning against the pigsty, watched Tail until she had disappeared in the house. Conny was all of six feet tall, nicely built, and good looking in a slightly uncomfortable way; her expression of cheerfulness looked a bit forced and pathetic.

'You don't mind my calling you Michael, do you?' she asked in her man-to-man voice. 'Life's too short for the nicer points . . . Well, anyway it's a relief to know my sow hasn't got swine-fever.'

'No, it's just a mild case of swine erysipelas. She'll be better tomorrow. The injections work very well.'

'You the new veterinary surgeon?' asked an old man, who had stopped his bicycle beside us.

'Yes.'

19

'This is Mr Oldfellow,' Conny introduced us. 'We just call him *the* old fellow.'

'Friend of the Crosbys before Conny here was born.' He pointed to a small thatched cottage a few yards from Conny's farmhouse. 'That's where I've lived these fifty years. Crosby used to say to me, "If I go before you Oldfellow, look after my girls for me." '

'And we've looked after you ever since,' said Conny. 'Tell me, Michael, isn't it Mrs Pitt's day at Tit House?'

'Of course,' said Oldfellow. 'Just what I was thinking. You come and have supper with *me*, Mr Morton.'

'And we?' enquired Conny.

'Oh no, you don't like my cooking.'

'I wonder how *you'll* like it Michael. But anyway, the old fellow will put you in the picture about our village . . . he doesn't miss a thing.'

'Good night, Conny. I'll take another look at the sow sometime tomorrow,' I promised.

'Will you?' she sounded anxious.

'I won't charge you for it.'

'Oh good, thanks.'

The old fellow's cottage was packed out with large pieces of Victorian furniture which had been polished for many years and shone in the light of the oil-lamp. On the table in the centre of his sitting-room lay a form, and while the old fellow fetched plates and cutlery I glanced at it.

It *wasn't* anything from the Ministry of Agriculture but it had something to do with elections to the Parish Council. The old fellow had filled in his name, age and occupation. According to himself his occupation was *gentleman*. That somewhat confirmed Mrs Pitt's statement that Conny was working her fingers to the bone.

The old fellow's fingers looked gentlemanly white and clean.

'A pity Conny didn't marry Jenkins of the nursery,' he said, placing a large dish on a tile in the centre of the table. 'Farming's a hard life for a single woman, and Tail isn't any help either . . . Now if she married Thornton . . .'

'I thought Thornton and the Crosby girls . . .'

'I'm not saying relations are as cordial as they might be. That business with our bull and his cow . . . But what I say is forgive and forget. It was a long time ago. Now, Conny would let things be, but if there's one thing she can't stand it's a man telling her a woman's hopeless as a farmer. Conny's as good as him any day, it's just that she doesn't have his money.'

A mongrel dog had come and was sniffing at the parcel of sausages on the table. It looked as if its father had been a hound which had defected from the pack, while the hunt had stopped for a pint, and found a black poodle bitch.

'Rex! down!' The old fellow snatched the sausages Rex had licked and put them into the dish. 'Go find the rat! . . . as I was saying, Mr Morton, nowadays it's Thornton who has the money, though some of us know it isn't always come by in the way he makes out . . . It was funny last year, everyone losing beasts with the foot-and-mouth except him. Said he was lucky, he did. And then he went thankful and gave a cheque to the vicar. Now, watch!'

He had arranged the sausages side by side, and poured some colourless liquid over them. He now put a lighted match into the dish. Suddenly there was a hiss and the whole dish seemed to catch fire. The flames shot up a foot high, turned bright blue and kept on flickering over the sausages until all the liquid had disappeared.

'Flamin' sausages,' said the old fellow. 'It's my special.'

'What did you use?' I asked, 'pure alcohol?'

'Don't know what it's made of. The doctor gave me an ointment . . . that gave me a rash, and it was no use for cooking sausages, so last time I went to see him I asked for my usual bottle.'

'What for?'

'For rubbing my back when it's sore. The *ointment* was no use for cooking sausages.'

As I left Conny's piggery I found Tail inside my car.

'Was it flaming sausages?' she asked.

'Yes.'

'You were lucky. They're not bad. Did he tell you about our bull and Thornton's cow?'

'Two people have told me.'

'It's a feud.'

'I think it's silly,' I told her.

21

'You went to see Miss Sabina, didn't you?'

'How do *you* know?'

'I was in the garden looking for our Danny . . . the cat. I don't like Miss Sabina; she poisoned a kitten I had.'

'That's nonsense. Miss Sabina wouldn't have anything to do with poisons.'

'Not chemical ones, but a piece of rotten meat.'

'Look here, Tail, you don't know, do you.'

'I find out . . . always. I might have to act in a detective story; you know, a man gets poisoned and his wife . . .'

'Yes, but here no one's poisoning anyone, Tail.'

There was a silence while I started the car and wondered how I was going to get rid of Tail.

'Sanseverino,' she said dreamily, 'tell me, was it a horse or a play . . . I can't remember.'

'Neither can I. And it's time you went to bed.'

'If my husband ever says *that* to me I'll kill him . . . Good night. Ring me up if you remember about Sanseverino.'

# CHAPTER 2

'Sanseverino; I'm inclined to suggest he was an animal,' said Sir Roger. 'Yes, I think if you approached the competent authorities, Morton, the fact could be established that . . .'

'That Sanseverino was a horse,' said his wife, flatly.

Lady Beverley was at the wheel of her estate-car, driving us from Sir Roger's racing stables back to his house. She was surrounded by flapping ears and tails, a constant eddy of movement produced by three restless dachshunds.

Sir Roger kept removing them from her shoulders or preventing one or other of them from getting entangled in the gear-lever. He was surprisingly agile for a heavy man, and he seemed to enjoy the struggle with the dogs. His eyes were invisible behind thick spectacles but his thin-lipped mouth was crescented upwards in a benevolent grin.

'Extraordinary thing,' he said. 'We've got six of these little brutes and no one knows which three to take in the car except Beverley. I say, Beverley, why did you take Eleven, Twelve and Fifteen today?'

'Because Thirteen, Fourteen and Sixteen would have barked,' she told him.

'But they didn't bark yesterday!'

'That's why I took them yesterday . . . One must be fair to them.' She turned to me. 'The dogs expect to go out in the car every day. So I always take the three that aren't going to bark.'

'She always knows,' said Sir Roger, admiringly.

Lady Beverley turned the car into a path at the back of her house. There was a pencilled note pinned to the gate-post: 'We regret annoyance caused to anyone who hears our dogs bark between 12 p.m. and 2 a.m.' Behind the notice three brown, fluffy dachshunds were barking their heads off – clearly out of time; it was only 6 p.m.

The three dogs raced behind us to the back door and there

23

joined forces with the three tumbling out of the car. What with a jetplane screeching overhead and the barking of the dogs I missed half of what Sir Roger was telling me.

He was pointing to some dustbins which were fitted with thick rubber-rings. '... hushbins,' he was shouting. 'Beverley dislikes noise.'

Beverley had gathered up the dogs in her arms and bundled the six of them into a sun-loggia beside the door. This door as well as the others that led into the drawing-room was fitted with some pneumatic gadget that prevented it from slamming. In fact all doors shut behind us with a somewhat exhausted-sounding sigh.

'Well now,' Sir Roger sat down in a tall-backed antique chair. 'What did you think of my stables, Morton?'

'First rate. I didn't know you had twenty horses.'

'They're not all mine. The establishment's been expanded so that we can train other people's horses.' Sir Roger watched his wife mix martinis. 'I think the results of the past few months have been encouraging. Our investments have fully justified my expectations; we can look forward to consolidating . . .'

'Roger,' said Lady Beverley, handing me my glass. 'Roger, *please.*'

'Oh, sorry.' Sir Roger took the martini she was offering him on a tray. 'Got a Company Meeting in the morning,' he said. 'Well anyway, I wanted to tell you about my Russian decision, Morton. Though I let our Russian friends know that we are always open to negotiations I pointed out in no uncertain terms that we are standing firm,' he paused to take a sip, 'on our original offer. And we'll meet any contingency arising out of the situation with . . .'

'Roger,' said Lady Beverley, 'You're *not* in the House . . . the Russian horse – Princeling the Second – is going to be trained at our stables,' she interpreted.

'That sums it up.' Sir Roger gave his wife an appreciative smile. 'Of course I have private reasons for meeting the Russian demands halfway, which . . .'

'Roger wants to pinch the Russians' jockey,' said Lady Beverley.

'I wouldn't put it quite so bluntly.'

'But you do, don't you?' Lady Beverley refilled our glasses from a silver cocktail-shaker. 'Roger wants Atsy-Catsy.'

'Is that his *name*?'

'Of yes. He's of Greek extraction . . . Atsy-Catsy is Greek for *comme ci comme ca*. But that jockey isn't *so-so*. He's got good hands.'

'Hands!' Sir Roger exclaimed. 'He is the best judge of pace-riding I've ever seen. And he gets the last ounce out of his mount . . . hardly uses his whip at all . . . The Russians have agreed to let Atsy-Catsy stay with us; I dissuaded them from importing a Russian trainer. My Cecil's equal to training their Princeling along with the others. I've arranged for you to be in charge of the veterinary side, Morton.'

I thanked Sir Roger.

'Pity things can't be arranged so easily in international politics,' said Lady Beverley.

'It *wasn't* easy,' Sir Roger told us. 'Not by any means. Had to get round Atsy-Catsy with horse-to-horse talk; you know the kind of thing – that training a horse is four-fifth experience and one-fifth intuition; that the last fifth is the one that counts; that Atsy-Catsy was the man to provide it and he'd only be able to do so with a trainer who didn't interfere . . . Cecil in fact. We both agreed that you mustn't let a horse get bored and that each horse is a law unto itself and has to be studied individually. In the end Atsy-Catsy was dead keen on having Princeling here with us.'

'It's Noel Murless,' I said, 'who's got these ideas, isn't it? He also advises underworking rather than overworking a horse.'

'That *is* a point, Morton, a very good point. I'll suggest it to Atsy-Catsy. Or perhaps *you* had better do it.'

'Why?' asked Lady Beverley. '*Is* there a chance of Princeling winning the King Edward the Seventh Stakes?'

'There most certainly is,' said Sir Roger.

'I thought our Herakles was the better colt.'

'There's not a lot between them at level weights.'

'I see.' Lady Beverley's dark Cornish face looked thoughtful. 'I wonder . . . Did you put it to the Russian Ambassador that people in this country will think it rather odd that a Russian horse should compete in a Royal Stakes. After all, one of the Russian gimmicks is that they're anti-royal.'

'I tried, but it wasn't any good. It's the King Edward Stakes they want, not the Ascot Gold Cup. And don't ask me why. Top-policy, I expect.'

25

'Like sending the first man to the moon,' I suggested. 'First victory of the *Russian People* over a royal institution.'

Lady Beverley sat up. 'Yes, that's it. Roger, we can't let them have the King Edward Stakes. If Atsy-Catsy's as good as you say . . .'

'Don't worry, my dear.' Sir Roger's benevolent face had gone hard. 'Princeling is *not* going to win.' The fanaticism in his assertion made it clear to me how Sir Roger had become chairman of one of the biggest development companies in the country, and an M.P. *and* a successful racehorse owner.

'Beverley,' he said, after a silence in which only the distant barking of the dachshunds could be heard. 'I meant to tell you, we're expecting Atsy-Catsy for dinner tonight.'

'Roger, *no*! I've invited a couple who know Mr Morton . . . they're just back from *America*.'

'That's all right my dear. We want that jockey to . . . well, broaden his mind in the field of – er – international relations.'

'We must make the boy feel at home,' Lady Beverley whispered in my ear. She smiles at Atsy-Catsy across the dinner table. 'Those stupid Americans,' she told him in a confidential tone of voice, 'they just lapped it up.'

'Please?' The little jockey looked puzzled. 'What mean lappeditup?'

'They certainly did,' said Mrs St George Clemens, who had heard – luckily – only the second part of Beverley's statement. 'Broadway was packed with people waiting to see us leave the theatre . . . shouting "author! author!" And when he appeared several women fainted; I wish you'd been there, Michael.'

'A vet wouldn't have been much help.' My remark didn't sink in. Perhaps it was just as well; Mrs St George Clemens was re-living the triumph of her husband's play in New York. She had no doubt that *Three Brassières to Bond Street* was the greatest thing since Shakespeare.

But I didn't mind listening to this success-story; I was happy to meet Claire and Tiger again. It was some satisfaction to see that their marriage, which I had precipitated, was working as it should. The two of them made a striking pair; Claire in a lilac dress that matched her eyes and the two lilac-pointed Siamese cats she wore on her shoulders, Tiger with his rust-coloured beard and rust-coloured velvet tuxedo.

'But we're glad to be home again,' Claire was saying. 'I think Chou-en-Lai is going to have kittens again.' She stroked the little Siamese on her right shoulder. Mao-tse-Tung jealously nozzled Claire's pale hair. 'You see, Michael, they *know* I'm talking about them . . . You'll look after Chou-en-Lai again, won't you?'

'Yes, of course. Who's the father this time?'

'Well, we suspect Tail's tabby . . . Chou's got rather a thing about tabbies. But we don't really mind. Chou-en-Lai's the sort of cat that needs a healthy sex life – not a bit like a thoroughbred Siamese. I sometimes wonder whether Mao-tse-Tung would have been the same if I hadn't had her doctored; you know, it worries me.'

'Mao's perfectly happy,' I assured her.

'Mao-tse-Tung.' Atsy-Catsy had listened to Claire with a frown of concentration. 'I understand. Mao-tse-Tung, Chou-en-Lai,' he spread his hands palm up in a gesture of bewilderment, 'they big problem for Russian people . . . they great men, but sometimes is too hot in the head. Nikita Khrushchev . . .'

'You're absolutely right my boy,' Sir Roger interrupted him. 'Now, as I was saying . . . I agree with you; I too prefer head *lads* to girls but . . .'

'They not even *look* girl,' said the jockey with contempt. 'They very meagre.'

'Meagre?' asked Sir Roger.

'He means thin,' suggested Lady Beverley, 'lean.'

Sir Roger looked interested. 'Like this?' he asked, pointing to his slim wife and the even leaner Claire.

Atsy-Catsy nodded, 'Yes, meagre.'

Lady Beverley, Claire and Tiger began to talk at once. Tiger's booming baritone won. 'Working on another play,' he informed us.

'He's finished almost half,' said Claire. 'Tiger found it very difficult to concentrate in London; the quiet in Craftly is just what he needs . . . Oh Michael,' she put her hand on my arm, 'we *are* grateful to you. You see, Beverley, it was Michael who introduced us to Miss Skeffington. When she came to Tiger's first night in New York she happened to mention that she was selling Craftly Manor. I sent off a cable to Daddy at once.'

'Wasn't the house pretty dilapidated?' I asked.

'Well, yes,' said Tiger. 'But Claire's making a marvellous job of it.'

'Do you remember my flat in London?'

I was not likely to forget it; that lounge with two walls painted lilac, the colour of her cats, two walls striped lilac and mustard yellow; the black ceiling with marks on it like dusty footsteps, the paper-replicas of pheasants that hung suspended on threads from the ceiling, the organ-sized white record-player, the quilted satin Easter-eggs which were the beds of Chou-en-Lai and Mao-tse-Tung . . .

'And the whatnots,' Claire was saying, 'I picked up in New Orleans . . . I didn't mean to buy so much in the States, but I just fell for the southern colonial style. Beverley, you should see those houses . . . the Americans are so civilised.'

'Americans,' Atsy-Catsy was telling Sir Roger, 'they *savages*, all savages.'

'Beverley dear,' I took it Sir Roger's kick under the table was meant for his wife, not for me. 'Why not let *Olive* serve the coffee?'

'It's already in . . .'

'Darling,' said Sir Roger, 'you've done enough. *Olive* can serve the coffee.'

She got up from the table rather hurriedly. 'Coffee in the library,' she announced before letting the door sigh shut behind her.

Sir Roger allowed Tiger to finish his cheese; he gave Claire time to rearrange her cats, and strolling towards the library he explained to Atsy-Catsy the points of a good greyhound.

'A head like a snake
a neck like a drake
a back like a beam
a belly like a bream
a foot like a cat
a tail like a rat.'

Atsy-Catsy, staring at the floor, was still trying to work that one out when Sir Roger put a hand on his shoulder and propelled him towards the coffee-table.

Suddenly the jockey lifted his head. There was in his eyes the sort of expression I'd seen on a child's face when I'd given her a fluffy kitten. What in fact confronted us was no kitten but the back view of a parlourmaid of a width roughly equal to her height.

She put down the tray and rolled towards a door on the far side of the room. 'Olive,' said Sir Roger, 'will *you* serve the coffee.'

'Yes, sir.'

'Sit down, sit down everyone.'

Olive clumsily lifted the coffeepot, Lady Beverley watched the fragile cup she was filling, and Atsy-Catsy watched Olive.

'Please,' he said, jumping up from his chair, '*I* give everybody.' He went and took the cup out of Olive's hand and gave it to Claire.

Claire said she thought it had been 'sweet' of Sir Roger to introduce Olive to Atsy-Catsy; the poor little Russian was bound to be lonely being in a foreign country for the first time in his life. Tiger, with surprising perspicacity, disagreed; he suggested Sir Roger wasn't the kind of man to consider the more human side of a foreigner.

The two of them had insisted on my having a 'nightcap' with them and on showing me their house.

'Well, Michael, what do you think of it?' asked Claire.

I said, 'Very original.'

She sat down on the floor in front of the log-fire and leaned against Tiger's knees. 'Do you remember? You said exactly the same the first time you saw my London flat.'

I almost said that Craftly Manor *was* exactly the same, but that wouldn't have been quite true. In this house of thick old oak beams the black ceiling was even more depressing and the lilac and mustard striped walls looked frightening; one couldn't tell whether the waviness of the stripes was due to uneven walls or to an uneven struggle against the effects of Tiger's brandy.

Besides there was no escape from that room. Apart from a vast fourposter bed on the floor above the house was empty and likely to remain so until the furniture from America arrived. In the kitchen, which Miss Skeffington had kept well furnished with tins of sardines and newspapers, there now stood a solitary refrigerator which purred in a disgruntled way; no doubt it had never been meant to stand so uncomfortably on a bumpy uneven brick floor.

But Claire was quite happy about her housekeeping. They were managing, she told me, with trays in front of the fire. Did I remember the deep-frozen chops, chips and peas I used to have with them in her London flat? Well, I'd be welcome to the same at Craftly Manor any time I cared to drop in. Once the furniture was in they might even try those deep-frozen haddocks; Tiger had the most wonderful food-ideas.

It was inevitable; from 'food-ideas' Claire brought the conversation round to Tiger's literary ideas, and at two in the morning she persuaded Tiger to let her read me part of his new play. But then I felt that anything likely to distract me from seeing lilac and yellow snakes wiggling on the walls was bound to be pretty good.

'There's a cryptoneurous connection between *Three Brassières to Bond Street* and Tiger's new play *Three Corsets to Curzon Street*,' she explained.

To me it was crystal clear. 'So he's kept to a London background,' I said.

'Exactly.' Tiger leaned back with a grunt of satisfaction.

'Darling, don't interrupt . . . I wouldn't be reading to Michael if I didn't *know* he understands.'

'London setting,' I felt pleased with myself. I was getting the hang of it at last. Obviously, Tiger had got *something*; those hard-headed people on Broadway hadn't cheered or fainted for *nothing*.

'Well . . . we're inside a bicycle-shed,' explained Claire. 'A sort of lean-to. Hetty – an elderly woman of about forty – is leaning against a disused gas-cooker. Jack is working a hand-pump trying to inflate a bicycle-tyre.

JACK: Curzon Street, that's where it was.

HETTY: The way he went for that haddock.

JACK: If I could go back to Curzon Street . . .

HETTY: Cut clean through it, he did.

Jack's pump slips. The valve jumps out of the tyre. Tyre deflates with a hiss.

HETTY: Cut clean through it, he did. It wouldn't have happened in Wandsworth.'

'Better explain,' said Tiger.

'Oh yes,' Claire agreed. 'You noticed the last line, Michael?'

'Yes, haven't I heard it somewhere before?'

'Of course you have! How clever of you to spot it. You see Tiger had a fabulous idea; in this play he's actually drawing certain features from *real life*. Well . . . listen.'

HETTY: Cut clean through it, he did. It wouldn't have happened in Wandsworth.

JACK: I know it was in Curzon Street, that time . . .

HETTY: So I said to him, if you did that in Wandsworth . . .

JACK: If I don't go back to Curzon Street . . .

HETTY: In Wandsworth . . .

JACK: In Curzon Street . . .'

Claire looked up with shining eyes. 'You see the rhythm, Michael . . . how it speeds up as the conflict breaks into the open.'

I was no longer looking at the walls; I didn't dare to. The lilac and yellow snakes seemed to be inside my head. And there was Wandsworth and Curzon Street and the beastly bicycle tyre that kept getting deflated, and the brandy I kept drinking because I needed *something*.

'Well?' asked Claire.

I tumbled to it that she'd stopped reading, but all I could do was stare at the black ceiling and duck in case it came down any lower.

'Terrific, isn't it?' she asked.

'Terrific,' I said. 'Got to go home.'

'I know how you feel,' said Claire warmly. 'When I read this act for the first time *I* just wanted to be alone . . . and think . . . Oh Michael, it was mean of me to forget; poor Chou-en-Lai. I'm almost sure she's having kittens, but will you examine her?'

'Tomorrow.' I was sure if I touched Chou while I saw everything in yellow and lilac Chou would know about it and I'd get my face scratched.

'Yes, of course,' Claire agreed. '*Three Corsets to Curzon Street* has that effect on one . . . it takes *me* hours to get back to earth.'

The earth outside seemed full of pot-holes and ridges, but I managed to find my car somehow. I made a resolution and I stuck to it; I drove the bubble at exactly ten miles an hour, a speed which suited us both.

As I passed Farmer Thornton's place I noticed a light in his kitchen window, and while I wondered whether he too had a stomach-ache a dark figure slid across the yard towards Conny Crosby's piggery.

I slowed down to five miles an hour and leaned out of the window. There *was* someone about but before I could recognize any detail the silhouette had merged with the dark bulk of Conny's hedge.

A couple of days later the rumour was all over the village; Thornton had lost Petunia. One story went that the cow had been bitten by an adder, another that Thornton had shot her because she'd broken a leg. Yet another version maintained that Thornton's cow hadn't died at all but changed hands.

I had come to accept the last as the most likely account when Tail produced the weirdest story of all. Petunia, she told me, had been taken away all right; she'd been carried out of her byre upside down at three in the morning. The carcass had been taken to a waiting truck and driven away by Thornton himself.

I said, 'One of these days your tales will get you into trouble, my girl.'

As usual, she had been waiting for me inside my car while I had examined Conny's sow.

'It's not a tale.' She seemed genuinely annoyed. 'I *saw* old Thornton.'

'Then it was *you* I saw prowling about his yard in the small hours.'

'Oh, you *did*,' she didn't seem to mind. 'Well then, you know I'm not telling lies.'

'Listen Tail,' I felt if there was a scandal brewing it was not my business. 'I saw you and no one else.'

'You must have been too late to see the others. And I know something else; old Thornton's had men in at night several times.'

'Does your sister know about your night-excursions?'

Tail put on her 'inscrutable' expression. 'When the time is ripe I'll tell Conny.'

'Why have you told *me*?' I asked, wishing she hadn't.

'Oh, just in case.'

'Of what?'

32

'You could work out what old Thornton's up to, couldn't you?'

'No, I *couldn't*. I've got enough to do without keeping tabs on people who haven't consulted me.'

'There you are!' Tail opened the car-door and managed to scramble out without detracting from the drama of her exit. Her timing was quite professional. 'Thornton *hasn't* called you in. Don't you think that's a bit peculiar?'

I did find Tail's logic somewhat disturbing. If a farmer's prize cow was sick I would have thought he'd call in his vet; if she died I'd hardly have expected him to drive the carcass away at three in the morning. There *was* something odd about Petunia's demise. But I couldn't see myself paying Thornton a prying visit.

It was Conny who stopped my car as I was passing her piggery on my way to Tit House. She and Thornton had been standing by her gate, glaring at one another.

'Michael, will you tell him?' she asked, before I was out of the car. 'He's been saying things about Myrtle. *Did* she have swine-fever?'

'Certainly not,' I told Thornton.

'Well, then you're just lucky,' he said to Conny. 'The way you keep your animals it's a wonder any of them are sound.'

Conny drew herself up to her full six-feet height but she still looked fragile beside Thornton. 'What's wrong with my sties?' she asked, pointing to the buildings at the far end of the yard. 'They're as good as your cowsheds, Dave, and well you know it.'

'Who's saying anything about your sties? What about the cesspool?' Thornton seemed to enjoy Conny's annoyance. 'Stinking ditches are out of date. If you used modern methods of farming...'

'Modern methods cost money.'

'An efficient farmer can afford them.'

'You don't have to be an efficient farmer to make money, Mr Thornton. You can do very well if you have no conscience about Ministry of Agriculture regulations.'

'Better be careful, Conny.' I was surprised to see Thornton obviously angry. 'With this kind of loose talk someone might get hurt.'

'Are you...'

I thought it was time I intervened. 'Thornton, stop pulling Conny's leg. Why don't you help her get rid of the ditch instead of shooting pigeons for me. I'm getting a bit tired of pigeon-pie.'

'*There* is gratitude for you,' said Thornton, accepting my let-out. He grinned at Conny. 'Maybe I *will* give you a hand with that ditch of yours.'

'Thanks. I don't need any help. You're busy enough with your cows.' There was something in the way Conny said it that made Thornton turn his back on her without another word.

'Cup of tea?' he asked me. 'Come on in, Mr Morton, I was just going to have one myself.'

There was a big coal-fire in his kitchen and the kettle was simmering on the hob. Thornton still looked uneasy, and as he poured the water into the teapot he muttered, 'Jealous bitch.'

'You're being unfair,' I told him. 'Conny's pigs are pretty good. She's doing all right.'

'I reckon she is. But Conny and that Tail have other ideas; can't get it out of their heads that their dad was a dairy-farmer. What they've forgotten is the troubles that go with cattle; the better your herd is the more you stand to lose.'

'Did you lose animals in last year's foot-and-mouth outbreak?' I asked.

'Haven't my pals in the village told you? . . . No, I was lucky. But that doesn't mean to say I'm safe this year. Whiteley – not fifteen miles from here – has lost thirty-two head of cattle since last week.'

'I know. But the Vet Investigation Department moved in smartly. Kenton's in charge. When I spoke to him this morning he sounded quite hopeful. He said Whiteley's herd's the only one affected in the county.'

'Rubbish!' Thornton slapped the kitchen table. 'You boys want to come down to earth. How often do you manage to keep foot-and-mouth inside one farm? It spreads like wild-fire no matter what you do. There's only one remedy; immunise the cattle. Vaccinate the livestock all over the country. That's what they do abroad, and it works.'

'So does our system,' I told him.

'It does, does it?' Thornton had jumped up, and was

34

striding up and down between window and fireplace. 'I dare say it works on paper . . . vaccinating the livestock would cost the country a packet. The British taxpayer couldn't afford it. Slaughtering sick beasts is cheap at the price. Whose price, Mr Morton?'

'You get compensation – in full – for every animal that has to be killed.'

'Oh sure. But what about the income you lose? Six to eight weeks before you can replace your animals . . . before they earn you anything. What about the cost of transporting new stock to your farm? Thirty bob a head on a hundred head of cattle isn't chickenfeed. What about your cowman's wages . . . twelve pounds a week or more. Good cowmen don't grow on bushes; if you're lucky enough to have one you can't afford to sack him because of foot-and-mouth. Before you know where you are you're in the red; working farmers don't *have* much capital.'

I made a few sympathetic noises, but Thornton wouldn't be pacified.

'Let me tell you something else.' He stood towering above me, his face hot with emotion. 'Do you know how long it takes a man to build up a pedigree herd that suits his land? Twenty years . . . maybe longer. Twenty years is a big chunk out of a man's life. Much good would it do me if the Ministry gave me sixteen hundred guineas for my bull Roderick. Does that take into account his future performance . . . 'cause it doesn't. I reckon Roderick would be impossible to replace.'

There was so much feeling in what Thornton had said that I became sure he wasn't thinking of entirely hypothetical animals. 'What was the matter with your cow Petunia?' I asked.

He straightened up, rather abruptly. 'Broken leg,' he snapped. 'Had to kill her . . . I might have known you'd hear a lot of lies; that's what happens when you're surrounded by a bunch of damned women. If Conny and that Tail aren't spying on me as if I were a criminal, Miss Sabina's accusing me of God knows what. As if she owned those bloody tits.'

# CHAPTER 3

There were as many birds inside as outside Tit House. In the drawing-room the tits were hammering away at a piece of wood specially provided for them because of its juicy knot-holes. There were tits with black sidewhiskers, tits with black skull-caps and tits with bright blue wings. Many of them, showing their egg-yellow waistcoats, were hanging upside down or balanced like acrobats in an all-out effort to get every bead of resin out of the wood.

Mrs Pitt, damp cloth in hand, was looking on. 'It isn't that I've got anything against them, Mr Morton, but the work they make! When Miss Sabina asked me if I could come in a couple of hours on Saturdays I *said* I'd oblige, but it wouldn't happen in Wandsworth; I'd at least get a Saturday afternoon to meself . . . Mind you, I feel sorry for Miss Sabina. It's that owl what's causing . . .'

'Where *is* Barney?' I asked.

'Lor! You can't leave her alone for a minute!'

We searched floor and cupboards, nesting-boxes and chairs. Eventually I discovered Barney huddled into the cushions of a settee. The little owl, not surprisingly, had sought shelter from the icy draught in the room. A second bout of diarrhoea had weakened her so much that she swayed when I put her back on the parrot-perch.

I took her to the kitchen, which seemed to be the only warm place in the house, and impressed upon Miss Sabina that Barney would die if she were left in the drawing-room. I also gave Miss Sabina a bottle of chlorodyne.

'Give her four or five drops in a dessertspoonful of water, Miss Webb.'

'I'd rather not, Mr Morton. I'm sure Barney wouldn't be sick if it weren't for Thornton's chemicals. He must have used that spraying machine of his.'

'I doubt whether Barney had the strength to go outdoors.'

'But the fumes, Mr Morton, the fumes. It's murder to the birds. It's all so unnecessary. In my father's time they managed very well without those deadly chemicals. Farming's become a farce. People like Thornton do an hour or two's genuine work and then they go off shooting innocent pigeons or chasing young women.'

'Not Thornton, surely.'

'Yes indeed. I may not be able to leave Tit House very often – *someone* has to protect the birds – but I am not uninformed of village affairs. I assure you Thornton lets those poisonous chemicals do his work for him while he spends his time pursuing our mutual neighbour Conny Crosby.'

'Then your information *is* inaccurate. My impression is that there isn't much love lost between your two neighbours.'

'When it comes to persecuting my birds they're solidly united, I assure you. Conny's cats are as destructive as Thornton's . . .'

'Miss Webb, the medicine I'm giving you for Barney is *not* a chemical. It's made from a plant, and Barney should *have* it.'

'Miss Sabina ma'am,' Mrs Pitt put her head through the door. 'There's a patient just arrived . . . we can't get her wheelchair in the front door.'

There were movements in the jungle-thickets of the garden, odd thuds and flurries of snapping twigs. As I slowed down my bubble I discovered that the 'grounds' were full of people with legs or arms encased in plaster. They were lying on the wet mush of rotting leaves, sleet dripping from above, clutching binoculars as if they were essential weapons.

I watched a female member of the Beginner-Birdwatcher Brotherhood of the Post-Skiing-Fracture-Fraternity, still gripping her binoculars, struggle to her feet with the aid of a stick. The plaster on her leg was scribbled over with signatures and what looked like doggerels.

'Hi,' she greeted me. At close quarters she was a dumpy redhead of about twenty with the long-nosed good looks of a thoroughbred filly. 'You the electrician?'

'No, the vet,' I told her.

'Holy cow, I'm gonna die if they don't fix that radiator thing in my room,' she said. 'When I think I could have stayed in my central-heated hotel in Pontresina!' She shivered and looked utterly miserable. She was the first American I'd ever seen looking like a waif. 'Say, is it warm in your surgery?'

'Not bad. Want to come for a cup of coffee?'

'Sure, I'd just love it.'

I had some difficulty in getting Elizabeth's leg out of my car but eventually I managed by grasping her round the middle and pulling. She was a nice armful, heavy but not in the wrong places.

While we drank our coffee in front of the breakfast-room fire she told me that the skiing-holiday in Switzerland had been her first trip abroad. When she'd broken her leg, by wrapping herself round a tree, Dr Schwersteiger had advised her mother to send her to Tit House. She'd thought it would be all right; she was fond of animals and she'd believed it would be fun watching the birds. It wasn't; it was 'too darned cold.'

But she'd have to stay until her mother and her current boy-friend had done wintersporting, and they had no intention of returning to England for another month. Meanwhile, with her leg in plaster, Elizabeth wasn't able to do the rubber-necking she'd planned, she was cold and she was bored.

'Back home there's something to do,' she told me, hobbling round my surgery. 'I can always go riding or somethin'. I've got three Appledor ponies.'

'Appledor?'

'Yeah; that's a special breed we have in Tennessee. I kinda miss them . . . Mom's bought me the whole of Sartre in French and Thomas Mann in German, but I haven't opened a book since I've come to Craftly; it's too cold.'

'You're studying languages?'

'Yes. It's easy for me though; my Pop was German and Mom's Russian, so she speaks French . . . Mom's crazy about riding too. We're going to Ascot . . . but that won't be for a heck of a time.'

She sounded so blue that I wanted to help. 'Would you like to see some horses that are going to run at Ascot?'

'I sure would.' Elizabeth's face began to look animated. 'Where?'

'There are two in training in Craftly. I'm going to see them this afternoon.'

I parked the bubble at the corner of the gallops from where Elizabeth could see the horses approach and the final furlong without having to leave the car. If Sir Roger did turn up I didn't think he'd mind this young American watching the training of his colt.

Further down the field Cecil, Sir Roger's trainer, was keeping his eye on a stopwatch while Atsy-Catsy pushed out Princeling at full stretch. The Russian colt, head into the wind, black tail flying looked magnificent. So did Atsy-Catsy; he and his horse seemed so much at one that I couldn't imagine this jockey ever coming a cropper. On reaching the 'post' he straightened up and sat back with armchair-ease. I could not see him pull Princeling up; the colt appeared to slow his pace in response to a slight pressure of the jockey's knees.

Cecil put the stopwatch in his pocket. 'Can't see Herakles beating him,' he said, shaking his head, 'Certainly not with that cough or whatever it is . . . You'll see for yourself. Our head lad's down with 'flu, but Atsy-Catsy says he'll take our colt round for you . . . Decent fellow, young Cat.'

While 'young Cat' had dismounted, Olive had appeared. In a sheepskin jacket she looked even more enormous than in her uniform. She waited, looking rather bored, while Atsy-Catsy was talking to his horse.

'Hurry up, Cat,' she called. 'We'll miss the bus.'

Just then a stableboy came running along with Herakles. Atsy-Catsy went up to Olive, talking to her chiefly with apologetic gestures of his hands.

'You said we was going to the pictures, you did,' shouted Olive.

More hand-signals from Atsy-Catsy.

Olive's face had gone scarlet. 'Well, you know what you can do with yourself! It's bad enough going out with a fellow who don't understand what you're saying. But I'm not going to be stood up by anyone, see . . . least by a foreigner what doesn't even speak English. *I* am a member of the English Countrywomen's Association, see!' She turned her back on Atsy-Catsy and waddled off like an outraged mother-duck.

The little jockey stared after her with bewilderment, but after a while he shrugged his shoulders and came over to us. 'I go,' he announced, mounting Herakles.

Sir Roger's colt began by rearing, giving a curious high-pitched snort. Atsy-Catsy didn't change his hold on the reins; he just talked to Herakles and presently the colt trotted off amicably.

I could see nothing wrong with his performance. Atsy-Catsy sat him quietly, letting him go at an easy pace that showed what a beautiful mover he was. By the time he did let the colt stride on it was obvious that Herakles was enjoying himself. All the same I decided to examine him immediately after the work-out.

When Atsy-Catsy brought him up to us Herakles again reared, danced backwards, and gave peculiar snorts and gurgles.

Cecil's mouth drooped pessimistically. 'He does all right with *Atsy-Catsy* handling him, but I don't like that cough.'

'No cough,' said the jockey.

'Well, what is it then?'

'Happiness.'

Cecil's long face grew longer. 'Happiness?'

The jockey put his cheek against Herakles's and murmured something in a foreign language. The colt's ears went up, he nuzzled Atsy-Catsy's face and made noises that sounded as if he'd swallowed a speaking mouse.

'You see?' Atsy-Catsy smiled.

'No,' said Cecil.

'Easy,' said the jockey, patiently. 'Herakles like speaks; you speak, he speak back.'

'It's possible,' I agreed. 'But I'll take a look at him.'

While the lad took Herakles back to the yard Atsy-Catsy walked with me to the car. I told him in monosyllables how much I'd liked the way he'd handled the colt.

Elizabeth looked warm and animated. 'Gee, that was great,' she said, when I'd introduced Atsy-Catsy. 'If *I* could ride again . . .'

Atsy-Catsy sympathetically studied her plaster-leg. 'Bad. You broke fet-lock?'

'No,' Elizabeth suppressed a giggle. 'I broke hock; just above chestnut.' Suddenly she broke into another language, Russian judging by the pleasure in Atsy-Catsy's eyes.

While I drove the bubble to the yard Atsy-Catsy ran beside us, talking to Elizabeth through her open window. He stayed with her while I examined Herakles.

Apparently the colt understood his owner's language as

40

well as Russian. I found no evidence of a cold, no inter-ference with respiration, but when I talked to Herakles he answered back much as he had done with Atsy-Catsy. For the moment I was satisfied of his soundness but I decided I'd keep an eye on him.

When I returned to the car the jockey had gone but the effect of his personality was still there in Elizabeth's smile. 'He's great,' she said dreamily. 'He'd sure make a pile of dough in the States.'

She was no less warm and expansive when I dropped her at the gates of Tit House. 'I figure this place is okay.'

'Drop in for coffee,' I offered. 'Any time you feel cold.'

'That's mighty nice of you, Michael . . . Maybe I could give you a hand in your surgery sometime.'

There was only one pair of hands I wanted in the surgery – Julia's. And when I got back to the house she was there, waiting for me beside the fire in the breakfast-room. She had taken off her skirt and was sitting curled up in a pair of red velvet briefs, a black sweater and a pair of fur-lined boots. I could have shouted with joy, seeing her familiar dainty figure dressed in the inimitable familiar style.

Instead I just hugged her and pulled her down on the settee. I was so starved of all this and Julia too that I could hardly breathe. The fresh scent of her hair almost drove me round the bend.

'Stop it,' Julia gasped, 'stop it I like it.'

'Let's get married.'

'No.' Julia clung to me as if she too had found bachelor-dom a trial.

'You're crazy, darling.'

'I'll marry you the moment we have a home of our own. We *must* have a place for our animals.'

'But we haven't got animals, Julia.'

'We shall have though.'

'Of course; after we've found somewhere to live.'

'There you are!' Julia said in her I'm-always-right voice. 'We can't get married until we've got our own home . . . Darling, I've been looking at dozens of houses.'

'Any possibles?'

'No. But I'll go on trying. I realise now *you* will never have the time to go house-hunting.'

'Why not wait until I'm back in London? Meanwhile we could live here and . . .'

Julia shook her head. 'It's no good Michael; you've said yourself we can't get married until we have a home of our own.'

It was no use arguing with her. The best I could do was to give her a good week-end; make her feel at the end of it that she didn't *want* to go back to London.

I opened one of Phil Brogan's bottles and made champagne-cocktails; I turned down the lights and put on a record of 'Never on Sunday'. Julia took off her furry boots and snuggled up to me, warm and relaxed. I felt happy and forgiving; Julia *was* illogical and hot-headed, but she was mine and well worth having. In all fairness to her it wasn't surprising I'd fallen for her; I'd known for a long time that I was the sort of man who got involved with impossible people – a variation of being accident-prone.

About ten both of us began to feel hungry and went looking for supper. Mrs Pitt had left a cold pigeon-pie, and there was some soup in a pan.

Julia had just re-heated the soup when there was a loud knock on the kitchen door. Almost immediately it was flung open and Tail came hurtling in. She was wearing a pair of stiletto-heeled shoes, no doubt Conny's, and a somewhat moth-eaten fur coat in the roaring-'twenties-style which had recently become fashionable again.

Tail, scarlet fingernails outstretched in a gesture of heavy drama, threw herself into my arms. 'Darling,' she sobbed, 'come quickly! Come at once. A terrible thing has happened. *Please* Michael.'

'What nonsense is this?' I was annoyed with Tail, especially when I noticed Julia's ice-cold expression. 'You silly little . . .' I was about to call her names when I noticed that she was crying. The tears were genuine enough. 'What is it Tail?'

'Rex . . .'

I allowed her to stay in my arms and stroked the damp hair out of her eyes, aware all the time that Julia was watching and that Tail in her get-up looked disgustingly old – eighteen at least.

'Oldfellow's dog,' she managed to get out at last. 'He's been run over.'

42

She told me a sports car had come tearing down the lane as Rex was following the old fellow's bicycle; it had hit Rex's head and left him lying in the road unconscious. Though the driver must have been aware of the accident he had not stopped.

While Tail described the first-aid given to Rex, Julia had left the kitchen. She returned dressed in her fur boots, skirt and coat, tying on a head-scarf.

I opened the door for Tail and told her to run along, I'd be with Rex in a few minutes.

'We'd better take morphia,' I said to Julia.

'We?'

'Aren't you coming?'

'Certainly not. If I hurry I'll catch the last train home.'

'Darling, you don't understand.' It was monstrous that Julia should be fooled by Tail's masquerade; ridiculous. 'Tail's only . . .'

'I'm not blind, Michael,' said Julia. 'The first thing I saw when I arrived here was a cup with lipstick marks. But I made allowances . . .'

'One of my animal-owners,' I said. There was no time to explain about Tit House, the Post-Skiing-Fracture-Fraternity, the evidence of Elizabeth's lipstick on a cup.

'I am asking no questions,' said Julia, frostily. 'Your friend Tail has made it quite obvious that I'm in the way here.'

'Listen, damn you!' I shouted. 'Tail's only . . .' But Julia missed the information that Tail was a child of twelve. She'd banged out of the kitchen and I knew she wouldn't listen to me if I did follow her.

Rex was lying on the table in the old fellow's cottage, with Tail and his master talking to him and stroking his shivering flanks. His white and brown mongrel-face was streaked with dry blood and there was a gaping wound on his forehead. Rex did not seem to be in pain, but his rapid shallow breathing indicated that he was badly shocked.

I injected a sedative before examining the dog. Luckily there were no bones broken; and though Rex was suffering from concussion I found the skull undamaged. I stitched up the gash and put Rex in his basket while still dopey from the light anaesthetic I'd given him.

43

Rex curled up and went to sleep but I still didn't like the sound of his breathing.

'We'll have to watch his heart,' I told the old fellow. 'I'll stay for a while.'

'Is he going to be all right?' asked Tail. She was still wearing that ridiculous fur coat but her face, wet with tears, looked childish and very tired.

'Don't you worry about Rex. He's doing quite well, and there's nothing hurting him. It's time you went to bed.'

'I couldn't sleep,' she said. 'I'd just be thinking . . . Couldn't we play rummy?'

'It's nearly midnight,' said the old fellow. 'If Conny wakened and found you out . . .'

'She never does . . . I mean, she won't,' Tail corrected herself. 'Conny isn't awake at night.' She went and fetched a dog-eared pack of cards from the dresser. 'Just one game,' she coaxed us.

'All right,' we agreed, 'just one game.'

Tail lost, so of course we couldn't stop until she'd won at least one game, and then the old fellow made cocoa for her and gave me a glass of his powerful rosehip wine.

By the time I'd listened to Rex's heart once again and taken Tail to the window which was her private entrance to her house it was two in the morning.

So as not to waken Conny I let my car run out of the yard without switching on the engine. I had just reached the road when a coupé came shooting out of Thornton's farm, missing my bubble by a fraction of an inch. According to the old fellow's description it might have been the sports car which had hit Rex. But what worried me even more was a distinct impression that it had been an Alfa Romeo, a car not owned by anyone in Craftly yet oddly familiar to me.

When I saw Rex on the following morning he was asleep. His heartsounds were weak but more regular, and I thought he'd got over the worst of his accident.

Tail agreed that the Alfa Romeo I'd seen sounded like the car which had hit Rex, but she admitted not having seen it before. The old fellow said he seemed to remember someone in the village driving a foreign car like that but he hadn't seen it about for a long time.

Claire and Tiger, whom I visited afterwards, were positive

that they knew *someone* with an Alfa Romeo but they couldn't remember whether it was John or Winkey or Clarence. I changed the subject, partly because I had no solid grounds for suspecting the Alfa Romeo, partly because I had other worries.

There was the 'Julia situation' which I'd been unable to tackle because Julia was either out or not answering the 'phone, and there was the Chou-en-Lai situation.

Claire had called me because the little Siamese was in labour. It was soon clear to me that, this time, Chou-en-Lai's tabby-mate had been larger than was good for her. She was not meant to bear those tabby-sized kittens, yet I was reluctant to spoil her beautiful coat by delivering her offspring surgically.

It took me more than an hour of manipulation, which made me feel as exhausted as Chou-en-Lai, to get the kittens born and even so I had to put in three stitches. But Claire was satisfied and Tiger, glad to see her relieved of the 'birth-strain', insisted on my staying to lunch.

'There's no point in your going to London now,' Claire agreed. 'Julia won't listen to you while she's in that mood. Write to her. Explain about Elizabeth's lipstick and about Tail . . . and don't forget to tell her you miss her.'

'And encourage her pigheadedness?'

'Better not.' Tiger put some slices of frozen haddock under the grill. 'A dignified note's the thing . . . come down to Craftly when you've got over your temper and we'll talk things over like *adults*.'

'That's a wonderful idea, darling,' said Claire. 'Better tell Julia she'd be welcome to stay with us . . . You know, you can't afford gossip in the village. Besides . . .'

I knew what she was thinking. Basically her marriage had not changed Claire; she was still the coca-cola puritan in shaggy lilac tights who daringly talked of a 'healthy sex life' as other people might recommend the uses of liver-salts.

'*Three Corsets to Curzon Street*,' she said, balancing the plate of grilled haddock on her lap, 'throws a much stronger light on the woman's sex life than Tiger's first play . . . *Three Brassières to Bond Street*. You remember the scene in the lean-to, when Jack is trying to inflate the bicycle-tyre? Hetty says "the way he went for that haddock" . . . well, you immediately *know*, don't you? When I read this scene to

Caraway of the *London Roundabout* – cold critic that he is –
he had tears in his eyes; he said he'd never heard a more
moving statement of the problem.'

'That's splendid,' I congratulated Tiger. 'Have you
finished the play?'

'Not yet.' He frowned. 'There are difficulties . . .'

'Of course,' said Claire, '*Three Brassières* was a purely
imaginative play . . . relatively easy. Tiger's new technique
of taking features from *real* life is much more complex . . .
more demanding.'

'I suppose he's got to mix with ordinary people,' I suggested, 'find out about them.'

'Mix with them,' said Claire, thoughtfully, 'yes, up to a
point. But he doesn't have to go so far as to *find out* what
they're like. For instance in the second act of *Three Corsets
to Curzon Street* . . .'

'I'm sorry, Claire,' I said, putting my empty plate on the
hearth-rug. 'I'll have to be going.' It was one day when a
reading from Tiger's play would have driven me up those
mustard and lilac striped walls. 'Got to see a dog.'

'The one that was hit by the Alfa Romeo?'

'I don't know whether it *was* an Alfa Romeo.'

'The Duke of Alanspring!' exclaimed Tiger. 'Doesn't he
have an Alfa Romeo?'

'Darling,' Claire gave him an affectionate smile. 'You *are*
absent-minded. The Duke's in the States. Don't you remember, he came to your First Night. Besides, he hasn't had a car
for five years or more.'

'I say, Claire, you're right. But when he did have a car it
was rather a powerful thing, wasn't it?'

I walked out quickly, carrying the remains of the haddock
to the kitchen. Chou-en-Lai, in her basket, stopped licking
her kittens, sniffed, and gave her peculiar Siamese baby-cry.
Her demand for a meal was the best proof that she had
recovered from her difficult confinement. I had not recovered. All I wanted was to read the Sunday papers in front
of the fire, and sleep.

As I passed Conny's piggery Tail came running out.
'About that sports car,' she said. 'I saw it again.'

'Where?'

'Coming out of The Lion carpark. There was a man
driving.'

46

'What did he look like?'

'Couldn't see. A lorry got between us.'

'Then it might have been *any* car and *any* driver.'

'It *was* the car that hit Rex. Don't you *want* to find out?'

I told her I didn't want to go in for guesswork. But for the rest of the day vague recollection of an Alfa Romeo kept coming into my head with uncomfortable persistence.

Seeing the owner of the Alfa Romeo justified my uneasiness. I had been watching the training of Sir Roger's Herakles and the Russian colt when I saw him walk across the field with one of the stablelads. There was something familiar about his thin, tall figure in tight-trousered tweeds, the face with the somewhat incredibly even suntan.

I suddenly remembered the one and only man I knew whose tan came out of a bottle – Captain Sidney Franks, the horse-doper I had once incarcerated in Miss Skeffington's horsebox, the man I had warned off horses, the owner of an Alfa Romeo. With the sale of Miss Skeffington's Craftly Manor to Claire and Tiger he no longer had a home in Craftly, yet there he was, watching the Ascot candidates, and on friendly terms with one of Sir Roger's stablelads. I doubted that Sidney was visiting his old haunt for sentimental reasons.

When he saw me he came up to me like a man. 'Well, look who's here,' he said, grasping my hand, 'once a horse-doctor always a horse-doctor, what!'

'Hello,' I said, with deliberate lack of enthusiasm. 'What are *you* doing here? I took it you'd finished with horses.'

He ignored the implication. 'You know how it is, Michael . . . when you've been a trainer, horses are your first love. You can't keep away from them.'

'I remember we agreed you *would* keep away from them.'

'Don't be so unfriendly, man. Nowadays I only have an amateur's interest in racing.'

'I don't think Sir Roger would like you taking any kind of interest in his colt.'

'He wouldn't mind; I have old friends in Craftly. Besides I'm more interested in the performance of the Russian colt. I think he's a good bet for the King Edward Stakes, don't you?'

'There are months between now and Ascot.'

'Well, I can't see the Russians risk another defeat such as the Grand National . . . That jockey of theirs is the best thing I've seen in the saddle for years. An attractive lad he is too.'

'Better keep away from him, Sidney.'

'Don't make a habit of warning me off. And don't be nervous, old chap; I'm minding my own business these days.'

'What *is* your business?'

'I'm in commerce.'

'On your own?'

'I have a partner.'

'Oh yes?'

'It's time you stopped being suspicious of me,' said Sidney, self-righteously. 'I'm doing a good job.'

'A job allowing you plenty of free time.'

'Now what does that mean?'

'You're in Craftly quite a lot, aren't you?'

'Not that I know of.'

'I do know,' I told him. 'I suppose Farmer Thornton's one of your old friends.'

He suddenly looked less dapper, more like the shifty individual I'd first seen in Soho. 'Prying's a bad habit of yours. One of these days it'll get you into trouble.'

'Will it?'

He ran his eyes over me, and no doubt remembered that he was dealing with a rugger-player. 'Live and let live,' he said. 'Our – er – difference of opinion is a thing of the past. Since then I haven't touched a horse. Anyway, I don't see why you should object to my visiting my friends in Craftly; Dave Thornton's got no interest in horses, so where's the harm?'

There was no answer to that one. I didn't believe in Sidney's attachment to his friends in Craftly, I felt certain there *was* harm in whatever he was doing here, but there was nothing I could put my finger on other than the possibility that Sidney had hit the old fellow's dog.

Neither Cecil nor Atsy-Catsy appeared to know Sidney, nor had they noticed him observing the colts before. The stablelad who had been with him said he'd met Sidney Franks a few days previously in The Lion, the Captain had bought him a beer and asked whether anyone would mind if he looked at the Russian colt. Since a lot of people were taking an interest in the Russian entry for Ascot the lad had thought the request was quite natural. I couldn't be sure that it was other than innocent curiosity.

After I had given Princeling a routine check Atsy-Catsy accompanied me to Herakles's stable. He was very proud of the improvement in the colt's 'speaks' and gave a remarkable demonstration of a conversation with the horse during which Herakles produced some new and thoroughly un-horse-like noises.

I pointed out to Atsy-Catsy that a thoroughbred race-horse had no business to be a freak and suggested that Herakles should not be encouraged to 'talk'. Atsy-Catsy disagreed, politely but with truly Russian stubbornness.

A good horse, he argued, had to have character – a personality – a soul in fact. The remarkable thing about Sir Roger's colt was that it liked men better than other horses. Herakles had an irresistible urge to communicate his feelings for man, especially for his rider. If the rider accepted the colt's overtures and reciprocated there was nothing they could not achieve together. Because of his peculiarity Herakles, in Atsy-Catsy's opinion, stood a better chance of winning the King Edward Stakes than Princeling, his own horse.

'Capitalist' society was doing strange things to the little Russian. His English had improved rapidly and he was using the language in a very outspoken manner – not only with regard to the relative merits of horses.

'I guess,' he said, 'I was wrong about multiple things. You remember? Eating dinner with Sir Roger I say the Americans is savages. Is not true . . . is stupid lie.'

'I'm glad you've changed your mind.'

'Americans love horses,' he said in support of his newly found convictions. 'Is intelligent people; is warm and decent inside like . . . like cabbage.'

It seemed Elizabeth had done some useful public relations work. She was waiting in the yard as we came out of the stables, and her manner of greeting Atsy-Catsy *was* 'warm and decent'.

I asked her what it had to do with cabbages.

'It's a Russian saying,' she told me. 'You know the way

cabbages are all rolled up tight . . . I guess they're clean and warm inside . . . How did it go today, Cat?'

'Great,' said the jockey, 'just great, honey. How's your leg?'

'They're going to take off the plaster in a couple of weeks.'

'The doctor is very happy?'

'Sure; he says the leg will be as good as new.'

They stood gazing at one another, their public conversation apparently exhausted. They were too courteous, both of them, to speak Russian in front of me.

'We go out?' asked Atsy-Catsy, bravely breaking the deadlock.

'We could have tea in your room if you like,' suggested Elizabeth.

'I *like*,' he said. 'I like much. Moment, I fetch cake.' He made off towards the harness-room.

'Isn't it a pity about his name?' asked Elizabeth. 'He hates it . . . even prefers people calling him Cat.'

'Couldn't he use his surname?'

Elizabeth shook her head. 'It's even worse . . . it means something like he-with-the-warts . . . I think it's great, the way he hasn't let his name give him the fantods. In his place I'd have gotten as nutty as a fruitcake.'

Lady Beverley's estate-car came dashing into the yard. She smiled at Elizabeth, and leaned out of the window. 'How are you getting on . . . walking better?'

Elizabeth's reply was drowned by the barking of the dachshunds inside the car. It seemed to be the one day when Lady Beverley had taken out the wrong trio of dogs.

'. . . come to dinner again, Elizabeth,' screamed Lady Beverley, struggling with a fluffy brown dachs bent on hurtling head first into the yard. 'Mr Morton . . . nine o'clock . . . Roger . . . the others . . . Kenwood.'

Before I could disentangle the message, if indeed it has been one, from the noise of the dogs, Lady Beverley had stepped on the accelerator. Her car almost knocked for six the armful of biscuits Atsy-Catsy was carrying out of the harness-room, swerved round the corner and disappeared in an explosion of mud.

# CHAPTER 4

Olive, in white cap and apron, did not say she would announce me, so I took it that Sir Roger *was* expecting me at nine o'clock. She showed me into a room, furnished like a glossy office, which I had not seen before. The door sighed shut behind her.

I looked at the latest number of *The Farmer and Stockbreeder*, took out my pipe, filled and lit it, and wondered for the second time that evening why the Craftly cattle were making such a noise. Even with the windows shut I could hear a continuous lowing. Was the restlessness of the beasts a symptom of foot-and-mouth disease? I decided to look it up when I got home.

By half-past nine there was still no sign of my hosts, though I did hear enthusiastic crowd noises from a television-set. I thought it strange of them to keep me waiting while they watched what sounded like a good match.

At a quarter to ten, uncertain whether to go or stay, I began to wander about the room. I was passing the large teak executive desk for the umpteenth time when I noticed the plan on the blotter.

It was a sketch on the headed paper of the Radiant Homes Development Company, apparently drawn to scale, with pencilled notes on the margin. The one beneath the letter-heading read 'Craftly Development'.

I think I'd have become interested in the plan even if Radiant Homes had not beaten me to the house in London which Julia and I had wanted. As far as I could remember Radiant Homes had not been in existence a couple of years ago. It was fascinating to see how a company such as this 'developed'.

The drawing was roughly eggshaped, and I soon recognised the plots of land. One side, a long curve, was marked as the holding of the Radiant Homes Company, the rest of the circumference was divided between the properties of Farmer Thornton, of Conny Crosby and Miss Sabina Webb, and the elongated centre of the egg was taken up by the

Jenkins's market-garden and nurseries. Conny's piggery and Miss Sabina's 'bird-sanctuary' adjoined Sir Roger's Radiant Homes plot on the sharp ends of the 'egg', with Thornton's pastures and rough-shooting grounds stretched in between.

The names of the different owners were jotted down at the side together with notes concerning their interests; Sabina Webb – birds, quackery; Thornton – dairy-cattle, shooting; Conny Crosby – young sister, survival; Alan and Beryl Jenkins – tomatoes, baby, cars.

Beside Miss Sabina's name there was also a question-mark and a cross. The meaning of the cross became clear to me when I looked at the letter attached to the plan; it was the Minister's refusal of the Radiant Homes development plan. The proviso that building would *not* be against policy if the company acquired adjoining land, not less than an acre, was heavily underlined. The cross and the question-mark against Miss Sabina's name indicated, I thought, that Sir Roger considered hers the most likely land to come into the market; she was elderly; she'd have to die some time.

But at the back of the plan I found another note concerning her. 'Alternative,' it stated, 'offer Sabina Aberdeenshire site. Almost certainly prolonged social approach. See Beverley.'

Beverley's 'social approach' was apparent the moment I opened the door of the drawing-room. It was after ten and I had become annoyed and tired of being kept waiting.

Lady Beverley and Miss Sabina were sitting with their backs to the door watching the biggest television-screen I'd ever seen. Miss Sabina, a large whisky beside her, was leaning forward in her chair, her back as expressive of tension as the face of the ex-heavyweight who was refereeing the boxing-match in progress.

The welter-weight in the dark shiny pants was driving the welter-weight in the light shiny pants up against the ropes. Light Pants performed a dexterous turn, got himself with his back to the centre of the ring and slogged Dark Pants on the back of the neck.

'Rabbit punch,' shouted Miss Sabina. 'Now, now! no rabbit-punching!'

Light Pants managed to land a second one of the same kind.

'Referee! Referee!' called Miss Sabina.

The three fluffy dachshunds began to bark and rage round Miss Sabina's chair.

'Fourteen,' reprimanded Lady Beverley, 'sit down. Fifteen, Sixteen, quiet there! Sit!'

Dark Pants, though looking a bit punch-drunk by now, was rallying. For a while he flailed about with both arms, leaving himself wide open to Light Pants' attack, but then he saw his chance and squarely landed an uppercut on his opponent's chin.

'Follow up,' advised Miss Sabina, loudly. Her stringy little fist performed a right hook to Dark Pants's left. 'Move in . . . move in *now*!' Her fists were hooking right and left indiscriminately.

Dark Pants was tiring again, going into a tight clinch with Light Pants, which Light Pants used for a few nasty low jabs. Since Dark Pants retaliated with some quick head-butting there was little to choose between the two, and Miss Sabina refrained from calling upon the referee.

The commentator announced that Light Pants had a cut under the eye.

'Serves him right,' said Miss Sabina.

A cut under the eye, repeated the commentator, but it appeared to be only a slight one. There was no blood; no sign of the eye closing up.

'Pity,' said Miss Sabina.

Light Pants was not so sure that his eye wasn't closing up. He kept touching it with an air of surprise, thereby giving Dark Pants another chance of crowding him to the ropes.

'Here's your chance!' shouted Miss Sabina. 'Go on, boy; follow up!'

She gave a sigh of disappointment when Dark Pants, obviously weary, hit nothing more useful than his opponent's glove.

The spectacle of Miss Sabina's participation in the match was so enthralling that I'd willingly have watched to the end of the round. Unfortunately the raging of the dachshunds had begun to get on Lady Beverley's nerves. She gathered all three in her arms and got up to eject them.

'Hello,' she greeted me. 'Come to watch the end of the match?'

'Wasn't I supposed to see Sir Roger?' I asked. 'At *nine*.'

'Of course . . . and the others.'

'I haven't seen anyone but your maid.'

'Oh Lord!' Lady Beverley dropped the dachshunds. 'It's that stupid girl Olive . . . Where have you been?'

'In . . . I suppose, the office.'

'That's what I was afraid of . . . Olive *will* mix up the office and the library. I'm sorry. Roger does hate being kept waiting; I'd better take you to the library right away. The others are staying with us, of course, but they'll be wanting to go to bed soon.'

*I* was feeling rather sleepy. 'I'll come again, tomorrow.'

'Oh no; Sir Ludley's leaving first thing in the morning. He came down specially . . . Roger said it *was* rather important to get everyone together.' She walked to the door, ignoring the fact that the dachshunds got out first, scattering in three different directions. 'Come along, Mr Morton.'

Miss Sabina gave a cry of distress. Light Pants, despite his cut eye, had succeeded in punching Dark Pants in the stomach and landing the knock-out blow while his opponent was doubled up.


The five Members of Parliament assembled in the library were as mixed a clutch as I'd seen anywhere outside the House. Sir Roger (Labour) introduced Sir Ludley Morrows (Labour), Mr Smythe and Mr Barrys (Conservative) and Mr de Cross Anatole (Liberal). My impression was that they had nothing in common other than that their doings and opinions took up a lot of space in a lot of newspapers.

'We've done some useful preliminary work,' said Sir Roger. 'I move we adjourn for refreshments.'

'I second that,' Mr Smythe clapped Sir Roger on the back, 'yes, I certainly do . . . Brandy? Just the thing, just the thing; be interested to taste your stuff, Roger. I'm rather in a quandary about re-stocking; my grandfather's brandy's done . . . we're right down to my father's stuff now. Trouble is, my old man had no palate for brandy. Now *there's* a queer thing . . . no palate for brandy but believe me when it came to selecting hocks for his cellar the old man was first-rate, quite first-rate. Must open a bottle of that Rüdesheim for you sometime.'

'Rüdesheim,' said Sir Ludley, 'I had a good bottle the other day, when I lunched with the Earl of Bolney . . .

though I don't think it was up to old Richard's standards
. . . you know, the old Duke of Alanspring.'

'Frightful snob,' Mr Barrys murmured in my ear, 'old
Ludley. Only reason he came in with us on the greyhound
syndicate was that his *good friend* the Duke of Alanspring's
got one.'

I almost admitted to knowing the Duke's hound.

'I heard,' said Mr Barrys, still in his confidential voice,
'that there's something fishy about the Duke's hound . . .
he gets the jitters when he sees a hare, or something of the
kind. Someone told me the Duke's in the States having the
dog treated by an animal psychiatrist.'

I could have confirmed the story, but I didn't because the
Duke's dog had been a patient of mine.

'What interests *me*,' Mr Barrys informed me, 'isn't the
psychology of greyhounds but the mentality of the crowds
that attend *greyhound racing*. Think of the numbers that go
to the tracks regularly; the National Greyhound Racing
Society alone represents sixty-four tracks. What do people
see in dog racing?'

'*I* can tell you.' Mr Smythe had joined us. He was smiling
indulgently at his younger fellow-Conservative. 'People just
like a bit of a fling and a gamble. I know, I do. That's why
I'm all in favour of keeping our Kenwood.'

Mr Barrys frowned. 'I disagree most strongly, Claude.
We'll give the public an erroneous impression if we continue
to hang on to that dog.'

'Oh, look here, Bertie, you were as keen on buying Kenwood as I was.'

'Yes, but for different reasons. I felt, as a Member of
Parliament, it was my duty to mix with the man in the street,
to be seen in popular public places, to know how ordinary
people feel!'

'Come off it, Bertie. Sniffing around the canaille won't
earn you promotion in the House,' said Mr Smythe. 'Even
Roger's got a sounder reason for going to the dogs. He
doesn't rub shoulders with the canaille, but he watches. He
wants to know how they tick . . . he does find out, and then
he goes and tells his tame executives what'll make the man
in the street buy a Radiant Home rather than the better
built house round the corner.'

Mr Barrys laughed, with his mouth only. 'You're an old

cynic, Claude; and if the Party doesn't get rid of a few like you we'll lose the next election.'

Mr Smythe ignored the jibe and turned to Mr de Cross Anatole. 'Moved into your new house yet, Leicester?' he enquired.

'No, not yet. We've got to get rid of the trees first.'

'You're *not* going to cut down those fine old oaks, are you?'

'Certainly,' said de Cross Anatole. 'Couldn't live in that jungle.'

I remembered a recent Sunday-paper profile of de Cross Anatole. As an undergraduate he'd spent several months in the Kalahari desert; it had been his spiritual home, and he'd written a book about it. Since then he'd wanted to return to his desert but life had put too many obstacles in his way; on the death of his father he'd considered it his duty to continue the family's liberal tradition in politics; his wife said the children needed him, and she herself preferred the south of France. So, instead of travelling the desert, de Cross Anatole had moved from country-mansion to country-mansion, cutting down the trees wherever he lived and leaving throughout the country a trail of country-mansions named *Kalahari*.

Sir Roger had brought in a large brindled greyhound which looked as sleepy as I felt.

Mr de Cross Anatole stroked the animal's narrow head with real affection. 'What do you think of him, Morton?' he asked me. 'Beautiful creature, isn't he? There's only one animal I find more attractive to look at, and that's the little gazelle you meet on the fringes of the Kalahari.'

'Go ahead, Morton,' Sir Roger shoved the dog over to me, 'take a look at him. Tell us what you think of Kenwood.'

I found Kenwood a sound and splendidly built animal, and I said so to the five owners who had settled down round a paper-strewn table. The papers, I noticed, were newspaper racing results and programmes from different greyhound tracks.

Mr Barrys didn't seem to like my report; Sir Roger looked thoughtful.

'Are you sure, Morton?' he asked.

'The dog's as good as the best I've seen racing at Wimbledon.'

Sir Roger looked concerned. 'But what about his glands? There may be something wrong with his glands, don't you think?'

'Why?'

'One can't put one's finger on it exactly; it just struck me that there may be something odd about Kenwood's thyroid. I mean . . .'

'Hrrm,' Mr Smythe interrupted. 'Our chairman means we've got us a dog that rarely loses a race; and that's been – er – inconvenient lately.'

'Exactly.' Sir Roger's tone of voice made it clear that if there was going to be any 'brutal' frankness *he* was going to be brutally frank. 'It's been a nuisance, Morton. Kenwood's had too much publicity lately. You know the kind of thing, *syndicate of M.P.s are on to a good thing*.'

'And why *shouldn't* we be?' asked Sir Ludley, plaintively. '*Ordinary* people don't object to a bit of tax-free income.'

'Quite,' said Sir Roger, implying that Sir Ludley was *after all* verging on the 'ordinary' despite his friendship with dukes and the like. 'The papers have taken to calling Kenwood *the House of Commons winner*, the *mixed Members' unearned income coup* . . . Well, Morton, it's become embarrassing . . . very embarrassing indeed. You see, originally we bought Kenwood for one purpose – for one purpose only; the Betting and Gaming Act had come before the House and we felt the only right thing for us to do was to study greyhound racing from the inside . . . discover the snags for ourselves.'

Mr Smythe grinned. 'But as far as our Kenwood's concerned there haven't been any snags. He's been a cert all along.'

'Precisely,' said Mr Barrys, coldly. 'If Kenwood hadn't been a cert – as you so elegantly put it – the question of selling him wouldn't arise.'

'It hasn't arisen yet,' Mr Smythe pointed out. 'Mr Chairman, am I right?'

'Yes indeed,' Sir Roger agreed. 'I'm in favour of . . . er exploring other avenues. That, gentlemen, is why I put to Mr Morton the suggestion that Kenwood's thyroid may be . . . er . . . out of sorts.'

'It isn't,' I told the syndicate, firmly. If they wanted a quack to tinker with the dog's hormones I wasn't going to be their man. 'Kenwood happens to be ideally built for speed, he's young and he's fit.'

'Mm,' Sir Roger scratched his thick white hair. 'That does pose rather a problem, doesn't it.'

'Not in the least, Mr Chairman,' said Mr Barrys, 'all we've got to do is *sell* the dog. We'll get a decent price for him.'

Sir Ludley picked up some of the newspaper cuttings. 'A decent price! But nothing *like* the money Kenwood's earning us.'

Sir Roger looked almost embarrassed. 'The money's beside the point, Ludley.'

Mr de Cross Anatole looked happy for the first time since the discussion had started. 'You're absolutely right, Roger. Why not keep Kenwood for the pleasure he gives us? And there's no reason why we shouldn't bet on him, provided we give our winnings to charity. I mean . . . one can drop a word in the right quarters and you'd have first-rate write-ups in no time at all.'

'I support this suggestion,' said Mr Barrys.

'I don't,' said Sir Ludley and Mr Smythe in unison.

'Too much like a publicity stunt,' decided Sir Roger. 'I'm not against publicity stunts, gentlemen, but they mustn't be quite so obvious or they defeat their object.'

'Surely,' de Cross Anatole sounded exasperated, 'what *matters* is the dog. I'm firmly against selling Kenwood because one cannot be sure that another owner – or owners – would take care of him as well as we do. A noble creature like Kenwood . . .'

'Yes, yes,' Sir Ludley cut in. 'There's all that, we know. But we've got to be practical. Let me put the problem to you *clearly*; if we sell Kenwood we lose the revenue from his future performance. If we don't sell him and give our winnings to charity someone will have to spend valuable time on book-keeping; the maintenance and training of the dog costs us about two pounds a week . . . and there are transport expenses. All this has to be worked out in relation to Kenwood's winnings. We can't be expected to pay for the dog out of our own pockets *and* give away his winnings.'

'I don't see why not.' de Cross Anatole was puzzled.

'No, *you* wouldn't. *I* suggest we hang on to Kenwood. Only sensible thing to do.' Sir Ludley's voice rose to a sturdy-fellow pitch. 'I don't give a damn if the newspapers jabber about the *mixed Members' unearned income coup*. I say, this is a case for showing courage.'

Mr Smythe laughed. 'Come off it, old chap. The dog's fun – that's why *I* want to keep him. You do because you like the winnings and de Cross Anatole because he likes the dog. So why not . . .'

Sir Roger got up. 'Exactly what I was going to suggest; Barrys and I will sell our shares in the syndicate but you . . . by all means . . . hang on to yours.'

Mr de Cross Anatole looked slightly stunned. 'I say . . . I'm not sure . . . considering the best interests of Kenwood . . .'

'I assure you,' said Sir Roger, 'my first consideration *is* Kenwood's well-being . . .'

Apart from being superfluous I suddenly felt slightly sick. I got up and told the syndicate that I didn't think I was needed at this stage. They agreed and thanked me for my 'services', and I said I'd find my own way out.

It was easier said than done. The passages and the hall were in darkness; Miss Sabina must have gone home, Lady Beverley and the staff had presumably retired for the night. Only the barking of the dachshunds gave me an idea how to find the back door, and my car.

It seemed to me the dachshunds had a perfectly legitimate reason for barking – for once. The night was full of noises, the noises of restless cattle. It was peculiar. Cows, at least numbers of them, didn't normally moo and roar at one in the morning.

# CHAPTER 5

Even with the engine of the bubble-car spluttering away I could tell that the lowing of the cattle became louder as I approached Farmer Thornton's fields. Tired as I was my curiosity got the better of me.

When I reached the stile leading to Thornton's land I drove the bubble on to the verge, switched off my lights, and got out. The night was black except for the odd moment when the clouds parted and let the moon flash out. It was very cold in a damp unpleasant way and the moment I'd climbed over the stile I almost lost my shoes in the mud.

I told myself I was a fool to bother about a lot of silly cows but I squelched on, sinking ankle-deep into the mud, making a mess of my best suit. I didn't have a torch and I didn't strike matches because there were only a few left in the box which I wanted to save in case I lost my way back.

The cattle-noises led me across a field, a patch of bramble-scrub that tore at my clothes, and across a second field. Then, at last, I could actually make out the darker darkness of the herd. It looked as if the four-hundred-odd head of cattle belonging to Thornton had all been packed into a relatively small field. On climbing over the last stile I had to push away a couple of cows before I could put my feet down on the other side.

As I stood among the cattle, wondering what to do next, the herd began to calm down. The animals stopped milling around, fewer of them lowed or roared. It seemed my muddy walk had got me nowhere.

A cleft in the clouds showed me a drier way back to the road, past Thornton's house, across his yard. The cows appeared to have got over their attack of hysteria and didn't seem to mind my shoving them out of the way.

I was approaching the gate to the orchard, wondering whether I hadn't imagined the noise, when I heard the raised voices of two men. I recognised Thornton's voice, the other – I felt almost certain – was that of my horse-doping friend Sidney Franks.

'I kept *my* part of the bargain,' he was saying.

'I'll soon know whether you've done the job or not,' said Thornton. 'If you have you'll get your money.'

'I've had to pay . . .'

'I've given you a fiver for your expenses and that's all you're getting tonight.'

'If I'd known you were going to play me a dirty trick . . .'

'Better keep your mouth shut,' said Thornton. 'You'll be lucky to get anything at all. If you think I've forgotten you killed Petunia . . .'

'That wasn't my fault, Dave,' whined Sidney. 'That cow died . . . well, it was an accident.'

'It wouldn't have happened if you'd known what you were about. *I* had to tell you. And you didn't organise things properly tonight either . . . the row the cattle made must have roused the whole village.'

'How was I to know?'

'You *should* have known, that's all . . . what am I going to say if people ask what was the matter with my beasts?'

'Tell them someone else's cow got in with your bull. It wouldn't be the first time such a thing's happened in Craftly, would it?'

'You damned dirty little . . .'

'Now, now!' said Sidney. 'Let's not call one another names. That wouldn't be wise. After all, we're in this together . . .'

'If you don't shut up you'll find out whether we are or not. Another word out of you and you can go whistling for your money.'

'Well, well, stop fussing about nothing.'

'You call my herd *nothing*?' Thornton sounded hurt as well as angry.

'I didn't mean your herd, Dave,' Sidney's voice had become ingratiating. 'I know as well as the next man what your animals mean to you. Would you be taking such risks if you didn't feel like you do . . . Don't think I don't understand. When I was training horses I got so . . .'

The two of them had walked away and I could no longer hear what they were saying. One thing was certain; Sidney had found a new racket and Thornton was up to something illegal. I had an idea what they had been doing but there was nothing I could do without positive proof.

I was not likely to find such proof at two in the morning, in the middle of a muddy field. I waited a few minutes and then made my way towards Thornton's house. There was a light on in the kitchen but I managed to get past without being seen. In the yard I came across the Alfa Romeo, well hidden behind a shed.

Though I had a two-mile walk along the road to where I'd left my bubble I no longer felt tired. I was too preoccupied with what I had heard. There was no doubt that Sidney and Thornton had committed a breach of the law, but even if I *could* prove it, was it up to *me* to act on privately gathered information?

There was a problem that would never arise in my city practice. The one thing I hadn't expected when I agreed to do a locum in the country was that I might finish up with a bad conscience whatever I did in a case such as Thornton's.

I considered 'phoning Phil Brogan; after all it was *his* practice. But Phil was a sick man; I'd be worrying him. Besides wouldn't it be shirking responsibility to wash *my* hands of that business? Of course, there was always the alternative of 'forgetting' what I had heard.

I kept thinking in circles until I went to sleep, and I came to with a feeling of having dozed for a few minutes only. The joys of country life, I reflected bitterly, listening to the shattering row of the false dawn. Dark as it still was the birds were solidly united in music; in comparison the Trumpet Voluntary was a *sotto voce* affair. Using what strength of mind I had left after my late night with the syndicate of M.P.s and the cows I persuaded myself back to sleep.

The next thing was that Patty, the black kitten, had an attack of playfulness and began to chew up the cord of my pyjama-trousers. And a few minutes later someone was throwing pebbles at my window.

It was Tail of course.

'Don't you ever sleep?' I yelled at her.

'At my age one doesn't need much sleep.' She sounded like the old fellow. 'There are more important things than sleep.'

'Such as?'

'Let me in and I'll tell you. Anyway your breakfast's cooking. It's sausages and bacon today.'

'Thanks for telling me . . . I hate surprises. What do you want?'

'A don't like shouting,' she called out in the voice of a Frinton landlady. 'Am A to be admitted or not? A have something of importance to communicate to you.'

'Oh, all right.' By now I was awake anyway.

Tail kept her her new role even after I'd let her in. 'There was,' she informed me, 'a disturbance last night.'

'Oh yes?'

'The animals of our neighbour, Mr Thornton, were restless. They disturbed our slumber.'

'I bet *you* didn't slumber.'

'Well, I didn't,' said Tail, in her normal voice. 'Look Uncle Michael . . . look what I found in Thornton's field.' She took a grubby white face-flannel from her pocket and unrolled it on my breakfast table. It contained a large hypodermic syringe with some liquid at the bottom. 'Well?' she asked excitedly.

'Well what?' I wondered how much Tail had guessed.

'Isn't it one of those things you keep in your surgery?'

I looked at her, reminding myself that for all her virtuosity Tail was only a slip of a child. 'Yes,' I said. 'It *is* one of those things.'

'Has Thornton pinched it from you?'

'Don't be silly, of course he hasn't.'

'Did you lose it then?'

I thought it would be simplest to tell her that I must have dropped the syringe out of my bag.

'Oh,' she sounded disappointed. 'All the same . . . I bet old Thornton stuck the needle into some cows last night.'

'What gives you that idea?'

'The cows made a noise like . . . as if somebody was doing something nasty to them.'

'That's nonsense, Tail. Look here, would Thornton do anything to hurt his own animals?'

'No,' Tail admitted. 'But there *was* something funny going on . . . Don't pick it up in your fingers,' she said, as I lifted up the syringe. 'You *are* clumsy; I didn't touch this thing at all . . . 'cause of the fingerprints. If the police want to investigate . . .'

'I'm sure it isn't a case for the police,' I said, feeling not a bit sure. 'Thank you very much for bringing my syringe back. Here's the reward.' I gave her half a crown. 'And now, off you go.'

'O.K., thanks.' Her dramatic sense had been disappointed, but the half-crown appeared to be some slight compensation.

'Don't know what's come over the animals,' said Mrs Pitt, clearing away the breakfast dishes. 'The noise last night was something awful! It wouldn't have happened in Wandsworth, Mr Morton. I mean to say, decent folks are entitled to their sleep. And there were them cows kicking up as if they was in agony; as if the day hadn't been bad enough what with the trouble we had about Barney.'

'I thought the owl was well again.'

'Well!' Mrs Pitt was indignant. 'I should say so. Took herself off, she did and not so much as a "thank you" for all we done. Miss Sabina was in a state . . . had us hunting all over the place for Barney . . . me and the patients and all. Poor lady . . . she can't see it's nothing but ingratitude; she thinks Mr Thornton killed Barney with them chemicals.'

I took the syringe and retreated to the surgery. Tail's find had confirmed my own theories; there *was* something fishy about the alliance of Sidney Franks and Thornton. But whatever I did I first had to know what the liquid in the syringe was, which would almost certainly tell me why Thornton's cows had been given injections.

I wrote to Eric Goff of the London Laboratory asking him to analyse the liquid for me, put the note into a box with the syringe, and went along to the village post-office. When Mr Tucker gave me the receipt for the registered parcel I wondered just how much trouble I was asking for.

As I turned into the High Street a car drew up beside me. 'I was just going to see you, Michael,' said Renton, of the Veterinary Investigation Department. 'Can you spare a moment?'

I said I could and he asked me to accompany him to The Lion. As soon as we entered the private room of the local I realised that the V.I. Department were preparing for the worst. A large map of the county had been pinned to the beams and the map itself was studded with little coloured flags. At a table in front of it a clerk and John Porter, Renton's second in command, were studying a stack of files. The place looked like an army headquarters in the thick of war.

Tom Renton walked up to the map and silently moved one of the red flags a few inches nearer to Craftly village. 'That's the position now, Michael,' he said.

'So you think we're going to have foot-and-mouth here.'

'I hope not. It's all of ten miles away. I just want to tighten up preventive measures in your area to be on the safe side. You'll give us a hand?'

'Of course.' Phil Brogan had given me an idea what this would mean; the whole cattle and pig population would have to be kept under surveillance, animals would have to be laboratory tested, and if one of them was found suffering from foot-and-mouth disease an investigation into the source of infection would be carried out. And such investigations were as wide and arduous as any police-hunt for a mass-murderer. The virus that caused foot-and-mouth disease was no less a killer.

'We've traced the route by which the infection has spread.' Renton pointed to a black flag. 'There were two infected cows at the market . . . here. The day after one of them, which hadn't been sold, went on to market *here*. Both had been sold several times over. It's taken us a longish time to trace the movements of those beasts . . . the familiar story; the dealer who handled them was trading under a false name.'

'Still,' Porter looked up from his files. 'We're pretty sure of the boundaries of the infection now. With a bit of luck the Craftly lot won't catch it.'

'Yes, I think so too,' agreed Renton. Both he and Porter looked so drawn and tired that their optimism was doubly impressive.

'What do you want me to do?' I asked.

Renton thumbed through some type-written sheets and handed me a list of names and addresses. 'Could you deal with this lot?'

I said I would. It was a longer list of cattle- and pig-owners than I had expected and some of them had large herds. When I noticed Thornton's name on my list I wondered whether access to his animals would help or hinder me in the investigation I had started off my own bat.

Back at Phil's house a geranium pink vintage car was sitting in the yard, and in the car sat a great airedale, as upright and straight-backed as a human dignitary with arms folded across his chest. The car belonged to Miss Sabina, and it was Tail who had made it memorable to me. She'd said the colour of the car reminded her of the teats of Conny's sow Myrtle – it was 'teaty' pink and the old fellow had told her that type came off the production-lines in pairs and only a sucker would buy one. I still didn't know whether Tail's remark had been as guileless as I believed it to be.

Miss Sabina was first in the queue of waiting animal-owners. 'Did you hear the appalling noise, last night?' she asked as I showed her into the surgery.

'I wasn't at home,' I said, 'forgetting that she had seen me at the Coolcrows'.

'I wasn't aware of it myself while I was watching . . . television. But I am told there was a lowing of cattle all evening, and I certainly heard it half the night.'

I suggested, feeling mean, that the staff of the Veterinary Investigation Department might have caused a disturbance.

'I doubt it,' said Miss Sabina, grimly. 'I shouldn't be in the least surprised if there were a connection between the noise of Thornton's beasts and the disappearance of my owl.'

I tried to persuade her that owls were not as sociable as tits; being night-creatures, that hours kept by a human household didn't suit them.

Miss Sabina was less than half convinced. 'Young man, I've studied birds all my life. *If* poor Barney is alive she'll come home. But I fear something dreadful's happened to her. I've made up my mind, I need an assistant who'll help me protect my birds. I have a dog . . . a *large* dog.'

'The airedale outside?'

'Precisely. Jock belongs to my sister. Anne was going to send him to a kennel while she's abroad. I told her he'll be much more useful at Tit House.'

'Won't Jock scare your birds?'

'They'll get used to him . . . There's only one thing that worries me . . . the *smell*. I'd like you to examine Jock.'

Jock followed me into the surgery wagging his thick

66

stumpy tail, obviously eager to please. A large dog he was, as large as a calf, but I doubted whether he'd protect Tit House, let alone the tits. Jock was the kind of soft-hearted giant that would respond indiscriminately to the friendliness of his household, to people in the streets, marauders and burglars. I found nothing wrong with him; he was a strong, sound two-year-old.

I noticed no *smell* until I looked at his teeth. The teeth were perfect, but Jock's breath wasn't; it was like the breath of an alcoholic who'd forgotten to swallow his chlorophyll tablets.

I asked Miss Webb whether she knew what the dog had eaten.

'Only a biscuit,' she told me. 'He's fed in the evening . . . What *is* the smell, Mr Morton?'

'If Jock were a man I'd say its beer.'

'Beer!' Miss Sabina frowned. 'It's outrageous!'

'Not of the dog. Someone must have given it to him.'

'Yes indeed, and I have an idea who is responsible. It must have been that dreadful American.'

'Who? Elizabeth?'

'I see she's introduced herself to you too. Frightful young woman. If dear Dr Schwersteiger hadn't personally recommended her I wouldn't have her at Tit House; she's more interested in horses . . . and jockeys than in birds. Yes, I'm sure the culprit is Elizabeth.'

'Why should she give your dog beer?'

'I fear it's partly my fault. You see I allow my patients visitors in the morning . . . the birds don't mind, provided all strangers leave before lunch . . . and provided visitors don't wear plastic raincoats or hats. The patients are allowed to receive their friends in their bed-sitting-rooms. This morning the foreign jockey called on Elizabeth. They must have been drinking beer, though it's strictly against the rules of Tit House. The patients are not allowed to keep alcohol in their rooms . . . except whisky, which I myself supply at a special price . . . I should have spoken to Elizabeth before; I actually saw beer-cans in the dustbin. Yes, it must be Elizabeth . . . drinking beer out of cans *is* an American habit, isn't it?'

'Perhaps. But beer isn't nearly as strong as whisky,' I said. 'If Elizabeth wants to offer her visitors a glass . . .'

67

'A *can* of beer,' Miss Sabina cut in, 'No, I can't permit a thing like *that*. With a dog in the house it's positively dangerous . . . I do hope Jock hasn't come to harm.'

I assured Miss Sabina that the surreptitious drink had not hurt the dog and escorted the two of them to their pink car. Jock, as large and dignified as a lord mayor, took the back seat and was told not to breathe down Miss Sabina's neck.

Most of the other animal-owners who came to the surgery commented on the noises of the past night. A smart woman with a chocolate poodle said she and her husband had moved to Craftly recently to escape the din of London; now she was not sure they hadn't 'jumped from the frying-pan into the fire'. The people who owned pigs or cattle wondered whether the restlessness of the beasts had anything to do with foot-and-mouth disease. Most of them guessed that the disturbance had been on Thornton's land.

Several times during the day I found myself wandering into the yard or the garden, listening. But the village was quiet except for the chugging of the odd tractor, the usual bird-chatter, and an occasional heartbroken sob from the little donkey that belonged to Dr Eller's grandchildren. Towards evening the sun came out and brought a scent of spring; a few crocuses had opened out and the early irises had broken through their leaves, their petals adroop like spaniel-ears.

I hoped it would be as warm and peaceful when Julia came. She had at last accepted my explanation for Elizabeth's mark on the cup and Tail's appearance. She'd promised to come for the week-end and I was determined to make her stay. If Claire and Tiger repeated their invitation there was no reason why she shouldn't give up her job and stay for the rest of my locum. If I put it to Julia that . . .

The telephone rang. I'd been so absorbed in the charms of the countryside and the charms of Julia that I said, 'Hello darling.'

There was an embarrassed grunt at the other end of the line. The caller had a message from Mr Thornton. His Scotch collie had a sore paw; would I call in please.

Robbie had a wood-splinter in his right forepaw. It was only just under the surface and I managed to pull it out with my fingers. It seemed very odd to me that Thornton had not dealt with it himself.

The collie shared my views; he clearly didn't regard me as a vet but as someone who'd come to play with him. He fetched a piece of wood, pushed it into my hand and let me know that it was for throwing. When I did throw it Robbie caught it in mid-air coming down heavily on his forepaws. The splinter had done so little damage that the dog had forgotten it already.

'It'll heal up soon, won't it?' asked Thornton.

'There's nothing to heal,' I told him.

Thornton muttered something unintelligible, went to the kitchen dresser, and unhooked a couple of pewter tankards. 'A beer?' he asked.

'Thanks.'

'How's the foot-and-mouth?' He put one of the tankards in front of me and sat down across the table. 'I heard it's getting nearer.'

I suddenly realised he'd also heard that I'd been in The Lion with Tom Renton, and that he was nervous. He wanted to know *why* I'd seen Renton. The splinter in Robbie's paw had been providential.

'Foot-and-mouth may spread or not,' I said. 'You yourself know what it's like.'

'Yes.'

We sat there in silence. Robbie put his piece of wood on my knees, begging me to throw it again. While playing with the dog I kept my eye on Thornton; he was so uneasy that I felt almost sorry for him. The moment I'd finished the beer he jumped up.

'I want to show you my bull,' he said abruptly.

'Anything wrong with him?'

'No.'

He led me through the orchard into the field where the cattle had been assembled on the previous night. Now only one animal was there, a truly splendid Ayrshire bull.

'That's Roderick the Second,' Thornton sounded like a boy who was introducing his first girl-friend to his mother. 'What do you think of him?'

'Best of the breed I've seen.'

'A man wouldn't want to lose an animal like him.'

I agreed.

'I mean . . . I could never replace him,' Thornton almost pleaded. 'He was the son of Petunia.'

'The cow you lost?'

'Yes. Reared both of them myself . . . funny thing about Petunia; when she was born her forelegs were so weak she couldn't get up on them. Old Whiteley said "sell her to the butchers" . . . but, well, somehow I couldn't do it. I got the vet to put splints on her forelegs; I had to get her to keep them on for five months.' He smiled. 'You'd never have known the trouble I had with her if you'd seen her a couple of years later . . . Old Whiteley was on to me every year, but I wouldn't have sold her to my own father.'

'If she was such a poor calf why *did* you keep her?'

'Oh, I don't know . . . it was the way that little scrap looked at me. She'd stare you straight in the eye, and then she'd try and try to lift herself on those thin legs. Guts . . . that's what she had, right from the day she was born.'

It crossed my mind that Thornton was putting on an act to enlist my sympathy and to make me 'overlook' his illegal actions, in case I *had* discovered what he'd done with his herd. He had shown me Roderick for a purpose. But the story of Petunia had come out spontaneously, of that I felt certain. To Thornton his animals meant more than bread and butter. He'd reared most of them himself, he knew their merits, their tempers and oddities, and they were part of his life, perhaps the most important part. Who was I to keep him in suspense?

I told him that Renton had asked me to take care of foot-and-mouth prevention routine in my area, and that his farm was on my list.

He nodded. 'That'll mean a lot of extra work for you . . . Don't bother about *my* animals. If one of them were sick I'd be on to you right away.'

'By then it would be too late.'

'What do you mean?'

'How much land is there between you and the nearest dairy-farm?' I asked.

'That would be Brook's . . . thirty acres I'd say.'

'Not bad. You're still free to sell cattle, but I'd rather you didn't.'

'Why's that, Mr Morton?' He was feigning surprise.

'In case any of your animals are carriers of the infection without actually being sick themselves.'

'Oh, I don't think so . . . but anyway I wasn't going to sell.'

'We'd better be careful, Thornton.'

He gave me a quick, harassed look. 'Anything you want me to do?'

'Yes. Keep a close check on your herd; to be on the safe side scrub your cowshed walls, stalls, troughs; spray your bedding and manure clamps with antiseptic. And see that your labourers change and scrub up before they go out.'

'You make it sound as if I *had* an animal with foot-and-mouth,' he objected. 'I'm telling you . . .'

'You lost Petunia, didn't you?'

'All right, I'll do as you say. I suppose it's in my own interest.'

'It's in everyone's interest . . . And next time Robbie has a splinter in his paw take it out yourself, won't you?'

In the High Street I passed Jock. The airedale was trotting along the pavement all by himself. I had the impression that he was turning in towards The Lion.

# CHAPTER 6

On Friday I actually saw Jock walk into the local, as purposefully as a regular customer. It didn't surprise me that Miss Sabina's pink car was *not* in the car park. On the other hand there was Claire and Tiger's Daimler 'sports' and Lady Beverley's run-about with three of her dachshunds pawing the windscreen and barking at the moon.

I decided to follow Jock. Sir Roger and Tiger were leaning at the bar, Claire and Lady Beverley sat perched on stools, and between them Jock was breathing hard at Mao-tse-Tung on Claire's shoulder. The Siamese cat seemed quite unworried; she regarded Jock's rough brown teddybear head with an expression of disdain. Jock gave a low growl. Mao-tse-Tung yawned. Everyone in the pub laughed, and Jock stalked off to the far end of the bar greeting a man he appeared to have met before. The man ordered a half-pint in a bowl.

'Have a drink,' Sir Roger invited me.

'Perhaps I should take that dog home,' I said.

'Oh no, sir.' The landlord poured Jock's beer into a pudding-basin. 'Jock's here most nights; we usually ask the last customer to drop him off at Tit House.'

Lady Beverley smiled. 'Miss Sabina's given Jock up; it was an unequal struggle from the start. Now she just doesn't think about him until closing-time.'

Sir Roger gave me a whisky. 'Boxing for her, beer for him; fair enough.'

'Got a home for the kittens yet?' I asked Claire.

'We'll keep them a bit longer. Chou-en-Lai is such a marvellous mother; we don't want to upset her . . . Michael, we're celebrating. The American furniture's arrived. You *must* see it. Roger and Beverley are coming too . . . we're going to have smoked haddock.'

I excused myself and told her that I was expecting Julia; I'd be fetching her from the station. Claire and Tiger said they'd be pleased to have Julia staying with them.

'We've got one of the guest-rooms decorated.' Claire

removed Mao-tse-Tung's tail from her mouth. 'Tiger thinks it's most successful . . . a gunmetal-grey wallpaper, clerical purple curtains and black paintwork.'

'Sounds lovely,' said Lady Beverley. 'What's the colour of the furniture?'

'Well . . . it's natural amboyna wood . . .'

'African,' explained Tiger, 'it's the wood of the *ptero-spermum indicum*. The tree grows mostly in . . .'

'Morton,' Sir Roger drew me aside. 'Have you been visited by – er – a member of the cultural staff of the Soviet Embassy?'

'No.'

'Good, good . . . The Russians have made an approach suggesting modifications . . . which would radically alter certain aspects of our original agreement. Apart from a grave shortage of suitable accommodation . . .'

'Roger,' interrupted Lady Beverley. 'Roger, *no*.'

'Thank you my dear,' he smiled at his wife. 'As I was saying . . . with goodwill on both sides it will be possible to avoid unfortunate incidents such as . . .'

Lady Beverley shook her head. 'Oh Roger! . . . He means the Russians wanted to send down a supervisor, someone to keep an eye on Atsy-Catsy. So Roger sent a *stiff letter* . . . you know the kind of thing . . . *it would be much appreciated if you had the kindness* etcetera . . . Anyway, we let them know we won't put up their supervisor and we won't let him put up a tent. Since then a couple of Russians have been here twice. They said they were interested in watching Princeling's training. But they met Elizabeth and asked her a lot of questions.'

'Did Elizabeth mind?'

'No,' said Sir Roger. 'She conducted herself admirably. But I consider it an infringement . . .'

'He means,' his wife interpreted, 'that Elizabeth is our guest while she's at our stables. The Russians had no business to question her.'

Sir Roger put down his glass. 'In fact it's my considered opinion that the situation demands tact and firmness from all in charge . . . very well, Beverley, very well . . . I mean if they come snooping round your place tell 'em where they get off. As long as they're paying for Princeling to be trained at my stables, he's going to be trained my way . . . without interference. And they're not to get information of any kind from my *vet*.'

'Roger,' Lady Beverley must have noticed my reaction. 'You don't have to tell a veterinary surgeon how to behave. Vets have *ethics*.' She made it sound like a disease. 'You do understand, Mr Morton, I'm sure.'

'How does Atsy-Catsy feel about his compatriots coming down from London?' I asked.

'He's in no way concerned,' said Sir Roger. 'I have intimated to him in no uncertain terms that I'd fully support him in his . . . oh, very well, Beverley . . . if he wanted to change employers.'

A little later Sir Roger 'intimated' that Kenwood was about to change his owners. It was easy to think of Sir Roger as a slightly absent-minded bureaucrat of the House and the board-room until he revealed the ruthlessness underneath his jargon. I felt almost sorry that I hadn't stayed to observe the collapse of his colleagues' hopes of keeping the *M.P.s unearned income coup*.

He ordered another round of drinks, coca-cola for Claire and Tiger, a half-pint for Jock, and whisky for the rest of us. The Lion was getting a bit too small for the village, he pointed out; the population of Craftly had grown considerably within the past year or two. The village could do with another pub . . . something attractively modern with a juke box; in the near future there was bound to be a good deal of development . . .

The Lion certainly had become crowded. Looking round at the faces of the shopkeepers, craftsmen and farmers beside us I could see what they thought of Sir Roger's planning; there was no mistaking the stares of disapproval or obvious dislike.

Lady Beverley had just said they'd better be going when Thornton and Conny Crosby came in. The people nearest the door looked at one another and made way for them. Undoubtedly most of that crowd knew of the feud between Thornton and the Crosbys.

Thornton, holding Conny's arm, made for the bar. 'Make it two Scotch, Bob,' he said, glancing at Conny as if he expected her to pass out if she didn't get her drink quickly. Conny did look sick, very sick.

\* \* \*

74

'By the morning it'll be all over the village,' said Thornton, 'May as well tell them, eh Conny?'

'All right, Dave.' The drink had helped her; she was looking less dazed. 'There's been an accident,' she told the people around them, 'the Jenkinses.'

'Jenkins the nurseries?' someone asked.

'Yes,' said Thornton. He gave Conny a cigarette and lit it for her. 'Car-smash, right outside Miss Crosby's house.'

'Ah, I always knew it,' said an old man. 'That Alan Jenkins . . . car-crazy, that's what he is . . . always has been.'

'Quiet, Dick,' said the postmaster. 'Anyone hurt?'

'Alan's dead,' said Thornton. 'So's his wife and the baby.'

The silence spread throughout the bar.

'How did it happen?' someone asked at last.

Thornton put an ashtray beside Conny. 'He must have skidded . . . head-on collision with a lorry. The lorry-driver and his mate are all right. The car was like . . . just like crumpled paper.'

Sir Roger moved closer. 'Did they have any relatives, Thornton?'

'There's an uncle and aunt in Guildford. We've 'phoned them.'

'No – er – *close* relatives?'

'Parents? No, Alan's parents were killed in the war.'

'And his wife's?'

'She was brought up by the relatives in Guildford.'

'Stop it!' Conny turned on Sir Roger. '*I* know what you're thinking . . . Never mind about the Jenkinses . . . maybe their land will be for sale. That's it, isn't it? Get in fast . . . buy the Jenkinses land for your nasty little Radiant Homes bungalows . . .'

'Conny,' Thornton tightened his grip on her arm.

'It's true.'

There was a murmur of agreement all around us.

Sir Roger took off his spectacles; without them he looked sad – almost vulnerable. 'You're upset, Miss Crosby,' he said kindly, 'very understandable in the circumstances. This . . . horrible accident must have been a grave shock to any witness . . . If there's anything I can do . . .'

'Not yet,' said Conny, 'the land's not for sale *yet*.'

'Miss Crosby!' Sir Roger's voice was quietly emphatic. 'I really cannot discuss business matters at *such* a time . . .

Good night.' He looked at his own party and walked to the door. Tiger, Claire and I looked at one another and stayed put. Only Sir Roger's wife followed him out.

'Michael, shouldn't you have gone with them?' asked Claire.

'Silly question, darling,' said Tiger.

'I'm going to pick up Julia . . . I'm taking Jock home,' I said rather more loudly than necessary.

'You do that, Mr Morton,' the landlord agreed. 'That dog's had a pint and a half . . . But don't drive him in, sir. If you drop him at the gate he'll go into the house by himself. Miss Sabina doesn't like cars driving in at night . . . on account of her birds.'

Jock followed me willingly. He took the seat beside me and didn't seem to mind the low roof of the bubble; he kept his head down as if he'd known the snags of travelling in my car all his life.

By the time I let him out, at the gates to Tit House, the car was reeking with the smell of beer. I opened the windows, hoping the smell would disperse by the time Julia took Jock's seat.

Mrs Pitt was too well-mannered to say clothes like Julia's 'wouldn't happen in Wandsworth,' but she obviously thought so. Julia was wearing pale blue furry slippers and a thick white sweater which concealed her pale blue shorts so that she looked as if she wore nothing under the sweater.

'Wicked,' said Mrs Pitt, putting a plate of scrambled eggs in front of Julia. 'If you ask *me*, an accident like that wouldn't have happened in Wandsworth. It's them bad roads . . . though it's the country, they shouldn't be allowed. That's what *I* say. It's wicked . . . Sir Roger being after poor Jenkinses land; mark my word, before we know where we are there won't be a real village left in England; not a *real* village that is.'

'Then it'll be more like Wandsworth,' suggested Julia, trying to cheer up Mrs Pitt.

'Oh no, Miss!' exclaimed Mrs Pitt. 'It wouldn't be right. You don't want Craftly looking like Wandsworth. Craftly's a *village*!'

'She's wonderful,' said Julia, when Mrs Pitt had left us to ourselves. 'Here, Patty!' The black kitten jumped from the

76

chair on to the table and accepted a piece of scrambled egg.

'Don't ruin her manners,' I told Julia. 'She'll be as bad as her mother. Old Patty used to steal slices of meat from the table and take them down on the floor; if Fiona or Phil saw her they'd pick up the meat and put it back on the plate.'

'How sweet!'

'Darling Julia, *that* was the reason I never had lunch in their house while *they* lived here.'

'I see.'

But Julia didn't see. She was wholly absorbed in the antics of young Patty, who was absorbed in pulling a piece of toast out of the rack. It was no good; once Julia and I were married I'd have to get used to sharing plates with cats, dogs, and possibly a monkey or two. However, I was sure a vet's wife *had* to be fond of animals and there I could rely upon Julia.

She picked up the kitten and came to sit on my knees in front of the fire. She took the morning paper out of my hands and put it on the floor. 'What's the news, darling?'

'I've hardly seen the paper,' I reminded her. But it didn't occur to her to retrieve it. 'Foot-and-mouth outbreak in Scotland . . . it's still spreading.'

'I meant the foreign news.'

'Don't know . . . It'll still be America versus Russia, a draw.'

'Never mind. Happy?'

I brushed the kitten off, and kissed her. I was still kissing her when the door opened and a man's voice said, 'Oh, sorry.' It was Eric Goff of the London Laboratory.

'Do come in,' said Julia, in her reassuring Girton voice. She slid off my lap as if she'd been sitting in a chair.

I introduced Eric and over-emphasised that Julia and I were about to be married. He congratulated us, and apologised for bursting in without warning; he was spending the week-end with friends nearby and he'd thought it would be a good idea to discuss that hypodermic syringe I'd sent him for analysis.

'It may be rather boring for your fiancée, Michael.'

'Not at all,' said Julia.

Instead of explaining that no one could dismiss Julia if she meant to stay I told Eric that Julia was used to assisting me in the surgery – that she knew a great deal about veterinary practice.

'Well, it looks to me like a case of *mal-practice*,' said Eric. 'Where did you get this syringe?' He took it out of his briefcase and put it on the table beside his chair. 'I take it that it isn't yours or you'd have been certain what was in it.'

'No, of course it's not mine. It was brought to me by . . . a child who'd found it in a field.'

'Do you know whose field?'

I said I didn't. At the same time I had no clear idea why I wanted to keep Thornton's name out of it.

'What did you find?' I asked.

'Well, your guess was correct. The liquid was a vaccine against foot-and-mouth . . . I'd say a foreign vaccine. What with foot-and-mouth disease in this area you know what *that* means.'

I knew very well. It was illegal in England to immunise animals against the disease, and Thornton had broken the law. What made it an even greater offence was that Thornton had got his herd vaccinated at a time when foot-and-mouth disease had broken out in the neighbourhood. If the Veterinary Authorities wanted to trace the carrier of the disease it would no longer be possible because Thornton's vaccinated animals would confuse the laboratory tests. It would be impossible to establish whether they were vaccinated beasts or beasts carrying and therefore spreading the infection without actually being sick themselves.

'It's pretty serious,' said Eric. 'Incidentally this is the second case of illegal vaccinations within the past two months. Same thing happened in Scotland, also on a farm on the borders of a foot-and-mouth outbreak.'

'What happened?' I was feeling hot under the collar.

'Case pending against the farmer. He gave the name and address of a vet who was supposed to have advised him to have his animals vaccinated. The police haven't found any such person . . . Judging by the lab-tests of the Scottish cattle I believe the vaccine used was the same as the stuff in your syringe.' He took a sheet of paper from his pocket and gave it to me. 'Here's the analysis.'

'A vaccine made from killed virus?'

'That's it. What's your next move, Michael?'

'It depends . . .'

'Take my advice, hand over to the Veterinary Investigation Department and the police will do the rest. It's a bad business.'

I told Eric I didn't want to rush things, and I asked him not to mention the test he carried out for the time being – certainly not until we'd had another talk.

'Well,' he agreed, 'I hope you know what you're doing . . . *I* wouldn't take such a risk, not for my best friend. Oh, one does sympathise with a farmer who hates the idea of seeing his cattle in a mass-grave. Any good farmer would rather have his beasts than the money-compensation. But while we have a national policy of slaughtering sick beasts and carriers individual farmers *mustn't* be allowed to take the law into their own hands. We *can't* risk losing the whole country's livestock because a handful of farmers decide to vaccinate their animals. If the Veterinary Investigation Department are unable to trace the carriers of the disease . . . because of a few blackleg farmers . . . anything might happen.'

'Michael,' said Julia, 'we *must* find out who's been vaccinating animals.'

'Leave it to me.'

Eric got up. 'All right, but I'm glad it's none of my business. I'm only a chemist . . . Anyway, don't stick out your neck.'

As soon as he was gone Julia demanded to know *everything*.

I didn't tell her of the quarrel between Thornton and Sidney Franks on the night the herd was 'restless', nor where Tail had found the syringe. It was not that I couldn't trust Julia; I just wanted to think things over.

So I told her about foot-and-mouth vaccination in general. Eric's analysis was not uninteresting either. Vaccines, I explained, were made from the virus that caused foot-and-mouth disease. There were two types; a vaccine in which the virus had been killed with chemicals so that animals injected with it became immune from the disease without getting infected, and a vaccine made from the live virus. The 'live' vaccine was perhaps more effective, but animals injected with it actually had the disease and were therefore capable of infecting others.

I was relieved to know that Thornton's animals had not been given 'live' vaccine. Though they were capable of confusing laboratory tests they would not *spread* infection.

What Thornton probably did not realise was that vaccines were not as much of a panacea as he seemed to believe. There wasn't only one type of foot-and-mouth disease – there were seven types, although only three of them affected animals in Europe. In England an animal, to be really safe from the disease, would have to be injected with at least three different viruses. If it was injected with one only it could still contract the two other types of foot-and-mouth, one at a time.

I was certain of one thing, a horse-doper like Sidney Franks was the last person who should have been allowed to handle the immunisation of cattle, even if it *had* been legal.

As I told Julia the technical details my own ideas were beginning to clarify. Thornton's cow Petunia, much to his grief, had died and he'd accused Sidney of making a mistake. It probably meant, firstly that Sidney had been asked to try out the vaccine on one animal only and that he'd experimented on the wrong cow; secondly that he had originally experimented with another vaccine – 'live' vaccine – which had actually given Petunia the disease.

Thornton's anxiety for his herd must have been extraordinarily strong or he wouldn't have given Sidney a second chance. The syringe proved that he had.

Another curious facet of the case was that Thornton had told me the truth when he said he'd been 'lucky' in not losing animals in the previous year's outbreak of foot-and-mouth disease. If he *had* had his animals vaccinated before there would have been no need to do it this year. But luck alone would not have been enough to protect his herd in the middle of an epidemic; I thought his hygienic measures had been exceptionally strict and therefore effective.

I believed they must have been. The fact that Petunia almost certainly died of foot-and-mouth without spreading it to other animals showed how well Thornton understood the dangers of infection.

Thornton was a first-rate farmer. And I suddenly realised that it was one good reason why I had not taken Eric Goff into my confidence, why I was not admitting to Julia that I knew the person who had been acting against the law. Once I had admitted to myself that I disliked the idea of taking action against a good farmer other excuses for shielding him piled on top. I remembered the way he'd talked about

Petunia, the reason he gave me for rearing the weak calf against almost hopeless odds.

But as a vet I had to consider how Thornton's action was likely to affect other farmers. If the area of the present foot-and-mouth outbreak increased, if the disease did spread, my friends of the Veterinary Investigation Department were bound to start the hunt for the carrier-animal all over again. If that happened, Thornton's vaccinated cattle might be the cause of concealing the animal responsible for the epidemic; as a result there would be a danger of the epidemic killing beasts which wouldn't have died if Thornton had not committed his illegal action. So much for the worst that could happen.

At best there was a theory that might save Thornton from prosecution and other farmers from losing their animals, *if* it worked. I visualised the development map of Craftly I had seen in Sir Roger's study. On that 'egg' of land Thornton's was the only dairy-farm; his farm constituted something of a barrier between the area afflicted with foot-and-mouth and the part of the county where – so far – the cattle were healthy.

The theory I recalled had cropped up time and again when the present policy of slaughtering versus the possible policy of vaccinating British livestock was discussed. It was a compromise; the possibility of vaccinating all beasts along a 'belt' of country to create a barrier of animals immune from foot-and-mouth disease between sick and healthy beasts.

The advantages of such a compromise were that the epidemic might be halted more quickly than with the present methods of slaughtering-plus-detection; the disadvantages that a 'barrier' of immunized animals would make almost impossible the detection of those beasts that were causing the epidemic.

Because there were arguments against the barrier-theory it had never been put into practice in this country; it was illegal. And even if I believed that the theory might work in the case of Thornton's herd it was still illegal. Thornton had still broken the law by vaccinating his herd, and I – if I concealed my knowledge of his action – was, as Eric Goff had put it, sticking out my neck.

I couldn't afford the luxury of sticking out my neck; I was

a veterinary surgeon and if I were struck off the register –
as I would be if I were caught – I had nothing to fall back
on, no money, no 'bent' for paper-hanging, gardening or
selling juke-boxes.

'You're impossible, Michael,' said Julia, nibbling my ear.

'Yes darling?'

'I've been talking to you for the past ten minutes . . . you
haven't heard a thing, have you?'

'Yes, I have,' I lied.

'Then why aren't you pleased?'

'About what?'

'You *haven't* been listening. Now I *know* I'm right. You *are*
in trouble.'

'Nonsense.'

'Well, if you aren't now you soon will be if I leave you to
your own devices. *I said*, I'm going to stay right here in
Craftly, and I'm going to see to it that you don't do anything
stupid . . . stop laughing. I *have* got more sense than you.'

'What about your job?'

'The zoo will just have to find someone else for giving
lettuce to the Asian goat.'


Inevitably Julia got the whole of the Thornton story out of
me. She'd been hurt when I showed no enthusiasm for
having her in Craftly, I'd had to 'unhurt' her by giving my
reasons for not wanting her around. After that she'd told
me to remember our engagement, and announced her intention of sharing my troubles as a fiancée as she would in
future as my wife. We embraced with solemnity – a thing
we'd never done before – and the final result was that Julia
arrived back on Monday complete with more luggage than
the roof of the bubble could stand. But with the help of
Tiger's Daimler sports car I got her installed at Craftly
Manor.

I had to admit to myself that Julia had taken me by surprise. I'd expected her to disapprove of Thornton's 'crime'
and I'd even been prepared to defend my hesitation in
handing him over to the authorities. Instead, Julia, despite
her claims to having more sense than I, strongly supported
me. She agreed it would be 'horrid' to hand over a farmer
who was so fond of his cows. She agreed that it wasn't
Thornton who should pay the penalty for breaking the law,

but Sidney Franks. Sidney would *have* to be stopped from leading astray other farmers and probably causing foot-and-mouth disasters all over the country.

I had to see Thornton and I had to make Thornton realise that Sidney could not be allowed to continue his new line of 'business'.

It was an interview I didn't relish. Though I'd meant to tackle it on Monday I was almost glad of the trouble with Julia's luggage because by the time we got up to the gun-metal and purple guest-room it was too late for me to call on Thornton.

On the following day, when I was visiting farms on Renton's lists, I was too tired; besides Thornton was busy. I saw him shovelling gravel from a truck into the ditch of Conny's piggery.

# CHAPTER 7

When I visited Conny's pigs on the following day Thornton had just finished levelling the ground where the ditch had been. He and Conny were still admiring the results when I returned from checking animals and sties in the cause of Tom Renton's anti-epidemic campaign.

'Isn't it an improvement?' asked Conny, as if it had been her idea to get rid of the quagmire.

'Well, you won't have so many flies about the place,' said Thornton, modestly. 'What do you think of the pigs, Mr Morton? They're all right, aren't they?'

I thought there was some anxiety in his question. 'Yes, they're fit . . . I wanted to see you about . . .'

'We're having a meeting here,' Thornton interrupted me. 'It's to do with Jenkins's land.'

'Won't you stay, Michael?' asked Conny. 'You see there's a rumour that Alan's aunt will put up the market-garden for auction. So people in the village felt we should get together and discuss what can be done to stop Sir Roger from buying it for development. We'd like to have you in on it.'

'Bit awkward for Mr Morton,' said Thornton, 'being Sir Roger's vet. He'll hear all about the meeting in any case; you can't keep anything quiet in *this* village.'

'You're right.' I was grateful to Thornton. 'But if I hear what happens at your meeting I won't tell Sir Roger. I'll drop in tomorrow, Mr Thornton.'

I was about to leave the two of them when Tail came flying into the yard, face white, hair more than usually dishevelled, clothes impressively disarrayed.

She threw herself into Conny's arms and gave a heart-rending sob.

'Tail!' Conny stroked her hair. 'What is it, love? What's the matter?'

Tail pointed at Thornton. '*He* is trying to murder me.'

'Nonsense,' said Conny.

'It's not; it's not . . . He's blinded you with the *ditch*!'

84

Our laughter made Tail sob with such passion that Conny began to look worried.

'He's going to shoot me at sight.'

Conny tried to see Tail's face, but it remained stubbornly hidden against her jersey. 'Tail, have you been to the copse?'

'Oh no. I *know* they shoot pigeons there.'

Thornton grinned. 'I bet I know where she's been . . . in my south field, the one I told her to keep away from. Isn't that right, Tail?'

'The bullet just missed my head,' Tail ignored Thornton's question. 'He's trying to get rid of me . . . and . . . and no one's doing anything to stop him.'

'But Dave's been here all afternoon,' said Conny.

'Ah, yes,' Thornton winked at Conny, 'but one of my men might have been shooting. Harry now . . . he's keen on shooting with his crossbow.'

'It *wasn't* an arrow,' protested Tail, 'and it wasn't Harry . . . It was Bill shooting rabbits and . . .'

Conny succeeded in detaching Tail. 'You must stop telling these stories!' Tail's face had left a chalky mark on her jersey and she was rubbing it off. 'You know perfectly well that Bill wouldn't hurt you. He'd be in a fine state if you got in the way of his gun. So you just keep out of the south field my girl.'

Tail gave her sister a 'haunted' look. 'Well, I've warned you. *That* man . . .'

We didn't find out whether Tail had any other charges to bring against Thornton because Miss Sabina's pink car had drawn up. Jock bounded out and went straight for Tail's cat. The cat misinterpreted his advance, flew up the lilac tree by the gate and left Jock standing underneath wagging his tail.

'This dog simply loves . . . pussies,' said Miss Sabina, not without bitterness. 'But of course I do understand that cats have their uses on a *farm*. What would happen if Sir Roger were allowed to build Radiant Homes is unthinkable . . . unthinkable! We'd be overrun with cats, not even *working*-cats, *and* children! My dear Conny, it *is* good of you to take steps . . .'

'Oh, no, no. I'm not,' Conny looked at Thornton. 'It just happened because I told Sir Roger . . .'

'Indeed,' Miss Sabina's voice rose to a pitch suited to a

large audience. 'The whole village admired you for your brave defence of our countryside. Your stand at The Lion will give us courage to fight . . .'

'Golly,' whispered Tail. 'She looks just like the woman in the picture, Uncle Michael. You know the one . . . there are five or six Sabinas, and some men are trying to carry them away and the women are fighting them . . . It's in my art-book; you know *The Rapture of the Sabines*.'

'You tell Conny about it,' I advised her.

Two or three other cars had arrived and people were converging on the gates. The old fellow, strolling across from his cottage, nodded at them. 'Never come here, they don't,' he grumbled, 'only when they want something. I told Conny to keep out of it. But no, not she. "This is a village," she says, "and if I can help it, it's going to stay a village . . . not one of your suburbs with no one having any land." Unselfish, that's what she is, our Conny. Now Dave Thornton . . . he just doesn't like Sir Roger, on account of Sir Roger bringing that court case.'

'What court case?' I asked, thinking of the vaccinated cattle.

'About Dave's cows getting into Sir Roger's paddock . . . it cost Dave twenty pounds . . . Preserving the country-side they call it!' The old man watched the arrival of the local carpenter. 'Maybe it's right, maybe they have *private ideas* about poor Jenkins's land. There isn't much land to be *had* these days.'

'They can't all want Jenkins's land,' I said.

'Well,' said Tail. 'The vicar wants a new church hall, and the cricket club wants a better pitch, and . . .'

'Tail,' said Conny, grabbing her young sister. 'Go and wash the powder off your face. And while you're about it take off that nail-varnish.'

'Can I come to the meeting?'

'No, Tail . . . Dave wants a wash; you can put out a towel for him . . . a *clean* towel.'

'I can't do *everything* in this house,' Tail achieved a fine tragic expression, '*and* look after Mr Thornton as well.' She looked round the guests, making sure she'd been heard, and then turned her back on us as wearily as an overworked housewife.

\* \* \*

86

'Thornton's in the shed,' said Tail, 'cutting wood.' She was sitting on Thornton's gate, almost certainly waiting to tell me something. 'You know the meeting last night? . . . They made Conny the secretary.'

'Of what?'

'The Craftly Rural Preservation Society of course.'

'Good.'

'It wasn't. Nobody really wants to *buy* Jenkins's land . . . except Miss Sabina. And she hasn't got the money. So in the end they made a sub-committee – that's the vicar – and he's to study the problem . . . Are you visiting Thornton's cows?'

I explained to her it wasn't 'proper' for a vet to discuss his patients, and that interested her sufficiently to let me get away.

As usual, her information had been accurate; Thornton *was* in the shed cutting wood. He stopped, reluctantly I thought, and offered me the block for a seat.

'I want Sidney Franks's address,' I told him. It seemed the simplest way of letting him know that he'd been found out; and I did indeed want that address.

'Sidney Franks?' he asked, examining the blade of his axe.

'You know who I mean.'

'Fellow who used to work at the Manor?'

'Yes.'

'No,' Thornton shook his head. 'I wouldn't know where he is nowadays. Never did know him well.'

'Well enough to let him vaccinate your herd,' I said. 'It's no good Thornton. I've got a lab-analysis of the stuff he used . . . it was a foreign vaccine.'

'The dirty . . .'

'I didn't get it from *Sidney*.' I realised I'd get nowhere with Thornton unless I put my cards on the table.

I proved to him beyond a doubt that I knew what he had done to his herd and when I suggested that Sidney had first used a wrong vaccine on the wrong cow he didn't deny it. Nor did he contradict when I told him that I was sure Petunia had died of foot-and-mouth and that he was more than lucky she hadn't spread the infection to his other animals.

'I kept her isolated from the word go . . . and afterwards I burnt all the stuff from her stable . . . and I disinfected . . . What are you going to do, Mr Morton?'

If I had any doubts in my mind the wretched, defeated expression in the man's eyes would have decided me to 'stick out my neck'.

'Your animals are immune from foot-and-mouth now. Provided the epidemic doesn't spread any further they won't do any harm. If the epidemic does spread it'll be too bad for you . . . and I'll probably have to apply for a job as somebody's cowman.'

'Mr Morton, I . . .' Thornton was gripping the axe so hard that his knuckles went pale. 'I don't know what to say . . . you're taking a shocking risk.'

'I know. And you've got to realise that I must get hold of Sidney Franks. I know the fellow; if I warn him off the vaccination racket he'll stop it. He's got to be stopped or he'll kill off half the animals in the country.'

'I hadn't thought of that,' said Thornton.

'No; but I've got to think. We don't want Sidney to get picked up for illegal vaccinations, and *I* can't keep quiet about your deal with him unless I can be absolutely certain that your herd's the last Sidney laid his hands on. I'm pretty sure it wasn't the first. There's been a case similar to yours in Scotland. The farmer's been caught, but not the fellow who immunised the animals.'

'I see. Yes, Sidney's got to be found.'

'That's why I'm here,' I told him.

'It's no good,' said Thornton, unhappily. 'I haven't got an address. He came to *me*, every time.'

'Have you paid him?'

'Yes . . . four or five days ago.'

'Do you remember the number of his car?'

'I never thought of looking . . . He didn't mention a place either. I know that, because I was wondering where he gets the vaccine.'

'Try and remember all you can . . . people, for instance, anyone else he might have visited here.'

Thornton promised, and I was sure he meant to help all he could. But I wasn't hopeful. I knew Sidney.

'Everything all right?' asked Julia.

'Everything's all wrong. Thornton doesn't know where Sidney Franks is to be found.'

'Oh.' Julia's 'oh' sounded less concerned than I'd expected. She led me through Claire's lilac-and-mustard lounge into the dining-room. 'What do you think of it Michael? Isn't it heavenly?'

I wouldn't have called that room heavenly even if I'd been in a happier frame of mind. The walls were covered with a paper with a heavy abstract design in reds and black; looking hard one could make out coal-mines, blast-furnaces, and figures which might have been intellectual conceptions of workers on the dole. A table and a dozen Victorian kitchen-chairs were lacquered red, there was an iron contraption that looked like a work-bench, and the curtains were black with grey streaks.

'The curtains are marvellous; so right.'

'Are they?'

'Can't you see it, Michael?'

'Well, the streaks make them look as if they were torn.'

'That's it!' Julia said delightedly. 'They look absolutely in tatters. You see, the whole room expresses . . .'

I grabbed her, shut my eyes and kissed her. She was wearing black shorts, presumably to match *the* room, and her bare legs felt warm and smooth.

'Stop it, Michael!' she pushed me away. 'Someone's coming.'

'Let them. If you are going to turn into a miserable little puritan in this house . . .'

Claire came in, carrying a large platter, followed by Tiger with Chou-en-Lai and Mao-tse-Tung tucked under his arms. The cats followed the platter on to the table and Claire swept them off. 'We're having haddock and anchovy balls . . . they'd give Chou and Mao indigestion,' she explained, putting the cats into their satin-quilted Easter-eggs. 'Michael, Julia's a great help. Tiger hasn't cooked a meal since she arrived.'

I thought the haddock as well as the anchovies were well camouflaged; the fishcakes tasted more like haggis. 'You mean Julia's made . . . this?'

'She has. Isn't it wonderful . . . Tiger's been able to concentrate on the play. It's finished.'

I congratulated Tiger.

'Thanks.' He stared at his fishcake. 'Of course I still have to alter a scene in the last act.'

'No . . . no you mustn't,' said Julia and Claire almost in unison. 'It's perfect.'

'No,' said Claire, 'don't tell Michael. Let him judge for himself. Imagine,' she demanded of me, 'the bicycle shed where Jack is blowing up the tyre . . . and trying to tell Hetty he's been in Curzon Street . . .'

'I thought he did tell her,' I said, 'right in the beginning.'

'Oh, Michael!' exclaimed Julia, sounding almost ashamed of my lack of sensibility.

Claire just ignored it. 'Well, in the scene that worries Tiger, Hetty suddenly confesses that she actually *knows* Curzon Street. Isn't it terrific!'

'Absolutely in orbit,' murmured Julia, nudging me into making an appropriate noise.

'You see, Tiger!' Claire affectionately grasped her husband's hand. 'I knew Michael would understand at once. If *Three Corsets to Curzon Street* were similar to *Three Brassières to Bond Street* Hetty's reaction would have to be . . .'

'You aren't listening,' Julia accused me.

'I'm worried.'

'Why, Michael? . . . oh, I see. Sidney Franks.'

'I can't have him vaccinating other farmers' cattle.'

'No, you can't . . . isn't it wonderful how Tiger worries about a scene until he's got it absolutely . . .'

'I've got to find Sidney.'

'Yes . . . I think Tiger's right. The climax . . . you know, Hetty confessing that she knows Curzon Street, *should* come in the last scene.'

'I can only think of one way,' I told Julia. 'I should think Sidney's still going to race meetings.'

'What I mean,' Julia's eyes were shining with — what I assumed — artistic inspiration, 'Hetty's corsets, and Jack's attitude to the corsets that lead him to Curzon Street . . .'

'Julia,' I almost shouted at her. '*We* shall be going to Lincoln races.'

'Why?'

'To try and find Sidney.'

'Oh yes . . . Well, when Jack actually gets to Curzon Street . . .'

'Tiger won't have to worry so much about the production,' Claire was telling me. 'Skip's doing it all . . . exactly as Tiger worked it out. The only snag's Larry. You see Skip and Larry have a tie-up; it's rather awkward because it just isn't the kind of role . . . well you know how it is. Skip says Larry will be livid.'

'Julia,' I pleaded.

She took my hand under the table. 'I'll come out with you, darling.'

'No, it isn't *that*. I just remembered, the Lincoln meeting may be on the same day as Hurst Park. I couldn't go to both; and I'd better go to Hurst Park because Sir Roger's colt will be running. Will *you* go to Lincoln for me?'

'Why do you want me to go to the races on my own?'

'To find Sidney, if he's there.'

'Oh, Sidney.'

'You remember him, don't you?'

'Of course; he used to take me out to dinner.'

'That's the fellow. You'll go?'

I never got an answer out of my Julia because Claire had reached the point where Tiger almost agreed with her that the 'climax' – Hetty's confession that she *knew* Curzon Street – should come at the end of his play. And Julia, her grey eyes bright with excitement, was listening to Tiger's remarks about the 'inner meaning' of the corset-theme.

The 'inner meaning' escaped me; and as soon as I decently could I escaped the great playwright's house. I felt I could have taken the blast-furnace-and-tatters decoration of the dining-room, Julia's enthusiasm for it, the fish-balls that would have given the cats indigestion, but *not* Julia's in-difference. It seemed unfair that she should discover a passion for modern drama just when I most needed her moral support and some practical help in tracing Sidney Franks. I arrived home weighed down by my responsibilities, those I should never have taken on and those – such as the beginning of the calving- and lambing-season – which were inescapable in a country practice.

When I saw the big car in my yard my stomach turned over and I got a taste of those fish-balls in my mouth; I'd had enough for the day; if that car meant an emergency I just wasn't equal to a foaling mare or a sick cow.

I parked the bubble close to the front door; I had some foolish notion that the owner of the car wouldn't bother me if I slipped into the house quickly. But I was still groping for the right key when he was beside me.

'Mr Morton?' he asked, with a heavy foreign accent.

'Yes?'

'I have to communicate with you.'

'Write me a letter,' I suggested.

'*Nyet*, now,' he said, pushing past me into the house.

I asked him into the surgery, hoping that the hard chairs would discourage him from prolonging his business. He introduced himself as a cultural official of the Soviet People – a Supervisor – but he didn't give his name. He said he understood I was veterinary surgeon to Sir Roger Coolcrow and therefore to the colt Princeling, owned by the Soviet People. *He* was directly responsible to the Soviet People; above all it was his task to ensure Princeling's success at Ascot. There was to be no repetition of a performance by Russian horses such as their failure at the Grand National.

'I didn't expect you to win the Grand National,' I told him.

'Why not?' he asked sharply.

'For one thing you knocked the guts out of the horses before they arrived. Why *did* you send them by train?'

'How else?'

'It's a long way from Russia . . . too long a journey for thoroughbreds. You should have flown them over.'

'Impossible,' said the Supervisor. 'Let a horse travel by jet . . . like . . . like Nikita Khrushchev! Impossible!'

Class distinction was not a profitable subject for discussion. I was tactful, or so I thought, and suggested that Princeling – being an English colt – would do better than his predecessors who had suffered from that enormous journey.

'Princeling,' said the Supervisor, 'is a *Russian* horse.'

'Yes, of course.'

'What is your impression of our jockey?'

'Atsy-Catsy? He's first-rate.'

The Russian nodded. 'He is reliable?'

'Certainly. Surely you wouldn't have sent him if you yourself didn't think so.'

'He *was* reliable. Now? One cannot say. He goes about with dubious people . . . *Americans*.'

'If you mean young Elizabeth, there's nothing dubious about her; she just likes horses.'

'She speaks Russian.' He made it sound like a crime. 'We do not approve of the situation.'

'If this situation worries you then you'd be worried no matter where you put Atsy-Catsy and Princeling . . . anywhere in England.'

'*Many* people in England speak Russian?'

'Thousands.'

The Supervisor gazed at the shining bullet-shaped toes of his boots. 'There are other problems,' he said. 'Sir Roger's trainer wanted Princeling to run at Hurst Park.'

'That's sensible. He *should* be out on a course once or twice before Ascot.'

'No,' said the Russian. 'We do not wish him to be seen.'

'You mean you want him to be a mystery horse until he runs at Ascot?'

'Yes. We do not want publicity too early. First he must win the King Edward Stakes.'

'Why not the Ascot Gold Cup?' I asked.

'It is policy in Mowcow.'

'I suppose it's a matter of principle,' I suggested, trying to sound as earnest as he did, 'A Russian horse defeating English horses in a Royal Stakes.'

'That is so.'

'Well, you can be sure Sir Roger is doing his best to help you; his trainer's good, Princeling is well looked after and Atsy-Catsy . . .'

'Our jockey speaks with Sir Roger's colt Herakles. It has been reported to me. I do not like it.'

'Can I do anything for you?' I got up, yawned, and made it obvious that I wanted to go to bed.

Surprisingly, the Supervisor took the hint. He rose, black boots creaking. 'I have communicated my views,' he declared. '*You* advise Atsy-Catsy accordingly.' He walked past my desk, and then suddenly pulled up. There, of all things, lay a letter from our embassy in Washington. The Duke of Alanspring had written that his greyhound was beginning to respond to psychiatric treatment; he'd been induced to eat hare and his analyst hoped it was the first step towards making him *run after* hares on race-tracks. The Duke was hoping to stay on at the Embassy; by not wasting money on hotels he expected he'd be able to maintain himself in America for another two or three months, by which time he expected his dog to be cured of his hare-allergy.

The Russian Supervisor stared at the letter, and I stared at *him* wondering whether I should offer to let him read it. I decided against. If what I'd heard of Russian suspiciousness was true he'd probably have persuaded himself that I was showing him a top secret document in code, for the express purpose of insulting him.

I told him rather ineffectually, that I had patients in other countries.

'Okay,' he said, giving me a penetrating stare. 'You understand! No communications between Atsy-Catsy and the American, no communication between our jockey and Sir Roger's colt Herakles. No racing by our horse at Hurst Park. No nothing.'

'No nothing,' I agreed.

# CHAPTER 8

There is much to be said for letting things slide. If you are made to promise something and you don't do anything about it the advantage is yours; few people have the energy or the tenacity to exact a promise *and* see to it that you keep it. True to this principle I did nothing to carry out the wishes of the Russian Supervisor, even when I heard Atsy-Catsy talking to Herakles or saw him hand-in-hand with Elizabeth at Hurst Park races.

I had other worries. The maternity season had broken; Conny's number two sow Angelface had produced a litter with two weak piglets which needed much care; Lady Beverley's dachshund Thirteen was in a pregnancy with sickness, and almost every day I had to attend the birth of foals, calves and even lambs which had grown in an awkward position for getting themselves born. All this on top of pussies and bitches owned by people who wanted them 'doctored', 'put down', or treated for ailments from abscesses to old age.

Flat racing had come at the wrong moment for me. I'd have got out of attending Sir Roger's perfectly fit Herakles at Hurst Park if it hadn't been for the necessity of finding Sidney.

I'd given Julia a fiver for losing on the horses and sent her to Lincoln with instructions *not* to go out to dinner with Sidney if she did find him. I'd lunched at Hampton Court, aware how much I'd have enjoyed flowering trees and sun if Julia had been with me, and driven on to the racecourse in a mood of pessimism.

I missed the first race because Lady Beverley asked me to be a darling and take dachshunds Eleven, Fourteen and Fifteen for a walk round the course, and the second race because Sir Roger gave me a beer and made me read a bunch of newspaper cuttings about the greyhound Kenwood. Sir Roger was wondering whether the syndicate of M.P.s shouldn't have sold Kenwood after all. 'Kenwood, the parliamentary dog, gone into recess,' said one cutting,

'The M.P.'s unearned income coup, one of the most consistent winners for the past twenty years, is suffering from a broken heart over his change of ownership. Liberal M.P. Mr de Cross Anatole considers that the dog's poor performances in recent races are due to . . .'

Sir Roger handed me another beer. 'Publicity for Leicester de Cross Anatole . . . and the Liberal Party . . . that's all we achieved with our respect for public opinion. I'd recommend a change of policy if I could be certain that Kenwood would not abuse our confidence.'

'You mean you'd buy him back,' I translated, 'if you could be certain that he won't win *every* time.'

'Precisely. The assets could be invested in the cause of charity, as has been suggested. As regards the administrative difficulties of such a scheme I take an optimistic view of . . .'

'Herakles,' I interrupted him. I swallowed my beer, and made off to the enclosure.

The colt's chestnut coat was gleaming in the sun and the white blaze on his nose gave an impression of long-faced donnish calm. One felt that here was a horse with the build as well as the temperament of a winner. Cecil, the trainer himself, was leading Herakles round, probably because Herakles was chortling and gurgling and Cecil *had* occasionally succeeded in making the colt stop 'talking'.

Atsy-Catsy was watching the exchange between Herakles and Cecil with obvious disgust. 'He will make Herakles unhappy,' he said, 'it is so wrong, so wrong.'

'He'll never make it,' said Elizabeth, waving to Coops, Sir Roger's jockey. 'Catsy sure told him what to say to Herakles, but he always forgets; he gets kinda loco inside about the last furlong.'

There was no sign of Sidney in the paddock, so I wandered back to the next most likely place – the bookies' stands. The odds against Herakles were shortening.

I spotted the white Alfa Romeo three or four minutes before Herakles's race. Not a bad time, it occurred to me; all eyes would be on the course. Already heads were turned towards the starter.

The car was locked, its windows shut tight, but I made up my mind to get inside. It was less risky than letting Sidney continue his vaccination racket. I opened my penknife and carefully inserted the small blade under the window. As I'd expected it was framed in rubber and a little levering and pushing soon made it possible for me to pull down the glass beside the passenger-seat.

The glove-compartment contained nothing but a box of sweets, the other pockets fistfuls of unpaid bills addressed to a W. C. Beauchamp Esq. I was beginning to wonder whether I'd got into the wrong Alfa Romeo when I saw a Garage Service card beneath a tailor's account. At the top was a crossed out name, Capt. Sidney Franks, and an address in Eagle Street, W.C.1, on the opposite page was the name and address of W. C. Beauchamp – presumably the new owner of the car.

I had just returned sweets and bills to their respective compartments when the door of the car was flung open and I was half pulled half lifted on to the grass.

'Got you, damned thief!' a stout red-faced gentleman bawled into my face. 'Oh no, you don't?' He hung on to my arm with one hand, to my collar with his other. A break-away was out of the question. 'Never can find a damned policeman when you want . . .'

'Can so!' I contradicted, slurring the words like a drunk. 'Get you for speeding ev-vy time, Dicky. Vemember Dicky . . . that time . . . races in York . . . with Lola.' I gave him a friendly punch in the stomach. 'You dog . . . Dicky! Dicky . . . dog . . . Want to go out with you 'tnight, Dicky. Foun' your car,' I swept my arm over the hundreds of other cars and almost over-balanced. 'Foun' your car out of aaall others. Less go to . . .'

'Hell!' said the owner of the Alfa Romeo, 'you're tight, old man.' He was sounding quite sympathetic.

'Not tight, Dicky . . . juss . . .'

'I'm not Dicky, old man.'

'Look here, Dicky, you can't treat me like that . . . after all these years. It's no way to treat 'n old . . .'

'Oh! For the love of Mike! Come on, let's have a drink.' He released his hold on me, and I stumbled off without another look at him or the car. I staggered on until I reached the paddock before I dared turn round. As I'd hoped he had not followed me.

There was great consternation in the Coolcrows' camp. Sir Roger kept talking of 'unforeseen circumstances' and 'unexpected developments'; Lady Beverley was asking Cecil what on earth could have made Herakles virtually stop on the bend after the second furlong, Coops was shaking his head and repeating an assurance that he'd never known a mount behave like that at Hurst Park – not at Hurst Park.

Herakles, head lowered and looking more than ever like a thoughtful don, was standing waiting for his horsebox with Elizabeth and Atsy-Catsy on either side of him whispering soft Slavonic words in his ears.

Elizabeth looked up with tears in her eyes. 'Michael, this would never have happened if Catsy had been riding him . . . It sure wouldn't have happened. That Coops . . . he's nothing but a hatchet-boy.'

'No, honey,' said Atsy-Catsy. 'Is good jockey, Coops. But Herakles,' he rubbed his cheek along the colt's nose, 'he is not like different horses.'

Herakles nuzzled Atsy-Catsy and made peculiar grunting noises.

'Not to be unhappy,' Atsy-Catsy consoled him. 'Not to be unhappy.'

I had for some time noticed a black-coated man who was watching us as if he were being paid for it. All at once I realised that he *was* undoubtedly being paid for it, that he was in fact the Russian Supervisor with the bullet-shaped toe-caps, and that he was not only seeing Atsy-Catsy in conversation with Herakles but also in the company of the 'dubious' American, Elizabeth.

'Do you know the man over there?' I asked Atsy-Catsy.

The little jockey swung round as if he'd suddenly remembered something. 'Aich,' he sighed. 'It is the Sasha again. In England I do all things wrong.'

'You must explain to him,' I told Atsy-Catsy, 'that you can't live in England as if you were in Russia. You can't live among people – especially racing people – like a recluse.'

'Explain to Sasha? Is not possible. Sasha is very clever; he live in England five years and know nobody . . . very intelligent.'

I wondered whether the 'intelligent' Supervisor had witnessed my 'drunkenness' beside the Alfa Romeo. If so there was no telling what conclusions he'd arrive at, especially seeing me completely sober so soon after.

'Michael,' Elizabeth took me by the arm and drew me

aside. 'I guess Catsy doesn't want to go back to Russia. Will they make him?'

'It'll be up to him, surely.'

'I get kinda scared. There's no place we can go if . . . you know what.'

'Well, if . . . anything happens you can always come to me,' I said, like a fool.

It was all very well playing the protector but it only needed a few cases of foot-and-mouth on the wrong side of the present boundary and I'd have nothing to protect Elizabeth and her little jockey with – no income, no home. My future looked less promising than theirs. And my only piece of luck was in my pocket, the Garage Service card with Sidney's address.

Eagle Street was a narrow lane full of back doors, and at most of them stood mighty lorries which were being unloaded. My bubble got stuck between a newspaper van and a British Railways pantechnicon until I thought of driving along the pavement. There it got held up by brewers rolling barrels of beer into one back door and coalmen carrying their sacks through another. Eventually I managed to wedge in between the coal lorry and a van which advertised 'Culpa. Potters. Since 200 BC. Telephone: Pennyvale 4343.' I put the bubble hard up against the wall so that it hid the 'no parking' notice, and set off on foot.

The entrance to Sidney's flat was yet another back door, a yard of tea-chests, and a narrow stairway which changed – after the second floor – from grubby stone to creaking wood. It ended, surprisingly, on a carpeted landing with large white-painted doors. I rang the only bell I could see and a door on the opposite side opened almost at once.

The boy who stood there seemed disappointed to see a stranger. He was a thin lad of nineteen or twenty in a pair of black jeans, a black jersey that came down to his knees and off one shoulder and a red shirt with a pattern of teddybears.

'Yes?' he enquired, brushing back the fair fringe over his eyes.

'I'm a friend of Sidney's. Is he in?'

'No.' The boy stood and I stood. Eventually he wilted against the door. 'Can I do anything?'

'When do you expect Sidney back?'

'Not tonight.'

'It's rather urgent.' I decided to take a chance. 'It's about the . . . pharmaceutical products.'

'Well . . . better come in. I'm Bobo, his partner.' He managed to lead me through a toy-sized hall full of mirrors into a gold and white lounge before folding up in an enormous shell-shaped armchair. There were three others like it, a cocktail-cabinet encrusted with sea-shells, and a flood-lit tank of tropical fish.

Bobo touched a button on a thing I'd taken for a super tea-table and suddenly the room sounded like Tit House; the sounds of birds came from everywhere, from the ceiling and the corners, from behind curtains and out of the cocktail-cabinet.

'Stereophonic music,' said Bobo. 'Isn't it ghastly?'

I agreed it was. But instead of switching it off Bobo increased the volume and presently a kind of heavenly choir came bawling at us from every direction.

'Listen!' I shouted. 'I must get hold of Sidney right away.'

'Can't,' Bobo shouted back.

'Where is he?'

'Abroad.'

I went up to the 'tea-table', put my hand under it, and found a few knobs. After some twiddling I managed to soften the racket.

'That's the vox humana,' exclaimed Bobo.

'When's Sidney coming back?'

'Tomorrow.'

'I'd better meet him. Where?'

'Newhaven.'

'He's coming back by boat from Dieppe . . . with his car?'

'Of course.' Bobo burrowed deeper into his chair and stared at the fish.

'He's bringing in more vaccine?'

'They sometimes eat each other,' said Bobo, gazing at the tank. 'But you've got to watch for hours and hours . . . or you miss it . . . Why do they eat each other?'

'Well, you shouldn't mix those monodactylidae with . . .' I pulled myself up just in time. I didn't want Bobo to know that I was a vet.

He'd paid no attention. 'There,' he said, 'see the black fish on the right? He's going to kill the little blue one in front. Maybe he won't get her now . . . Mean thing, he'll probably do it when I've gone to bed.'

'Bobo, this is important,' I tried again. 'You must tell me; has Sidney gone abroad to buy more vaccine?'

'Vaccine? . . . Oh . . . bottles. He always brings back bottles.'

'Have you got any of them here?'

'Ask Sidney . . . Got her! No, the blue one was too fast for him. He'll get her though; sure to, when I've gone to bed.' The black fish had settled down and was sleepily nuzzling a wisp of greenery. Bobo flicked a speck of dust off the stereophonic 'tea-table'. 'It was the black one who got my striped fish; isn't he gorgeous?'

'Bobo, are you going to meet Sidney?'

'Meet him? Oh, in Newhaven. No, that's business. Sidney never worries me with business.' He turned a couple of knobs under the 'table'. African drums started thumping all around us and a tin-whistle-voice in quadruplicate wailed 'It's bla-a-ack mao-aw-gic, bla-ack maw-awjick!'

Bobo's mouth had fallen open and his head was ticking sideways in a kind of epileptic beat that made the blond fringe jump all over his face.

I went and took a quick look round the flat – bedroom, kitchen, bathroom, roof-garden. No sign of foot-and-mouth vaccines. As I let myself out I saw Bobo, sleeves pushed up above his elbows, with both hands in the fishtank. But that didn't mean, I told myself, he'd been other-worldly about Sidney landing at Newhaven.

With the harbour in sight and a Channel steamer on the horizon Julia suddenly remembered that she'd come to New-haven with me to make sure I didn't get into trouble. She stopped talking about Larry being livid because there was no role for him in Tiger's play, she stopped talking of the play itself and became 'realistic'.

'Michael,' she said crisply, 'I don't think there's any need for you to go running after Sidney.'

'Why have we gone to Newhaven then?'

'Yes, I should have thought earlier. But we can always feed the seagulls . . . What I mean; Phil Brogan will be home in two or three weeks and we'll be going back to London.'

'I see. So, if there *is* a spread of foot-and-mouth and the Vet Investigation Department does find out that Thornton's herd's been vaccinated I'll be well out of it. At worst they'll come to the conclusion that Phil employed a locum from London who knew nothing about country practices.'

'That's it,' Julia agreed. 'Let's buy some bread for the gulls.'

'There's one little detail you've forgotten.'

'Have I?' She touched her ears, making sure that she *hadn't* come out without those Indian turquoises she always wore.

'You've forgotten about the cattle *all over* the country.'

'But there are lots of vets . . .'

'And only one that knows *who* is carrying out the illegal vaccinations. If I don't stop Sidney thousands of animals might die . . . unnecessarily.'

'We've got to find Sidney,' said Julia, as if we'd only just decided upon it. 'What are we going to do?'

I stopped at a telephone box and rang up Customs and Excise. Someone had told me the thing to do if one wanted one's voice to become unrecognisable was to put a handkerchief over the receiver. I covered it with *two* thicknesses of handkerchief.

I told the person who answered that this was 'London' calling, and when a more senior voice came to the 'phone I explained 'we' had received private information that a man by the name of Captain Franks was about to land with a consignment of drugs. Whether he offered to pay duty or not those drugs – vaccines – were to be 'held', as they were for illegal use, and Captain Franks was to be 'investigated'.

My clipped tones must have satisfied the Customs Officer because he promised to carry out my instructions. He asked whether 'we' knew the number of Captain Franks's passport or the registration number of his car and when I told him 'we' didn't and he'd better adopt 'our usual routine' he seemed to know what was required.

We drove on to the harbour station, asked for passes at the gate for 'meeting Julia's father' and were admitted. We could see the boat approaching the quay. It seemed fairly empty, there were only a few cars awaiting their owners, so the chances were that Sidney would be dealt with quickly.

I was glad of that; I wanted the wretched business to be over as soon as possible. After talking to the Customs Officer I'd been tempted to turn round and go back to Craftly; the thought of handing Sidney over to the authorities gave me no satisfaction whatever. Before I'd 'phoned Customs and Excise it had seemed the best way of stopping Sidney's activities; now, watching the passengers disembark, I wasn't so sure. I had once stopped Sidney from doping racehorses; couldn't I have given him another chance? I didn't think Sidney was a criminal; a misfit, yes; amoral, certainly. But so were lots of other people and no one put them in jail.

By the time the first cars came driving into the customs shed I felt certain I could have made Sidney 'go straight' without landing him in prison. Now it was too late. All I could do was stand at a door guarded by a policeman and watch the customs officers open boots and doors.

'Anything to declare?'

One old man was charged on that extra litre of wine while his wife, carrying a bag of little trees, was being ignored. The customs officer was probably a gardener too. A young girl with flowing hair was made to pay on a roulette wheel. A couple with a baby were allowed through with a suitcase full of furry toys.

The officer turned their attention to an elderly man with a Tyrolean hat in an elderly Rover. A tool box, suitcases and a set of golf clubs were turned out of his boot, loose clothes were taken from inside the car and spread on the table. An officer was taking up the carpet of the car and another had opened its bonnet.

'Why are they going to town on *him*?' asked Julia. 'He looks rather a nice old thing.'

'Maybe they know he's smuggling diamonds.'

'He isn't the type.'

Sidney didn't look 'the type' either. He drove in a practical estate-car and sat back at ease until one of the customs officers invited him to pass the Rover. The first thing he showed the officer was a silver cup. His deeply tanned face looked happy and animated and the customs officer was listening to him with obvious interest. Next Sidney produced a saddle, pointing out some feature of the cantle. The officer nodded.

Before I had begun to guess what was happening Sidney was back in his car, while the owner of the Rover was still standing among his scattered possessions looking rather surprised and bewildered. Sidney eased his car to the gates, gave the customs officer a farewell wave and drove on to the road.

'They thought your call was a hoax,' said Julia. 'They must have done.'

'Or our friend Sidney was travelling under another name.' I didn't know whether to be glad or sorry that he'd got away. 'Judging by his performance he was probably travelling as a clean-limbed British sportsman.'

'So was the man with the golf clubs.'

'But he didn't look the part . . . Well, we won't catch up with Sidney now, not with the bubble,' I told Julia. 'Might do it by train.'

We were lucky. We found a garage for the car and just managed to catch the train to London. I wasn't very clear what we'd do when we got there, except go to Eagle Street.

Bobo was in the middle of feeding lobster to the tropical fish. On a table in front of the tank a lobster-meal for two was set out, which confirmed that we'd arrived before Sidney.

Julia didn't like it when I suggested her keeping Bobo company while I waited for Sidney in the street, but when Bobo put on a stereophonic record she changed her mind. When I left them she was showing Bobo how to dance the cha-cha.

I took a walk round the courtyard. The shabby doors with the name-plates of various companies suggested a warren of store-rooms, so did the smells of damp paper, sulphur or rotten eggs, beer and printers' ink; not a bad place for Sidney's purposes.

It was almost an hour before his car drew up outside. And he got to work at once. Throwing the saddle, the silver cup and some riding-clothes on the front seats he lifted out a wooden packing-case. And suddenly I knew what I'd do with it and him.

'I shouldn't bother unpacking,' I said.

He straightened up with a jerk. 'Michael! I . . . er . . . didn't see you. That's a pleasant surprise,' he added, heartily.

'Let's say a surprise. Come on, put that case back in the car. I want to talk to you.'

'Sure, how about a drink round the corner.'

'Let's go up to your flat; Julia's there.'

'Good.' He locked the car and then unlocked it again. 'Mustn't leave this lying about in the street.' He picked up the cup and handed it to me. 'Been pot-hunting in Sweden . . . come on up; top floor.'

'I didn't know you went in for show-jumping.'

'Well, I'm getting a bit long in the tooth for it. But I enjoyed Sweden.'

'It must be a good story,' I said, following him into the flat. 'The customs officer seemed to like it.'

He didn't react; there was Bobo's cheek to pat and Julia to be complimented on looking more beautiful than ever. He said he hadn't been able to get the striped fish for Bobo but he'd brought home a new stereophonic record – he'd fetch it. So down we went again, myself close on his heels, to fetch the record which Bobo put on at once. It was both sentimental and noisy.

Sidney gave us some gin-mixture from his sea-shell cocktail cabinet and I made him take his glass out on the roof-garden. I told him I knew about his vaccination racket, that I had proof of his activities, and that I could have had him arrested at Newhaven but decided to give him one more chance.

'I never knew you were so attached to me,' he said. There was no charm about his sun-tanned face now. He'd found my Achilles' heel; my 'weakness' in protecting Thornton and so making myself an accessory to his law-breaking. 'I appreciate what you've done, believe me.' That too was pretty double-edged.

I had to make the fellow believe that I was 'fool enough' to hand him over regardless of the consequences to myself; I felt sure he did take me for a bit of an ass. I went back to the lounge and called Julia, through the din of music. 'I want you to take a taxi to Knightsbridge. Go to Uncle Simon's and wait for me.'

'Another drink?' offered Sidney.

'No. Listen, both of you. If I'm not at Simon's within three-quarters of an hour, Julia, ring the police and give them the lab-analysis, the syringe and the other . . . evidence. If that gets *me* into trouble I'm prepared.'

'What do you . . .' Julia almost gave me away, but I'd

105

pinched her in time. 'All right, Michael,' she said, looking at her watch. 'See you in forty-five minutes.'

Sidney made an instinctive move to stop her from walking out, but I got in front of him and he had enough sense to realise he'd be in for a painful rugger-tackle.

'A man's got to live,' he whined, mournfully. '*You* have got to live.'

'Not your way, Sidney.'

'Why blame me? It's Thornton . . .'

'You don't know a thing about farmers such as Thornton, or what it means spending half a lifetime building up a good dairy herd. Better stop arguing. Come on, let's go.'

'Where?'

'We're getting rid of your vaccines, in Knightsbridge.'

Sidney drove so fast that I was afraid we'd be run in for speeding, not a desirable situation in a car full of contraband. But Sidney was determined to get to Knightsbridge before Julia rang the police, and I thought it would be poor psychology to admit to him we'd been bluffing. After all, I wanted him to stop his animal rackets for good.

Though we reached the Mews without being booked my problems were by no means over. How was I to get several crates of bottles into my Uncle Simon's house, and dispose of the contents without taking him into my confidence? He certainly wouldn't have approved of the way I'd handled the Sidney–Thornton affair. Despite our being partners he was quite likely to wash his hands of the crates *and* me.

But Julia had done some fast thinking. She had told Simon and Muriel we'd been buying china for our future home and wanted to store it in my room. Simon looked quite pleased to see Sidney and myself carry the crates upstairs. Running our practice single-handed had been hard work. When I told him I'd be back in harness by the end of the month he was so relieved he'd have allowed me to move in a fourposter bed and a couple of elephants as well.

The car emptied, Sidney and I, feeling pretty empty ourselves, said good-bye. He asked me how he was going to make a living now, and I told him a versatile fellow like him was bound to make out.

'Animals are my life,' he declared.

106

'They *were*, Sidney,' I told him. 'If I find you interfering with animals again it'll be jail for you.'

'What about a pet shop?' he asked. 'I never thought I'd come down to small fry . . . but I dare say I could make something of tropical fish . . . maybe a few birds.'

I could see no harm in it; at least, not yet. 'I don't see why not, provided you keep on the right side of the law.'

'Naturally,' he said, with great dignity.

Julia and I set to work in my room. We poured the vaccine down the handbasin and then soaked the labels off the bottles. A consignment that size had paid Sidney between three and four hundred pounds – free of tax. With several shopping-trips abroad it hadn't been a bad one-man business. He'd told me it was easy to take a car full of crates through the customs; the officers were more interested in little things such as opium and diamonds. But a man had to be quick in assessing the customs officers; some had to be shown a bit of paper – a richly rubber-stamped *permit* for bringing in chemicals for a 'controlled experiment', others convinced of their shrewdness or experience hardly bothered to look inside the cars.

We were busy returning the unlabelled bottles into their boxes when Simon knocked at my door. He came in before we had time to put the covers on.

'Good Lord!' he gazed at the neat rows of screwtops. 'What . . .'

'Isn't it maddening,' said Julia, looking furious with me. 'Michael was supposed to bring up our china, and look what we've got instead!'

'Well, what is it?'

'Bottles,' I said.

'I didn't think they were teacups. What are you going to do with them?'

I had an inspiration. 'I collected them for the Animal Dispensary . . . they're always short of bottles.'

'They won't be any more,' observed Simon.

'Not if you take them round to the Dispensary for me.'

'As if I didn't have enough to do,' complained Simon. But I knew he'd tell Muriel to deliver them. 'All right, Michael, but you can just carry this lot down again. *I* am not going to slip a disc . . . You're staying for supper?'

'We're staying the night,' I told him. The de-labelling had taken so long that we'd missed the last train.

In the morning I was wakened by electric drills, lorries and landslides of caving-in walls. A crane, its teeth hanging on to an assortment of bricks and mud, swung past my windows and on a scaffolding workmen were chipping away at what had been, only a few months ago, the 'desirable mews-residence' of Alfred Donizetti, Manufacturer of Society Gloves.

Julia came into my room almost in tears. 'Have you seen what they're doing to our mews?'

One couldn't help seeing. A notice-board the size of a cottage announced, 'A Radiant Homes Company development scheme. You too can live in Knightsbridge. Leave the Top People in their dingy out-of-date stables. WE are building for you, the MEGATON MAN. The Knightsbridge of the future is for YOU.'

'Not for *me*,' said Julia. 'I wonder what Wandsworth is really like . . . I *hate* Sir Roger.'

Faced by the destruction of our personal London village I felt as Julia did. Why did those jovial-faced millionaires in their cosy cocoons of parliamentary and board-room clichés have to go about tearing down nice mad little houses, putting up flats that looked like animal-cages in a laboratory or railway signal-boxes? And not content with London the megaton-minded gentlemen were shaking the fences of the green-belt laws, sniffing out the weak spots, and advancing their boundaries acre by good agricultural acre.

'Let's stop Sir Roger from building in Craftly,' said Julia.

'Let's,' I agreed. 'How?'

'We'll think of something.'

Back in Craftly the message-pad beside the telephone looked like a railway time-table for trains between London and the sea on August Bank holiday. Mrs Pitt had begun to record the calls in block letters but towards the end of the second page her writing had deteriorated to a worried scrawl.

'Monday 6 a.m. Sir Roger – horse
Monday 8 a.m. Lady Beverley – bitch
    do    8.30 a.m. Lady Beverley – horse
    do    8.55 a.m. Sir Roger – horse

| | | |
|---|---|---|
| do | 9.45 a.m. | Lady Beverley – bitch and horse |
| do | 10.30 a.m. | Miss Sabina – blackbird |
| do | 11.45 a.m. | Miss Conny – sow Angelface |
| do | 12 a.m. | Mrs Jones – cat |
| do | 12.15 p.m. | Mr Lock – foal |
| do | 12.27 p.m. | Mr Thornton – calf' |

And so it went on throughout Monday and Tuesday. All Craftly seemed to have united in making me feel guilty for having deserted my patients. Since I couldn't tell anyone, with the exception of Thornton, that I'd been away on the essential job of dealing with Sidney I knew I'd be in for comments, some aggrieved, some outraged.

In London I could have pleaded the dramatic confinement of a great dane or a 'heroic' operation on a TV star's pussy. But not in Craftly. The whole village was bound to know at what time Bill's foal was due, when the airedale Jock got home from The Lion, why Conny's sow Angelface spent a sleepless night, or when dachs Thirteen was going to have her pups.

# CHAPTER 9

There was a change in the atmosphere of the Coolcrows' house, but for a moment I couldn't make out what had happened. Then I realised that the notice at the gate, apologising for the barking of dogs between 12 p.m. and 2 a.m., had gone and that the dachshunds weren't – as usual – barking out of time. The sighing of the noiseless doors seemed very loud; it made me think of the obtrusiveness of small noises in a sick-room.

Five of the dachshunds were in the morning-room, where Lady Beverley was waiting for me, but none greeted me with the frenzied yapping which I'd come to expect. The fringed ears didn't rise, the plumed tails didn't wag; the dogs just drooped around in an oddly undecided way close to the doors of the sun-loggia.

Lady Beverley was too worried to comment on my absence; she only said she'd been sitting up with Thirteen all night, wondering whether to find another vet. Thirteen had been sick and she thought the pups might be born prematurely.

As she showed me into the sun-loggia where Thirteen was lying in her basket four of the dachshunds remained standing while the fifth followed me so closely that he was almost squashed in the door. Lady Beverley picked him up and was about to eject him when he struggled free and fled behind Thirteen's basket. He sat there mutely, his slender large-eyed face pleading, muscles taut and ready to evade anyone who'd try to catch him.

'Is he the father?' I asked.

Lady Beverley said he was and she'd kept him away from Thirteen in case he made her nervous or started barking. But Thirteen seemed pleased to see him; when Fifteen leaned over her basket and licked her face she made an effort at wagging her tail.

'Fifteen, *sit*,' I ordered.

Fifteen, used to total disobedience, looked at me, head cocked sideways in the characteristic dachshund posture; he

110

looked at his sick mate and then quietly sat down at some distance from her basket.

Thirteen had a temperature and when I examined her belly she made a sharp movement which ended in a yelp of pain. The pain, I thought, was due to a not uncommon deformity of the hip – a dysplasia – in which the femoral head had shrunk causing a looseness of its articulation with the acetabulum. Though it was not normally a painful condition a bitch carrying a litter large for her size was liable to suffer. The fever was another matter. I found no obvious reason for it but there was the possibility that it was caused by the death of one of her pups. If that was the case the others, though premature, had a chance of survival provided I could get them out soon.

Fifteen was watching every move I made and when I explained the position to Lady Beverley he kept looking at us as if he understood that there was some difficulty.

'I want to take Thirteen to my surgery,' I said, 'but my car is out of action.' There was no need to tell her that Julia was fetching it from Newhaven.

'I'll lend you mine, Mr Morton . . . You'll drive slowly because of Thirteen, won't you? The brakes aren't working properly, but it'll be all right if you're careful.'

Brakes or no brakes I accepted her offer. Thirteen was weak and there was no time to be lost. We put her basket in the back seat. As I switched on the engine I heard a howl that sounded almost human in its misery. Fifteen was flinging himself at the windows of the loggia with such force that he was liable to knock himself out.

'Let him come,' I said.

'He'd make a nuisance of himself.'

'I don't think so.'

Lady Beverley opened the french windows; Fifteen came hurtling out, fringed tail and ears flying, and leaped straight into the car.

The brakes were not only not working properly; they weren't working at all. Going down the hill from the Coolcrows' house into the High Street my only hope was that nothing should cut across my bows. Miraculously nothing did. I got through the lane and managed to stop the car a couple of feet from my front door.

With Fifteen quietly watching me from a corner I debated

111

with myself what to do with the little dachshund bitch. I finally rejected the method of inducing labour; the fever was apt to interfere with normal labour-spasms. If my theory of a dead pup was correct I'd have to use forceps without being able to see exactly what I was handling and there was a danger of aggravating her hip condition.

The alternative was a caesarean delivery, a method I didn't like using on a young bitch. But it was safer for the mother and certainly for this particular litter of pups. I'd have felt happier about it if Julia had been there to assist me; I didn't much like working the anaesthetic machine with my elbows.

There was no getting rid of Fifteen. When I picked him up to put him in the waiting-room he wriggled, whimpered and finally escaped back into the surgery. There he made such a show of being quiet and sensible that I let him stay, hoping he wouldn't go for my ankles while I was in the middle of operating.

If anyone had told me, before Thirteen's pregnancy, that one of Lady Beverley's dachshunds was capable of remaining silent and motionless for an hour I wouldn't have believed it. But Fifteen did. Though his eyes remained fixed on the operating-table he didn't stir until he heard the thin voices of the pups. Only then did he come a few paces closer, nose lifted towards his offspring.

Two of the five pups were dead; the rest looked more viable than I'd dared to hope. Thirteen was slow in coming out of the anaesthetic, but her breathing was better than before the operation.

While I wondered whether she'd be able to feed her pups and what would be the best way of rearing them, Fifteen had approached the operating-table and got up on his hind-legs. He tried to jump on but slipped on the polished lino and tumbled backwards. But he'd given me an idea. It was worth trying.

I picked him up and put him on the table with his family. He gave Thirteen a perfunctory sniffing-over and then switched his attention to the pups; he gave each a tentative lick, seemed to decide it *was* his job and began to clean them up in earnest – as thoroughly and gently as a mother.

Dachshunds had never been my favourite dogs but Fifteen's behaviour struck me as so extraordinary that I

112

decided to find out more about the breed. Perhaps, as with certain other pets, their noisiness and excitability were characteristics acquired in the course of riding in cars instead of hunting, of living in centrally-heated drawing-rooms and being fed out of tins.

I was mentally 'writing up the case' for a learned journal when Fifteen and I were startled by a great crash and the slow splintering of wood. In the hall I collided with Julia.

'Watch out!' she gasped. 'Don't go near it!'

Lady Beverley's car did look pretty fearsome. It had crashed straight through the front door and was standing with its nose pointing at the surgery door.

'It tried to run me down,' said Julia. 'I was just closing the door . . . and it came after me.' She was looking very white.

'We need a drink,' I told her, leading her into the surgery. A whisky and the newborn pups soon helped her to recover. We examined the damage; Phil needed a new front door and Lady Beverley's car would have to be unbuckled and fitted with a new headlamp. I could have sworn I had put the car in reverse, but when I checked it was in first gear.

'Never mind about the car,' said Lady Beverley, affectionately stroking Thirteen's head. 'We'll deduct the damage from your bill.'

'Have the brakes fixed,' I suggested.

'Yes, I'd better . . . I'll pay for that myself.'

'Thank you.'

'After all, we don't want the car to damage *our* house . . . No, don't go Mr Morton. My husband wants to see you.'

'Professionally?' I asked.

'Yes. It's about Princeling.'

I took out Phil's consultation slips. 'Then perhaps you'd sign these.'

'Two of them?' she asked. 'I don't recollect calling you in *twice*.'

'If I am to see Sir Roger now it'll be my second consultation today.'

Lady Beverley looked as if she might argue. But since she was probably uncertain whether it *was* a vet's job to fetch a bitch and return her complete with pups and mate she took my slips with silent ill grace and scrawled her name on them.

Whether it was a result of her displeasure or not, Sir Roger kept me waiting for more than half an hour and when he finally appeared he did not, as usual, offer me a drink.

'I'm taking you round to the stables,' he said. 'Want you to take a look at Princeling.'

'Anything wrong?'

'Better judge for yourself . . . There's been no *accident*.'

Princeling, as far as I could see was his usual fit self. There was no apparent reason for Sir Roger's early morning telephone calls during my absence.

'Lucky you got back in time,' he said.

'In time?'

'Our Russian friends have seen fit to make representations through the person of their Supervisor . . .'

'He's been here again?'

'Precisely. Our talk ended in deadlock. Developments are not promising. If circumstances were more propitious I'd consider the possibility of making an issue of it.'

I gave Princeling a lump of sugar, which gave me time to translate Sir Roger's statement. 'The Russians want to take Princeling away from you?'

'That is in fact the position.'

'To another training establishment?'

'I received no definite information. There are indications that our Russian friends take too serious a view of their jockey's social activities . . . which, in the light of our agreement, hardly justifies the drastic steps they're contemplating.'

'If they want Princeling back you can't stop them.'

'I hold very strong views concerning the welfare of my charge. In my opinion it would be directly against the best interests of Princeling to effect a move at this stage of his development. I told our Russian friends in no uncertain terms . . .'

'Did the Supervisor ask you to consult me?'

'He did intimate that it would be desirable . . .'

'The Russians want me to say whether Princeling's fit to be moved or not?'

'Yes, I think we can put it like that.'

'Princeling *is* fit.'

'Well, Morton,' Sir Roger put his hand on my shoulder. 'We mustn't let considerations of the colt's *present* condition stand in the way of – er – the wider implications. In my opinion an arduous journey is liable to disrupt his stability. I fully expect you to support my endeavours to . . .'

'Sir Roger, have you ever thought about the meaning of the word "vetting" . . . vetting something?' I asked him. 'It means giving something or someone an indisputably reliable test. The word vetting came into being because vets – veterinary surgeons – acquired a reputation for being . . . reasonably honest, and thorough.'

'My dear fellow,' Sir Roger's pressure on my shoulder increased. 'Of course, of course . . . though I fail to understand this – er – observation in connection with our present problem.'

'It isn't a problem, Sir Roger. Princeling is fit to travel and I don't think you can tell the Russians anything else. And if you did they'd have every right to ask *why* their horse shouldn't stand up to a journey. They'd probably accuse you – and me – for not looking after Princeling as well as we should have done.'

'This aspect of the situation hadn't occurred to me,' admitted Sir Roger. 'I'll give it my consideration, Morton . . . certainly. The trouble is, recent pressure of work has been such that I haven't been able to devote as much thought to my racing interests as is necessary.'

I learned something about the nature of Sir Roger's 'pressure of work' when I visited Thornton on the following day. Thornton appeared uncommonly inattentive.

Normally he would have given me a hand in examining one of his cows; this time he just told me where to find her. The cow had lost its calf, and even when I told Thornton it was possibly due to the cattle-disease that had given Phil Brogan undulant fever he didn't seem concerned. He'd isolated the cow and done all he could to prevent her infecting other animals, but that was just routine. He asked me no questions and it was I who had to tell him when we could expect the results of laboratory tests.

He was no more responsive when I told him I'd run Sidney Franks to earth and that we could be pretty sure he wouldn't carry out any more foot-and-mouth vaccinations.

'Sidney's thinking of starting a tropical fish business,' I said.

It was the kind of thing that should have amused Thornton,

but he didn't move a muscle. He thanked me, rather flatly, for 'all my trouble' and mentioned he'd heard that Tom Renton might give the Craftly area the 'all clear' from foot-and-mouth within the next week or two.

'A beer?' he offered, as if he didn't care whether I accepted or not.

'What's on your mind, Thornton?' I asked while he was filling the tankards.

He almost banged them on the kitchen table. 'Then you haven't read about Sir Roger's speech?... No, not here; in his own constituency. Building-land isn't enough for him... now he's after the cattle-breeders... as if he knew the front from the behind of a bull.'

'What's it all about?'

'It started with that speech. All high and mighty; *for the good of the country* and all that tripe. Sir Roger Coolcrow M.P. deplores that cattle stock improvement's in the *wrong hands*. The present day pedigree cattle-breeder isn't capable of producing an *economical* animal. He hasn't got the *resources*. What the country needs is big livestock companies... with British and American capital... to produce more uniform pedigree animals.' Thornton wiped his mouth as if he'd just been spitting at Sir Roger. 'I suppose he thinks selling 750 gallons of milk per cow is chickenfeed.'

'Not everybody has animals as good as yours,' I told him. 'Sir Roger isn't altogether wrong.'

'Well, it's difficult for the small farmer... the profit per gallon's down to between sixpence and eightpence. But big companies isn't the answer; not for the small farmer. Not for me either; and that's what I told him. If he comes in here again I'll...'

'He came to *you*? What did he want?'

'The lot.' The way Thornton held his tankard I half expected it to crumple like tinfoil. 'He made me an offer for my herd and the land; said I could keep the house... and work for him as his manager... And do you know why, Mr Morton? Jenkins's land's up for auction and Sir Roger's sure he'll get it. So what he reckons he'll do is this; he'll take the acre he needs for building those damned Radiant Homes and he'll turn the rest over to dairy-farming. Start another commercial company... Seeing that he himself lives in Craftly he doesn't want *too much* building develop-

116

ment here . . . he wants to keep it nice and countrified. But its got to be countrified *and* pay. So he gets a bright idea. Put the remainder of Jenkins's land together with Thornton's and one can work up to eight hundred or a thousand head of cattle . . . quite a start for a Radiant Cows Development Company. And as an afterthought he goes and sees Conny and makes an offer for the piggery.'

'Bit of a nerve. I suppose he's found out by now that Conny's the secretary of the Craftly Preservation Society.'

'*He* knows . . . Let *her* know that he was sure the Society didn't stand a chance . . . But if he thinks he'll have a walk-over at the auction he'll get a shock.'

'There are other people after Jenkins's land?'

'*I* am after it . . . if I have to work like a black for the rest of my life.'

'Is it worth it?'

'I reckon I'll manage somehow. And Conny's pigs could pay better . . . Constance and I are getting married in the winter.'

'Congratulations.'

He gave a brief smile. 'I reckon we'll give Sir Roger Coolcrow, M.P., a run for his money. Maybe he knows about making millions but there's one thing he doesn't know . . . and that's a *real* village.'

I was driving out of his farm when he came running after me. 'Mr Morton . . . about Conny and me; don't tell anyone. It's on account of the kid. She and I . . . well we're getting on all right, but she's a funny one, that Tail.'

'That Tail' was lying in wait for me on the road to Tit House; or rather, she was sitting on a white pony which was nibbling the grass verge. She was wearing pink tights, a white shirt with a life-sized picture of Sammy Tin – the latest pop-star – on the chest, and a top-hat that looked as if the death-watch beetle had been at it. Her blonde hair was sticking out under the brim like Scotch broom. I wasn't clear whether her latest act was 'the Sammy Tin gang', or 'Lady Godiva'.

'This is Pegasus,' she introduced her pony. 'Dig it?'

'Dig what?' I asked.

'Well, he's in orbit, isn't he.'

'Yes, he's a beauty.'

'So he's Pegasus . . . flying horse, see? Old Thornton gave him to me. The old fellow said Dave Thornton must be mad about Conny if kissing her was worth a horse . . . And he – I mean Thornton said – Conny's hair smells nice, so now she keeps washing it.' Tail stroked the pony's neck. 'But Pegasus and I don't mind. Dave Thornton's house is nicer than ours.'

'Now what do you mean?'

'You *are* a square! Conny's going to marry Dave of course. But don't tell them I know . . . 'cause I want a record-player . . . Uncle Michael, will you be Pegasus's vet?'

'Yes, of course.'

'You can't be his vet sitting in your car. Come on, examine him!'

I got out and patted and pinched Pegasus in all the right places. 'Don't give him so much to eat,' I told Tail.

'Thank you, doctor . . . Are you going to see Miss Sabina? Because her blackbird's flying about again. I know, because she said one of our cats almost got it.'

The blackbird had met with a strange accident. It had got into a drawer of mending-wool and when it tried to fly out one of its legs, enmeshed in the threads, had become dislocated. As a result the bird had been unable to take off or land and I'd recommended keeping it under a wire-mesh meat-cover.

'The blackbird's all right,' Tail informed me, 'but Jock's in trouble . . . Watch me!' Pegasus, feeling her heels, un-willingly lifted his head. 'Go, Peg, go!' The fat little pony went into a jogtrot. 'Come on, Uncle Mike!' shouted Tail, 'I'll race you!'

I kept my bubble well behind her and escaped into the drive of Tit House before she could say she'd won. I'd just got out of the car when I saw one of Tail's predatory tabbies streak into the bushes with a bird in its mouth.

I went after her and got my hand on her hindquarters; she wriggled free and leaped over the wall. But, in her hurry, she'd dropped the bird. It was a coal-tit, somewhat stunned, but apparently still unhurt. As I waded out of the thicket some missile nicked my ear, whizzed past, and struck a tree. It was easy enough to find, being an airgun dart with a bright red top.

In the drawing-room Miss Sabina was still clutching the airgun. She looked so belligerent, she might have been watching the heavyweight championship of the world.

'You didn't hit the cat,' I told her, 'but you nearly brained *me*.'

'It would have been the fault of the cat,' she said philosophically. 'I'll put some sticking plaster on your ear.' She took a large roll of the stuff out of a drawer, cut off a piece with gardening shears, and tried to fix it. 'Oh dear, you've got such pointed ears, Mr Morton . . . But I think that'll do. You'll have a whisky, won't you?'

I said I would, forgetting for the moment that her whisky was something 'special' from Acharacle. Luckily she had to fetch a new bottle from her store, which gave me time to look round for a discreet receptacle. I noticed several pots of oakleaf geranium in strategic places; and I noticed a few more startling things as well. Under one chair lay Jock, the airedale, under several other chairs stood or lay a scattering of blue-tits, coal-tits and robins. Jock, most unlike himself, didn't even move his tail when I patted him; with his great head hidden between his front paws he looked like a flat-out brown doormat. As to the birds they might have been little coloured pebbles for all the reaction I produced by picking them up and putting them down again. They were alive all right, but quite impervious to the world.

Turning towards the mantelpiece to take a look at my ear I saw that the mirror had been replaced by a large illuminated parchment in a carved gold frame. It appeared to be a declaration by Dr Schwersteiger, Dr Med., Dr Phil., Dr Theol., of Switzerland. It said, 'Hearty Congrats for the anniversary of the Beginner-Birdwatcher-Brotherhood of the Post-Skiing-Fracture-Fraternity (Founder-Lodge).
Ploffskin, Pluffskin Pelican jee,
We think no birds so happy as we!
Plumpskin, Skiskin, Pelican jill,
We think so then, and we thought so still. (Edward Lear?)
This enterprise is not to be subject to appraisement but to the orders of excessive profits.'

'Isn't Dr Schwersteiger wonderful?' asked Miss Sabina, coming in with a bottle and glasses. 'Such a tribute to Tit House! Look at the goldleaf on the capital letters . . . Dr

Schwersteiger did all this work himself. I felt very moved.'
She gave me a whisky and I stepped closer to one of her
potted plants.

She tossed down a glass of her firewater and turned back
to Dr Schwersteiger's parchment. 'Believe me, Mr Morton,
he's given me new courage. When I wrote and told him about
the auction of Jenkins's land he immediately sent me a
hundred Swiss francs towards the fund.'

'The fund?'

'Yes, Mr Morton. I've opened a fund to buy Jenkins's
land so that we can extend the bird-sanctuary of our
Brotherhood. Dr Schwersteiger's support has been a great
spur. I immediately got in touch with my Scottish friend
and he's made me the sole agent for Acharacle whisky for
the south of England. That'll bring in a steady revenue.'

'But you'll need money pretty soon,' I suggested, 'if you
want to buy that land. The auction's in less than a fortnight.'

'My bank will advance the money *if* I have securities . . .
Well, now there's the whisky agency . . . and the boxers'
appointment ought to arrive in time . . . The Liverpudleian
Boxers' Benevolent Board have given me a firm undertaking; they're going to use Tit House as a rest-home for
their permanently punchdrunk cases . . . Dr Schwersteiger
assures me the punchdrunk won't be incompatible with my
post-skiing fracture cases.'

I said I wished her success. And I meant it, although she
didn't take her eyes off me until I'd swallowed the whole of
that pernicious whisky.

But I wasn't going to risk another helping. 'What's happened here?' I asked, picking up one of her comatose tits.

'It's inebriated,' she said.

'I suspected it. Is Jock . . . inebriated too?'

'That dog! He started the whole thing. You see, two nights
ago he was taken home from The Lion by *complete strangers*.
Of course they didn't know that Jock was to be dropped at
the gate. So they roared up to the house in their frightful
sports car and upset my birds. I felt it really was time I put
my foot down; and yesterday I tied Jock up in here. He
*didn't* get to The Lion. I'm afraid it rather upset him. When
I came down this morning,' Miss Sabina swept her arms
over the prone creatures under her chairs, 'that's what I
found. Jock had knocked down a bottle of my whisky . . I

smelled it at once though they hadn't left a drop. Do you know, Mr Morton, the tits were even pecking the carpet!'

'They'll survive.'

'That's what I really wanted to ask you. They won't come to any permanent harm?'

'I shouldn't think so. And of course Jock's an alcoholic already.'

'I beg your pardon, Mr Morton!'

'I mean Jock . . . tolerates alcohol quite well.'

'Well, that sets my mind at rest; though an accident of this kind gives me so much extra work. I have to be on guard against cats *all the time*.'

'Couldn't you keep the windows shut?' I suggested.

'And penalise tits who had the decency *not* to become inebriated! Certainly not!'

I explained to Miss Sabina that even an airgun could be something of a murder-weapon, warned her against winging one of her bird-watching patients, and exacted a promise that she wouldn't shoot until I was out of her 'grounds'.

At the gate I was stopped by Elizabeth putting her stick across my path. With her leg out of plaster, she was able to wear tight trousers; and she was showing off her rich curves with unselfconscious innocence.

'Gee, am I glad to see you!' she greeted me. 'I felt kinda scared with you away and no one to go to.'

'But there's Miss Sabina, and the Coolcrows.'

'Sure; but they wouldn't be any good if the Russians got up to some real monkeyshines.'

'Well, I wouldn't . . .'

'You'd help us; you said you would. You see, that supervisor-guy's going to take Princeling some other place. And Atsy-Catsy figures it'll be Russia . . . and then they'll send him back to Russia too . . . and . . . well, Cat doesn't wanna go.'

'He could apply for asylum on political grounds. I'm sure Sir Roger would help him.'

'But Cat wants to go to the *States*. And he doesn't wanna do anything right now . . . in case the Russians *aren't* sending Princeling to Russia. He's kinda set on riding at Ascot.'

'Well, what can *I* do?'

'Nothing right now I guess. As long as you're around.'

'Don't do anything silly, Elizabeth.'

'Silly? Sure I won't. I don't mind telling *you*, Michael; I'm going to marry Cat. I've written to Mom about it and she says it's okay . . . and when she gets over from Switzerland she'll see our Ambassador and fix things. Atsy-Catsy's going to change his name . . . we'll be called Atkinson . . . You see how it is, we just gotta keep out of trouble with the Russians until Mom gets back.'

'Couldn't your mother come now?'

'You don't know Mom. She just got her ski-certificate third class. Next week she's gonna try the second class. If *she* doesn't get a medal she won't be fit to do a thing for me and Cat . . . But it's okay now *you're* here.'

'I'm just a vet,' I reminded her.

'Sure,' she said, placidly. 'I guess you're kinda used to managing . . . mad bulls and things.'

# CHAPTER 10

The Russian Supervisor looked more like a 'thing' than a 'mad bull' when he did turn up at my surgery. He'd got caught in an April shower; his suit was wet, his face crumpled with care.

'Aich,' he sighed. 'Aich, such trouble . . . such trouble.' He unseeingly accepted the whisky I gave him, murmured something like 'Poruskie', tossed it back, and absent-mindedly held out his glass for more. 'Sir Roger said maybe Princeling is not fit for a journey.'

'Princeling's perfectly fit,' I assured him.

'Maybe Princeling would be very sick in the aeroplane?' he asked, hopefully.

'I thought you people didn't take animals by air.'

'This time, yes. All at once everything is different. You are *sure* Princeling will not drop dead in the aeroplane?'

'As sure as anyone can be.'

'Then he must go to Russia.'

'What about Ascot?'

'This year,' he said, heavily, 'Princeling will not run. We withdraw.'

'But why?'

'It is all my fault. I did not interpret correctly the directive from Moscow. I did not allow Princeling to run at Hurst Park or Windsor.'

'Well, you *said* your colt was to be a surprise at Ascot . . . remember? It wasn't to be seen before.'

'I was wrong,' the Supervisor dejectedly stared at his bullet-shaped toecaps. 'I did not interpret correctly. Princeling belongs to the Soviet People. The Soviet People want a good working racehorse – sometimes he wins, sometimes he loses, and then he wins again. You see?'

'No,' I admitted.

'Like this. If Princeling loses at Ascot the people say "Soviet horse is not good, we have been cheated," if he wins people say "Soviet horse is a great hero." '

'I'm sure you're quite wrong about it.'

'You do not understand the Soviet People . . . If Princeling had run at Hurst Park and Windsor it would have been good; sometimes he wins, sometimes he loses and everyone would have said "is good working racehorse" . . . *good*, but not a personality-cult. The Soviet People do not want Princeling to become a personality-cult; that is what I did not interpret correctly.'

'Perhaps we can think of some way out,' I said, weakly. I felt sincerely sorry for troubled Toecaps.

He suddenly sat up and listened. There were sounds from the kitchen, sounds of breaking crockery. 'You are *not* alone in the house,' he accused.

'I *told* you, I am.'

'A lie!'

'Come on, see for yourself.' It was Mrs Pitt's day at Tit House, and Julia wouldn't have done anything in the kitchen without first letting me know she'd come.

The Supervisor stalked out in front of me, arms flexed. He had biceps as large as young rabbits. He stopped at the kitchen door, listened to the faint scratching noises, and flung open the door with his foot.

In the middle of the floor, surrounded by bits of broken earthenware, sat Patty eating the remains of a steak and kidney pie, her bushy black tail quivering with enjoyment.

'Catushinka!' exclaimed the Supervisor. He scooped up the kitten, tenderly cuddling it against his broad chest. 'It was hungry the catushinka! The poor little one!'

'This cat eats non-stop,' I told him.

'That is true; in Russia *I* have a cat like this. But my Alyosha has a white nose . . . Come, we must talk.' His face all love and gentleness, he stopped Patty from returning to the steak and kidney pie, embraced her more firmly, and led the way back to the surgery.

There was a ring at the door, and I went to answer it. An elderly lady in a tweed suit stuck a collection box in my face.

'I am here on behalf of the vicar,' she announced. 'We are hoping to buy land for a new village hall . . .'

I put a coin in the slot and returned to my guest.

'The Soviet People are disturbed about Atsy-Catsy.' He pronounced it Atsycatchioff. 'It is only natural we want him to return to the Motherland with our horse.'

Another ring at the door. This time it was a small boy in a schoolblazer. 'I'm the cricket club,' he said. 'We want to buy a new pitch you see, so Mr Black said you see . . .'

'Here you are.' I put a coin in his tin, wondering whether I wasn't defeating some object or other by supporting both the village hall and the cricket pitch.

By way of apology I gave the Supervisor another whisky. Patty had gone to sleep across his stomach.

'Today,' he said, 'I could not find Atsycatchioff. I could not find him at the stables and not . . .'

'Excuse me. Someone at the door.'

The man who was extending to me a wooden box with the picture of a robin had a plastercast on his arm. I'm a patient at Tit House,' he introduced himself. 'You may have heard that the Beginner-Birdwatcher-Brotherhood of the Post-Skiing-Fracture-Fraternity have . . . er . . . ambitions to extend the bird-sanctuary. I hope you're prepared to support . . .'

I supported with sixpence and returned to the surgery.

'Atsycatchioff was *not* at Sir Roger's house either. I confirmed . . .'

'Damn that bell.'

'Damn,' the Supervisor agreed.

My latest caller was a white-haired gentleman in a clerical-style suit. He was holding a sheaf of pamphlets.

'I'm a representative of the Berkeley Brethren of Christ, sir. Do you believe in God?'

'Yes,' I said, 'do you?'

He glowered and turned his back on me with a scathing 'I bid you *good* afternoon.'

'Good afternoon.'

The Supervisor was still sitting tight.

'You were saying,' I reminded him, 'that Atsy-Catsy was not at Sir Roger's. I shouldn't worry if I were you. After all, jockeys have to keep fit. He's probably gone for a long walk in the country.'

'I am afraid . . .'

I had no chance of hearing why Toecaps was afraid. The doorbell was clanging for the fifth time. And there was Tail.

'I'm busy,' I told her.

'The Russian's here, isn't he?'

'How do you know?'

'Well, his car's here,' she said, reasonably. '*I* know where Atsy-Catsy and Elizabeth are.'

'Then don't tell me.'

'They're sitting in Dave Thornton's south field.'

'That's none of your business, Tail.'

'It's yours though.'

'Certainly not.'

'Oh yes, it is. Listen,' she grabbed my head and put her lips to my ear. 'They're coming here after dark. That's what Elizabeth said. Don't tell anyone.'

'You bet I won't. Don't you tell anyone either.'

'What do you think I am, Uncle Michael . . . Where are you going to put them?'

'I don't have to put them anywhere.'

Tail frowned and pinched in her mouth; she really did manage to conjure the expression of a 'stern and upright member of society.' 'Well,' she said, 'I hope I'll always do my duty.'

'I hope you will,' I said, lifting her on to her pony. 'And *please* don't go about telling stories . . . not about this.'

Patiently the Supervisor repeated the account of his efforts at finding his jockey. '. . . And at Tit House,' he wound up, 'I saw only people with broken arms or legs . . . and an old lady. She told me to take my hat off and then she made me threats with a gun.'

The daylight was fading fast. I had no doubt that Tail's information about the imminent visit of Elizabeth and Atsy-Catsy was accurate. Her information always was. Somehow I had to get the Supervisor out of the house before they arrived; but the Supervisor, despite his worries, looked exasperatingly comfortable. The whisky appeared to have dried and relaxed him, and Patty in his arms was purring away like a well-oiled machine – no doubt making the Russian feel at home.

'When's Princeling due to fly to Russia?' I asked, trying to introduce an element of hustle.

'Tomorrow evening.' He wriggled as if he'd suddenly discovered a darning needle under his seat. 'It will be great trouble if Atsycatchioff does not fly *with* the horse . . . I am staying *here*.'

I suddenly felt sweat on my face; and I remembered that detectives could pinpoint suspicious characters by the sweat on their upper lip. 'We've got to find you a room,' I told the Supervisor. 'Hang on. I'm going to ring The Lion.'

'I can maybe sleep here in the car.'

'Oh no, you can't. Our police wouldn't allow it. It's illegal.'

'Illegal?' The word had made *some* impression.

'Something to do with the sanitary laws,' I assured him, lifting the receiver.

'Darling, you must let them stay,' said Julia.

Elizabeth and Atsy-Catsy were sitting side by side holding hands. They looked like a couple of hungry, chilly kids waiting to be fed. Someone had probably seen them make for my surgery. And the Supervisor's parting shot had been that he didn't mind staying at The Lion; he'd probably pick up information about the jockey in the pub; he knew from experience that English pubs were good for picking up information.

'I guess we could go back to that field,' said Elizabeth.

'Don't be silly.' Julia prodded me. 'It's too cold to stay out all night.'

'So it is,' I had to agree. 'You're forgetting one thing Julia. This house is wide open . . . remember the accident with the front door? There's no lock on it yet. It isn't as safe here as you think.'

'Would the Russian come back?'

Atsy-Catsy nodded. 'If he think I am here, he come with force.'

'Then there's only one thing to do,' declared Julia. 'We keep a watch on him. We'll go to The Lion.'

'And leave these two alone?'

'The Supervisor wouldn't expect us to, would he?'

'Good,' said Atsy-Catsy. 'You go, we stay.'

He had stubbornly refused to leave the village, but I had to try once again. 'Look, all this panic's quite unnecessary. If you went to London now . . .'

'Is not possible.'

'I guess not,' agreed Elizabeth. 'You see, Michael, he doesn't wanna go on account of the colt. That horse'll get mighty upset. That's what Cat says and when it's to do with a horse Cat sure knows what he's saying.'

'But the horse is going to Russia.' I was beginning to feel

exasperated. 'And Atsy-Catsy's *not* going to Russia . . . so there's nothing he can do for the horse in any case.'

'Is not *our* horse,' he said. 'Is Herakles. If Supervisor take away Princeling it is Herakles will be very unhappy. If Herakles is unhappy he do silly things. I must stay for Herakles.'

'But Cecil and Coop are handling him perfectly well now.'

'When Herakles is happy, yes. With Herakles unhappy,' the little jockey spread his hands palm up. 'Who knows what he will do.'

It was futile to argue with them. They'd clearly made up their minds to be in Craftly until after Princeling had gone, and if I didn't find them somewhere to stay they'd probably both catch pneumonia in the fields. There was only one place in the whole house with a key in the lock and that was the tiny boxroom adjoining my bedroom. I was aware that a bedroom wasn't the 'proper' place to send these youngsters to, but in the circumstances the finer points had to be ignored.

We had some sandwiches and cocoa, I showed them to the bedroom with instructions not to put on lights, and then Julia and I went off to The Lion.

It was a cold, starry evening and we needed no flashlight to guide us through the potholes of the lane. Julia was uncommonly quiet.

'Scared?' I asked her.

'Not really.'

'You're a dead loss,' I told her. 'You're supposed to be the one who keeps us out of trouble. There'll be *some* scandal if the papers get hold of this story.'

'They won't,' Julia sounded reassuringly pigheaded. 'Michael, we *couldn't* let them down . . . a couple of foreigners with nowhere to go. Isn't it typical of Sir Roger that he didn't let them stay at his house? Just because Atsy-Catsy's going to the States. I bet if he'd promised to become Sir Roger's jockey it would have been a different story.'

'What did you expect?'

Suddenly Julia giggled. 'First Sidney, now this . . . You know Phil was right about a country vet needing nine lives like a cat. This village *is* dynamite.'

\* \* \*

128

The pub looked more 'dynamic' than usual. All along the bar stood groups of farmers and tradesmen discussing the committee meeting of the Craftly Rural Preservation Society, which was going on in the lounge next door. At their elbows stood a good many tins and collection-boxes, and the walls were hung with posters which – they proudly told us – were the work of Claire and Tiger.

The posters invited people to the Cricket Club's spring fair, to a church bring-and-buy sale, to a church coffee-morning, and to a Tit House jumble-sale. Over the huge old log fireplace a notice read, 'these premises have been temporarily rented by Craftly's Church of St Mary.' In the 'premises', the size of a modern kitchenette, the church had installed a one-armed bandit which was being fed sixpences nonstop.

With magnificent impartiality the landlord had arranged the collection-boxes in a manner that gave Miss Sabina's Tit House an advantage at the counter, presumably because she *hadn't* been able to provide a one-armed bandit or a spring fair. Each of her boxes had a picture of a robin and a typed notice. 'While the Beginner-Birdwatcher-Brotherhood recognises a relative justification for land being used for purposes of food production, your attention is drawn to the poisonous chemicals used by modern farmers. They are a lethal menace to our feathered friends. Please help us to give them a larger home.'

At the far end of the bar I saw the Russian Supervisor in earnest conversation with Tom Renton of the Vet Investigation Department. Near the door stood Claire and Tiger with their neighbour, Farmer Lock, and the old fellow. Julia said under her breath that we'd better stay near the door.

'What'll you drink?' invited Tiger.

'Coca-cola, thanks.' It was one evening when I meant to avoid anything stronger.

Claire was absent-mindedly fondling the lilac-pointed Siamese on her shoulder. 'Mr Oldfellow's been telling us some interesting things about the old families of the village.'

'The Crosbys,' he nodded ponderously, 'have been here since Domesday; they're in the book.'

'Oldest family in Craftly,' agreed Mr Lock. 'When they made Conny the secretary of our Preservation Society I said right away, "that's as it should be." '

The old fellow looked pleased, aware of his new importance. 'Conny's a fine girl. There's not many could have organised the Society as fast as her.'

'They say Major Uckthorpe's given the Cricket Club several hundred,' said Lock.

'That's right. And I heard Miss Ponsonby-Pluck's given a big cheque to the vicar.'

'But everybody will be bidding *against* each other,' said Claire. 'Isn't that a bad thing?'

The old fellow smiled. 'Well, we all have our private ideas. If you ask *me*, I'd say it would be best if Jenkins's went to someone like yourself . . . someone famous who's been brought up in the country, someone who wouldn't do no harm like building.'

There was a murmur of assent. 'There's something in that,' said Lock. 'It does a village a lot of good having someone famous living in it.'

'It's kind of you,' said Claire, warmly. 'But you see we wouldn't have time to take on Jenkins's nurseries. I can hardly manage the land we have . . . the orchard . . . vegetables . . . kitchen-garden. And my husband's been busy with his own work . . . Oh, Michael! Has Julia told you our news? Larry loved the new play . . . he was terribly nice about it, though he must have been disappointed that there's no role for him. And we've got Dame Patty to play the lead . . . When he heard about it Tiger changed the third scene in the first act . . . you know the one about Wandsworth . . .'

Tom Renton and the Russian Supervisor had moved closer. The Russian seemed determined to get away, Tom Renton equally set on prolonging the discussion. 'I'm not satisfied,' he was saying, 'that we've got to the bottom of it. All right, we've taken our usual measures . . . we've killed the animals with foot-and-mouth *and* the animals whose lab-tests have been positive . . . we've taken all sanitary measures and stopped the movement of cattle in the affected area. But in my opinion we still don't know why an epidemic stops where it does, do we?'

'No,' said the Russian, edging closer to the door.

'I've been making a study,' continued Tom Renton, 'a long-term study of animals on the *fringes* of epidemics . . . I have certain theories, and if they turn out as I hope we might be able to develop a strain of cattle with a natural resistance to foot-and-mouth . . . Of course it would change our policy for the whole country. And if we still got the odd outbreak of foot-and-mouth we'd be able to cope with it by vaccinating the animals across a belt of country . . . in fact making a barrier of immune beasts between the sick and the healthy. I think we'd lose fewer animals. I'm working on a paper . . .'

The Russian muttered something and dived for the door. At the same time Julia turned and managed to block it.

'Have a drink,' I invited him, heartily. 'You haven't met . . .' I introduced the old fellow and Lock, Tiger and Claire. What made the Supervisor stop with reasonably good grace was the cat on Claire's shoulder.

'Very fine cat,' he complimented Claire, 'puss, puss.'

The cat turned its head in disgust and evaded the Russian's hand by moving from Claire's right shoulder to her left.

'She doesn't listen if you don't call her by her name,' said Claire. 'It's Mao-tse-Tung.'

There was an awkward silence. At last the Supervisor smiled, 'Mao-tse-Tung.' The little Siamese turned and allowed him to scratch her behind the ear. 'Very fine cat,' he said, 'I think you have made a compliment to . . . Mao-tse-Tung.' He tossed back my double Scotch, excused himself and walked out.

'A *kitten*,' murmured Julia. 'That's it.'

I knew what she meant. I took Claire aside and asked her whether she'd part with one of Chou-en-Lai's kittens. For a moment she was reluctant but when I explained it was really important to keep the Supervisor occupied – where I could keep an eye on him – she agreed. As I left I saw her in a huddle with Tiger.

By cutting across the churchyard I caught up with the Supervisor just as he was disappearing through my front door. I ducked behind my car, wondering what on earth I could do if he did find Elizabeth and Atsy-Catsy. Except at rugger I'd never knocked anyone down and it was inconceivable that I should start now.

I saw the flicker of a flashlight move about the downstairs rooms and then in the rooms above. But there was no sound. After about ten minutes the Supervisor came out – alone. Suddenly he gave a jump. There was a scampering noise and Patty streaked across to my car. She sat down beside the right front wheel, and there was nothing I could do about it. The Supervisor went after her. Fortunately he managed to get hold of the cat first time. 'Catusha,' he murmured tenderly, 'Catushinka.'

For a while he played with Patty and when she was purring he set her down on the doorstep; he took a quick look at the windows of the house and walked off. There was something hesitant about his behaviour, as if he had not convinced himself that the house *was* unoccupied. I thought of the American cigarettes Elizabeth smoked; it was too late to give her English ones now.

I got back to The Lion before he did; and there was Claire clutching a pretty unmanageable kitten which looked more Siamese than tabby. Jock had joined the party and was trying to befriend the kitten but the kitten only boxed his face. Disgustedly Jock turned away and accepted the remainder of Farmer Lock's pint of beer.

'All right?' asked Julia.

'So far.'

The little lounge next door was getting noisy. There were sounds of scraping-back chairs, and voices. The door opened just as the Supervisor was coming in at my end.

'Get Tiger to make a speech,' I said to Julia, making for Thornton and Conny who were still surrounded by the rest of the Craftly Preservation Society committee.

I managed to get into the scrum, watched by the Supervisor. But when I looked again the Russian was fully occupied with the kitten.

'I want you to do something for me,' I told Thornton, drawing him aside. 'Atsy-Catsy doesn't want to return to Russia.' I explained the situation without making much impression on him. But when I mentioned that Sir Roger had refused to have Elizabeth and her little jockey in the house Thornton's caution vanished.

'All right, Mr Morton. What do I do?' he asked.

'Go to my house – the front door's open – up to the main bedroom. They'll be in the boxroom next door. Tell them who you are. Tell them I've asked you to take them to your place for the night. I'll keep the Supervisor here somehow.'

'Don't worry, Mr Morton. I'll manage it. I'd better have

132

a pint with Conny and the others first . . . It'll look better.'

But the Russian didn't appear to have noticed my talking to Thornton. He was cuddling the kitten, his face a study of kindliness and good nature.

'. . . express the hope,' Tiger was winding up, 'that our guest will long remember this evening and that we'll have made *some* contribution towards better understanding between our two nations.'

Everyone, including the committee of the Craftly Rural Preservation Society applauded, the landlord produced drinks on the house, and several people called, 'speech! speech!'

'Let him have his drink first,' I said. Thornton was getting through his pint pretty fast. He was edging Conny along to the door behind us.

'You have to reply,' I said to the Supervisor.

'It is the custom?'

'Certainly.'

'I do not know of such a custom in a public house.'

'You've never had a presentation evening in a public house, have you?'

'No,' he agreed. 'It is with much pleasure,' he raised his voice, 'that I accept this generous gift. It is a poetic justice that you give me the son of Chou-en-Lai.' On the name Chou-en-Lai Thornton and Conny slipped out of the bar. 'He is a finer cat than my cat Alyosha who has a white nose . . .'

I looked at my watch. By car it would take Thornton no more than two or three minutes to reach my house; in about the same time he'd be past The Lion on his way home. If I allowed five minutes for him to get Elizabeth and Atsy-Catsy from the boxroom and out of the house a quarter of an hour would see us through.

The Supervisor had arrived at the cat he'd owned before Alyosha of the white nose, and it didn't seem unlikely that there'd been a cat or two in his life right back to his boyhood. Eight minutes, I counted, ten, twelve; he'd come to the first kitten of his childhood; fourteen minutes. The applause took another fifteen seconds and by the time it ended I'd put a double whisky in the Supervisor's hand. All clear!

Tom Renton was saying good night to the landlord. He

had Jock by the collar, so evidently it was his turn to deliver him at the gates to Tit House.

'Michael,' he said, in passing, 'I meant to have a talk with you.'

'Back to normal?' I asked.

'Just about. I think we're finished with the foot-and-mouth. I'm clearing up, so I'll be here most of tomorrow. Drop in some time, will you? I've got one or two queries.'

Queries. I suddenly felt weaker than the kitten the Supervisor was cuddling. I had an idea what those queries might be. Tom Renton had asked me to check a list of farms. And I *had* been round the lot, more than once, taking specimens, sending them to the lab and giving Renton the results as they came through; I'd done my job and more except that I'd left out Thornton's herd because I had known beyond a doubt that Thornton's cattle would show a *positive* reaction. Thornton's animals would have been condemned to death. So – well – I hadn't reported on them at all.

Was it possible that Tom Renton had caught me out *now* when the danger of foot-and-mouth had passed and events had proved my gamble justified?

All night long, tense and unable to sleep, I tried to find an answer to this question – by racking my brains in remembering all I knew of Tom Renton. I'd met him as a student, when he was the youngest of my lecturers. He'd changed to his present job because his chief interest was cattle and the breeding of better stock.

Tom, despite the first-rate work he'd done in epidemics, was above all an academic person. He was the kind of man who'd always be involved in some 'long-term study' or other. What would his reaction be to a colleague who had jettisoned his professional ethics by withholding information from the Veterinary Investigation Department, who had broken the law, and taken it upon himself to prejudge the outcome of a foot-and-mouth outbreak?

My thoughts went round in circles. Perhaps Tom's queries were quite small unimportant things. Perhaps they concerned what I feared. Was this to be the end of me as a vet? I couldn't imagine any other kind of life for myself. And there was Julia, Julia who always supported my most harebrained enterprises when she sensed how strongly I felt about them.

134

At dawn, with the chorus of birds in full voice, I went to sleep from sheer exhaustion. I was vaguely aware of Patty settling down on my shoulder, and then I began to dream. I dreamed I was lying on an operating table and Tom Renton was standing there with a syringe, saying I'd have to be put down. Julia was arguing that he should first try the other serum because one couldn't kill a man just like that. And Tom was telling her not to be foolish; didn't she remember I was responsible for infecting a whole herd? He was putting the needle to my arm when it suddenly occurred to me to jump off the table.

I came to lying on the floor beside my bed with Patty's claws in my shoulder. From downstairs came the sounds of Mrs Pitt cooking breakfast. 'Condemned man's breakfast' I thought sombrely. If Tom Renton had tumbled to what I'd done it would be my last as a vet.

# CHAPTER 11

There was no time for ascertaining my future, one way or the other. When I looked into The Lion immediately after breakfast Tom Renton hadn't yet arrived, and I was committed to examining Princeling before his journey.

His horsebox had arrived already, the Supervisor's car was there, and Cecil told me the colt would be taken away as soon as I was through. As I'd expected the colt was in first-rate condition, but I took my time looking him over from head to tail. When I filled in the familiar 'Certificate of Examination as to Soundness' I wondered whether I'd ever again be able to sign a document beginning 'I certify that I have this day examined at the request of . . .' and ending 'In my opinion the colt was sound at the time of my examination.'

I made a copy of the certificate for Sir Roger and gave the Supervisor the original. While Princeling was taken to the horsebox he was scanning the fields.

'No Atsycatchioff,' he said, staring into the morning mist, his fingers playing with his kitten's ears. 'He will not be on the aeroplane.'

'What will be the . . . consequences?' I asked.

'To *me* there will be consequences. I must report Atsycatchioff missing. I must say he was taken by the Americans and . . .'

'Surely not. He was taken, if at all, by one little American girl who fell in love with him.'

'The Soviet Culture Department, of which I am the member, does not provide for love.'

'Couldn't you introduce a new clause?'

'I am not enough important. But I have good record,' he brightened a little. 'Five years I have been in Britain and I have not a single English friend.'

'You made friends last night,' I reminded him.

'Not a single English friend,' he repeated, emphatically. 'But now I shall be called back to Moscow.'

'To explain what happened?'

'No, no. The Culture Department will have made the decision before I arrive. Maybe they give me smaller post, maybe they put me into re-education place . . . maybe they say I must go to Siberia.'

I said I was sorry.

'About Siberia? Is not so bad for *me*. I think many years ago, "Sasha, one day you will do something bad, you will be sent to no comfortable place." So, when my brothers and me are young men, we go to Siberia and build a good strong house. Now we *have* good strong house.'

Sir Roger's Jaguar came sweeping in, with Lady Beverley and three of the dachshunds inside.

'Formalities concluded?' asked Sir Roger.

Cecil handed him the copy of my certificate. He read it carefully, put it in his wallet, and then shook hands with the Supervisor. 'It's to be profoundly regretted that the Ascot potentialities of your colt won't be brought into play . . .'

During Sir Roger's speech and the Supervisor's counter-speech a girl had brought Herakles into the yard. She was trying to saddle the colt, but he was dancing backwards and shaking his head. When I went up and spoke to him he made noises in his throat and gazed at the horsebox. The white blaze on his nose quivered; he again reminded me of a don – an apprehensive one.

Princeling, inside the box, was behaving quite well but there were slight noises of scraping and stamping and I had the uncanny sensation that Herakles knew what was happening. He was suspicious of the situation. He didn't like it.

When the horsebox, followed by the Supervisor's car, had driven off I suggested to Sir Roger that Herakles should have a sedative; the colt was showing too much of the whites of his eyes.

'I don't believe in doping,' he snapped at me.

'Neither do I. But even Atsy-Catsy – in whose eyes Herakles can do no wrong – thinks the colt might get badly upset. He's been brought up with Princeling . . . they've been training together. You know horses make friends as people do.'

'I suppose your theory is that Herakles failed at Hurst Park because Princeling wasn't there.'

'It's quite possible. That as much as the fact that Coop didn't yet understand the colt.'

'Well, Coop understands him now.' Sir Roger suddenly turned on his wife. 'These dogs of your! *Must* they bark their heads off! If you can't control them you'd better send them to a kennels.'

'You're in a filthy mood, darling,' said Lady Beverley. 'I think you should take Mr Morton's advice. *I* don't think Herakles looks too happy.'

'You know nothing about horses. There's not going to be any doping in my stables . . . Morton, while you're here I'd like you to take a look at . . .'

'I'm sorry,' I said. 'I have a surgery.'

Again I couldn't fit in the interview with Tom Renton. My waiting-room was full of animal-owners, a variety of cats, small dogs and a couple of rabbits.

The baby rabbits belonged to an independent little boy about ten who handed them to me with a request to make them well quickly or they'd die.

He was right about their condition.

'I've got eight little rabbits,' he told me.

'How many mothers?' I asked him.

'Just the one.'

'Was she your first rabbit?'

'Yes, and she's white and grey, and one ear's white and the other's grey . . . I don't think she likes Tony and Thumper.'

'These two?'

'That's right.'

'Then *you* must look after them,' I told him. 'You see, your doe's had too many children and she can't look after them all. So Tony and Thumper have gone hungry.' I explained to him he'd have to bottle-feed the baby rabbits with lukewarm milk and water three times a day for two weeks, then twice until they could manage greens, bran and table-scraps.

'Thanks,' he wrapped them up in a piece of blanket and returned them to their basket. 'Mum said I'm to ask you, is it on the Health Service?'

'No, there's no health service for animals.'

He held out sixpence. By the expression on his face he'd had other plans for the coin.

'Don't tell anyone,' I said, 'but this time there's nothing to pay.'

The next owner was a lady who'd brought three kittens to be 'put down'. She said she couldn't possibly murder the little creatures, but she appeared to be quite happy about my killing them. That handful meant I'd once again go round the village trying to find homes for them.

My last patient was a toy poodle belonging to a lady whose husband was 'in the City'. Trixie, she'd told me, had disgraced himself at two of her cocktail parties; on one occasion he'd 'made a smell' while being cuddled by a guest, on another he'd been sick into the turn-ups of a friend's trousers.

'But he's perfectly all right with the family,' she said. 'He just can't be trusted at parties, precisely when one wants a dog to make a good impression.'

'He doesn't like *parties*,' I told her.

'But that's just when I want him there . . . You know, it gives people something to talk about.'

I thought I'd better be polite to the poor fish. 'Look at it from Trixie's point of view,' I suggested. 'He's very small, but normally he's fairly safe from being trodden on. Then, suddenly, he finds himself surrounded by masses of legs with big feet, and he knows that every one of them might hurt him. It must be rather frightening to a little dog. And, you know, *people* sometimes get sick when they're scared.'

'I hadn't thought of that . . . There's nothing the matter with him?'

'Nothing?'

'You can send us your account.'

I knew as soon as she'd said it that here was an account that wouldn't be paid for a long time, if at all. But that would be Phil's worry. I'd be back in London within a week; sooner if Tom Renton had found me out.

Much as I wanted that interview over I didn't take the car. I walked along to The Lion pretending I wanted a 'breather' for thinking things out. I didn't of course; if I had such a thing as a mind it was blank.

Crossing the High Street I was almost knocked down by Sir Roger's Jaguar flying towards The Lion at an indecent speed. As I turned the corner a horse, ridden by Atsy-Catsy, came galloping down the other road at right-angles to Sir Roger's car and at the same moment I saw Herakles – riderless – flying through the cobbled lane, parallel to the High Street, which led into the car-park of The Lion.

Even at a distance I could see the whites of the colt's eyes. He was slipping wildly on the uneven cobbles, and a terrified mother had pushed her children up against the wall. I realised if I didn't at least break the speed of the bolting Herakles he'd come to grief in the traffic, damage himself or damage passers-by.

I'd just managed to block the exit from the car-park into the road when Herakles came thundering up. I leaped at him, and by some miracle landed with my stomach on his back. The sudden weight on him made him rear, but though he slipped he didn't fall. By the time Atsy-Catsy reached us I had Herakles practically under control, and he allowed the jockey to lead him away.

Tom Renton was standing in the doorway of the pub. 'Come on in,' he called. 'I always knew you were a bloody fool.' He was more shaken than I. 'Better have a drink, Michael . . . Well, I never thought you could stop a bolting horse with a rugger-tackle.'

I wished he'd get on with our interview. When I'd thrown myself at Herakles I had been aware that anything might happen; oddly enough it hadn't worried me. And the un-worried mood persisted throughout my first whisky. But I couldn't be sure how much longer I'd feel that I *could* take what was coming to me.

'Know how it happened?' asked Tom.

'I wanted to give the colt a sedative this morning,' I said. 'Owner doesn't believe in *doping horses*.'

'That sounds like Sir Roger Coolcrow.'

'It is.'

'Will he get Jenkins's land, do you think?'

'He can afford to bid higher than the village people.'

'You might get farmers from other parts of the Country at the auction. I've seen it advertised all over the place.'

'Tom,' I couldn't stand the nice normal gossip any longer.

'You said you have some . . . queries. Let's get down to it.'
'All right. Might as well get it over.'

\* \* \*

Tom Renton pulled up a chair for me in front of his im-
provised desk. The files and papers on the table had been
arranged in stacks and looked ready for packing. On the
map of the county, behind Tom, the position of the
little coloured flags had changed to a final, clearly defined
pattern.

Those foot-and-mouth flags, scattered over a roughly
arrow-shaped part of the country, stopped at a curved belt of
land which could only be Thornton's. Along that belt the
flags were white, meaning that the laboratory tests of the
animals there had been negative – that the animals were free
from infection. The flags beyond that line were also white,
indicating that the animals over a wide area *had* been tested
and found healthy.

The work of checking this large animal-population had
been enormous. It had meant that almost every vet in the
county had taken on the work of two men, as I knew well
enough from my own experience. To avoid unnecessary red
tape the vets, including myself, had reported infected animals
only and simply ticked off on their lists those farms where
the tests had proved the animals free from infection.

Tom Renton turned round. 'Well, Michael, see anything
striking about this map?'

I recalled what he'd said in the pub on the previous
evening; about his long-term study of animals on the fringes
of an epidemic, about developing a foot-and-mouth resistant
strain of cattle and the possibilities of applying the barrier
method. It was just possible that this interview would turn
out to be nothing worse than an academic discussion. But
there was one thing of which I felt certain; whatever Tom
asked of me I would not mislead him.

'Well?' he asked. 'Any ideas about this pattern?'

'Just that no farm on the other side of this strip of land
was affected.'

'Exactly. It looks . . . well, as if the attack of the virus had
been broken against a solid wall . . . a *barrier*.' Tom took a
file from one of the stacks and opened it. 'I've been looking
up your reports . . . the dairy-farm which seems to have
acted as a barrier belongs to Thornton, one of *your* farmers.

141

I see you ticked him off on your list, so his animals must have been negative. You're sure they *were*?'

'No.' It was the moment for telling him what had happened, but now that the inevitable question had come I didn't know where to begin.

'Let's get this straight, Michael. You did get lab. reports on Thornton's animals?'

'No . . . I knew what the results would be. Thornton had his herd vaccinated.'

'*You* knew that and didn't report it?' Tom had risen from his chair and was standing over me.

'That's about it,' I said foolishly.

'Damned idiot! Do you realise what you've done? You'll be struck off the register.'

'I know.'

'You do?' As he stood there the anger went out of his eyes and he just looked tired, a prematurely middle-aged man who had thought he'd finished a gruelling job, only to find that there was, after all, no end to it. 'Listen,' he said 'You've got a city practice, haven't you?'

'Yes.'

'You know nothing about cattle?'

'I'm not going to plead ignorance.'

'No . . . it wouldn't help, anyway.' He lit a cigarette and picked the match into small shreds. 'No, incompetence is no excuse for a vet.'

Somehow Tom's discomfiture helped me. 'I'm not incompetent,' I said. 'I found out by chance that Thornton had vaccinated his herd. I knew I should report it, and I didn't.'

'For God's sake, why? Why?'

'I suppose first of all it was Thornton's *cattle*. Have you seen his herd . . . the bull Roderick?'

'Yes. I took a look round this morning. It's certainly one of the finest herds I've ever seen . . . But a dislike for slaughtering good animals is no excuse.'

'I didn't think it was. I *would* have reported the illegal vaccinations if it hadn't been for the lie of the land. If there's any chance at all of the barrier-method working effectively it was here . . . It was worth trying out.'

'And you were prepared to stake your future on it.'

'I don't know . . . How can one stomach any kind of

142

future if it means just one long legitimate track . . . never daring to step off in case one gets bumped?'

'Most of us do stick to the track. We've made it ourselves.'

'*I* haven't made it.'

'Don't deceive yourself, Michael. You're not an anarchist . . . But I know how you feel. Changes in the law . . . progressive changes . . . aren't carried out until a majority feel they can no longer tolerate the outdated regulations. And the majority are always slower in advancing than the individual . . . But that's getting us nowhere.'

'Well, I've landed myself in nowhere, and that's all there is to it . . . I'll let you have the lab-analysis of the vaccine in the syringe found in Thornton's field . . . then you can make your report.'

'And get you struck off the register.'

'I suppose so.'

'I realise, of course, that the risk you took probably stopped the epidemic much sooner than if there *hadn't* been this barrier of immune animals . . .'

'Cut it out, Tom,' I begged him. 'It's over and done with.'

'That's what *I* am thinking . . . It was the second time that Thornton's saved his herd. Last year's epidemic was due to a different virus, but that's neither here nor there. I had a long talk with Thornton this morning, and I was most impressed with his hygienic measures. The fact that he managed *twice* to save his herd from infection is due as much to his good management as to the topographical position of his farm . . . And that is what I'm going to report to my Department. Seems to me, the topographical part of it could be useful . . . in the future . . . in an argument for adopting the barrier method . . . And now we could do with a beer.'

I felt bemused. Was Tom Renton so much of a bureaucrat that he was perfectly satisfied now he had all the material he needed for an administratively tidy report? Had he already forgotten that his report would mean the end of me as a vet?

'After this little lot,' he said, cheerfully, 'I couldn't possibly stay in the Vet Investigation Department.'

'Good Lord! *You* aren't going to resign?'

'No option . . . that is, if I don't spill *all* the beans. And I'm not going to.'

'Tom, I couldn't possibly let you do that.'

'Arrogant young devil, aren't you.'

'*I* put myself in the wrong. I'm not expecting you or any-one else to carry the can.'

'Spoken like a man.' He was laughing at me. 'You *are* an idiot, Michael. I'm not being noble, you know. But the position is this: thanks to your luck and good judgement you haven't done any damage despite the fact that you've violated the law . . . ethics . . . the lot. I think it would be wrong to have you kicked out of the profession. And I've seen the way to avoid it.'

'Yes, but what about yourself?'

'You've made me come to a decision. I've thought for some time about leaving the Vet Investigation Department. I've always been more interested in research. There's a job for me at the Research Institute at Pirbright. They're work-ing on a vaccine against foot-and-mouth.'

I went back to Phil's house at a fast trot. The way I felt I *had* to trot since only the physical peculiarity of a breast-bone six feet long could have enabled me to fly. I vaulted over the gate, and then I heard the telephone shrill with the kind of persistence I automatically associated with ill-tempered animal-owners.

Sir Roger did sound ill-tempered. 'Morton, where the hell have you been? I've been trying to get you for the past hour or more.'

'Obviously I wasn't gettable,' I said, not caring whether I offended him or not.

'I'll be glad when Brogan's back.'

'No doubt.'

'Make no mistake, I'll inform him of your conduct.'

'Don't forget to inform him that I risked breaking my neck to stop your colt from getting himself converted into mincemeat . . . under *your* car.'

'Impertinence!' Sir Roger spluttered. 'I take a very serious view of your conduct. Your negligence was deplorable!'

'My *negligence*.' I couldn't believe I'd understood.

'I *said* negligence. You leave a horse in a state of bad shock . . . a horse which might have injured himself . . . and disappear into the pub.'

I slammed down the receiver. I didn't feel in a mood for pointing out that I too might have been somewhat 'shocked', that Atsy-Catsy had been there to take charge of Herakles, and that – in any case – Herakles wouldn't have run amok if I'd been allowed to give him a sedative.

The telephone rang again. I was tempted not to answer, but it might have been another animal-owner, someone who really did need me.

'Mr Morton?' This time it was Lady Beverley, and she was wearing her Cornish charm. 'I'm most terribly sorry my husband was rude just now. You'll forgive him, won't you? But you see, he's had so many worries lately... The Russians and their horse . . . The Development Company plans . . . Atsy-Catsy . . .'

'You wouldn't *have* Atsy-Catsy in your house.'

'Well . . . it's rather difficult for my husband as a Member of Parliament . . . Anyway Catsy's at our stables *now*. That's really why he wanted you; Herakles is quiet now . . . at least while Atsy-Catsy's with him . . . but he's got a gash, about three inches by one in the skin of his right foreleg. Cecil says he should have some stitches.'

'All right, I'll come.'

'It's awfully sweet of you, Mr Morton . . . Oh, and my husband says if you still think the colt needs a sedative he won't object.'

I gave Herakles a sedative *before* I stitched him up. The injury was a superficial one, but it was a pity he'd have a scar for the rest of his life.

Atsy-Catsy told me he was moving to the cottage of the old fellow, Sir Roger paying for his room, and Elizabeth had returned to Tit House. They'd stay for two or three days until one could be sure that Herakles was all right and until Elizabeth's mother arrived from Switzerland. She'd be in London by the end of the week and they were to join her at the Savoy.

Sir Roger himself turned up when I was about to leave the stables. He didn't apologise for anything, but he invited me up to the house for a drink, which I declined.

I was just putting my case in the car when a lady in a tweed suit approached. 'I am here on behalf of the church,' she said, sticking her collection box in Sir Roger's face. 'We are planning to buy land for a new village hall, and I hope . . .'

145

'Madam,' said Sir Roger, obviously fighting for self-control. 'You don't appear to know who I am. Let me assure you you're wasting your time. The land in question will *not* be available for a village hall, a cricket-pitch or anything else because *I* shall buy it.'

# CHAPTER 12

'But Daddy doesn't buy things he doesn't want,' said Claire.

'Doesn't he buy things *you* want?' asked Julia.

While Tiger began to clear the dinner-table Claire took a tired-looking potato-chip out of Chou-en-Lai's mouth. No doubt it would have given Chou indigestion.

'*Do* I want Jenkins's land?' she asked, putting Chou with her kittens.

'Well, you're so clever at making things look different.' Julia glanced admiringly at the abstract blast-furnaces on the walls, the black and grey curtains which gave such a convincing impression of being in tatters. 'I'm sure you could do *something* with Jenkins's nurseries.'

Claire smiled. 'You're sweet, Julia. But the trouble is there's acres and acres of Jenkins's land; it's not like doing things with four walls, a floor and a ceiling.'

'But you've got hedges and ditches at Jenkins's . . . and a lot of glass.' Julia conveyed something of the exasperation she felt at the thought of Sir Roger 'winning' the auction. 'There must be something one can do with glass.'

'Grow tomatoes,' said Tiger.

'Or build a swimming-pool. No,' Claire shook her head. 'One acre would be enough for a swimming-pool. Daddy would want to know what I'm doing with the rest of the land . . . He isn't mean; it's just that he won't buy things if he doesn't see a future for them.'

Julia kicked me under the table, and I said, 'If there's one thing that has a future it's land.'

'Yes, for building,' said Claire, with unexpected perspicacity. 'But we don't want to build, do we?'

'You could build a modern church,' suggested Julia.

'There is a church in Craftly isn't there?' asked Tiger.

'Not a Catholic or a Presbyterian one,' said Julia.

'That's true, Tiger.' Claire looked questioningly at her husband. 'If we built a church the rest of the land could be used as a cemetery, couldn't it?'

'I think the swimming-pool's a better idea . . . We could have a zoo as well. Actually my next play's going to be set in a zoo.'

'Tiger, how marvellous!' In her excitement Claire failed to see Mao-tse-Tung stealing the remains of our haddock. 'Tiger, darling, it's a wonderful idea.'

'Well, someone's written a novel with a zoo-background . . . so that part isn't original,' admitted Tiger. 'What's new is the old man who's going to be *in* the zoo. He's going to be keen on apes and he'll hate the giraffe.'

'Terrific,' Claire turned to Julia, 'you see it, don't you?'

'Not . . . quite,' said Julia, humbly.

'It's psychological . . . Jung; that's the ancestral memory part . . . the apes. And Freud . . . spots . . . inkblots . . . the giraffe. It'll be fabulous . . . the *real* anti-play.'

'No story, of course,' explained Tiger.

'And no dialogue,' said Claire.

'None,' confirmed Tiger. 'I thought maybe I'll handle the whole thing with noises. . . you know something like the air going out of the bicycle-tyre in *Three Corsets to Curzon Street* . . . and of course a balance of monologues.'

'Will there be a part for Larry?' asked Claire.

'Darling,' Tiger looked pained. 'You should know better. I can't possibly consider *actors*.'

'Stupid of me,' murmured Claire.

'No, not really . . . I've got some notes for the new play. Would you like to see them?'

I got up and excused myself, saying I had a lot of paper-work to get through before handing over to Phil Brogan; Phil, now completely recovered, was due home in a couple of days.

Julia accompanied me out. Her kiss felt a bit absent-minded and depressed.

'He's going to get it,' she said.

'Who's going to get what?'

'Oh, Michael! Don't you ever remember things to do with your *private* life? You said you'd stop Sir Roger buying Jenkins's nurseries.'

'I said we'd think of something.'

'Claire's father's our only hope.'

'Not much of a hope unless you can make Claire mad keen on that land.'

'Mad keen! I've got it.' Julia pressed herself against me with positive fervour. 'Thanks a lot, darling.'

'For what?'

'For the idea you've given me. It must work. It *must*.'

'Look, Julia, don't worry if your idea – whatever it is – doesn't work out.' I knew it would be futile to ask her what she planned to do. Julia was superstitious about divulging intentions; she believed the cold shower of discussion weakened those delicate shoots. 'Sir Roger hasn't yet got the land.'

'There isn't much time,' she said, vaguely.

'Thornton will make a strong bid. And the Cricket Club . . .'

'They don't stand a chance.'

'Don't be too sure. There's a lot of money in this village; perhaps not among the farmers, but the business people who travel up to town can well afford the odd thousand. *They* don't want housing estates in their village, not when it's taken years to *have* a village. The megaton men *must* have places in the country . . . the country's *the thing*; so they can't let the country disappear from under their Bentleys.'

'I'm not taking any chances,' declared Julia. 'And even if Grey and Hollow *are* dealing with other properties first *we* are going to be at the auction at three.'

We were not at the auction at three. Julia and I were about to leave the surgery when Mrs Eller, the doctor's wife, arrived carrying her Yorkshire terrier Tim. Though the little dog was bleeding profusely Mrs Eller didn't flap. She had, she told me, seen men in worse condition recovering perfectly well; 'medical' people were so dependable.

Tim was an inveterate chaser of cats bigger than himself and a good many old scars told the story of his courage as a fighter. But he hadn't been equal to Mr Lock's tough ginger farm cat. Ginger had not only torn a piece off his left ear, she had also managed to lay open Tim's left eyeball, an injury that endangered the terrier's sight.

'Better go,' I told Julia, 'I'll follow you as soon as I can.'

Julia slipped off her coat. 'No, I'll give you a hand.'

'I'm sorry,' apologised Mrs Eller. 'You were going out.'

'Only to the auction,' said Julia, as if it meant nothing to her.

'How nice,' said Mrs Eller. 'I hope you'll manage to buy Jenkins's . . . it's ideal for a young couple. I'll come to you for my tomato plants. And I do think you should grow carnations . . . such useful flowers for people in hospital . . . Now, Timmy, don't be afraid.'

Timmy wasn't afraid, just thoroughly miserable. I first coped with his eye and gave him penicillin. That took half an hour in which Timmy bravely growled but didn't complain. But when I dealt with the lesser injury, applying crystals of Permanganate of Potash to his ear, he barked with a ferocity of which only a very small dog is capable.

Mrs Eller wanted to carry him home, but he wouldn't have it. He wriggled and twisted until she put him on the floor and then kept still while she put on his lead.

'Let me pay you now,' she said.

'That's all right. I'm sure Phil wouldn't charge a doctor's dog.'

'Well, it's kind of you. But I'm sure there's something wrong . . . wasn't it a dog that gave him undulant fever? Oh no, it was a cow; Primrose I think . . . Do tell me how's Phil's sister? The one who went to Kenya . . . such a charming girl. I always remember those runner-beans she grew, fourteen inches long, but they were as tender as little ones.'

Julia put on her coat; Timmy knew better, he lay down on the floor and went to sleep.

'I wonder,' mused Mrs Eller, 'whether Phil's sister grows those beans in Kenya. It's important nowadays, what with Africa so restless. One never knows about Africa, but if Kenya went native those runner-beans would remain as a little plot of England, or perhaps . . . they *are* Brogans . . . Ireland. I can't get used to the idea of Ireland as a republic . . . such poor taste on the part of the Irish. But I think the Brogans are all right; Phil's grandmother used to live in Craftly. And certainly Miss Brogan . . . oh yes, Moira was her name . . . she knew how to grow vegetables. Maybe *you* will grow runner-beans at the nurseries. Oh dear! How inconsiderate of me, you want to go and *buy* Jenkins's . . . Thank you so much, both of you.'

At the door she stopped and inhaled the strong scent of hyacinths and narcissi. 'Of course bulb-growing's quite lucrative, I've been told. We haven't got a local firm for bulbs. You must think it over.'

Julia gave me a look of appeal, which Mrs Eller intercepted.

'Off you go,' she said, briskly. 'You'll see my husband at the auction . . . I hope he doesn't buy another potting-shed . . . Do stop him if you can.'

As we walked into the former foot-and-mouth H.Q. at The Lion the auctioneer was in the middle of describing a 'desirable property' in the heart of the country.

'Out in nowhere,' Tail whispered to me. 'It's the one where the bedrooms get flooded.'

'Who lived there?' someone asked the vicar.

'Mrs . . . too bad, I've forgotten her name; trust *me*,' he chuckled. 'Used to call on her every second Tuesday.'

'Vicar,' the president of the Ladies' Guild tapped him on the shoulder. 'Have you got the letter from the bank?'

He palpated his pockets, searched inside his coat, and gave up. 'I've forgotten my spectacles; trust *me*.'

The president shook her head and sighed, making it obvious to all but the vicar that he was alone in being amused about his untrustworthiness over worldly details.

'It's all right,' said Farmer Lock. 'I've got the figures.'

'Come on, ladies and gentlemen,' appealed the auctioneer. 'What am I bid? Come on, give me a start! It's a nice small-holding, I assure you. I inspected it myself and . . .'

'*He* inspected that potting-shed,' Dr Eller told Conny and Thornton. 'It was alive with death-watch beetle. Grand-children burnt it on Guy Fawkes' night . . . Got to get another.'

Julia leaned across. 'Doctor, your wife told us to stop you.'

'She doesn't trust things she hasn't seen. But she'll be disappointed if I don't buy *something* . . . How's our Timmy?'

I told him Timmy would recover.

'Five hundred?' The auctioneer sat back and gave an imitation of jovial laughter. 'Now look here ladies and gentlemen, I haven't come here to play tiddlywinks with you . . . This is business, and believe me whoever's lucky enough to get Orchard Corner . . .'

Sir Roger walked in and took a seat in the front row.

'Fancy that,' said Mrs Pitt to Miss Sabina. 'Fancy him doing his own bidding.'

The bidding went sluggishly. I thought about a third of

151

the fifty-odd people had come for a bargain, perhaps the Gascoigne and Alfa-Laval milking units or the Bamford grinder, a third had come for the entertainment, and the rest were waiting for the auction of Jenkins's.

Julia, her fingers maltreating a handkerchief, kept looking at the door. 'Perhaps I should 'phone.'

Just then the auctioneer began to extol the virtues of 'a fine property known as Jenkins's Nurseries.' There was a rustle of sitting-up movements throughout the room.

'Give me a good start, ladies and gentlemen,' invited the auctioneer. 'Shall we say five thousand? Though I'd call that a *moderately* good start . . . the cottage alone is worth that much. Three thousand? Well, well! Who'll give me four? Three thousand five hundred, the gentleman at the back.'

People turned round to see who was bidding. Neither of the two men who had made offers came from Craftly. Julia's handkerchief split noisily.

'Four thousand?' asked the auctioneer. There was no bid from the two strangers.

'Three thousand six hundred,' said the vicar in a loud voice.

'Sir, I've got as good a sense of humour as the next man, but . . .' the auctioneer caught sight of the dog-collar and stopped himself. 'I've got to consider my reserve price, ladies and gentlemen. Though I, personally, would like to oblige the church I must be realistic . . . Who'll give me four?'

'Four thousand,' offered Major Uckthorpe, the Cricket Club.

Claire and Tiger appeared, with Jock squeezing through the door behind them. Julia sank back in her chair like an exhausted sprinter, Claire waved to us and took Tiger to the back-row; Jock wandered up to the platform and spread himself at the feet of the auctioneer's clerk who had prob-ably befriended him in the bar.

'Four thousand five hundred, anyone?' enquired the auctioneer.

Miss Sabina nodded her head.

'Five,' said Sir Roger.

'Five thousand five hundred,' bid Thornton.

'Six.' Sir Roger's tone implied that he hadn't got all day.

'Six-five,' said Thornton, trying to sound as casual as Sir Roger.

'That's better,' approved the auctioneer, 'but not enough for Jenkins's. May I have seven thousand?'

Sir Roger nodded his head.

'Seven-five?' asked the auctioneer.

There was a silence. It seemed the two original bidders, the church, the cricket club and the bird-sanctuary were out of the running.

'Seven-five,' said Thornton. Conny looked at him anxiously; Tail was beginning to enjoy herself.

'Eight,' offered Sir Roger.

'Eight-five,' Thornton was losing his temper.

'Nine?' asked the auctioneer.

Sir Roger assented with a raising of his programme.

'Nine-five,' shouted Thornton.

Sir Roger's programme moved again.

'Ten?' The auctioneer looked at Thornton, who nodded.

'Ten-five,' said Sir Roger.

Conny put her hand on Thornton's arm. 'No more, Dave. You promised.'

'Ten-five,' repeated the auctioneer. 'Any advance on ten-five. Now you *know* it's worth more than that, ladies and gentlemen. Eleven? Very well; ten-five . . .' The hammer went up. Julia clutched my hand.

There was a growl at the back of the room.

'Tiger,' Julia sighed.

'Eleven,' acknowledged the auctioneer. 'At the back there.'

Sir Roger turned round. 'Eleven-five.'

A deep, rumbling noise from Tiger.

The auctioneer sat back contentedly. He knew his work was virtually over. The programme in front kept going up, alternating with grunts from the back. Thirty thousand, forty thousand, forty-five thousand, forty-five-five . . .

Sir Roger, sounding angry, bid forty-six and this time there was no challenge. There was a pause. The only sound in the room came from the airedale who was padding, tongue out, towards the door that led to the bar.

'Forty-six-five.' The auctioneer raised his hammer. 'Any

advance on forty-six-five?' He began to count, still watching his audience. The hammer came down. 'Forty-six thousand five hundred. Sold to the lady at the back.'

Sir Roger shot out of his seat. The lady at the back was Claire. 'There's some mistake,' he said. '*Mine* was the last bid.'

'No, sir. I'm sorry. The lady raised her programme *after* your final bid.'

'Nothing of the sort! I object. I'll take steps . . .'

'You can put in a complaint in writing, sir,' said the auctioneer, 'but it won't get you anywhere. Plenty of people here who saw the lady make her bid, isn't that right?'

There was an enthusiastic murmur of agreement.

'This is unprecedented . . .'

'Quite right,' the auctioneer cut Sir Roger short. 'Unprecedented it is. In my forty years as an auctioneer I've never had a complaint of this kind . . . But no hard feelings, sir. Better luck next time. Got to be a good loser,' he added with fatherly tolerance.

Sir Roger, looking like a rotten loser, got up and walked out, slamming the door with a chairmanly crash.


'You're not to go,' said Tail, catching Julia and me at the door. 'They've got a surprise.'

'Who are *they*?'

'You'll see.'

The auctioneer's clerk had cleared away his papers, the landlord and the barman were taking away the stacking-chairs, and about half the audience had left or were about to leave.

Claire and Tiger stood surrounded by people congratulating them on their purchase. Miss Sabina suggested their growing soft fruit on Jenkins's land, presumably because her birds were fond of raspberries. Thornton and Conny informed them how many cows or pigs they could rear on a farm that size. Tail suggested their starting a riding-school and Dr Eller was saying that bulb-growing was a paying proposition.

Farmer Lock recommended poultry; chickens in batteries were easiest for people who didn't know much about farming. Half a dozen other farmers, all people whose animals I had tested for foot-and-mouth, stood around discussing among themselves what *they* would do with Jenkins's; and several ladies argued the merits of a cat versus a dog-kennels. Mrs Pitt told us she'd been to auctions when she and Pitt got engaged but she'd never seen the like of this; 'it wouldn't have happened in Wandsworth.'

Claire, looking somewhat flushed, removed Mao-tse-Tung from round her neck and put the Siamese in her bucket-bag. 'Actually,' she began a little uncertainly, 'I don't think we'll have room for a farm . . . You see Daddy's bought Jenkins's for us . . . You know, an outdoor theatre with gardens; he's going to put it on a sound financial basis . . .'

'The Craftly drama festival,' said Tail, dreamily.

'Well, yes. We'll have a lake with mallard ducks and swans . . . shrubberies, a park. And the glasshouses – if we don't repair them – will fall to bits, and then they'll make a wonderful setting for Tiger's plays . . . It was *Julia's* idea.'

'I approve,' said Miss Sabina, breaking the silence. 'If Craftly becomes well known there'll be less danger of people putting up Radiant Homes and the like. I don't think my birds will mind *civilised* audiences.'

'We'll have a *few* cows,' mused Claire, 'and probably a donkey and a few sheep . . . just for the big lawn where people will picnic. We must make them *feel* they've come to a country festival.'

The barman had spread a white cloth on the auctioneer's table. The landlord and the old fellow came in with two enormous roasting tins full of sausages; Elizabeth and Atsy-Catsy followed with platters of halved bridge-rolls.

I joined Tiger, who was standing a little apart, no doubt gathering material for those revolutionary plays with a basis in real live-life. 'You'll be able to make the drama-festival pay?' I asked.

'Oh yes,' he assured me. 'Father-in-law says we can't go wrong provided we charge a minimum of ten guineas a seat . . . make Craftly-theatre the *thing*. And of course you charge people a couple of guineas for parking . . . ten shillings for cloak-rooms; or rather tents. Then there's the programmes; a guinea each.'

'It's going to be absolutely in orbit,' said Tail.

'*I* think it'll cost the earth,' said Conny, passing us with several bottles of whisky.

'Ready?' asked Thornton.

'Doctor,' the old fellow looked worried. 'My prescription! Did you remember?'

Dr Eller took a couple of medicine-bottles out of his pockets. 'That it?' he handed them over, with a smile. 'Leave a bit for rubbing your back, won't you!'

Thornton clapped his hands. 'Friends!' The friends finished whatever they'd been discussing but gradually did stop talking. 'Friends! It's been quite a day, hasn't it? I know some of us had other plans for Jenkins's; but I dare say no one's going to quarrel with having a park instead, and a festival of our own. That's not what I want to talk about though.

'Let's not forget the past few months in all this excitement ... our worries over having a foot-and-mouth outbreak next door to us ... our troubles in the calving and lambing season. Let's remember how much Mr Morton, our vet, has done for us ... now that he's about to leave Craftly. Phil Brogan, who's coming back to us, used to say that a vet – if he's to survive in our village – needs nine lives. I reckon Mr Morton spent quite a few of *his* in the short time he's been among us ...'

Atsy-Catsy, his hand in Elizabeth's, had tears in his eyes. 'My passport,' he said, 'will be as Mr Atkinson ... it is all because of you.'

'You've been swell,' whispered Elizabeth. 'Mom's here ... she got her silver medal, so everything's okay.'

'... and so,' Thornton held out to me a fine all-purpose saddle, 'I'll ask Michael Morton to accept this gift, with our sincere thanks for all his help.'

I thanked everyone, rather incoherently, and then Tail – with her unfailing good timing – rescued me by asking when the food would be ready.

The old fellow poured the alcohol from the medicine over the sausages and put a lighted match to each dish. Dramatically high flames shot up, illuminating the foot-and-mouth map on the wall behind the table. For a moment I had the horrible illusion that the harmless white pin-flags were turning red on me. I wasn't a bit sure about the 'good judgement' with which Tom Renton had credited me; but the nine-lives-theory had worked for me as mysteriously as it seems to work for the scattier type of cat.

'We *could* get married in Craftly,' said Julia.

'What! House or no house?'

'I suppose it'll be *no house*,' said Julia, as if the question of 'roofs' had never troubled her.

'Such a clever idea,' said Miss Sabina, gazing into the flame-licked dishes. There were sounds of sizzling on the table and the sounds of Jock lapping a half pint under the table. 'I know . . .' she hesitated, 'this isn't the moment for truths, but I really *must* ask . . . This *isn't* one of your chemicals I hope?'

'Chemicals?' Thornton and Conny smiled at one another.

'I couldn't possibly eat anything that would harm my birds.'

'Chemicals!' The old fellow stuck a fork into the nearest baking-tin. 'Now *who* would cook with chemicals, Miss!'

'I *must* think of my birds.'

'Of course you must,' said Tail, every bit a tits' champion. 'But it's all right, *really* . . . They're only flamin' sausages.'

# THE ORIGINAL BESTSELLING VET BOOKS

## by

## Alex Duncan

**IT'S A VET'S LIFE
THE VET HAS NINE LIVES
VETS IN THE BELFRY**

A true and outrageously funny series concerning the exploits of veterinary surgeon Michael Morton, the animals in his care, and the owners the animals really owned.

'What Richard Gordon has done for doctors, Alex Duncan is doing for vets.' BOOKS AND BOOKMEN

'The author's fast and furious pace never conceals a hard core of veterinary experience.' THE COUNTRYMAN

'See how the Richard Gordon formula works just as successfully with animals.' PHILIP OAKES

'*Vets in the Belfry* is like its predecessors — or even more so — very funny indeed.' CATHOLIC HERALD

'Alex Duncan looks like becoming the Richard Gordon of the animal clinics.' LONDON EVENING NEWS

# ALIDA BAXTER

## FLAT ON MY BACK
## UP TO MY NECK
## OUT ON MY EAR

The hilarious saga in which Alida Baxter gets to the root of what living and loving in the '70s is all about — entirely dismembering her husband, sex and marriage . . .

'The funniest books I've read for years.' GOOD HOUSE-KEEPING

'In the long line of a writing tradition that includes Richard (Doctor in the House) Gordon, and James (Let Sleeping Vets Lie) Herriot . . . wholly worthwhile entertainers.' SMITH'S TRADE NEWS

'Ms. Baxter does a most difficult thing very well. She makes her life not only funny but interesting.' DAILY MIRROR

'Her honeymoon, a move to Germany, in-laws, out-laws — Alida treats them all like a slide on a banana skin. The result is just as hilarious.' ANNABEL

'Hilariously funny.' OVER 21

'Happily recommended.' FORUM

'Smiles all the way.' BOOKS AND BOOKMEN

Wyndham Books are obtainable from many booksellers and newsagents. If you have any difficulty please send purchase price plus postage on the scale below to:

**Wyndham Cash Sales,**
**123 King Street,**
**London W6 9JG**

OR

**Star Book Service,**
**G.P.O. Box 29,**
**Douglas,**
**Isle of Man,**
**British Isles**

While every effort is made to keep prices low, it is sometimes necessary to increase prices at short notice. Wyndham Books reserve the right to show new retail prices on covers which may differ from those advertised in the text or elsewhere.

1 Book    — 11p
2 Books — 17p
3 Books — 20p
4 Books — 26p
5 Books and over — 30p